Historical Materialism and Globalization

Interest in globalization has been growing over the last decade, and it has become clear recently that mass popular movements are increasingly concerned with the politics of globalization. In these circumstances, the revival of interest in historical materialism within international studies takes on a broader significance. In *Historical Materialism and Globalization*, pioneers of this tradition are brought together with innovative young scholars whose work will shape the next generation of critical international studies scholarship.

Now that Soviet-style socialism has collapsed upon itself and liberal capitalism offers itself as the natural, necessary and absolute condition of human social life on a world-wide scale, this book insists that the potentially emancipatory resources of a renewed, and perhaps reconstructed, historical materialism are more relevant in today's world than ever before. Rather than viewing global capitalism as an ineluctable natural force, these essays seek to show how a dialectic of power and resistance is at work in the contemporary global political economy, producing and contesting new realities, and creating conditions in which new forms of collective self-determination become thinkable and materially possible. It will be vital, topical reading for anyone interested in international relations, international political economy, sociology and political theory.

Mark Rupert is Associate Professor of Political Science, Maxwell School of Citizenship and Public Affairs, Syracuse University. He is the author of *Producing Hegemony* and *Ideologies of Globalization*. **Hazel Smith** is a Jennings Randolph Senior Fellow at the United States Institute of Peace, Washington DC, where she is currently on research leave from her post as Reader in International Relations at the University of Warwick. Her most recent book is *Democracy and International Relations*.

Warwick Studies in Globalisation

Edited by Richard Higgott and published in association with the
Centre for the Study of Globalisation and Regionalisation,
University of Warwick

What is globalisation and does it matter? How can we measure it? What are its policy implications? The Centre for the Study of Globalisation and Regionalisation at the University of Warwick is an international site for the study of key questions such as these in the theory and practice of globalisation and regionalisation. Its agenda is avowedly interdisciplinary. The work of the Centre will be showcased in this new series.

This series comprises two strands: *Warwick Studies in Globalisation* addresses the needs of students and teachers, and the titles will be published in hardback and paperback. Titles include:

Globalisation and the Asia-Pacific
Contested Territories
Edited by Kris Olds, Peter Dicken, Philip F. Kelly,
Lily Kong and Henry Wai-chung Yeung

Regulating the Global Information Society
Edited by Christopher Marsden

Banking on Knowledge
The Genesis of the Global Development Network
Edited by Diane Stone

Historical Materialism and Globalization
Edited by Mark Rupert and Hazel Smith

Civil Society and Global Finance
Edited by Jan Aart Scholte with Albrecht Schnabel

Towards a Global Polity
Edited by Morten Ougaard and Richard Higgott

New Regionalisms in the Global Political Economy
Theories and Cases
Edited by Shaun Breslin, Christopher W. Hughes,
Nicola Phillips and Ben Rosamond

Routledge/Warwick Studies in Globalisation is a forum for innovative new research intended for a high-level specialist readership, and the titles will be available in hardback only. Titles include:

1 Non-State Actors and Authority in the Global System
Edited by Richard Higgott, Geoffrey Underhill
and Andreas Bieler

2 Globalisation and Enlargement of the European Union
Austrian and Swedish Social Forces in the Struggle over Membership
Andreas Bieler

3 Rethinking Empowerment
Gender and Development in a Global/Local World
Edited by Jane L. Parpart, Shirin M. Rai and Kathleen Staudt

4 Globalising Intellectual Property Rights
The TRIPs Agreement
Duncan Matthews

Historical Materialism and Globalization

**Edited by Mark Rupert
and Hazel Smith**

Routledge
Taylor & Francis Group

LONDON AND NEW YORK

for Ellen Meiksins Wood – with appreciation for her scholarship, integrity and politics

First published 2002
by Routledge
11 New Fetter Lane, London EC4P 4EE

Simultaneously published in the USA and Canada
by Routledge
29 West 35th Street, New York, NY 10001

Routledge is an imprint of the Taylor & Francis Group

British Library Cataloguing in Publication Data
A catalogue record for this book is available from the British Library

Library of Congress Cataloging in Publication Data
Historical materialism and globalization/edited by Mark Rupert
and Hazel Smith.
p. cm. Includes bibliographical references and index.
1. International economic relations. 2. Globalization–economic aspects.
3. Materialism. I. Rupert, Mark. II. Smith, Hazel, 1954–.

HF1359 .H584 2002
337–dc21   2002069793

ISBN
0–415–26371–9 (pbk)
0–415–26370–0 (hbk)

Contents

Contributors

Peter Burnham is Reader in Politics and International Studies at the University of Warwick.

Alejandro Colás is Lecturer in the School of African and Asian Studies, University of Sussex.

Michael Cox is Professor of International Politics at the University of Wales, Aberystwyth.

A. Claire Cutler is Associate Professor in the Department of Political Science, University of Victoria.

Kathryn Dean is Lecturer in the Department of Political Studies, SOAS.

Fred Halliday is Professor of International Relations at the London School of Economics and Political Science.

Christian Heine is completing a doctorate at the London School of Economics in the International Relations Department.

Hannes Lacher is Assistant Professor in the Department of International Relations, Eastern Mediterranean University.

Mark Laffey is Lecturer in the Department of Political Studies, SOAS.

Kees van der Pijl is Professor in the Centre for Global Political Economy at the University of Sussex.

William I. Robinson is Assistant Professor of Sociology at the University of California – Santa Barbara.

Mark Rupert is Associate Professor of Political Science in the Maxwell School of Citizenship and Public Affairs, Syracuse University.

Hazel Smith is a Jennings Randolph Senior Fellow at the United States Institute of Peace, Washington, DC, where she is currently on research leave from her post as Reader in International Relations at the University of Warwick.

M. Scott Solomon is a Lecturer in the Department of Political Science, Syracuse University.

Bob Sutcliffe is Professor at the University of the Basque Country, Spain.

Benno Teschke is Lecturer in International Relations at the University of Wales, Swansea.

Ellen Meiksins Wood is Professor on the Graduate Programme in Social and Political Thought, York University, Canada.

Editors' introduction

Mark Rupert and Hazel Smith

Has historical materialism (HM) any relevance in an era of globalization? Of what significance is globalization within an historical materialist frame? Is the traditional vocabulary of HM – in which concepts such as 'class', 'state', and 'imperialism' loom large – adequate to understand, and to change, contemporary social conditions? Can there be a socialist project in an era of globalization, and what forms might it take? With an eye towards sites of struggle and transformative potential, this volume addresses the tensions and possibilities of globalizing capitalism – and historical materialist critique – at the dawn of a new century.

Perhaps ironically, during the last decade when liberal capitalism seemed to have attained a kind of global apotheosis, the study of international relations has witnessed a revival of intellectual traditions associated with the legacies of Karl Marx and his many and various interpreters. Entailing practices of critical scholarship, the traditions of historical materialism share a set of family resemblances: they aim at de-reifying the apparently natural, universal, and politically neutral appearances of capitalist social reality, explicitly to re-situate those abstract appearances in relation to the processes and social power relations implicated in their production, and thereby to enable their transformation by the human social agents whose socially productive activity constitutes their condition of existence.

Marx suggested that such a transformation might emerge out of the confluence of capitalism's endemic crisis tendencies, the polarization of its class structure and the immiseration of the proletariat and, most importantly, the emergence of the latter as a collective agent through the realization of its socially productive power, heretofore developed in distorted and self-limiting form under the conditions of concentrated capitalist production. Traditional interpretations of Marx tended towards mechanical and economistic visions in which the crisis tendencies of capitalism played themselves out 'behind the backs' of historical actors. Leninist interpretations re-injected a sense of historical agency into historical materialism, but did so by empowering a vanguard of professional revolutionaries to seize the state and transform social relations in the name of the oppressed. Viewed in the light of either of these interpretations, historical materialism may appear to have been discredited by the apparent robustness of capitalist economies and the failure of the oft-predicted final crisis to arrive, and by the degeneration of the Bolshevik revolution into a profoundly anti-democratic system of one-party rule.

But, as contributors to this volume demonstrate, there are resources within the traditions of historical materialism which counteract these regressive tendencies and which offer hope for a more enabling and participatory form of social organization than either liberal capitalism or Soviet-style bureaucratic socialism. These new historical materialisms share a scepticism towards mechanistic or vanguardist visions of social change. Progressive social change need not automatically follow in train behind economic crisis, nor can such change be enacted or imposed by a revolutionary elite acting in the name of the inert masses of the oppressed. Rather, progressive social change must be produced by historically situated social agents whose actions are enabled and constrained by their social self-understandings. This recognition highlights the practical, material significance of critical analysis. In an era when Soviet-style socialism has collapsed upon itself and liberal capitalism offers itself as the natural, necessary and absolute condition of human social life, the chapters in this volume insist that the potentially emancipatory resources of a renewed and perhaps reconstructed historical materialism are as relevant in today's world as ever.

Ethics and politics

Historical materialism has an ethical and political content in that it is a theory concerned with explaining the world in order to change it for the better. That change however does not come about automatically or simply because the world can be understood better through the instruments provided by historical materialist analysis. Change comes about through the self-organization and struggle of those social classes marginalized by capitalist social relations and those individuals and groups who are allied with them. What Marx understood as social classes – both in terms of those that benefit and those that are excluded from benefits of the system – are directly and in an everyday way engaged in class struggle with each other. This is a class struggle which is involuntary in the sense that, to secure their very existence, individuals within capitalist social relations *must* either earn a wage or salary and therefore constantly negotiate with an employer to maintain the means of existence, survival and life or, if they are owners of capital, they *must* constantly maximize their returns from the labour they employ and win out in the conflict with other owners of capital, again, because if they do not, their very physical survival is threatened. Class struggle is an imperative defining the way human beings relate to each other within systems of capitalist social relations – it is not optional and neither is it a condition of existence from which any individual can escape.

If class struggle is an imperative of capitalist social organization, it can take many different forms, be played out in many ways and take place in many different fora. Someone turning up late for work may not regard themselves engaged in class struggle but, unless their pay is docked, this person is retrieving their time and labour for their own purposes, not their employer's – this is a minor form of class struggle. A collective fight to maintain social protections – for instance in the fight to keep a minimum wage, to maintain welfare benefits for the elderly and the vulnerable – these also take resources from the owners of capital and redirect them towards those who work to produce that capital. This is also class struggle. And then there are the great conscious political struggles which have sometimes been informed by historical materialist theorizing and sometimes not. These include the great anti-colonial struggles of the nineteenth and twentieth centuries, the battles for the vote and the eight-hour day – and the fights for democracy and freedom and the struggle against poverty which continue worldwide. These are never 'just' economic conflicts but are fundamentally about the rights of people to have control over their own lives – to live a quality of life which is independent and dignified and free from oppression and poverty.

In the same way, those who own and control capital are engaged in everyday struggles for control of capital as well as the big, important and highly visible political and social conflicts of interest – between the owners and managers of capital and those who work to create capital, and among and between the owners and managers of capital themselves. Such struggles can be over the right to exclude small workplaces from the application of the minimum wage, the right to fire workers because of the insufficient 'profitability' of industries, such as in the airline industries after the 11 September bombing of New York and Washington D.C. in 2001, or perhaps the larger more overtly political issues – such as the right to decide who should be the political leaders of great nations (through funding political campaigns, access to high-level social and political networks and influence and sometimes straightforward bribery). These are also never just 'economic' battles. They are about struggles over the social division of the potential benefits that flow from capitalist organization of society – about who should have what and why – about, in other words, the politics of social existence.

There is no inevitability about the 'positive' outcome of class struggle. In the same way there is no sense here that historical materialist approaches can do more than help explain the world by providing a framework for analysis of empirical material. Historical materialist approaches do not obviate the need for painstaking empirical research. Nor does historical materialism offer glib or fundamentalist analysis that ignores the multivariate cleavages in contemporary society along lines of race, class, religion, age, gender, sexuality and geographical origin. Historical materialist approaches are informed by theories based on Marx's analysis of the modern world but they need not conflate Marx's theoretical enterprise with the task of carefully analysing historically constructed social and political life with all its complexity, multiplicity of tensions, and lack of linearity.

This book sets out to offer some explanations of this contested phenomenon called globalization, accepting that globalization in some way provides a shorthand marker to denote the breadth and depth of twenty-first-century international relations. But this, although an important purpose of the book, is not primary. Its primary aim is to show the pertinence and relevance of historical materialism as a theory of international relations – including that of contemporary international relations or globalization. The first of the three related objectives of the book, therefore, is to establish the relevance of historical materialist approaches to today's international social, political, economic and cultural life – to help explain this globalizing world. The second is to explain what is understood by historical materialist theories and how they can be used to make sense of, and change, the world in which we live. The third is to critically interpret and intervene in the politics of globalization. The book concludes with a historical materialist interpretation of the ideology and politics of what many contributors understand as 'globalizing capitalism'.

Relevance

The first part of the book demonstrates the relevance of historical materialist approaches to the study of globalization and international relations more generally. This part contains reference to some of the traditions of Marxian inquiry that have sought to understand 'globalizing capitalism' – its dynamics and trajectory (or, more accurately, its possible trajectories) – and investigates how some of these traditions of thought can be used to help us understand contemporary international relations – or 'globalization'. The concept of imperialism is reworked and dissected. An emphasis is placed right from the beginning on how historical materialist approaches help explain the world but also encourage its transformation.

In assessing the relevance of historical materialism to the era of globalization, contributors remind us of the continuities which relate contemporary global processes, and indeed possible future worlds, to the history of capitalism as an expansive form of social organization. Understanding historical materialism to imply a focus 'not on some transhistorical "economic" sphere, but on historically specific material conditions of social reproduction' (p.18), Ellen Wood argues that processes often called 'globalization' are not qualitatively new but represent instead the universalization of capitalist social relations. To the extent that territorial states (which existed prior to the eighteenth-century emergence of capitalist production in England) have been internalized, transformed and brought to maturity within capitalism's characteristic structural separation of the 'economic' from the 'political' (see also the chapter by Hannes Lacher in this volume), such states have become integral to the capitalist organization of social life. While acknowledging the increasing interconnectedness of international economic life, Wood argues that there is no reason to believe that globalizing capitalism entails the supersession of the territorial state by some supranational sovereign authority, nor of the national economic spaces which these political entities have organized. Indeed, capitalist globalization is likely to continue historical processes of uneven development, competition and rivalry across national states and national capitals. Contrary to those who argue for the emergence of a transnational capitalist ruling class and a nascent global state apparatus (compare, e.g., William Robinson's chapter in this volume), Wood suggests that market-mediated economic relations readily outdistance the social organization of political rule, so that globalizing capitalism is increasingly reliant on nation-states for the political mediation of local spaces. As 'a global system organized nationally' (p.37) globalizing capitalism is likely to generate an intensification of the contradiction between economic expansionism and the territorially defined forms of political

authority upon which capitalism depends for social stability and political reproduction. In the spaces opened up by this contradiction, Wood reminds us, there is
room for opposition and cause for hope.

Like a number of contributors to this volume, Bob Sutcliffe believes tendencies towards globalization to have been overstated, and he too questions the
representation of globalization as a fundamental discontinuity in social life.
Deploying metaphors of spirals and contradictions, Sutcliffe argues that – at its
best – historical materialist analysis leads one to 'think about change as something complex and many sided, and yet not totally random or chaotic' (p.43). For
Sutcliffe, globalization is not entirely new, nor is it simply a recurrence of long-
established patterns. Previous eras of international capitalist expansion – the era
of inter-imperialist rivalry preceding the First World War, and the neo-colonial
intensification of North–South relations of inequality following the Second
World War – have been the objects of sustained historical materialist analysis
and, Sutcliffe implies, it would be as serious an error to neglect the hard-won
insights of previous generations of Marxian theorists as it would be to accept
them uncritically as a template for understanding our own historical situation.
Spiral-like, capitalism is again entering a phase of intensified international
activity which retains some of the marks and contradictions of previous episodes
of imperialist expansion: 'Conflict between national capitals remains important,
and so does the exploitation, domination and marginalization of many countries
within the globalizing capitalist structure' (p.57). Recalling the classical Marxist
thesis that capitalism generates its own gravediggers, Sutcliffe notes emergent
forces of transnational resistance which may even now be coalescing around
these spirals and contradictions.

Insistent that historical materialists (of all people) must not shy away from
looking history in the face, Michael Cox situates contemporary Marxian analysis
in the wake of the Cold War and asks it to account for itself. With the tone of an
old friend and sympathetic critic, Cox broadly surveys Marxian and related
radical theory as it attempts to come to grips with the collapse of 'actually
existing socialism', globalizing capitalism and its contradictions, and the question
of US hegemonic power. Absent the emergence of a unified working class as
history's universal emancipatory subject, and with the taint of Soviet-style
socialism's ignominious collapse, the greatest challenge for radical theory in the
current period, Cox concludes, is not so much the critical analysis of emergent
tendencies in a contemporary capitalist world, but rather the formulation of a
coherent vision of an alternative possible world.

Elided from most contemporary discussions of globalization, Fred Halliday
notes at the outset of his chapter, are the crucial terms *capitalism* and *imperialism*.
'That this process is conducted for profit, with the aim of both subjugating and
incorporating, is the central dynamic, and secret, of the modern epoch' (p.76). As
does Sutcliffe, Halliday argues strongly for historical continuities in the expansion
of capitalism and suggests that a critical re-reading of historical materialist theories
of imperialism and neo-colonialism can teach us much about the hierarchical and
exploitative character of processes which may fashionably be subsumed, and

obscured, under the rubric of globalization. Most importantly, understanding contemporary processes in terms of capitalist expansion and domination holds out the possibility for political movements of transnational resistance: 'the task, common to both developed and developing countries, is that of bringing the processes of contemporary capitalism under democratic control, and of realising the emancipatory potential within advanced and subordinated capitalism alike' (p.88).

Mark Laffey and Kathryn Dean are likewise concerned with the ability of historical materialism to inform emancipatory political practices across an emergent global social formation, but underscore the dangers of responding to globalization with a reassertion of economistic forms of Marxian analysis. Such analysis not only reproduces conceptually capitalism's systemic tendency towards the domination of social life by the economic, it also marginalizes those forms of subjectivity and of struggle which are not reducible to the class categories of European modernity. Arguing for 'a flexible Marxism for flexible times', Laffey and Dean suggest that many contemporary Marxists have been unduly scornful of the work of Louis Althusser and have neglected his insights on crucial questions of subjectivity, ideology and the conditions of meaningful social action. Viewed in terms of a dialectically interpreted and revivified Althusserian conceptual field, capitalism and its economizing project appear dually threatened: on the one hand, by its own complex sets of contradictory logics and practices, distributed across various relatively autonomous aspects of the capitalist whole; and on the other by capitalism's articulation with various pre-capitalist or non-capitalist relations, identities and practices within concrete social formations. In both instances, difference becomes crucial to transformative agency. Indeed, central to Laffey and Dean's interpretation of globalization are the manifold tensions which must emerge between the economizing logic of capitalism and a world of cultural multiplicities. The flexible Marxism championed by Laffey and Dean 'offers hope of generating a critical theory that is attentive to the quite proper concerns of political economy without at the same time being blind to the importance and relatively autonomous causal power of difference' (p.103). Transformative political possibilities, they remind us in good dialectical fashion, are crucially related to the ways in which we understand ourselves in relation to the world around us.

Theories

Drawing upon Marxian categories and insights, contributors to the next part of the book consciously seek to develop historical materialism as a theory of international relations. In his contribution to this volume, Peter Burnham criticizes those – such as practitioners of neo-Gramscian international studies – who, he argues, would reduce class to 'just another "interest" in a methodology characterised by Weberian factor analysis' (p.113). Rather than reaffirming a Marxist-Leninist world-view with its deterministic methodology and statist political commitments, Burnham prescribes a return to Marxian conceptual fundamentals of class, labour, and struggle in order to reconstruct an 'open Marxism'.

> Class struggle ... lies at the heart of Marx's account of accumulation as capital must not only extract surplus from labour daily in the production process but must also ensure the successful reproduction of the total social circuit of capital through its three principal forms [the commodity-form, money-form and productive form of capital].
>
> (p.114)

On this view, capital is a *process* of self-expanding value in which, if it is to be successfully consummated in accumulation, must assume different forms as it completes its circuit. It is the pervasiveness of class struggle (more or less self-conscious), and the possibility of interruption at any point throughout this circuit, which creates real, if also open-ended, possibilities of systemic crisis and social transformation. Likewise, the state is understood as a relation in process: 'National states exist as political "nodes" or "moments" in the global flow of capital and their development is therefore part of the antagonistic and crisis-ridden development of capitalist society' (p.123). States attempt to facilitate accumulation by channelling class struggle into non-class forms, and managing the circuits of capital. Globalization, then, signifies a 'deepening' of international circuits of capital and corresponding challenges to political management of those increasingly complex circuits and their manifold contradictions.

In a wide-ranging historical survey of the emergence of Western philosophy, Kees van der Pijl suggests that Marx's revolutionary dialectical synthesis of materialism/idealism was often reduced by various followers and interpreters to a naturalistic and scientistic materialism unable to animate a transformative politics: 'the actual labour movement, if it adhered to an explicit philosophical position at all, more often adopted naturalistic materialism than Marx's historical materialism because manual labour in combination with experimental natural science was conducive to that perspective' (p.143). As globalizing capitalism transforms the social organization of production such that manual and mental labour are increasingly integrated in the 'collective worker' through the world-wide socialization of labour, van der Pijl suggests that the dialectical preconditions of human emancipation may be nearer than ever to realization.

Hannes Lacher both celebrates and criticizes the revival of historical materialist international studies which has taken place in recent years. In particular, he highlights the difficulties of Marxian scholarship – classical theories of imperialism as well as contemporary theories of the capitalist state – in providing an adequate account of the interstate system. While acknowledging that capitalist geopolitics are qualitatively different from absolutist or feudal geopolitics, Lacher offers a powerful theoretical and historical argument against the thesis that the modern state – and, by extension, the system of states – was born out of the very historical processes which gave rise to capitalism. Drawing on the work of Robert Brenner and Ellen Wood, among others, he argues instead that the emergence of a system of states, a process driven by the historically distinct politico-economic imperatives of absolutist rule, preceded the emergence of capitalist production relations and cannot adequately be understood as their product. Following the emergence of capitalist production relations in England, however, the dynamics of absolutist geopolitics were transformed and the system of territorial states was 'internalized' within, and became integral to, a distinctly capitalist system of social relations: 'Territoriality became exclusive with respect to political space only, while the privatization of appropriative power [in the hands of a capitalist class] allowed for the organization of surplus extraction across boundaries through the productive employment of contractually secured labour' (p.159). This insight generates a plethora of challenges for Marxian international studies, which is on this view obliged to untangle the complex and contradictory ways in which capitalist processes and relations have been shaped by the historical fact that capitalism's 'political space is fractured by sovereign territoriality' (p.160). Concurring with other contributors to this volume who emphasize inter-imperialist rivalry, Lacher argues that this structural disjuncture puts states in the position of rivalry:

> Whereas the state domestically stands apart from the competition between individual capitals, and seeks to regulate the economy through universal forms of governance like the rule of law and money, in the international sphere it is or can itself be a competitor seeking to promote the interests of its capital with political and economic means.
>
> (pp.160–1)

However, in contrast to some contributors – such as Wood, whose chapter strongly suggests that the states system is likely to remain into the indefinite future as the problematic political infrastructure of economically universalizing capitalism – Lacher views the persistence of territorially based rule as very much an open question in the era of globalization.

In response to the rise of 'social constructivism' as the newest (counter-) orthodoxy within international relations, Benno Teschke and Christian Heine argue that constructivists' criticisms of historical materialism are based on a systematic misreading of Marxian theory, neglecting its relational ontology and erroneously subsuming it 'under the deductive-nomological protocols of the natural sciences' (p.165). Launching their own critique, Teschke and Heine point towards contradictions and lacunae in the Weberian epistemology which underlies constructivism and undermines its attempts to understand neoliberal restructuring and globalization: 'We criticised this [constructivist] account because it treated "social purpose" as a domestic black box, failed to relate globalisation to capitalist crisis, and underspecified the fundamental relation between states and markets under capitalism' (p.175). A dialectical vision of historical materialism, the authors maintain, provides for a more compelling and politically empowering interpretation of neoliberalism and globalization insofar as it represents these as problematic and contestable responses to a crisis of capitalist profitability which had its onset in the 1970s. Further, they argue that globalization should not be understood in terms of the diminution of state power or the effacement of politics: 'neoliberalism is a conscious state policy that is not to be confused with the self-cancellation of the state' (p.182). Political struggles and correlations of social forces, which account for unevenness in the patterns of neoliberal restructuring, remain central to the processes of capitalist globalization.

Politics

The theoretical traditions identified by contributors to this book provide vocabularies for the political analysis of the globalizing world in which we live. Taking a brief from the famous Marxian thesis which understands historical materialism as being engaged in social critique as part of a political project of changing the world, contributors explore how the politics of globalization are being played out in today's world. Rather than viewing global capitalism as an ineluctable natural force, contributors seek to show how a dialectic of power and resistance is at work in the contemporary global political economy – producing and contesting new realities and creating conditions in which new forms of collective self-determination become thinkable and materially possible.

According to Alejandro Colás, globalization should be understood as integrally related to 'the class antagonisms inherent in capitalism' (p.191). The politics of globalization necessarily entails, as both cause and consequence, struggles between capital and labour – 'a process whereby the very policies and strategies developed by capitalists and workers in response to globalisation, themselves throw up new expressions of international class antagonisms' (p.192). Along with Burnham, Colás is strongly critical of neo-Gramscian interpretations of globalization, which he taxes with a top-down perspective which largely abstracts from the social relations of production, and hence reifies transnational ruling class agency and obscures the ongoing contestation of class power, especially as it unfolds unevenly across various local contexts. At the most abstract level, Colás argues that class must be seen as neither the subject of globalization (as in interpretations which emphasize ruling class agency), nor as its object (as in narratives stressing intensified subjugation and exploitation of global workers), but rather – as simultaneously the subject and object of these fundamental and contradictory political processes. Interpreting concrete class struggles, however, challenges Marxists to account for the ways in which capitalist social relations have been articulated with other, non-capitalist forms of social organization. 'It is this complex interface between the universality of capitalist social relations and their specific manifestation in different socio-historical contexts, which arguably defines international class-formation and reproduction' (p.205). A viable socialist politics for the new century, Colás suggests, can only be constructed on such a basis.

In contrast to a number of contributors to this volume whose attitudes towards the concept of globalization range from ambivalence to outright hostility, William Robinson embraces it as 'a concept useful intellectually and enabling politically', for it is this concept which enables historical materialist critique of a political process Robinson describes as 'the transnationalization of the state' (p.210). On this view, globalization represents an 'epochal shift' in which the displacement of pre-capitalist relations is completed and capitalist commodification is universalized, national circuits of accumulation are subsumed within global circuits, a transnational capitalist class emerges and the nation-state is tendentially transformed, superseded by and incorporated within a transnational state (TNS) as the political aspect of capitalist social organization. Deploying Gramscian concepts much maligned by some of our contributors, Robinson suggests that 'The TNS comprises those institutions and practices in global society that maintain, defend, and advance the emergent hegemony of a global bourgeoisie and its project of constructing a new global capitalist historical bloc' (p.215). Patterns of nation-state based political accommodation between capitalist and popular classes, and the constraints on accumulation which these have represented, have been increasingly vitiated by the transnational reorganization of capitalist power, displaced by the hegemonic project of the Washington Consensus. Robinson cautions his readers that there is nothing inevitable in these tendencies. Increasingly global, capitalism is nonetheless a deeply contradictory system and, like all hegemonic projects, the emergent TNS is both contestable and contested. To do so effectively, working and popular classes will need to extend their own political horizons, mobilize on a transnational scale, and construct 'alliances, networks, direct actions and organizations' capable of challenging the power of global capital.

Applying in an original and unorthodox way some core insights of historical materialism to the analysis of law, Claire Cutler argues that the law is a human social product and, having been produced in an historical context of capitalist dominance, is not class-neutral. Legal rules are a crucial constituent of property relations and privatized class power, and also form the 'legal culture' of a transnational bloc advancing a globalizing neoliberal agenda under the guise of naturalized representations of property, market, and capital. 'The globalization of the rule of law is an integral aspect of neoliberal discipline, which is expanding the private sphere of capital accumulation, while constraining potentially democratizing influences' (p.236). Cutler, too, adopts some of Gramsci's, insights in her analysis of capitalist globalization and transformations of international law, insisting that legal norms are also terrains of struggle fraught with implications for class-based power. 'The law can be used by the disenfranchised and dispossessed as a powerful instrument of change once the mythology of its inherent objectivity and neutrality is displaced by the sort of critical analysis provided by historical materialism' (p.251).

Class, state and the law are here discussed not as reflective of some transhistorical conceptual vacuum but are analysed as part of the recursive social relationships in which they are born and which they help to shape. Illustrating the thesis of this volume that globalization entails real social relations for real people which are often both oppressive and unequal but yet contain germs of emancipatory promise, this part includes an analysis of the contradictory nature of empirical reality for the electorate of the member states of the European Union.

Hazel Smith approaches the politics of European integration through a historical materialist lens. In particular, she focuses on the ways in which the language of individual rights embodied in the Amsterdam treaty of 1997 partakes of the contradictory character of liberal capitalist democracies. While the language of rights represents persons as abstractly equal individuals – the very representations which Marx attacked in his early critique of 'political emancipation' and his subsequent analyses of the appearances of contractual market relations – these representations are deeply problematic and potentially double-edged in the context of privatized capitalist powers ensconced in the economic sphere. European integration, and the promotion of liberal democracy, which now attends it, entail

> the contradictory normative project inherent to a capitalist logic which limits individual rights to a politics which is about facilitating capitalist exchange and, at the same time, provides what philosophers sometimes call 'the conditions of possibility' for emancipation through the collective exercise of those rights.
>
> (p.266)

To the extent that globalization represents the universalization of capitalist production relations and its associated political forms, struggles over the effective meaning and scope of 'rights' may become important terrains of struggle.

Like Laffey and Dean, Scott Solomon and Mark Rupert affirm the value of historical materialist analyses of globalization but are sceptical that the political processes involved can adequately be understood in terms of traditional Marxian categories of class. Drawing on neo-Gramscian insights regarding the mediation of political struggle through ideology, and the practical significance of social self-understandings and identities, Solomon and Rupert argue that

> the class-based relations of production under capitalism create the *possibility* of particular kinds of agency, but these possibilities can only be realized through the political practices of concretely situated social actors, practices which must negotiate the tensions and possibilities – the multiple social identities, powers, and forms of agency – resident within popular common sense.
>
> (p.293)

On this view, central to the politics of globalization will be struggles to counterpose visions of globalization/solidarity to dominant narratives of globalization/ competitiveness. While there are indications that such struggles are under way, Solomon and Rupert suggest that

> If such projects are to forge a unified resistance to globalizing capitalism, they must find ways to articulate class-based identities with other social identities and powers already resident and active within the popular common sense of working people in various parts of the world.
>
> (p.297)

Historical materialism as theory of globalization

That the contributors to this volume do not speak in a single voice should not surprise anyone familiar with the rich, complex and contradictory intellectual and political history of the Marxian tradition. It was never our aim to resolve the ambiguities, tensions and conflicts within historical materialism, or to produce a new party line on globalization. Rather we have sought to give voice to various currents within the tradition in order to demonstrate its continued vitality.

What we have in common is a view that historical materialism is relevant for both the theoretical understanding of globalization and for providing political analysis of how change might be possible within the limits and possibilities provided by globalizing capitalist social relations. Marxist concepts such as class, state and imperialism have not yet lost their ability to help frame the world and in some ways may be more pertinent than ever. There is more tentativeness, however, and less optimism, about the ability of historical materialist approaches to help challenge and, therefore, change social conditions. The bankruptcy of those actually existing socialisms and the lack of examples of democratic socialism as an end state have not helped. The Gramscian aphorism 'pessimism of the intellect, optimism of the will' is apposite here however. Given that there are many examples of democratic socialist practice world-wide, in various stages of revolutions, in solidarity struggles and in various collective enterprises world-wide, the next step for a further volume of historical materialist theorizing is perhaps to analyse the sites of political and social struggle where transformative practices and processes can be observed.

This volume identifies sites of struggle and transformative potential and addresses the tensions and possibilities of globalizing capitalism and historical materialist critique. Rather than foreclose the development of historical materialist thought, we have sought here its re-opening.

Acknowledgements and genesis

The editors of this volume first discussed at the Toronto International Studies Association in 1997 the possibilities of bringing together established scholars with younger scholars of Marx. We were particularly aware of the fine new work emerging from younger scholars in the discipline of international relations and wanted to find ways around which these scholars could be supported to form a 'critical mass' in the discipline. We were also aware of how difficult it had been, especially during the period of the Cold War, for serious historical materialist scholarship to be heard or published and how personally difficult it had been for those lone individuals who had braved what was at best marginalization and at worst what was often close to hostility when they had attempted to pursue any form of historical materialist intellectual agenda. Almost paradoxically, the end of the Cold War allowed space for the resurgence of such theorizing – partly because with the defeat of the Communist experiments, there appeared to be no possible threat from an 'academic' Marxism. Into this space climbed this project. Here Hazel Smith would like to thank all the scholars involved in the London

School of Economics historical materialist working group, led by Justin Rosenberg, all of them provided inspiration and confirmation that the historical materialist project was necessary, essential and timely. This book is also conceived of partly as a homage to those who have struggled to maintain a hearing for historical materialist approaches set out in this volume – many of whom we are proud to say are represented as contributors to this volume. It is of course invidious to pick out individuals but we do want to express special appreciation to Ellen Wood, whose work the word 'path-breaking' seemed designed for, and who has set standards for scholarly and political inquiry which she would with characteristic modesty be surprised to hear are standards which many would want to emulate but few could surpass.

Much of this volume has had to be put together while one of the editors was based in Pyongyang for a year with the United Nations, with all the attendant problems of communication (insufficient electricity – sometimes none at all – not enough voltage for faxes, no internet, no reliable postal service, etc.) and the other was coping with all the unfortunately now normal demands of modern academic life, which leave little time for 'research'. This book has been possible, in the end, however, because of the outstanding commitment of its contributors. They have not only submitted work that is of the highest scholarly standards but have submitted to the editing process with immense patience and forbearance.

We were very fortunate to secure support from Professor Richard Higgott of the Centre for the Study of Globalisation and Regionalisation at the University of Warwick, which resulted in generous financial backing such as to fund a workshop on historical materialism and globalization, at Warwick, in April 1999. The International Studies Association also financially supported the project. We are very grateful for all this support.

We hope it is not too much of a cliché to finish by saying that what we all share – editors and contributors – is a vision of scholarly work which involves a commitment to do our best to try to make the world intelligible, to explain and to understand, at the same time, never forgetting that 'the point is to change the world'. This book is not conceived as a 'threat' to conventional or ruling ideas about what constitutes good theory for understanding and explaining contemporary international relations and, most particularly, the phenomenon of globalization – but as a challenge to those theories.

Part I

Globalization

The relevance of historical
materialist approaches

1 Global capital, national states*

Ellen Meiksins Wood

Capitalist economies are all 'capitalist', despite their many national diversities, because they share certain common principles or 'laws of motion', a certain common 'logic of process'. In one way or another, they are all subject to the capitalist imperatives of competition, capital accumulation and profit-maximization. All national capitalist economies also exist only in relation to others, and capitalism has from the beginning been tendentially 'global'. Capitalist principles and processes are now more universal than ever before, and capitalist economies are, as we are constantly reminded, more interconnected and global than ever.

Yet there is no 'global economy' abstracted from the particular local, national, and regional economies that constitute it, or from the relations among them, whether among major capitalist powers or between imperialist powers and subaltern states. The general laws of capitalism and global economic forces manifest themselves in specific national and regional forms, and the global dynamics of capitalism continue to be driven by forces within, and relations among, national economies and nation-states. The emergence of capitalism was closely tied to the evolution of the modern nation-state, and that close link has shaped the development and expansion of capitalism ever since. The global economy as we know it today is still constituted by national entities.

My intention here is to explore the contradiction between the global sweep of capitalism and the persistence of national entities by tracing, in very broad strokes, some of the connections between capitalism and the nation-state from the beginning until now. The object of this exercise is not specifically to explicate the contribution that historical materialism can make to an understanding of 'globalization', but it should become clear why I believe that the interconnections between the modern state system and the development of global capitalism can be more fruitfully explored from the perspective of historical materialism than from more conventional theoretical vantage points.

For instance, the relations and the contradictions between the global and the national can be clarified by understanding the separation of 'economic' and 'political' spheres and the relations between them. But that separation is specific to capitalism. The 'economy', conceived as a distinct and separate sphere, is a notion that has meaning only under capitalism, where two fundamental and related conditions are met: first, all economic actors are market dependent – that is, dependent on the market for the conditions of their self-reproduction, and hence subject to the specifically 'economic' imperatives of competition and accumulation; and second, appropriation takes place not by direct coercive means, through the exercise of political or military power in the hands of the appropriators themselves (as, for example, in feudalism), but by purely economic means, the 'free' exchange between capital and labour in which direct producers are compelled by their propertylessness to exchange their labour-power for a wage. The economy as a separate 'sphere', in other words, exists only when the market regulates social reproduction and when exploitation is disaggregated into two separate 'moments', apportioned between two distinct agencies: the moment of appropriation by capital itself and the moment of enforcement by a separate state power.

The 'historical' in historical materialism allows us to explore the conditions and implications of this historically specific separation. Its 'materialism' focuses our attention not on some transhistorical economic sphere, but on historically specific material conditions of social reproduction, which not only affect all social spheres but constitute them as distinct spheres in the first place. From that perspective, we can explore a development like globalization not as some ahistorical natural process but as a truly historical one.

Joined at birth?

It is not at all uncommon to insist on the connections between the emergence of capitalism and the rise of the nation-state, or even to define capitalism as a system of nation-states. Typically, the connections are seen through the prism of one or another theory of 'modernity' or 'rationalization', according to which certain 'modern' or 'rational' economic, political, and cultural forms have developed more or less in tandem, combining a process of urbanization and commercialization with the formation of a 'rational' state. One particularly ingenious account suggests that the emergence of the absolutist state in early modern Europe freed the 'bourgeois' commercial economy from the dead hand of feudalism and landlordly power, separating political and economic spheres by concentrating sovereignty in a centralized state. Another influential explanation suggests that the European nation-state, in sharp contrast, say, to Asian empires, laid the foundations for capitalism because the organization of Europe into multiple polities, instead of in one over-arching empire, permitted the development of a trade-based division of labour, without the burden of massive appropriation by an imperial state which syphoned off surpluses that could otherwise have been invested.[1]

Let me propose a somewhat different account of the relation between the rise of capitalism and the nation-state. This account will be based on certain presuppositions which can only be stated here baldly, without elaboration, but which have been discussed at greater length elsewhere.[2] The main presuppositions are these: that capitalism was not simply the natural outcome of certain transhistorical processes like 'rationalization', technological progress, urbanization, or the expansion of trade; that its emergence required more than the removal of obstacles to increased trade and growing markets or to the exercise of 'bourgeois' rationality; that while certain European, or Western European, conditions, not least the insertion of Europe in a larger and non-European network of international trade, were necessary to its emergence, those same conditions produced diverse effects in various European, and even Western European, cases; and that the necessary conditions for the 'spontaneous' or indigenous and self-sustaining development of a capitalist system, with mutually reinforcing agricultural and industrial sectors, existed only in England.[3]

How, then, do these presuppositions apply to the relation between the rise of capitalism and the nation-state? We can certainly accept that capitalism developed in the distinctive context of the early modern European state, which was not itself created by capitalism – or, more precisely, that capitalism developed in tandem with the process of state formation. But, while there were certain common preconditions, not all European, or even Western European, nation-states developed in the same way. The French absolutist state, for instance, had an economic logic quite distinct from capitalist forms of exploitation or capitalist laws of motion. Notwithstanding France's 'bourgeois' revolution, we cannot take for granted its 'spontaneous' evolution into capitalism, in the absence of external pressures from an already existing English capitalism.[4]

The development of capitalism and the nation-state were intertwined in England in a very particular way. But to insist on the particularity of this English relationship is not at all to deny the close connection between capitalism and the nation-state in general. On the contrary, the particular nature of the English relationship only serves to emphasize that close connection. England was not, of course, alone in producing a sovereign territorial state, but it was, in the first instance, alone in producing a capitalist system. At the same time, the process that gave rise to English capitalism was accompanied by the development of a more clearly defined territorial sovereignty than existed elsewhere in Europe. The social transformations that brought about capitalism were the same ones that brought the nation-state to maturity.

As Marx pointed out long ago, precapitalist modes of production were characterized by a unity of economic and political power, specifically in the sense that exploitation was carried out by 'extra-economic' means – that is, by means of political, judicial, and/or military power, or what has been called 'politically constituted property'.[5] This unity – which cannot be effectively accommodated by a conceptual framework that takes as given the separation of the economic and the political, or their existence as distinct spheres – existed in a very wide variety of forms. For instance, many ancient empires employed state power to collect tribute from subject peoples, including their own peasants, and imperial office was the principal means of acquiring great wealth.

What was notable about precapitalist forms in Europe was the emergence of a fragmented state power, the 'parcellized sovereignty' of Western feudalism, which created a distinctive kind of extra-economic power, the power of feudal lordship. The fragmented military, political, and judicial powers of the state became the means by which individual lords extracted surpluses from peasants. At the same time, political parcellization was matched by economic fragmentation. Internal trade, for example, even when it extended beyond very local peasant markets, was less like modern capitalist forms of trade in an integrated competitive market than like traditional forms of international commerce, a series of separate local markets joined together by a carrying trade conducted by merchants 'buying cheap' in one market and 'selling dear' in another, or an 'infinite succession of arbitrage operations between separate, distinct, and discrete markets'.[6]

The feudal ruling class was eventually compelled to consolidate its fragmented political power in the face of peasant resistance and the plainly untenable disorder of aristocratic conflict. Parcellized sovereignty gave way to more centralized monarchies in some parts of Europe. But if feudalism was a precondition of capitalism, and if capitalism, with its separation of political and economic spheres, emerged in conjunction with a process of feudal centralization, the process of state formation took different forms in different places, and capitalism was only one of several outcomes of the transition from feudalism.

One effect was absolutism, which, instead of producing a capitalist economy, reproduced the *unity* of political and economic power at the level of the central state, while never completely overcoming the parcellization of feudalism. The most notable example is the absolutist state in France, regarded by many as the prototype of the emerging 'modern' nation-state. Formed in a process of state centralization that elevated one among many feudal powers to a position of monarchical dominance, French absolutism remained in many ways rooted in its feudal past.[7]

On the one hand, the bureaucracy that is supposed to be the mark of the French state's modernity represented a structure of offices used by office-holders as a kind of private property, a means of appropriating peasant-produced surpluses, what has been called a kind of centralized feudal rent, in the form of taxation. This was a mode of appropriation very different, in its means and in its rules for reproduction, from capitalist exploitation – depending, for example, on direct coercion to squeeze more surpluses out of the direct producers, instead of on intensifying exploitation by enhancing labour productivity.

On the other hand, the absolutist state never completely displaced other forms of politically constituted property. It always lived side-by-side, and in tension, with other, more fragmented forms, the remnants of feudal parcellized sovereignty. Aristocrats, the church, and municipalities clung to their old autonomous powers, military, political, or judicial. Even when these powers were fatally weakened by state centralization and hence no longer represented a fragment of parcellized sovereignty, they often continued to serve as a fiercely protected (occasionally revived or even invented) source of income for their possessors. At the same time, the central state, competing for the same peasant-produced surpluses, typically co-opted many potential competitors by giving them state office, exchanging one kind of politically constituted property for another. But the remnants of aristocratic privilege and municipal jurisdiction, together with the tensions among various forms of politically constituted property, remained to the end just as much a part of French absolutism as was the centralizing monarchy.

Elsewhere in Europe, the fragmentation of property and polity were even more marked, and everywhere, these fragmented forms of politically constituted property, like the centralized version, represented a mode of appropriation antithetical to capitalism. They were inimical to capitalism in yet another sense too: they fragmented not only the state but the economy. Instead of a national market, there were separate local and municipal markets (not to mention internal trade barriers) characterized not by capitalist competition but by the old forms of trade, not the appropriation of surplus value created in production but commercial profit-taking in the sphere of circulation. To put it another way, the parcellization of sovereignty and the parcellization of markets were two sides of the same coin, rooted in the same property relations.

The fragmentation of both economy and polity was overcome first and most completely in England. From the outset – certainly from the Norman Conquest – the English state (the emphasis here is on England, not on other parts of what would become the 'United Kingdom') was more unified than others in Europe, without the same parcellized sovereignty. For instance, when France still had its regional 'estates', England had a unitary national parliament, and when France (even up until the Revolution) had some 360 local law codes, England had a more nationally unified legal system, especially its 'common law' adjudicated by royal courts, which had become the preferred and dominant legal system very early in the development of the English state. But this unity was not simply a matter of political or legal unification. Its corollary was a degree of economic unification unlike any other in history, already in the seventeenth century constituting something like a national economy, an integrated and increasingly competitive national market centred on London.

Both political and economic unity can be traced to the same source. The centralization of the state in England was not based on a feudal unity of economic and political power. The state did not represent a private resource for office-holders in the way or on the scale that it did in France, nor did the state on the whole have to compete with other forms of politically constituted property. Instead, state formation took the form of a cooperative project, a kind of division of labour between political and economic power, between the monarchical state and the aristocratic ruling class, between a central political power that enjoyed a virtual monopoly of coercive force much earlier than others in Europe (the English aristocracy, for instance, was effectively demilitarized very early) and an economic power based on private property in land far more concentrated than elsewhere in Europe (in France, for instance, by far the most land continued to be held by peasants).

Here, then, was the separation between the moment of coercion and the moment of appropriation, allocated between two distinct but complementary spheres, that uniquely characterizes capitalist exploitation. English landlords increasingly depended on purely 'economic' forms of exploitation, while the state maintained order and enforced the whole system of property. Instead of enhancing their own coercive powers to squeeze more out of peasants, landlords relied on the coercive power of the state to sustain the whole system of property, while they exercised their purely economic power, their concentrated landhold-ings, to intensify the exploitation of labour by increasing its productivity, in conditions where appropriators and producers were becoming increasingly market dependent.

The weakness of politically constituted property in England, in other words, meant both the rise of capitalism and the evolution of a truly sovereign and unified national state. It also meant a more sharply defined territorial polity. In feudalism, the territorial boundaries of political sovereignty tended to be fluid, expanding or contracting with the reach of the lord's, or the monarch's, personal rule, his proprietary domain and family alliances. The centralizing monarchies of Europe certainly created territorial states in which the central more or less sovereign power exerted its predominant coercive force over a more or less well-defined territory. But the fluid boundaries of feudalism were never firmly fixed until personal rule was replaced by an impersonal state, and that could never be fully accomplished until the separa-tion of the political and economic, the moments of appropriation and coercion, private property and public power. Just as the separation of the political and the economic in capitalism ended the contestation of sovereignty among competing sites of politically constituted property, so did it detach the territorial borders of the state from the fluctuating fortunes of personal prop-erty and dynastic connections.

There were, to sum up, two sides to the historical relation between capitalism and the nation-state. On the one hand, that state was not itself produced by capitalism. The 'modern' state, together with 'modern' conceptions of territori-ality and sovereignty, emerged out of social relations that had nothing to do with capitalism, in the tensions between 'parcellized sovereignties' and centralizing monarchies.[8] On the other hand, the rise of capitalism, which took place in the context of a rising nation-state, brought that state to fruition – or, to put it more precisely, the particular form of English state formation belonged to the same process that brought about capitalism. The transformation of politically consti-tuted property into capitalist property was at the same time, and inseparably, a transformation of the state.

A state with an unambiguous sovereign power over a clearly defined territory did not come completely into its own until capitalist property had displaced precapitalist modes of appropriation – that is, until capitalist property displaced both parcellized sovereignty and the fragmented economy entailed by politically constituted property. The territorial nation-state was part of a more general European process of state formation, but a clearly defined territorial state with a truly sovereign power matured only when political sovereignty became both separate from and coextensive with a national economy.

Capitalism and inter-national relations

For those who regard capitalism as the consequence of commercial expansion when it reached a critical mass, there is something paradoxical about the development of English capitalism. England was certainly part of a vast trading network. But other European nation-states in the early modern period were also deeply involved in the system of international trade, as were non-European civilizations in Asia and the Islamic world, some of which long had trading networks more highly developed and extensive than the European. What distinguished England – and what was specifically capitalist about it – was not, in the first instance, predominance as a trading nation or any peculiarity in its way of conducting foreign trade. England's peculiarity was not its role in an outwardly expanding commercial system but, on the contrary, its inward development, the growth of a unique domestic economy.

What marked off England's commercial system from others was a single large and integrated national market, increasingly uniting the country into one economic unit (which eventually embraced the British Isles as a whole), with a specialized division of labour among interdependent regions and a growing, and mutually reinforcing, interaction between agricultural and industrial sectors. This market was also distinctive in the nature and extent of its trade in cheap everyday goods – the means of survival and self-reproduction – for a growing mass market.[9] While England competed with others in an expanding system of international trade, a new kind of commercial system was emerging at home, which would soon give it an advantage on the international plane too. Unlike traditional commercial systems, this one did not depend mainly on profits derived from 'buying cheap and selling dear', the carrying trade or arbitrage. This system was unique in its dependence on intensive as distinct from extensive expansion, on the extraction of surplus value created in production as distinct from profit in the sphere of circulation, on economic growth based on increasing productivity and competition within a single market – in other words, on capitalism.

Capitalism, then, while it certainly developed within – and could not have developed without – an international system of trade, was a domestic product. But it was not in the nature of capitalism to remain at home for long. Its need for endless accumulation, on which its very survival depended, produced new and distinctive imperatives of expansion. These imperatives operated at various levels. The most obvious was, of course, the imperialist drive. There was, to be sure, nothing new about colonialism, and Britain's major European rivals were just as much involved in the subjugation of colonial territories, in the oppression of colonial peoples, and in the slave trade. But here again, capitalism had a transformative effect. The new requirements of capitalism created new imperialist needs, and it was British capitalism that produced an imperialism answering to the specific requirements of capitalist accumulation, its particular need for resources, labour, markets, and increasing productivity. Above all, capitalism created new imperialist possibilities by generating economic imperatives that could reach far beyond direct political dominion.

Capitalism also expanded out from Britain in another and more complicated sense. The unique productivity engendered by capitalism, especially in its industrial form, gave Britain new advantages not only in its old commercial rivalries with other European states but also in their military conflicts. So, from the late eighteenth century and especially in the nineteenth, Britain's major European rivals were under pressure to develop their economies in ways that could meet this new challenge. The state itself became a major player. This was true most notably in Germany, with its state-led industrialization, which in the first instance was undoubtedly driven more by older geopolitical and military considerations than by capitalist motivations.

In these cases, the drive for capitalist development did not come from internal property relations like those that had impelled the development of capitalism in England from within. Where, as in France and Germany, there was an adequate concentration of productive forces, capitalism could develop in response to external pressures emanating from an already existing capitalist system elsewhere. States still following a precapitalist logic could become effective agents of capitalist development. The point here, however, is not simply that in these later developing capitalisms, as in many others after them, the state played a primary role. What is even more striking is the ways in which the traditional, precapitalist state system, together with the old commercial network, became a transmission belt for capitalist imperatives.

The European state system, then, was a conduit for the first outward movement of capitalism. From then on, capitalism spread outward from Europe both by means of imperialism and increasingly also by means of economic imperatives. The role of the state in imperial ventures is obvious, but even in the operation of purely economic laws of motion, the state continued to be an unavoidable medium.

Capitalism had emerged first in one country. After that, it could never emerge again in the same way. Every extension of its laws of motion changed the conditions of development thereafter, and every local context shaped the processes of change. But having once begun in a single nation-state, and having been followed by other nationally organized processes of economic development, capitalism has spread not by erasing national boundaries but by reproducing its national organization, creating an increasing number of national economies and nation-states. The inevitably uneven development of separate, if interrelated, national entities, especially when subject to imperatives of competition, has virtually guaranteed the persistence of national forms.

Nation-states and classes in today's universal capitalism

Today capitalism is all but universal. Capitalist laws of motion, the logic of capitalism, have penetrated ever deeper into the societies of advanced capitalism and spatially throughout the world. Every human practice, every social relationship, and the natural environment are subject to the requirements of profit-maximization, capital accumulation, the constant self-expansion of capital. At one extreme, in advanced capitalist countries, this means the penetration of capitalist principles into those social, institutional, and cultural spaces that even a few decades ago they had not yet reached. At the other extreme, it means the marginalization and increasing impoverishment of whole regions outside the advanced capitalist world. In a sense the class polarizations of capitalism are being reproduced in the North–South divide, together with the impoverishment of so-called 'underclasses' within advanced capitalist countries.

But to say that capitalism is universal is not to say that all, or even most, capital is transnational. The measure of universalization is not whether, or to what degree, capital has escaped the confines of the nation-state. We still have national economies, national states, nationally based capital, even nationally based transnationals. It hardly needs to be added that international agencies of capital, like the IMF, the World Bank, or the WTO, are above all agents of specific national capitals, which derive whatever powers of enforcement they have from nation-states – both the imperial states that command them and the subordinate states that carry out their orders.

There are many things to be said about capitalism today, and about its current relations with the nation-state, that lie beyond the scope of this chapter. Needless to say, a thorough examination of their complex interactions would, among other things, require a much closer inspection than is possible here of the many changes that have brought us from the early phases of capitalism to today's economic and political order. But the point here is that, throughout all the various phases or 'regimes' of capitalism, there has been one over-arching pattern: not the decline but, on the contrary, the persistence and even the proliferation of the nation-state. It is not just that nation-states have stubbornly held on through the universalization of capitalism. If anything, the universalization of capitalism has also meant, or at least been accompanied by, the universalization of the nation-state. Global capitalism is more than ever a global system of national states, and the universalization of capitalism is presided over by nation-states, especially one hegemonic superpower.

This is a point worth emphasizing. The conventional view of globalization seems to be based on the assumption that the natural tendency of capitalist development, and specifically its internationalization, is to submerge the nation-state, even if the process is admittedly still far from over. The internationalization of capital, according to that view, is apparently in an inverse relation to the development of the nation-state: the more internationalization, the less nation-state. But the historical record suggests something different. The internationalization of capital has been accompanied by the universalization of capital's original political form. When capitalism was born, the world was very far from being a world of nation-states. Today, it is just that. And while new transnational institutions have certainly emerged, they have not so much displaced the nation-state as given it new roles – in fact, in some cases, new instruments and powers.

Globalization itself is a phenomenon of national economies and national states. It is impossible to make sense of it without taking account of both uneven development and competition among national economies and without acknowledging the constant tension (the consistently contradictory relations between the USA and Japan spring to mind) between international cooperation and struggles for dominance among national capitalisms. Much of what goes under the name of globalization consists of national states carrying out policies to promote the international 'competitiveness' of their own national economies, to maintain or restore profitability to domestic capital, to promote the free movement of capital while controlling the movements of labour, typically by confining it within national boundaries, or at least strictly controlling its movements to coincide with the needs of capital, and always by subjecting it to disciplines enforced by nation-states. Even policies to create and sustain global markets, not to mention policies deliberately designed to forfeit national sovereignty, are conceived, implemented, and enforced by national governments. And nowhere is the nexus of global capital and nation-state more obvious than in the degree to which transnational organizations of capital like the IMF not only serve as the instruments of dominant states but also depend on subordinate states as the conduit of globalization.

If there has been a real movement towards transnational integration, it has tended to take the form less of globalization than regionalization. But even at the level of regional integration, the centrifugal forces of the nation-state are still at work. The global economy is constituted by regional blocs of unevenly developed and hierarchically organized national economies and nation-states. Even – or particularly – in the most ambitious, if not the only, project of transnational unification, the European Union, the tensions between cooperation and competition, or between integration and national sovereignty, are vividly on display. Real political integration, if it were possible at all, would, of course, simply create a larger state, whose purpose would be to compete with other national economies and states – and particularly the US superstate. But as it is, European integration has tended to mean growing competition among its national constituents, which is, if anything, intensified by monetary union. Nor has European integration transcended the contradictory logic of uneven development or the national exclusiveness that follows from it. In fact, the Union has brought into sharper relief the hierarchy of national economies. Major European leaders are generally quite open about the primacy of nation-states, and even those most committed to political integration persist in thinking about Europe as divided between an 'avant garde' or 'centre of gravity' and a periphery of marginal economies.

When we speak of global economic crises or downturns, too, nation-states and national economies invariably come to the fore. To be sure, crisis is never simply an Asian or Latin American crisis, nor is it a consequence of specific national strategies or policy failures, or the effect of 'crony capitalism' or any other specific and defective form of capitalism. Capitalist crisis is a consequence of systemic processes inherent in capitalism as such. At the same time, global crises are always shaped by the specific national forms of the global economy's constituent parts, each with its own history and its own internal logic, and by the relations among diverse and unevenly developed national entities.

It has been argued (by, among others, contributors to this volume) that, despite the persistence of national economies and nation-states, there now exists a 'global' capitalist class. Yet throughout the world of 'global capitalism', the principal economic actors and classes are still organized above all on a national basis. Each nation's working class has its own class formations, practices, and traditions; and while no one would deny that capital is far more mobile and less place-rooted than labour, we are still a very long way from a truly global capitalist class. No one is likely to have much trouble distinguishing US from Japanese capital, or either one from Russian or Brazilian, not only as regards their obvious cultural differences but also the divergent and competing interests among them. National classes are likely to persist precisely because global integration itself, whatever else it may mean, has meant intensified competition among national capitals.

To say, as Marx already suggested a century and a half ago, that capital acknowledges no national boundaries is certainly to say that capital is mobile and that capitalists place profit above national loyalties, so that they will move, whenever they can, wherever the imperatives of profit-maximization take them. But it certainly does not mean that they have no roots in, or no need for, the state or for their own nation-state in particular. Capital accumulation has always involved certain requirements of social order and stability which capital itself cannot provide, and market imperatives themselves require coercive enforcement (not least, to discipline the working class). These requirements up to now have been, and in the foreseeable future still promise to be, fulfilled above all by nation-states.

There are, needless to say, differences between capitalists whose main economic arena is their own domestic economy and those who operate on the global stage, deriving their massive profits from transnational movements of capital. To the extent that capitalists of the latter type have interests in common with others across national boundaries, as against the interests of their own compatriot capitalist classes, and to the extent that these transnational capitalists have certain international agencies at their command, they could (with great caution) be said to constitute a global capitalist class. But even they must rely on the coercive powers of national states. Even they – in some ways, especially they – rely on the preservation of territorially defined labour regimes and controls on the mobility of labour, which are always policed by national states and which depend on maintaining and strictly enforcing the principle of nationality.

It is no doubt true that national governments are now more than ever obliged to act in the interests of 'global' no less than local capital, including the interests of 'transnational' capital with its home base elsewhere. But this is significant not only because those capitalist interests are global but also because they need the nation-state to sustain them.

Of course the global economy is highly integrated, and of course massive and rapid movements of capital across national boundaries, especially in the form of financial speculation, are a dominant feature of the world economy. But not only is every transnational process shaped by specifically local conditions, the state is also its indispensable instrument. If 'globalization' means the decline of national capitalist classes and the nation-state, the transfer of sovereignty from the state to the organs of some kind of unified transnational capital, it certainly has not happened yet and seems unlikely ever to happen.

The new imperialism

To say all this is certainly not to deny that the relations between capital and nation-state take many different forms. The relations among advanced capitalist economies and among their national states are obviously very different from the relations between them and weaker national entities, and the room for national manoeuvre varies accordingly. Nevertheless, it is significant that all these relations are, in one way or another, inter-national.

Capitalism has, to be sure, made possible an imperial hegemony that need not rely on military conquest or political rule but dominates by means of economic imperatives and the 'laws' of the market. It is in this respect more than any other that globalization has moved beyond earlier forms of imperialism. Not only have the economic imperatives of capitalism extended into every corner of the world but new means have been found to implant them without the direct application of military force or political subordination: from 'structural adjustment' to disciplines imposed by capital lenders and speculators.

But the economic hegemony of capital requires the coercive support of the state in this domain as in every other, and the paradoxical effect of global capital's far-reaching empire is that it has become more rather than less dependent on nation-states, as increasingly global economic imperatives require local mediations. In a sense, the new forms of imperial domination by means of debt and financial manipulation, or even foreign direct investment, are what they are precisely because they provide a means of penetrating national boundaries, barriers that hardly existed for older forms of colonial domination by direct military means. That this new imperialism is no longer a matter of direct colonial domination and operates through the medium of national entities has implications, among other things, for oppositional struggles.

The other side of the new imperialism is a new kind of militarism. This one does not generally have territorial ambitions, and generally leaves nation-states in place. Its objective is not hegemony over specific colonies with identifiable geographic boundaries but boundless hegemony over the global economy. Instead of absorbing or annexing territory, this imperialist militarism typically uses massive displays of violence to assert the dominance of global capital – which really means exercising the military power of specific nation-states to assert the dominance of capital based in a few nation-states, or one in particular, the USA. These displays may have no clear objective, apart from demonstrating the capacity of US military force to move throughout the world at will, its freedom to navigate the global economy without hindrance, and enforcing the economic imperatives that make it possible for US hegemony to reach far beyond its direct political dominion.

Nevertheless, notwithstanding the 'Pax Americana' or in some ways precisely because of it, in the everyday life of global capitalism the major capitalist powers in general depend more than ever on local states throughout the world to operate globalization and enforce the demands of 'global' capital. If the economy is increasingly global, there is no commensurate political or military power to match, and nor is there ever likely to be. More likely is a growing disparity between the scope of the global market and the local, national instruments and coercive powers needed to sustain it. US military force – with or without the cover of international cooperation – is probably as close as the world will ever come to a global state power.

But the fact that the police force of last resort for global capital is still a national military force only serves to emphasize the persistent, if contradictory, relation between globalization and the nation-state. It is also clear that this global military power, for all its technological sophistication, is a very blunt instrument – as indeed it must be to sustain its long-distance and spatially unbounded dominance. It cannot provide the minute and local regulation required by capital in its daily transactions. High-tech bombs, however 'smart', are not the most effective instruments of economic order and stability. Capital has yet to find a more efficient way to meet those needs than a global system of multiple national states, each with its own legal and coercive apparatus.

What form of state 'corresponds' to global capitalism?

It is hard to foresee the day when capital will stop being organized on national principles. Existing nation-states may change their form. Some may fragment to form smaller national entities, while others may join larger regional associations. But the forces tending to prolong the historic connection between capitalism and the nation-state are very powerful, indeed rooted in the very nature of capitalism. Even the separation of the 'economic' and the 'political', the moment of appropriation and the moment of coercion, which makes capital dependent on an external agency of enforcement, tends to the preservation of the state as we know it, with its monopoly of coercive force within clearly defined, and more or less manageable, territorial boundaries. That tendency is reinforced by the uneven development of capitalism, which has preserved and proliferated the nation-state by differentiating national economies, a divisive effect perennially aggravated by the imperatives of global competition – imperatives not alleviated but intensified by globalization.

None of this implies that developments conventionally associated with the current 'globalized' world order are insignificant or negated by the persistence of national entities. Markets are certainly integrated, finance capital certainly sweeps the world in the flash of an electronic eye, the USA, together with other major capitalist powers, has certainly imposed globalization on the world economy, and global capital has certainly forged transnational agencies to advance its global class interests. The point here is simply that there is another no less essential feature of this economic order: a constant tension between the integration of the global economy and the centrifugal impulses of its constituent parts.

At the heart of this contradiction between the global and the national is the non-correspondence between capitalism's economic and political forms. It seems, on the face of it, self-evident that a global state (whatever that might mean) would better serve the interests of a globalizing capital, and it is no doubt tempting to think that the globalizing pressures of the economy will inevitably tend to globalize its political supports. The question, then, is whether the stubborn persistence of the nation-state, and the apparent lack of correspondence between economic 'base' and political 'superstructure', is simply a historical contingency or more deeply rooted in the nature of capitalism.[10]

My argument here is that, while capitalism's historic connection with the territorial state has continued to shape its patterns of reproduction, the persistence of that political form is not simply the result of tenacious historical legacies. The contradiction between capitalism's globalizing tendencies and its national form is not simply a transient confrontation between forces of the future and remnants of the past. It is not just a matter of capitalism's persistent inability to overcome a historic contradiction and grow into its 'proper' political form. The point is not simply that capitalism has so far failed to produce a global political 'superstructure' to match its global economic 'base'. The critical point is that there is an irreducible contradiction between two opposing tendencies, both of which are rooted in the nature of capitalism.

While capitalism did not create the nation-state, and nor did it invent state sovereignty or territoriality, its systemic logic has reproduced and reinforced the territorial state no less than the universalizing, globalizing force of the economy. It is, in other words, in the very nature of capitalism to intensify the contradiction between its expansionist imperatives and the territorial divisions of its original political (and economic) form.

Let us look more closely at the separation between the economic and the political in capitalism. Unlike other systems of exploitation, in which appropriating classes or states extract surplus labour from producers by direct coercion, capitalist exploitation is characterized by a division of labour between the economic moment of appropriation and the extra-economic or political moment of coercion. Underlying this separation is the market dependence of all economic actors, appropriators and producers, which creates economic imperatives distinct and apart from direct political coercion. This separation – which constitutes two distinct logics of process, each with its own dynamics, its own temporalities and its own spatial range – is both a source of strength and a source of contradiction.

On the one hand, the distinctive division of labour between the economic and political moments of capitalism, and between economic imperatives and political coercion, makes possible capitalism's unique capacity for universalization and spatial expansion. The economic powers of the feudal lord, for instance, could never extend beyond the reach of his personal ties and extra-economic powers, his military force, political rule or juridical authority. Nor, for that matter, could the economic powers of the absolutist state or any precapitalist empire exceed its extra-economic range. Capital, by contrast, is not only uniquely driven to extend its economic reach but also uniquely able to do so. The self-expansion of capital is not limited to what the capitalist can squeeze out of the direct producers by direct coercion, nor is capital accumulation confined within the spatial range of personal domination. By means of specifically economic (market) imperatives, capital is uniquely able to escape the limits of direct coercion and move far beyond the borders of political authority.

On the other hand, while the scope of capitalist economic imperatives can far outreach direct political rule and legal authority, the same disjunction that makes this possible is the root of an irreducible contradiction. The economic imperatives of capitalism are always in need of support by extra-economic powers of regulation and coercion, to create and sustain the conditions of accumulation and maintain the system of capitalist property. The transfer of certain 'political' powers to capital can never eliminate the need to retain others in a formally separate political sphere, preserving the division between the moment of economic appropriation and the moment of political coercion. Nor can purely economic imperatives ever completely supplant direct political coercion, or, indeed, survive at all without political support. This means that capitalism remains dependent on extra-economic conditions, political and legal supports, whose spatial range can never match its economic reach.

In fact, capitalism in some ways more than any other social form needs politically organized and legally defined stability, regularity and predictability in its social arrangements. Yet these are conditions of capital's existence and self-reproduction that it cannot provide for itself and that its own inherently anarchic laws of motion constantly subvert. To stabilize its constitutive social relations – between capital and labour or capital and other capitals – capitalism is especially reliant on legally defined and politically authorized regularities. The coercions that sustain these regularities must exist apart from capital's own powers of appropriation if it is to preserve its capacity for self-expansion. Furthermore, a system of market dependence, in which access to the means of subsistence is subject to the vagaries of the market (especially for the propertyless majority whose access even to the means of labour depends on selling their labour power), a system in which the economy has been 'disembedded' from other social relations, will also have a distinctive need for politically organized social provision.

It is also worth considering that the state in capitalist society, perhaps even more than in other societies, cannot rely on direct coercion alone and must also organize consent by other means. This means, among other things, that the differentiation of national entities is reinforced by differences in the cultures of legitimation that have accompanied the varied and uneven processes of economic development. At the same time, it is not the least of the many contradictions in the relation between global capital and the nation-state that, in their quest for social and political stability in the process of globalization, imperial states have not only consolidated the national statehood of subordinate states but sometimes encouraged 'public sector reform' on the model of Western liberal democracy. While it would be a mistake to exaggerate either the strength of this liberalizing impulse or its beneficial consequences, such reforms sometimes have the effect of opening new spaces for the politics of opposition, both against local regimes and against globalization – as has happened recently in parts of Asia and Latin America.

It is easy to argue that, as capital becomes increasingly global, its needs would be better served by a global state than by national states. But this remains at best a highly abstract theoretical possibility, and one that is constantly undermined by capitalism's own logic of process. The kind of legal and political order required to enable capital accumulation, and to preserve social stability in conditions of market dependence, is for all practical purposes inconceivable without clear territorial demarcations and sharply defined jurisdictions. New technologies of force have certainly extended the range of coercion, but the reach of direct legal/political dominion and civil order remains far more limited than the scope of economic imperatives, and it is hard to imagine how it could ever be otherwise.

A territorially fragmented political order may be less effective in managing transactions among globalizing capitals than in regulating relations between capital and labour. But within the range of practical possibilities, there can be little doubt that the territorial state is capital's best available option. Capitalism cannot tolerate the kind of fluidity that characterized political authority in precapitalist societies. It can tolerate it perhaps even less in the current conditions of globalization, when the deregulation of markets is aggravating the system's inherently anarchic and destabilizing effects. If, therefore, capital cannot have a global legal and coercive order coextensive with its economic reach (and even leaving out of account uneven development, which creates its own pressures against a unified global state), it must be able to move securely from one clearly defined political/legal order to another.

The social differentiation of national economies

The association between capitalism and the territorial state is not, however, simply a matter of mundane practicalities. It is not just the practical limits of political order that force capital to rely on the territorial state to carry out its regulative and coercive functions. Capitalism as a system of social relations also tends towards the territorial fragmentation of space and political authority. There is here yet another contradiction, which can, again, be brought into focus by contrasting capitalism with precapitalist forms and particularly Western feudalism.

The feudal system was, on the one hand, highly fragmented. Its 'parcellized' sovereignty represented a network of very local and personal social relations, which were at once political and economic. On the other hand, it was in the very nature of these relations that there were no rigid territorial boundaries between one feudal nexus and another. A feudal kingdom, constituted by a series of vertical relations of fealty, bondage and personal coercive power, and horizontal relations of family and dynastic alliance, was likely to have fairly porous borders, which could be breached or moved by extending, or contracting, the network of personal bonds and domination. Just as the feudal trading network was not an integrated global system but a series of arbitrage operations between one locale and another, feudalism as a social system was an aggregation of personal and local networks with permeable or moveable boundaries.

Capitalism presents a striking contrast. Its economic imperatives could indeed be said to have created a global order more integrated than ever before, maybe even a form of integration that for the first time constitutes anything even remotely resembling a global society. But the resemblance still remains remote. The development of that rudimentary global society is, and is likely to remain, far behind the contrary effect of capitalist integration: the formation of many unevenly developed economies with self-enclosed social systems of their own.

There is nothing else in the history of humanity to compare with the kind of social system created by capitalism: a complex network of tight interdependence among large numbers of people, and social classes, not joined by personal ties or direct political domination but inescapably connected by their market dependence and the market's imperative network of social relations and processes. This impersonal social system is uniquely capable of extending far beyond the reach of personal ties and direct domination, but it also has uniquely stringent conditions of existence.

A capitalist economy exists to the extent that it constitutes an integrated market within which market-dependent economic actors are compelled to compete. That market is integrated to the extent that economic actors are subject to certain common conditions, interdependencies and economic imperatives. The global economy is bound together by enough commonalities, interdependencies and common imperatives, to constitute a system of global competition. But global competition is still very far from the integrated market of a national economy in which capital and labour are subject to a truly common standard, not just a common standard of monetary exchange but social conditions sufficiently uniform to produce, among other things, a compelling social average of productivity and unit labour costs. If we think of all the conditions that determine the costs of labour and what Marxists call the 'socially necessary labour time' that constitutes the measure of value, we will have some idea of the social conditions of a unified capitalist economy.

Of course no national economy has ever neatly and completely coincided with such a uniformity of social conditions, but a well-developed capitalism certainly tends towards such a coincidence. At the same time, on the global plane, capitalist imperatives tend to produce a differentiated world of uneven social development. As capitalism brings less 'developed' societies into the orbit of its economic 'laws', it compels them to transform their social property relations to make them responsive to market imperatives. That social transformation will not and cannot create another capitalist society in the image of the dominant economies. It may not even constitute a self-contained and viable capitalist economy at all. But it will create a new self-enclosed social regime of market dependence.

Peasants, for instance, may be transformed from subsistence farmers into cash-crop producers, with all the social changes that entails. This transformation will certainly subject them to the imperatives of the global economy, but it will also enclose them in a new social system at home, which increasingly dissolves old social ties and replaces them with new economic dependencies, domestic hierarchies and class relations sustained and enforced by domestic state powers.

So the very forces that may tend towards the creation of a global society have solidified the boundaries between its constituent parts. Capitalist imperatives have produced a multiplicity of national units, each comprising a self-enclosed and territorially bounded social system. Developed economies maintain the conditions of capital accumulation by keeping intact their social regimes and civil order, while profiting from less-developed social conditions elsewhere. Subordinate economies are likely to reinforce those effects, in response not only to direct pressures from the dominant powers but also to impersonal economic imperatives – for instance, enhancing 'competitiveness' in the global market by exploiting their own low-cost social regimes.

The imperialism of social differentiation

Rich capitalist economies have, of course, regularly benefited from infusions of cheap migrant labour, legal and illegal, but these have always been strictly controlled, so as not to endanger the advantages of social differentiation among national economies. The benefits of immigration, including any effects it may have on lowering labour costs at home, depend on the preservation of low-wage economies abroad; and, in any case, those benefits have never outweighed the advantages of long-distance exploitation of low-wage economies elsewhere. Nor has capitalism ever been able to resolve the irreducible contradiction between its need for increasing consumer demand and its tendency to reproduce poverty. Each of these two opposing options, and both together, are consistent with, indeed compelled by, the logic of capitalism, whose market imperatives offer no less contradictory alternatives.

The major capitalist economies are, to be sure, finding new ways of exploiting the labour regimes of less-developed economies at a distance, but even these new methods both benefit from and reinforce the social differentiation of national economies. Even today's new patterns of migration, including the 'new' economy's dependence on the migration of skilled workers, confirms the continuing importance of national differentiation: the most dramatic example is the highly trained IT workers from India imported especially into the USA, which illustrates how capital can profit from appropriating skills produced in other national regimes (and typically non-unionized in their new home, though this may be changing) instead of paying for their more costly creation at home. Globalization may have replaced traditional means of remote-control exploitation, but the end remains the same. In any case, the difference is certainly not that older forms were mediated by the nation-state while the new one is not. On the contrary, now more than ever, imperialism is a matter of inter-national transactions.

Globalization as operated by the major capitalist states and their transnational agencies certainly seeks to foreclose the possibility of independent national development strategies in the world's poorest countries, by subjecting them to global market forces and 'structural adjustment'. There is no shortage of efforts to block avenues to development of the kind that created the last generation of economic 'miracles' in poor developing countries – development achieved by means of active state intervention within protected national economies. But the effect of this is not to dilute social differences and national states in the solvent of global economic forces. On the contrary, the effect is to aggravate the inequalities among national economies and to consolidate the enclosure of differentiated social regimes, presided over by national states.

For reasons inherent in the nature of capitalism, then, the global economy is, and is likely to remain, a differentiated aggregate of social systems, with very different social environments and very different labour regimes – and capital is likely to continue exploiting those social differences. While many poor economies are compelled to reproduce their own poverty, advanced capitalist societies will continue to sustain their own hegemony by combining, on the one hand, enclosed social orders at home, relaxing the boundaries only under the strictest conditions or, as in the European Union, extending them (up to a point) to embrace more or less comparable social regimes; and, on the other hand, an economic imperialism capable of penetrating other, very different but also nationally enclosed social orders. This tendency to reproduce the social differentiation of the world's national economies is no less powerful, to say the least, than the much vaunted capacity of a rising capitalist tide to lift all boats.

An equalization of social conditions throughout the globe would no doubt weaken this particular impulse to territorial division. But, whatever both advocates and critics of globalization may say about the homogenization of world culture by the spread of global capitalism, the dynamics of capitalist exploitation and competition, not to mention the ecological unsustainability of generalizing the system's destructive wastefulness, make a global uniformity of social conditions inconceivable. As long as capitalist exploitation, competition and uneven development continue to reproduce and reinforce the social differentiation of the world's national economies – and it is surely in their fundamental nature to do so – capitalism will continue to reproduce and reinforce the nation-state, or something very like it, in order to contain specific social systems, as for many other reasons.[11]

At any rate, however effective capital may be in escaping fixed territorial boundaries, it is very difficult to imagine how its extra-economic supports could ever do likewise. There are, and are always likely to remain, strict practical limits on the reach of direct coercion, and even stricter limits on the scope of a legally authorized coercive regime capable of governing the anarchy of capital from day to day. Capital is always likely to be torn between its need for global power and its demand for a spatially limited political and legal order, with local coercive mechanisms (and locally organized social provision) to manage its everyday life.

Conclusion

While it is true that capitalism did not invent the sovereign territorial state, the connection between the two is more than a historical contingency. Capitalism emerged in conjunction with the process of state formation, and just as it perfected the territorial sovereign nation-state by displacing politically consti-tuted property, so it has continued to reproduce and reinforce the division of the world into a multiplicity of nation-states.

In the earliest days of capitalism, when England's domestic economy more or less coincided with its national political regime, there was no obvious disjunction between the economic reach of capital and the political/jurisdictional reach of the nation-state.[12] But the growing disparity between the global economy and the territorial nation-state in no way signals the end of capitalism's need, however contradictory, for a spatially fragmented political and legal order. On the contrary, that contradiction results from the persistence of that need; and for the foreseeable future, it is most likely to be met by something like the nation-state. The strongest challenges to existing nation-states, to their boundaries or indeed to their very existence, are more likely to come from oppositional forces of various kinds than from the agents of capital or the impersonal forces of the market.

Competition and uneven development, which belong to the essence of capi-talism and have perpetuated national economies, would be enough to prolong the life of the nation-state. The intensification of competition and uneven devel-opment by globalization would be enough to intensify the contradiction between economic integration and national fragmentation. But even apart from all that, it is in the essential nature of capitalism that appropriation will always be separate from, and yet require enforcement by, legal, political and military instruments external to the 'economy', as well as support from extra-economic social institu-tions. It is also in the essential nature of capitalism that capital will, and must, always seek to extend its economic reach. So capitalism is always likely to be pulled in opposing directions by two contradictory yet equally essential needs: the economic impulses of capital will always strive to break through all territorial boundaries, while the extra-economic conditions of capital's self-reproduction will remain territorially rooted and spatially bounded.

The economic reach of capital will always, and increasingly, exceed the grasp of the extra-economic means required to reproduce and enforce it. However global the economy becomes, it will continue to rely on spatially limited constituent units with a political, and even an economic, logic of their own. The contradictions between these contrary impulses belong to the essence of global-ization as much as do transnational corporations, high-speed electronic movements of capital, or integrated global markets.

As for the political implications of these contradictions, the fact that capitalism is a global system organized nationally means two things: on the one hand, its systemic weaknesses and contradictions, its endemic crises, are not national in origin. They are global, and they are inherent in the system, rooted in capitalism's basic operating principles. This means that no specific national policy caused them, nor can any specific national strategy resolve or prevent them. On the other hand, because global capitalism is nationally organized and irreducibly dependent on something like the nation-state, national economies and national states can still be a major terrain of opposition. It goes without saying that struggles against global capitalism demand new forms of international solidarity. But it does need to be said, and constantly repeated, that the first battlegrounds are local, and the nation-state remains the central arena.

Whatever can be said about constraints on the power of the territorial state against global corporations, it remains their most vital support. No corporation can navigate, let alone dominate, the world without the collaboration of one or more states. The most effective political means of intervening in the global economy remains control of the national states that constitute, enforce, and implement it. And the nature of that intervention is still determined above all by the particular class forces embodied in the state. No existing transnational agency, nor, indeed, any conceivable form of 'global governance', will be answerable to popular and democratic forces as long as capital commands the nation-states that constitute the global system.

Precisely because global capital so badly needs the state, and because the state as the point of concentration of capitalist power is also the point at which global capital is most vulnerable, capital has a strong ideological stake in the myth that globalization means the disempowerment, if not the disappearance, of the nation-state. Challenging the hegemony of capital requires challenging that myth. If there is a growing distance between the global scope of the capitalist market and the local powers on which it depends, this cannot simply mean that capital is escaping political control. It means instead, or also, that there is a growing space for opposition.

Notes

* Parts of this chapter originally appeared in Wood (1999). I am grateful to David McNally for his comments on the original article and to Frances Abele for hers on the current one.
1 Many of those arguments are, of course, rooted in the work of Max Weber, although the underlying assumptions – concerning processes of modernization, urbanization, commercialization, and so on – go back further, especially to classical political economy and Enlightenment conceptions of progress. I discuss this idea of modernity, as it relates to conceptions of capitalism and the state, at greater length in Wood (1991). The theory of absolutism as a turning point in the transition from feudalism to capitalism, which liberated the bourgeois economy from feudal constraints, is developed by Perry Anderson (1974). For an explanation that stresses the importance of Europe's multiple polities in the development of capitalism, see Immanuel Wallerstein (1974, 1983).
2 Most recently, in Wood (2002a).

3 The conditions for such a capitalist *system* – a system of production, appropriation, and social reproduction driven *in its totality* by capitalist imperatives – seem not to have been present even in those parts of the Low Countries for which the strongest argument can be made for an early development of capitalism. For an argument on the early development of capitalism in some parts of the Low Countries, see Robert Brenner (2001: 169–238). I have raised some questions about Brenner's argument on the Low Countries in Wood (2002b).

4 For a discussion of 'bourgeois revolution' as non-capitalist, see Comninel (1987), especially the conclusion. See also Wood (1991, 2002a) for general discussions of the difference between 'bourgeois' and 'capitalist', and between absolutism and capitalism.

5 I owe this phrase to Robert Brenner, who has been using it in his work for many years.

6 This is how Eric Kerridge (1988: 6) describes traditional forms of international trade.

7 On the process of feudal centralization, contrasting France and England, see Robert Brenner (1985, especially pp.254–64).

8 I discuss the idea of 'sovereignty' and its emergence in a non-capitalist society in Wood (1991, esp. Chapter 3). In his doctoral dissertation, Hannes Lacher (forthcoming) discusses the non-capitalist origin of the 'modern' territorial state. See also his chapter in this volume.

9 England, in its domestic market, created a commercial system based in distinctive ways on commerce in the means of survival and self-reproduction – food and cheap commodities of everyday life. How this commercial system differed from the traditional European commercial system, with its dependence on the luxury trade and its contradictory interaction with commerce in the means of survival, particularly the grain trade, requires a more elaborate discussion than is necessary or possible here. (For more on this, see Wood (2002a).)

10 This question has been put in an especially challenging and illuminating way by Lacher (2000, and in this volume) arguing that the 'exclusive territoriality' of the contemporary state, which defies the globalizing tendencies of capital, is the product of that precapitalist historical legacy. At the same time, he shows how capitalism has 'internalized' the territorial state, which has become integral to capitalist processes of reproduction. My argument here, while it starts from many of the same premises, suggests that the reproduction and reinforcement of this historical legacy is more deeply rooted in the nature of capitalism.

11 The World Bank annual *World Development Report* (2000/2001), entitled 'Attacking Poverty', illustrates some of the contradictions. Even fanatical advocates of globalization have to acknowledge that, whatever claims they may make about the general rise of living standards, we have in recent years seen more, rather than less, social polarization between rich and poor among – as well as within – the world's national economies. The World Bank can always be relied on to give voice to global capital's contradictions on the subject of development and poverty. As usual, in the latest *Report* concerns about poverty express themselves in empty pieties and the insistence that 'growth' is ultimately the only solution – which means, of course, that the 'free' market, imposed according to the will of 'global' capital, must be allowed to have its way. The only real novelty in the *Report* is the introduction of the notion of 'empowerment'. The governments of poorer countries must, the *Report* argues, be more accountable to their poor populations and more sensitive to their needs, with policies designed to enhance social welfare. Apart from the vacuity of these pious sentiments, and the shifting of blame from globalization policies to the failures of local states, the most striking thing about this notion is that it neatly sums up the basic principles of globalization: let global market forces do their worst, while the responsibility for picking up the pieces must fall to nation-states – the very states compelled by global capital to implement and enforce its economic imperatives.

12 Of course, both England's national dominion and its domestic economy began to extend their reach very early in the development of the English nation-state. The multinational character of the British Isles was already a major factor in the formation of the Tudor English state, and England also sought ways of extending the reach of its economic imperatives beyond the capacities of its political and military dominion, already (it can be argued) in its early forms of colonialism. But that is another story, part of which is discussed in Wood 2002a.

Bibliography

Anderson, P. (1974) *Lineages of the Absolutist State*, London: Verso.

Brenner, R. (1985) 'The Agrarian Roots of European Capitalism', in T.H. Aston and C.H.E. Philpin (eds), *The Brenner Debate: Agrarian Class Structure and Economic Development in Pre-Industrial Europe*, Cambridge: Cambridge University Press.

Comninel, G.C. (1987) *Rethinking the French Revolution*, London: Verso.

Kerridge, E. (1988) *Trade and Banking in Early Modern England*, Manchester: Manchester University Press.

Lacher, H. (forthcoming) *The International Relations of Modernity: Capitalism, Territoriality and Globalization*, London: Routledge.

Wallerstein, I. (1974) *The Modern World System*, New York: Academic Press.

—— (1983) *Historical Capitalism*, London: Verso.

Wood, E.M. (1991) *The Pristine Culture of Capitalism*, London: Verso.

—— (1999) 'Unhappy Families: Global Capitalism in a World of Nation States', *Monthly Review*, July/August.

—— (2002a) *The Origin of Capitalism: A Longer View*, London: Verso.

World Bank (2000/2001) *World Development Report*, Oxford: Oxford University Press.

2 How many capitalisms?

Historical materialism in the debates about imperialism and globalization*

Bob Sutcliffe

The word on everybody's lips

Imperialism, wrote J.A. Hobson at the beginning of the twentieth century, 'is the word on everybody's lips' (Hobson 1902). A hundred years later, when capitalism once again seems to be entering unmapped regions, the word on everybody's lips is *globalization*. And globalization now, like imperialism then, is giving rise to new questions, fears and debates. On the right it produces a range of reactions from the triumphalism of pro-capitalist liberals to the pessimism of traditionalist conservatives and cultural nationalists. On the left there is a narrower spectrum of views: from socialists, post-Marxist radicals and environmentalists comes an almost unanimous negative verdict on globalization: it threatens to disempower all national states, undo all social gains and break down ecological defences.

The debates on imperialism of a century ago were also partly driven by terrible fears for the future. Writers like Lenin and Luxemburg in particular saw human society as being rapidly pulled by capitalism into an abyss of violence, war, destruction and barbarism unless it could be rescued by socialism. And yet the nature of that century-old discussion about international capitalism was strikingly different from today's. It was, perhaps surprisingly, more empirically probing. It was more historically conscious, looking for an understanding of contemporary changes in a longer historical context by seeing both their originality and their continuity. It was more theoretically grounded; and it was more political, spending less time lamenting the trajectory of the world and more on looking for contradictions of the process and for cracks in the enemy's armour. It was also, therefore, less pessimistic.

A crucial factor determining these differences is that the memorable debate on imperialism was conducted, to a much greater extent than today, largely within a methodological approach derived from Marx – in other words, using the tools of historical materialism including Marx's critique of political economy. Socialists on the eve of the First World War needed more than anything else to understand the nature of nations and their function in capitalism. And yet this was a question for which the answers bequeathed by the founders of historical materialism were particularly incomplete but where the political urgency was particularly great. The political need and the theoretical method combined to produce a flowering of bold and innovative extensions, adaptations and updatings of Marx's insights into the nature of capitalism. The rich harvest of writings of that time have rightly become points of reference for discussions of international issues throughout the succeeding century. Non-Marxist and anti-Marxist writers have probably devoted more energy to attacking Marxist theories of imperialism than to almost any other aspect of Marxism. This defensiveness has reflected the continued threat to exploiters, oppressors and their apologists, of socialist theory and in particular of historical materialism.

Historical materialism still has no ready-made answers to the new questions raised by globalization any more than it did to those of imperialism. But it does provide us with a long and illuminating history of attempts to analyse related problems and with a uniquely powerful set of tools with which we can try to reach a more complex understanding of the process: how much has changed, what is new and what is old, where are the strengths and weaknesses of a more global capitalism, who are the gainers and the losers, what are the sources of stability and instability, of growth and decline, which problems will globalization solve and which will it create, and what changes are taking place in the relative strength and importance of nations and classes? Just as they did a century ago, socialists today cannot just denounce the latest manifestations of capitalism; they need answers to questions about its trajectory, not to satisfy their curiosity but to know where and how to concentrate their political intervention.

Expressing his impatience with philosophers' contemplations about the world, Marx insisted that the point was to change it. But that, of course, is not the essential difference between historical materialism and other theoretical approaches. The world is full of people of all possible persuasions who wish to change it, including those who wish to make it in some sense more socialist. In these circumstances, to grasp what historical materialism teaches us, we might do better to invert Marx's famous dictum. Many people want to change the world; the point, however, is to analyse it. More precisely the point is to analyse it in such a way as to clarify the manner in which it can be changed. It is that combination which is the essence of historical materialism.

Marx's historical materialism: spirals and contradictions

In both his historical and his economic writings Marx often seems to see the world through the metaphor of spirals: movements which have some regular form but which take place in various dimensions at the same time and whose direction of movement may be complex, even ambiguous. Both in his broad account of human history and his detailed theoretical account of the production and realization of surplus value under capitalism the notion of the spiral is particularly clear. To simplify greatly, the grand historical spiral is the twisting movement of human society from a supposed egalitarian primitive communist origin through a series of exploitative societies based on class division, to return in the end to egalitarian communism but with productive power, needs and human capacity all greatly expanded. There are lesser spirals within that huge one; each one of them is the history of a form of class society, starting from progressive origins but eventually generating internal contradictions which become a fetter on human history; a new form of society can then arise and a further trajectory takes place, culminating in the transition from capitalism to socialism and the definitive end of class society (and the beginning of conscious history).

The other clear spiral, the circuit of capital, is what is basically explained by critical political economy, the new science which Marx believed became necessary to uncover the hidden and especially complex nature of exploitation under capitalism. Here the spiral represents the process of producing and reinvesting (accumulating) profit, what he called the expanded reproduction of capital. Capital is involved in a series of continuous circuits in which it can be seen as starting off as money, changing into productive commodities (raw materials, machines and labour power), which the capitalist purchases in order to combine them in the production or labour process. This is where workers produce more value than they receive (the value of their labour power). So more value (labour time) is embodied in the commodities which emerge from the production process than was embodied in those which went into it. The extra or surplus value (in other words unpaid labour) accrues to the capitalist when the new commodities are sold on the market and so the capital has returned to its original money form but in greater quantity. Marx used a famous simple formula to express this constant metamorphosis between money (M) and commodities (C) through which capital makes profits and expands: $M - C - C+ - M+ - C+ - C++ - M++$ and so on, a progression which is best understood as a spiral rather than a straight line.

The two spirals – that of world history and that of the capitalist mode of production – are similar in that, unlike the mathematical one, they are not smooth even in Marx's purest theoretical vision. The movement of history takes place through disasters, wars, struggles, revolutions and counter-revolutions, so the real world spiral is very irregular. And similarly the movement of surplus-value-seeking capital takes place through unpredictable and unstable markets, strikes and struggles over the production process and distribution and economic crises. Within the spiral, capital must both produce and realize surplus value and the conditions for each process are different and often in contradiction. Almost nothing that ever happens has an unambiguous or uncontradictory effect on the pursuit of surplus value. If wages rise, for instance, capital will lose because costs rise and gain because demand rises. Capitalism, more than any pre-market class society, is at best on a knife edge. In reality it tends to oscillate in cyclical movements of boom and crisis. And, although the crisis theory is never finally and fully developed the spiral image is there too: both in the early Marx of the *Communist Manifesto* (the idea of ever-worsening crises which with each return put capitalism more than ever on trial), and then much later in Volume III of *Capital* (the idea that each period of expansion may be longer, more intense and more internationally spread by the expansion of credit, thus making each inevitable crash so much more severe when it eventually comes).

If the spiral is an appropriate metaphor for the social world as seen by historical materialism, what are its virtues compared with another method of analysis which might resemble a different form of movement: for instance, a circle, a straight line or a random walk? The strength of the spiral model is that it makes you think about change as something complex and many-sided, and yet not totally random or chaotic. It encourages you to look for movements in more than one direction, which may have different, even contradictory, consequences, which are full of ambiguities and complex concepts, in which short-term movements may be very different in direction from long-term ones. To put it a bit crudely, it is a way of seeing that history can and usually does move both 'backwards' and 'forwards' at the same time, but it also provides some idea of what the notions 'backwards' and 'forwards', or progress and regress, mean. Marx's models may seem unconvincing when expressed in their purest simplified form, especially in the inspiring much-quoted summary passages of his writing; but when he writes about real events he tends to see simultaneously large patterns and small deviations, ambiguities, nuances, co-existences and contradictions. Too often, however, we want certainty and simplicity and so we try to impose simple patterns and categories on reality. Marx, like most politically active intellectuals, wrote sometimes for political effect and sometimes for analytical clarity, and so ranged between arresting oversimplifi-cations (the treatment of class in the *Communist Manifesto*) and extreme, nuanced detail (the treatment of class in *The Class Struggles in France*).

Marx was often, if not always, comfortable with the contradictions and ambi-guities which seem to be thrown up by his approach but many Marxists have been allergic to them. Take such questions as 'Is capitalism (at any particular moment) progressive?', 'Should communists support nationalism?', 'Is it possible to leap historical stages and build socialism without passing through capitalist development?', 'Is capitalism global?', 'Is a major capitalist crisis imminent?'. In Marx's hands historical materialism gave several answers to all of them. Sometimes it is possible to discern a systematic change in his positions (as some have claimed in the case of nationalism, or leaping stages). Sometimes his answer changed because the world had changed. But often the different answers simply reflect the fact that he seldom seems to have thought that a single, yes-or-no answer to such questions was possible or useful.

Taking as given the fact that there are no magic wands enabling everything to be understood, historical materialism's special claim to be taken seriously is the positive side of its especially large range of interpretations. Some combination of its wide variety of tools, general and particular, larger and smaller spirals if you like, produces at its best a method which does the following things with special power and subtlety:

- Recognizes the ways in which history repeats itself, while discerning the differences between the repeat and the first performance.

- Sees that the same event may have complex and contradictory effects (e.g. a rise/fall of wages on capitalist profitability, imperial expansion, globalization).
- Superimposes different ways of dividing social actors in a multi-layered map which allows us to see interrelations, overlaps and contradictions between class, nation, rural–urban residence (and in principle, even though Marx himself did not do it so well, race and sex/gender).

It is weakest when it:

- Suggests excessively teleological explanations of history. No particular end can be a certainty, and in Marx's personal conclusions he notoriously swayed between optimism and pessimism about the future.
- Tries to impose rigid stage theories on history (at a certain date everything is feudalism or everything is capitalism, everything is progressive, everything is retrogressive).
- Claims to discern unambiguous linear movements.

So, for example, it is a strength to see all history as the history of class struggle; but a weakness to reduce it to only a history of class struggle; a strength to see that developments can be progressive or retrogressive in relation to a socialist future; but a weakness to see that end like some kind of magnetic north which you always know if you are approaching or not; a strength to see the direction of change, but a weakness to assert too definitively that a particular qualitative transformation has definitively taken place.

If the other side to subtlety and flexibility may be confusion, indecisiveness and a failure to see woods for trees, there are ways around these difficulties. Marx's own writing is frequently a model of how to avoid such pitfalls and how to be both nuanced and decisive. This problem of how to combine the general and detailed elements in the historical materialist method is, of course, a major feature of the debates about imperialism and globalization which are the subject of the rest of this chapter.

Imperialism, mark 1

I think that it is useful to divide theories of imperialism into two generations: those which emerged just before and during the First World War and those which appeared after the Second World War. The concerns of both were strongly influenced by those particular historical circumstances.

The pioneer of the first generation was not a Marxist but a socialistically inclined liberal. J.A. Hobson regarded British imperialism, especially in Africa, as a fraud perpetrated on the nation by a group of financiers who needed legal and physical protection for their growing foreign investments (Hobson 1902). They invested overseas because growing inequality in the distribution of income depressed aggregate consumer demand in the home market. The remedy for imperialism was, therefore, state-sponsored income redistribution to restore the profitability of home investment. Like Marx before him and Keynes after, Hobson assigned great importance to underconsumption in particular historical circumstances without being a doctrinaire underconsumptionist.

Lenin scorned Hobson's redistributive remedies, saying that if capitalism could effect such a redistribution it would not be capitalism; but he eagerly devoured Hobson's empirical material and part of his theorizing on foreign investment. A central item of Lenin's five-point definition of imperialism was the predominance of export of capital over export of goods.

Lenin's presence in intellectual history these days is almost as scarce as his tenancy of his Moscow mausoleum is insecure. But, aside from his other claims to fame, in *Imperialism* (Lenin [1916] 1965) he made memorable and original use of the ideas of historical materialism. That capitalism had been 'transformed into imperialism' was shown by five new features: the decisive role of monopoly, the merging of industrial and finance capital, the predominance of export of capital over export of goods, the division of the world market between competing international capitalist monopolies and the completion of the territorial division of the world. The essence of Lenin's theory of imperialism, however, is not fully captured by these five empirical definitional points, nor even by his summary of them all as 'the monopoly stage of capitalism'; his central implicit idea was that imperialism was a stage of capitalist history which expressed Marx's expectation, stated in the often-quoted eloquent and inspiring passage in the Introduction to the *Contribution to a Critique of Political Economy*, that at some stage all forms of society become retrogressive. Imperialism for Lenin is the stage in which capitalism had entirely ceased to be historically progressive; socialist revolution, therefore, had ceased to be quixotic and became necessary, even urgent. What had brought progressive capitalism to an end was nationally based monopolies. A number of powerful, warring, capitalist nations were destined to engage in a ceaseless fratricidal conflict to redivide the world until social revolution intervened. In other words *Imperialism* was based on the idea that the globalization envisaged in the *Communist Manifesto*, though it would implicitly be desirable, was impossible. Imperialism was an epoch of aggression and destruction because the bourgeoisie could not draw 'from under the feet of industry the national ground on which it stood' as Marx and Engels had expected (Marx and Engels [1848] 1935). Globalization, seen by Marx and Engels as one of the historical 'tasks' of capitalism (and so part of its progressiveness), had become the 'task' of socialism. *Imperialism* in its time, therefore, was a product, but an unorthodox product, of historical materialism.

Imperialism became orthodoxy on the left partly because of the political dominance of officially Leninist communism but also because it seemed to contain ideas of tremendous power which, among other things, offered a perfectly convincing understanding of the First World War, as well as a justification for revolution. It is not surprising that, when World War returned only twenty years later, many wanted to see it as a continuation of exactly what Lenin had predicted. But that involved seeing the proximate cause of the war, the rise of Nazism, as no more than an extreme expression of national monopoly capitalism, an idea which simply seems insufficient to explain the hideous peculiarities of Nazism. Not surprisingly just about every organization professing orthodox Marxism (including Leninism) either careered grotesquely between extremes, or split, over the question of what political attitude to adopt to the Second World War (support for anti-Nazi 'democratic' capitalism, neutrality or, re-applying 1916 Leninism, revolutionary defeatism). Starting from a historical materialist perspective a number of writers have produced interesting and subtle accounts of aspects of Nazism. Alfred Sohn-Rethel, for instance, illuminatingly described the serious divisions in German big capital in the face of Nazism and so undermined any simple orthodox interpretation (Sohn-Rethel 1978). And when it comes to explaining the holocaust, the monopoly theory of imperialism has little to contribute. The most original and recent explanations look to very different elements of explanation than those which usually feature in historical materialist explanations (Mayer 1990). Failure both to generate an adequate theory of Nazism and to account for the absence of major conflict between the imperialist powers after the Second World War has left Lenin's overly simple attempt to see history as consisting of unambiguous and irreversible stages widely accepted in theory but relatively powerless in the face of events.

It was from Rudolf Hilferding that Lenin derived much of his thinking about monopoly and the state. Like Hobson, he is still best known for having been quoted approvingly by Lenin in *Imperialism*. His *Finanzkapital*, written in 1910, finally (thanks to Tom Bottomore) published in English in 1981, is not widely read. It is a very difficult book to characterize because it is so rich in ideas about many aspects of capitalism. At times he seems to prefigure most of the subsequent currents in the debate about imperialism and the international aspects of capitalism. What Lenin took from Hilferding was the idea that capitalism had recently passed into a new stage in which the structure of capitalist businesses, their relation to the state and the policies which they implemented had all qualitatively changed. Finance capital does not mean the predominance of banks but the fusion of all forms of capital into what he called its highest form, the trinity of industrial capital, commercial and bank capital and money capital (the Father, Son and Holy Ghost) (Hilferding [1910] 1981: 220). Giant monopolies take possession of the state and 'diplomacy now becomes the representation of finance capital' (Hilferding [1910] 1981: 330) and so conflict between nations might be intensified. Later he developed that into a theory of what he called 'organized capitalism' in which the existence of giant monopolies brought the possibility of planning, something which led other Marxists, including Lenin, also to enthuse about the organizational achievements of big business. (It should be noted that the standard Marxist theory of crisis at the time was the 'disproportionality' theory, in which crises were blamed on market anarchy. Hence the non-market allocation of resources within big companies was admired; and hence in part also Soviet planning took the ill-fated form of detailed central direction.)

One can easily see why Lenin found the pre-war Hilferding so useful in *Imperialism*. Hilferding himself, however, took a very much more nuanced view of the consequences of the monopolization process for international relations. He saw that it created two simultaneous and counteracting tendencies: one towards more conflict and the other towards new forms of solidarity and common interest between capitalist nations. He did not regard one as necessarily more powerful than the other and remained undecided about which tendency would prevail (Hilferding [1910] 1981: 332).

Hilferding's ambiguity about outcomes is underlined by the fact that Schumpeter, the 'bourgeois Marxist' (Catephores 1994) who believed that capitalist development would tend to produce free trade and world peace, was an even more enthusiastic supporter of Hilferding's views than Lenin. But Schumpeter added his own understanding to the effect that imperialism was not part of the nature of capitalism in general; quite the contrary. Imperialism was part of the character merely of German capitalism at the start of the century, due to the incomplete nature of the German bourgeois revolution and the maintenance of considerable social power by the reactionary landowning classes with their nationalist backward-looking aggressive policies. If Schumpeter seems ridiculous when he says that Britain, and more particularly the USA, were much less imperialist than Germany (because they were more completely ruled by the rational bourgeoisie), we should bear in mind that by imperialism he (and many Marxist analysts) did not mean colonial acquisition so much as economic and other forms of aggression based on national interest; and that a version of Schumpeter's idea of imperialism as social atavism has been creatively used to explain Nazism more satisfactorily than it is explained by the crude application of Leninist imperialism theory (Mayer 1990).

In more ways than one the odd-person-out of the first wave of Marxist imperialism theory was Rosa Luxemburg. Like Lenin, and unlike Hilferding, she did believe that the world socialist revolution was an immediate question since capitalism was mutating rapidly into an ever more destructive beast. But her argumentation could hardly be more different. She was not in the slightest interested in monopoly which she never mentioned, and very little interested in different states and their rivalries. She *was* interested in foreign investment, but for very different reasons from those of other writers. In fact she approached the whole question from another standpoint, and one which has frequently been denounced as mistaken. I believe it was much less mistaken than it can be made to seem.

Luxemburg's underconsumptionism was more thoroughgoing and doctrinaire than Hobson's. In *The Accumulation of Capital* (Luxemburg [1913] 1951) she made an ill-fated attempt to overturn Marx's algebraic argument in Volume II of *Capital*, where he expounded the conditions under which self-contained capitalist accumulation is possible. Luxemburg's analysis of all this is long and, by almost universal consent, mistaken. And her analysis of imperialism was ostensibly based on it. By imperialism she understood something much closer to the conventional meaning of the term (expansion and aggression of rich, especially European, countries into the rest of the world), than Lenin's special meaning (the monopoly stage of capitalism). She argues that imperialism was necessary because capitalism could not exist or survive as a self-contained system but had a permanent need to appropriate value from not-yet-capitalist areas. Imperialism was, therefore, system parasitism; and it was self-destructive since, once all the pre-capitalist world was absorbed, the necessary underconsumption of pure capitalism must result in catastrophic economic collapse. Her defence of this idea of imperialism was original but the idea was rooted in Marx's historical materialism.

Marx had argued that a considerable amount of capital was accumulated in the emergent stages of capitalism in not purely capitalist ways, through what he called primitive or primary accumulation, which means appropriating surplus labour in various ways from pre-capitalist activities. Although Marx wrote about this largely as part of the early history of capitalism there is no necessary end to primary accumulation and it could in theory take place at any time, as long as a non-capitalist realm exists. Luxemburg's theory of imperialism was a novel version of this idea.

The primary accumulation whose role in the birth of capitalism Marx had emphasized, Luxemburg regarded as an essential process during its whole life. She believed that underconsumption and the explanation of imperialism were inseparable. But in fact the possibility of extra-capitalist sources of capital accumulation at any moment in history, not just as the birth of the system, is in no way inconsistent with the denial of general necessary underconsumption. Luxemburg's 'primitive accumulation' theory of imperialism, therefore, has a life of its own quite independent of underconsumptionist errors of reasoning which partly lead to it.

She applies the idea in an illuminating way, especially in her account of how the pre-capitalist Egyptian peasantry are made to pay for the country's debt. It is a subtle and brilliant analysis of the way the ruling class of one mode of production appropriates the labour of the oppressed class of another. It is a method which has wide applications both in history and in today's world because it asserts the importance of a process (primary accumulation) which most Marxists had wrongly assumed to be long since superseded.

Luxemburg's second original stroke was to separate imperialism theory completely from nationalism. Other ideas about imperialism stressed opposition to nationalism in the dominant imperialist countries but legitimized other nationalisms. Luxemburg's imperialism was not primarily an imperialism of nations but of a predatory mode of production already operating on a world scale. Nationalism for her was not even a legitimate stage on the way to socialist revolution; it was in all senses a deviation. In this she echoed the young Marx.

As far as the historical materialist tradition is concerned I take Hilferding, Lenin and Luxemburg to be the most important writers on imperialism in the period around the First World War. The three had one thing in common, which is the sense that humanity had recently entered a crucial new phase. For Hilferding it was because the nature of the capitalist corporation and state had changed, for Lenin and Luxemburg it was because what kept capitalism progressive and (relatively) peaceful was exhausted: for Lenin because the monopolies had for the first time divided the whole world and so would be obliged to continue to struggle to redivide it, and for Luxemburg because capitalism was rapidly running out of non-capitalist regions and situations from which to supplement its own insufficient capacity to produce profit, its necessary life blood.

This first generation of imperialism theorists represented one of the high points of the application of historical materialist method to understanding the world of international relations. They wrote in a period of extraordinary theoretical fertility. They contributed not by being orthodox and exegetical but by being boldly revisionist and critical. After the crisis of the war the theoretical gains were either lost or soon crystallized into dogmas and new orthodoxies. Ironically perhaps, those ideas which seemed most powerful at the time have not proved so durable in understanding the world a hundred years on, while those which were more marginalized or ignored now seem to offer some insights. But the search by all of them for a way of applying general analytical principles remains a source of illumination.

Imperialism, mark 2

I call the second generation of theorists of imperialism those who have analysed the concept during the last three or four decades. (It is the intellectual family in which I grew up.) They have not always used the term imperialism and they have been principally concerned with relations between rich industrialized capitalist nations and the 'Third World' or capitalist periphery. In the immediate aftermath of the Second World War a widespread and successful anti-colonial movement based itself theoretically on the very obvious injustice of imposed foreign rule and the right to national self-determination, which as a principle almost no one denied. The second generation of imperialism theories arose as a reaction to the idea that the end of direct colonialism closed the book on imperialism. So they are all in a sense theories of neo-colonialism or neo-imperialism. The emphasis shifted from the political anti-imperialism of the colonial liberation movements to economic and cultural anti-imperialism. One of the most fertile of these theories, dependency theory, was (ironically in view of its own analysis of the world) an intellectual and political product of a part of the peripheral world where formal colonialism had hardly existed for well over a century (Latin America).

There is surprisingly little continuity between the first- and second-generation theories of imperialism. This is partly due to the special role of Lenin in the debate. Almost unique among the contributors to the first-generation theories, Lenin both died in his bed (supposedly) and subsequently enjoyed general reverence on the left. His book *Imperialism* was, at least for a time, at the top of the all-time world best-sellers' list and in orthodox, and even some not so orthodox, circles was uncriticizable. Yet, while Lenin had in the end espoused in theory a fairly radical national self-determination position, the relations between developed and underdeveloped countries were scarcely at all at the heart of his concept and theory of imperialism. He seems to have expected imperialism to accelerate the industrialization of poor countries, almost the opposite of what second-generation imperialism theory usually argued. And, unmentionable irony of ironies, the world of the 1960s looked not so much like the permanent inter-capitalist warfare predicted by Lenin, but much more like the world predicted by the person who argued that the First World War would not resolve all the contra-dictions existing between the main imperialist powers, that 'the subsequent peace will be no more than a short armistice', but that eventually 'there is nothing further to prevent this violent explosion finally replacing imperialism by a holy alliance of the imperialists', which he added for good measure would be domi-nated by the United States and return to a regime of freer international trade. I am referring to the 'renegade Kautsky' (Kautsky [1914] 1970; Wollen 1993). The vehement denunciation of Karl Kautsky by the Bolsheviks, for daring to suggest that there might be a capitalist world beyond the imperialism of the early twentieth century, helped lead to a general decline in interest in Kautsky's writing, which is only now beginning to recover.

The second generation of imperialism theorists had an (unstated and unstat-able) Kautskian perspective, based not on prediction but on observation, and one writer has drawn attention to the consistency of Wallerstein's world-systems theory with Kautsky (Wollen 1993). But they were in general less stage theoretical than Kautsky and indeed than all the other first-generation theorists. For all those writing at the start of the twentieth century imperialism was a new phase, stage or epoch of capitalism. It is true that one of the pioneering second-generation theo-rists, Paul Baran, author of the influential *The Political Economy of Growth* (Baran [1957] 1973), is associated (in this work with Paul Sweezy) with a theory of the monopoly stage of capitalism (Baran and Sweezy [1966] 1968); but most of the writers in the tradition of dependency theory (Andre Gunder Frank, etc.) and world-systems theory (Immanuel Wallerstein, etc.) see the polarization of centre and periphery as a permanent feature of capitalism since the seventeenth century. But if that eliminates the problem of an oversimplified attribution of stages of capitalism, it itself contains its own simplification, relating to the connection between mode of production and social system, that of simply defining the world as capitalist since the seventeenth century. These theories have been sharply criti-cized for implying a definition of capitalism based on markets and not production. But I think that the main problem with them is different: that they reject stage theories too thoroughly, and so they reduce 400 years of capitalist history to a few permanent features, the main one of which is the polarization between centre and periphery of a single world economy. This makes it very diffi-cult to identify important historical changes, even if we do not want to interpret them in the form of a rigid stage theory.

The strength of this second-generation imperialism theory is the way in which it has revealed the multiple sources of international economic inequality, the multiple forms of economic exploitation, and political dominance of the South by the North. Its weakness has been its inability to account for those developments which have not simply been a continuation of North–South polarization, for instance the extraordinarily rapid capitalist industrialization of a number of Asian countries during the last forty years. Lenin had expected imperialism to have such a result, though he did not attach much importance to it since it took place in what he regarded as an epoch of irreversible social retrogression. But the Leninist and the second-generation imperialist theorists coincide in the view that capitalism has now lost all progressive aspects. Such a totally negative position has been, I believe, a source of weakness in left analysis because it leaves the left with an insufficient explanation of the resilience of capitalism in the world, either economically or ideologically. Both rigid stage theories and more timeless theories like world-systems both in different ways set up obstacles to understanding historical change in a nuanced and dialectical way. With one the changes are regarded as too complete, with the other they are insufficiently noticed. To revert to the terminology of the second section, there are too many straight lines and not enough spirals.

Globalization, marks 1 and 2

There is not the slightest doubt that in the last few decades many of the national barriers to the global functioning of capitalism have been coming down. Most indicators of global integration of capitalist economies have been on the rise for some time. That there is globalization in this sense is beyond dispute. But many current ideas about globalization go much further than that: they argue that these changes have qualitatively changed the system, that it has entered a new and unprecedented stage.

It is possible to distinguish two generations also in theories of more recent globalization, as there were about imperialism, though now the speed of reproduction has risen. The first generation dates from the early 1970s and presented itself explicitly as a replacement for imperialism theory (Sklar 1976). A group of Marxist historians formulated a theory which they called post-imperialism, just before the epoch of post-everything. Their 'post-' referred more to Leninist than dependency imperialism theory. They argued that the capitalist class had ceased to be divided into different nationalities and had fused into a single international corporate bourgeoisie. Capitalism was so internationalized that national borders no longer had much significance and so nation-to-nation conflicts were being replaced by class struggle at the global level. The theory was presented with a lot of 'back to Marx' rhetoric, though the relation between the conceptual and empirical was problematic. Whether going back to Marx was justified by the fact that Marx had always been right or that the world had changed to make him right (again) was not made clear. The post-imperialist hypothesis regarded a network of multinational corporations as the form assumed by the modern global capitalist class. There was in this view quite a strong current of Schumpeterism: the idea that capitalism never ceases to be progressive, but also some notion that the globalization of capital will lead to the globalization of the working class also and therefore the development of an international revolutionary movement.

This is evidently a very similar conclusion to that found at about the same time in the work of Bill Warren (Warren 1980). The difference was that Warren was reacting especially to second-generation imperialist theory on the grounds that it had been responsible for the systematic substitution of nation for class and submerged socialism in a morass of nationalism. With Warren, too, there is plenty of 'back to Marx' rhetoric as well as the same ambiguity about whether imperialism really had existed and had gone away or whether it had never existed (i.e. Marx had been right all along).

Warren and the post-imperialists failed to gain much following for their proto-globalization hypotheses in spite of the fact that the more orthodox anti-imperialist left found them difficult to refute. There was a general unwillingness on the left at that time to abandon the notion of imperialism as the central feature of the world, which both versions of the proto-globalization idea demanded. Within a short time, however, with the exception of a few sceptics, most people had come round to some version of the hypothesis of globalization.

Globalization hypotheses are supported, sometimes very loosely, sometimes more rigorously, with a series of facts. I think that this empirical basis is very weak as I try to show in commenting below on some of the key facts which are frequently adduced to show globalization.

1   International trade is rising in relation to the value of production. It is true that trade has risen faster than production since 1950, although the fact tends to be greatly exaggerated by inappropriate measures. But its present relative level is not very far above what it was just before the First World War. Thus, relative to production, there is not an unprecedented level of international trade. Part (admittedly a small part) of the present large figure is due to the fact that some single countries have divided; and if the European Union is ever treated as one country international trade will decline enormously (Sutcliffe and Glyn 1999).

2   Foreign direct investment has risen in relation to the size of the economy. Again it is true that the percentage of foreign in total investment has been rising (much more erratically than trade). But here too the figures suggest that, at most, the relative levels of 1913 have been regained. Again there is globalization but not to unprecedented levels.

3   Foreign production has become more important than exports (an unconscious echo of Lenin's idea that the export of capital had become more important than the export of goods). Much is made of recent estimates that the value of sales by foreign subsidiaries became around 1990 greater than the total value of world exports (UNCTAD 1999). It is argued that this represents a qualitative turning point after which international integration of production dominates arm's-length transactions between the producers of one nation and another. I very much doubt the significance of this statistic. Many so-called foreign subsidiaries of multinational companies are little more than sales agencies for their parent companies. This means that exports may be counted twice, once in the figures for exports proper and again in the figures for the foreign sales of subsidiaries. The genuine foreign sales are, therefore, much smaller than they appear.

4 Much or even most international trade takes place between different branches of multinational corporations (intra-trade), thus suggesting that there is a very high degree of cross-border integration of productive structures. I have only been able to find two substantial studies of this question, for the USA and Japan. They both show some upward movement in intra-trade though it remains in the case of the USA a little over one-third, a figure which first began to be widely quoted as long ago as the 1960s. And again some of the intra-trade is simply sending goods to a sales subsidiary to sell in a foreign market, so for what it implies for the integration of the productive system it is not much different from non-intra-trade.

5 Multinational corporations dominate the world. Big corporations have dominated the world economy in some sense for rather a long time though probably never more so than the great trading companies in the eighteenth century. This argument, however, suggests that the degree of dominance has increased. This could be due to higher levels of monopoly and concentration. The evidence does not support that and globalization in many areas has increased competition. All big capitalist corporations are, and have been for some time, multinational in the sense that they export goods and invest abroad. A few have integrated production structures, hardly any either have internationally integrated managements or have lost a clear national identity (Ruigrok and van Tulder 1995; Doremus *et al.* 1998). Moreover, many common statements about the quantitative weight of multinational corporations are grotesquely exaggerated. Usually they wrongly compare the sales (not value added) of firms with the national income (value added) of countries or the world. I think that the best estimates of their importance is that the 100 biggest multinationals produce about 5 per cent of the world's GDP (2.5 per cent abroad); their share of the world's capital stock is a little lower than this; and all 44,000-plus multinational corporations (defined as such by UNCTAD) produce about 22 per cent of world GDP (7.5 per cent abroad) (UNCTAD 1999; Sutcliffe and Glyn 1999). That may be enough to dominate the world in some sense but it is much, much less than is frequently asserted.

Globalization hypotheses are more than just a series of statistical exaggerations. There are, as with everything, hard- and soft-core versions of the globalization argument. The soft-core one says simply that things are getting more global (for the most part undeniable), that this is producing more precariousness for human economic life and that the national state is losing the power to do anything about it. The world has become a single macroeconomic space so national economic policy can no longer exist and life is becoming an ever more cut-throat struggle of all against all. Some of that, I think, is true although it tends to accept too readily what the rulers of national states would like their electorates to believe (that they can do nothing to stop the consequences); and it tends to exaggerate the difficulties of producing a response; and that generates pessimism or at best a visceral anti-globalistic or nationalistic response. It also tends to create the nostalgic illusion that things were much better before.

By and large, however, this version of globalization, while it notes that there have been very rapid changes in indicators of globalization, tends to remain theoretically in the camp of second-generation imperialism theory. The North–South polarizing effects of the new global economy are emphasized and global institutions are seen as really being not so much global as ultraimperialist institutions of the rich, imperialist countries. The idea that multinational corporations from countries of the North are the main agents of economic exploitation is already present in second-generation imperialist theory, as is the idea of the powerless state in dependent countries. So, while earlier the proto-globalization ideas of Warren and the post-imperialists demanded a choice between believing in imperialism and believing in globalization, many new versions of globalization theory do not, and that has made them more digestible on the left. Globalization, in this interpretation, represents no new stage, though it is often held to mean a major intensification of long-established tendencies.

The hard-core version of globalization, however, goes considerably further to argue that the world is not only an economic unity but also a social unity with a unified global class structure. The capitalist class in particular has formed itself into a global class for itself. An immanent process has reached its completion. The post-imperialist theorists took this position and it is now quite common though it travels under a different name.

How does globalization in this sense relate to imperialism? In the first place, it apparently clashes frontally with the Leninist concept of imperialism. That took as a starting point the fact that different national capitalist classes were destined to be eternally fratricidal and incapable of forming a global ruling class. They would be constantly redividing the world at great cost to everyone. This is why capitalism urgently needed to be replaced. Post-imperialism theorists, as the name of their idea implied, accepted Leninist imperialism as appropriate for a particular epoch but believed it had been superseded. The strong versions of second-generation globalization theory imply, but seldom explicitly state, the same change of stage. Logically, the idea that the world is a single social and economic unit implies that nations no longer have any importance as social divisions and that the class struggle now pervades everything and has, therefore, assumed a global dimension.

Historical materialism, globalization and politics

So, the hard-core version of the globalization hypothesis, once again, may look like a return to what the young Marx and Engels argued. There is, however, a notable difference. Marx, Engels and many other nineteenth-century socialists more generally saw globalization as a development which produced welcome opportunities from the point of view of socialism. It could form the basis of an international working-class movement and dispel narrow-minded nationalist notions. Yet today globalization receives an almost universally hostile reception from the left. It seems to be assumed that it can only represent more complete capitalist control of the world and portends both resistential weakness and economic damage for oppressed and exploited classes.

At least at a superficial level there are some very striking differences between this widespread pessimistic reaction to globalization in today's left and the positions of the early practitioners of historical materialism. In 1848, Marx gave a speech in Brussels about free trade much of which would have delighted a 1999 demonstration outside the World Trade Organization with its devastating attack on free trade as nothing more than freedom for capital (Marx 1848). But just when he seemed to be leading up to a conclusion denouncing free trade, he concluded without hesitation that between protectionism and free trade he, as a socialist, would have to support free trade because it was destructive of the *status quo* and not conservative. In saying this he was not supporting capitalist free trade; he was looking, within the possible trends of the ruling capitalist system, for the best circumstances for the development of world socialism. The first generation of imperialist theorists also were unanimous in considering that the tendencies away from free trade in the early years of this century were reactionary. Even more, while today's left denounces the multinational companies as responsible for almost all evil, Lenin and others of the first generation of imperialism theorists lamented the fact that capitalism increasingly identified with a national interest instead of building world-wide economic units which would strengthen the development of a world working class and pave the way for a globally planned socialist economy. For Lenin and many others the huge capitalist corporation was a pointer to the new rationality of socialism.

In pointing to these contrasts between then and now I am not trying to say that it is appropriate simply to repeat what they said then. But we should try to answer the question of why there is apparently so much difference in the political answers offered by enemies of capitalism between these two epochs. Were they wrong? Or has the world changed so much that their answers have lost their relevance? I believe that correct answers to these questions would include some elements of 'yes'; but also many elements of 'no'. And if that is true should the left of today not also ask rather more insistently a third question: are we wrong?

Marx famously remarked (in 'The Eighteenth Brumaire of Louis Bonaparte', 1852), that human beings 'make their own history. But they do not make it ... under circumstances chosen by themselves, but under circumstances directly encountered, given and transmitted from the past' (Marx [1852] 1935: 99). What that surely means is that political action to be effective (to make history) cannot ignore existing forces and movements. Whatever political destination is desired for the future, the route is necessarily constrained by the partially unstoppable movement of the spirals of history. There are moments in history where there may be no alternative outcomes. But more usually a given economic or political situation can evolve in a range of different possible directions. But not in just any chosen direction. The art of applying historical materialism to the craft of politics is to identify the real alternatives, and to see how interventions can influence the development of reality towards the most progressive of those possibilities.

Lenin once said that 'there are no completely hopeless situations for capitalism'. Using the same logic we should say that also there are no unambiguously triumphal situations either. According to historical materialism, capitalism is not capable of attaining permanent stability. My interpretation of the historical materialist approach is that from the standpoint of an anti-capitalist movement, political action (the making of history) seldom involves either direct confrontation with the enemy, or putting the clock into reverse and returning to some pre-existing state. It involves applying the principles of certain eastern martial arts: seeing where the enemy's contradictions are and acting on these weaknesses by deflecting the energy of the enemy to one's own advantage.

Such an approach emphatically does not lead to a simple conclusion that globalization will in some automatic way produce global socialism. It clearly will not. But nor is it simply a movement in the opposite direction. Like all significant historical changes, while it creates new social problems it also creates both new political needs and new political opportunities.

The current pessimism about globalization is, I think, partly a legacy of a previously mentioned aspect of the Leninist way of looking at capitalist history: as a process where a historically progressive phase eventually but decisively, permanently and unambiguously, gives way to a stage in which capitalism can no longer be anything but retrogressive. If that is the case, then no change in capitalism can ever be welcomed, not even in the partial or sceptical or ironical way in which Marx welcomed some changes. Not only is this far from the spirit of the socialists of the nineteenth century but, more important, it seems to be a false assessment of the real possibilities of turning the present changes in capitalism to the advantage of exploited and oppressed people.

Many statements about globalization overestimate the strength, unity and consciousness of the capitalist class by assuming that recent changes are well planned, conscious and necessarily successful. Freer international markets, however, involve great danger for capitalists. They complicate the chain of conditions which have to be satisfied in order for surplus value to be effectively produced and realized and increase the dangers of instability. Capital, especially the most global kind, speculative capital, can easily be wiped out by international instability. It is no coincidence that George Soros has become one of the leading advocates of new controls on liquid capital movements. You do not have to have an all-out orthodox Leninist perspective, or to think that world war is round the corner, to see that fratricidal conflicts between capitalist enterprises and capitalist states threaten to break out almost every day. The global unity of the capitalist class and the supersession of the nation-state are largely myths.

If one problem with the pessimistic approach to globalization is that it sometimes does not see any political way out, another is that it sometimes advocates a backward-looking way out. Identifying globalization as the problem tends to suggest deglobalization -- nationalism or localism – as the logical solution. If history is a straight line and we do not like the road ahead there is nowhere to go but back; but if it is a spiral we have more possibilities. If the problem is identified as capitalism and not globalization, and if capitalism is global, then that suggests that anti-capitalism is the solution and that anti-capitalism must also make itself global, producing counter proposals not to globalization as such but to global capitalism and capitalist globalization. In part that means socialist and democratic globalization, an idea whose time should have come or rather returned. There seems to me to be no reason to think, as today's pessimists do, that larger social units (even the world economy) are more difficult to democratize than smaller ones (such as the village and the family).

In short, we would, I think, be entirely faithful to the method of historical materialism to recognize important new, but not unprecedented, elements of globalism in the current structure of world capitalism, but not to interpret that as some new stage or complete qualitative transformation; to accept that the nation-state remains important and necessary to the capitalist class, which therefore continues to be by and large national, although with increasing elements of international collaboration and in particular cases fusion. Far from being an accomplished fact, globalization, like any other major social and economic tendency, is partial, biased, ambiguous and contradictory. Conflict between national capitals remains important, and so does the exploitation, domination and marginalization of many countries within the globalizing capitalist structure. The real growth in the globalized aspects of capitalism, however, are great enough to require a resistance movement which can transcend national boundaries at the same speed as or, better still, faster than capital can. So far international resistance has lagged behind capitalist globalization. But there are increasing signs of a growth in international movements of non-capitalist classes. Part of the progressive aspect of capitalist development, as seen by Marx, was that, while developing the productive forces, it also developed the strength of the classes which would bury it. I believe that that process goes on and can be accelerated in the new period of globalization.

Note

I thank Jonathan Rée for very helpful comments on a draft of this chapter.

Bibliography

Baran, P. ([1957] 1973) *The Political Economy of Growth*, Harmondsworth: Penguin.
Baran, P. and Sweezy, P. ([1966] 1968) *Monopoly Capital*, Harmondsworth: Penguin.
Catephores, G. (1994) 'The Imperious Austrian: Schumpeter as Bourgeois Marxist', *New Left Review*, 205, May–June: 3–30.
Doremus, P., Keller, W., Pauly, L. and Reich, S. (1998) *The Myth of the Global Corporation*, Princeton, NJ: Princeton University Press.
Hilferding, R. ([1910] 1981) *Finance Capital: A Study of the Latest Phase of Capitalist Development*, London: Routledge & Kegan Paul.
Hobson, J. (1902) *Imperialism: A Study*, London: George Allen & Unwin.
Kautsky, K. ([1914] 1970) 'Ultraimperialism', *New Left Review*, 59, Jan–Feb: 41–6.
Lenin, V. ([1916] 1965) *Imperialism: The Highest State of Capitalism*, Beijing: Foreign Languages Press.
Luxemburg, R. ([1913] 1951) *The Accumulation of Capital*, London: Routledge & Kegan Paul.
Marx, K. (1848) 'On the Question of Free Trade', speech to Brussels Democratic Association (http://www.marxists.org/archive/marx/works/1848-ft/1848-ft.htm).

—— ([1852] 1935) 'The Eighteenth Brumaire of Louis Bonaparte', in *Marx–Engels Collected Works*, Vol. 11, Moscow: International Publishers, pp.99–197.

Marx, K. and Engels, F. ([1848] 1935) *The Communist Manifesto*, Marx and Engels *Selected Works*, Vol. 1, Moscow: Progress Publishers, pp.98–137.

Mayer, A. (1990) *Why Did the Heavens not Darken? The 'Final Solution' in History*, London: Verso.

Ruigrok, W. and van Tulder, R. (1995) *The Logic of International Restructuring*, London: Routledge.

Sassoon, D. (1997) *One Hundred Years of Socialism*, London: Fontana.

Sklar, R. (1976) 'Postimperialism: A Class Analysis of Multinational Corporate Expansion', *Comparative Politics*, October: 75–92.

Sohn-Rethel, A. (1978) *Economy and Class Structure of German Fascism*, London: CSE Books.

Sutcliffe, B. and Glyn, A. (1999) 'Still Underwhelmed: Measures of Globalization and Their Misinterpretation', *Review of Radical Political Economics*, 31 (1), March.

UNCTAD (1999) *World Investment Report 1999*, Geneva: UNCTAD.

Warren, B. (1980) *Imperialism, Pioneer of Capitalism*, London: Verso.

Wollen, P. (1993) 'Our Post-Communism: The Legacy of Karl Kautsky', *New Left Review*, 202, Nov–Dec: 85–93.

3 The search for relevance

Historical materialism after the Cold War

Michael Cox

Introduction

The modern history of historical materialism begins – some would say ends – with the collapse of actually existing socialism as a serious political project after 1989. Some might dispute this reading of events, and no doubt a few would insist that the value of Marxism as a method has little or nothing to do with what existed in the former Soviet bloc. As one reasonably sympathetic critic has argued, it is neither logical nor fair (in fact, it is most 'unfair') to assume that the collapse of authoritarian communism necessarily invalidates the insights of Marx or the utility of historical materialism (Thomas 1997). One might equally point to the indisputable fact that the history of Marxism is a history of crisis, and that the current crisis so-called is merely another blip in the evolution of a body of ideas that have constantly been revised from within and challenged from without. Thus why be too bothered about the current situation? (but compare Gamble 1999). Indeed, according to Alex Callinicos, the real 'crisis of marxism' did not begin in 1989 at all but 1977 when a certain French intellectual decided to launch a bitter attack on Marx and all his works (Callinicos 1982: 5–6). One could go on rebutting the charge, but in the end it would be faintly absurd, distinctly unhistorical and in a very important way 'unmarxist' as well, not to recognize the simple truth that while crises are nothing new to Marxism, there has never been anything quite so cataclysmic in the history of Marxism as the fall of the old communist regimes in Eastern Europe and the USSR; and whether we prefer to talk of a crisis of historical materialism or a crisis of a particular and peculiar type of social formation, it would be a nonsense-on-stilts to deny some sort of connection between what happened in the Soviet bloc after 1989 and the current travails facing radical theory in general and Marxist analysis in particular. The collapse of the left as an organized force in the world, and the rapid decline of academic interest in Marxism (one prominent international relations (IR) theorist recently suggested that constructivism had now replaced Marxism as the most obvious paradigmatic rival to realism and liberalism; Walt 1998: 32, 34), would seem proof enough of the argument that radical materialist analysis in general and Marxism in particular is facing difficult times (but see Wood and Foster 1997; and the chapter by Teschke and Heine in this volume).

The point of this short piece is not to mount a defence of Marxism against its many detractors, but rather to suggest that in spite of its current travails, taken together the collapse of the Cold War system, and along with it the old international rules of the game, could ironically provide radical theory with an intellectual shot in the arm. Nor am I the only one to suggest this somewhat iconoclastic idea. As has been observed by others, while historical materialism is in many ways an excellent surgical tool, it was never very good when it came to discussing nuclear weapons, arms control and the sources of Soviet conduct. In many ways, the Cold War conflict didn't really suit it and its passing (and substitution by a more materialist set of global relations) has created new intellectual opportunities which did not exist before. But this is not all. Precisely because radicals no longer feel obliged to defend the USSR, a political space has opened up that permits them to think more openly and creatively. As Stanley Hoffmann has noted, whatever one thought of socialism as a practical goal, historical materialism itself always possessed a rare ability to expose and explain. Unfortunately, too many Marxists became drawn into the Cold War and consequently were impelled to choose sides rather than develop an independent line of analysis. Now however the situation is far more fluid and less politically determined, and in these 'new times' there is now greater scope to realize the still unrealized potential in historical materialism (Hoffmann 1995: 35). Finally, as the doyen of liberal American historians has recently pointed out, the irresistible dynamic of our modern form of 'unbridled capitalism' makes very fertile ground indeed for radical analysis. In fact, as Arthur Schlesinger has already warned, there is a very real danger that in a world of 'low wages, long hours', 'exploited workers' and 'social resentment', Marxism could easily take on a new lease of life. Though John F. Kennedy's most favoured historian could hardly be expected to welcome this development (and doesn't) his observation about the consequences of capitalism is an acute one, which both critics and defenders of modern capitalism would be well advised to heed (Schlesinger 1997). Some it would seem have already done so (Gray 1998).

Whether or not Schlesinger's nightmare scenario is ever realized will of course depend in large part on the credibility and vitality of historical materialist analysis itself. Nothing after all is inevitable, and if Marxists fail as badly in their attempts to explain the shape of the post-Soviet world as they did in analysing the contradictions of the former Soviet Union itself, then Marxism has (and deserves) no future. It might therefore be useful to see how the varieties of Marxism, neo-Marxism and radical theorizing have thus far come to terms with a world they, and nearly everybody else for that matter, never anticipated. In what follows I shall therefore try to summarize a large, very uneven and deeply schismatic literature. In my brief review I will include many writers who some might not even include within the fold; and others who themselves would not be comfortable being labelled as Marxist. Robert Cox for example is often associated with Marxism, though he himself could hardly be described as orthodox (Cox 1981, 1983). The same might be said of Andre Gunder Frank whose most recent work seems to challenge the whole edifice of Marxist thought on the history of capitalism (see Frank and Gills 1993). Noam Chomsky moreover is no

Marxist. On the other hand, his writings on the new international order are highly critical of the *status quo* (Chomsky 1994). Furthermore, unlike many of the analysts mentioned in this chapter, his works have a fairly wide readership, especially outside the narrow confines of the international relations profession.

I have divided the discussion into four sections. In the first, I look at the way radicals have tried to come to terms with the death of actually existing socialism and the associated international result in the shape of the 'end of the Cold War'. In the second, I examine their efforts to decode the meaning of the term 'globalization'. The third part then sees whether or not radical analysts have developed a theory of crisis. Finally, the fourth part examines the way or ways radicals have tried to come to terms with American power. In the concluding section I explore what is by far and away the greatest problem facing radical analysis today (possibly its greatest problem throughout the twentieth century): identifying the source of political regeneration in a world where there is possibly as much, if not more, suffering than at any point over the last fifty years, but little sense that much can be done to alleviate it.

The end of the Cold War

The collapse of Soviet power and with it the end of the Cold War was as big a surprise to most radicals as it was to more mainstream analysts, perhaps more so because many on the Western left had a certain regard for 'actually existing socialism': quite a few out of a misplaced sense of political loyalty, some because they just didn't like capitalism, and others because they felt that the Soviet Union (whatever its faults internally) played an internationally progressive role by counterbalancing the power of the United States while underwriting numerous anti-imperialist regimes – especially in the less developed countries of what was then, but is no more, referred to as the 'Third World' (Halliday 1993).

Lacking a proper political economy of communism (for reasons which would take too long to discuss here) radical analysts have in the main tried to deal with the politically problematic question of the fall of official socialism not by confronting the problem head on, but rather by finessing the issue. They have done so in a number of different ways.

The first way, quite simply, has been to deny that the regimes in Eastern Europe or the former Soviet Union were genuinely socialist. Thus what 'fell' between 1989 and 1991 was not the real article, but some odd hybrid which had little or nothing to do with what American Marxist Bertell Ollmann once tried to describe as 'Marx's vision' of the new society. This inclination to deny the socialist authenticity of the former USSR can in fact be found in the writings of many radicals, though it is perhaps most strongly articulated in the work of Hillel Ticktin, editor of the journal *Critique*, and the only Western Marxist to have developed a detailed political economy of the USSR before its disintegration. According to Ticktin (who was one of the few radicals to have ever lived in the USSR for any extended period of time) the Soviet system was not just repressive, but economically far less efficient than what existed in the West. For this reason he did not believe that what he termed this 'economy of waste' could endure over the long term. This view – first articulated as early as 1973 – in turn became the basis of a very specific politics which meant that Ticktin at least was somewhat less surprised than other Marxists by the Soviet Union's subsequent collapse. Indeed, in his opinion, until the USSR passed from the stage of history, there was little chance of a genuine 'new' left ever emerging in the West (Ticktin 1992).

If Ticktin detected deep and life-threatening economic flaws in the Soviet system, this was not the position of most socialists. Indeed, one of the more obvious ways in which other radicals have tried to come to terms with the fall of the Soviet Union, has been to imply that the system did not have to go under at all: and the only reason it did was because of ill-fated attempts to reform the country in the 1980s. Thus one of the better informed socialist economists has argued that although the Soviet Union had its fair share of problems, it did not face a terminal crisis. What brought it down, in the end, was not its flaws but Gorbachev's contradictory policies (Ellman and Kontorovich 1992). The American radical Anders Stephanson (1998) also insists that there was nothing inevitable about the demise of communism in the USSR. In his assessment it was largely the result of what he terms 'contingency'. Halliday too has suggested that the Soviet system did not (in his words) 'collapse', 'fail' or 'break down' (1994: 191–215). Rather, the Soviet leadership after 1985 decided – albeit for good objective reasons – to rule in a different way: and did so not because of massive internal difficulties, but because the Soviet elite finally realized that the USSR could neither catch up with nor compete with the West. Once this became manifest, the ruling group effectively lost its historical nerve (Halliday 1995).

The argument that the old Soviet system might not have been suffering incurable economic cancer has also led certain radical writers to the not illogical conclusion that if the system was not doomed because of its internal problems, it was in the end external factors which caused it to implode. This is certainly implicit in the influential work of Halliday who, significantly, says little about the USSR's domestic weaknesses, but a good deal about the impact which Western economic performance had upon Soviet elite perceptions. Others have stressed a more direct connection. Thus in the view of the Dutch Marxist, Kees van der Pijl, though the final transformation of the Soviet system was the result of several factors, one should not underestimate the role played by the United States and its declared objective of quite literally spending 'the Soviet Union into bankruptcy' (van der Pijl 1993). Robert Cox appears to have come to much the same conclusion in his writings. Like van der Pijl, Cox accepts there is no simple explanation of what happened in the former USSR after 1985. Nonetheless he still concludes that 'the arms race provoked by the Reaganite phase of the Cold War was too much for an unreformed Soviet economy to sustain' (Cox with Sinclair 1996: 217). Michael Ellman has also laid great stress on the importance of US strategy: taken together, Reagan's rearmament programme, Star Wars, and US support for anticommunist guerrillas throughout the world, were, in his opinion, 'key external factors' in bringing about Soviet economic collapse in 1991 (1993: 56).

But if the left has faced very real problems in coming to terms with the fall of the Soviet Union, it has tried to compensate for this in two very different ways.

One has been to understate the impact which communist collapse has actually had upon the 'essential' nature of the international system. Hence, in the view of Noam Chomsky (1992), there is nothing 'new' at all about the new world order: the rich remain rich, the poor South remains the poor South, and the United States still remains in charge. Robert Cox concurs. The new international system, he thinks, looks very much like the old one. Indeed, in the most basic of ways, the Cold War he argues has 'not ended' at all and its more basic structures continue 'to live in the West' in the shape of high military spending, in the operation of its intelligence services and in the unequal distribution of power among the various states (Cox with Sinclair 1996: 34). This also appears to be the position of the doyen of world-systems theory, Immanuel Wallerstein. Unfortunately, in his metastructural (and highly abstract) output over many years, one had no real sense that the Cold War ever had much meaning at all. Thus its conclusion was unlikely to have a great deal of impact upon a world-system that had existed since the sixteenth century, which had been in some fairly unspecified 'crisis' since the late 1960s, and would presumably remain in crisis until it came to an equally unspecified end twenty or thirty years down the historical line (Wallerstein 1979, 1996).

Finally, if writers like Wallerstein have tended to minimize the impact of the end of the Cold War, others have argued (perhaps rather more convincingly) that its passing has in fact created new political spaces that did not exist before. This is more or less the position adopted by Bogdan Denitch. Starting from the not unreasonable assumption that the division of Europe rested upon an illegitimate form of Soviet domination over the East, and a legitimate form of American hegemony in the West, Denitch concludes that in the new united continent there are now great opportunities. Unlike many politically active Marxists, Denitch is no utopian. Thus in his view the new openings are unlikely to free the workers from the grip of capitalism. Yet 1989 does make possible the deeper integration of Western Europe and upon this basis, Europe – in his opinion – will be able to develop a new social democratic third way between a highly dynamic but politically unacceptable American-style liberal capitalism and a moribund Soviet-style communism. This hardly amounts to the same thing as world revolution. Nonetheless, in a post-communist world, the possibility of building a new progressive Europe is one that should animate intelligent radicals more than pointless calls to man barricades which nobody wants to build and few want to stand behind (Denitch 1990: 3–14).

New world economic order: globalization

Though analysts like Denitch have tried to find some crumbs of comfort from the events of 1989, overall the collapse of planning in Eastern Europe, followed as it was by the adoption of radical market strategies in countries such as Poland and the Czech republic, had (as we have already suggested) an enormously debilitating impact upon Western Marxists. Yet the pessimism did not last long, and the few Marxists who managed to survive the baptism by fire began to take intellectual heart somewhere around the mid-1990s. There were two reasons for this. One, obviously, was that the transition in the former communist countries turned out to be far more problematic than most market triumphalists had originally antici-pated. In the case of Russia of course the so-called transition to something better and higher soon turned into a minor tragedy for the Russian people (see Cox 1998). The other, equally important, reason was the birth of a new world order in which economics assumed centre stage. In fact, it almost looks now as if it required a healthy dose of capitalism to re-ignite radical analysis and provide the intellectual left with a clear focus. But perhaps we should not be so surprised by this. In an age of geo-economics where even staid bankers were now prepared to use words like 'capitalism', where the former editor of the London *Times* talked menacingly of the 'coming depression' (Davidson and Rees-Mogg 1993), and an American President paid tribute to a book which speculated in almost Leninist terms about the coming economic struggle for dominance between the great powers in the twenty-first century (Thurow 1992), it was almost inevitable that some Marxists would take heart! Having been ground under politically since 1989, it looked to some of them at least (and at last) that historical materialism had finally come of age.

Rather than trying to provide a detailed reconstruction here of a single 'neo-Marxist' analysis of late twentieth-century capitalism (one which has yet to be written), it might be more useful to briefly point to some of the issues now being debated in the growing left-wing literature. Not surprisingly, one issue that has been discussed more than most is 'globalization'. While there is no agreed radical view on the subject, four quite reasonable questions have been asked of the concept since it literally exploded on to the academic agenda in the early 1990s.[1]

The first has perhaps been the most challenging: namely, what exactly is so new about the idea? As many on the left have argued, the apparently novel thesis that national economies have become mere regions of the global economy and that the productive forces have expanded far beyond the boundaries of the nation-state, is not novel at all.[2] Indeed, one of the first writers to advance the argument was no less than the abused and much ignored Karl Marx, who in the *Communist Manifesto* made it abundantly clear that the central feature of the capi-talist epoch was the 'universal interdependence of nations'. Moreover, this simple but critical idea ran like a red thread through Marxist thinking thereafter. It was, for instance, repeated by Lenin in his 1916 pamphlet *Imperialism* in an effort to provide a materialist explanation of the First World War. Trotsky also deployed very much the same argument in his critique of Stalin's claim that it was possible to build socialism in one country. And later theorists of dependency took it as read that until the less-developed countries could break away from the spidery economic web of the world market, they had no chance of overcoming the limits of backwardness (Baran 1957; Frank 1969). Globalization might have become a fashionable concept in the 1990s among those desperately looking for a 'relevant' topic now that traditional security questions no longer seemed to be interesting. But like most intellectual fads and fashions it was only a recycled version of a very old idea. In fact, according to Burnham (1997), even the idea itself was not a very good one.

The theme of continuity is also developed in the work of Hirst and Thompson (1996). However, rather than attacking mainstream academics for failing to recognize the radical antecedents of the concept, they question whether or not globalization is even an accurate description of the world economy in the late twentieth century. In a much-cited study whose underlying purpose is as much political as it is economic, they conclude that the image of globalization has for too long mesmerized analysts.[3] In their opinion the theory can be criticized on at least two grounds. The first is in terms of its descriptive power. In their view the 'present highly internationalized economy is not unprecedented' at all; indeed, 'in some respects the current international economy is less open and integrated than the regime which prevailed between 1870 and 1914'. Moreover, 'genuinely transnational companies appear to be relatively rare' (p.2), while the world economy itself, far from being genuinely 'global', is still very much dominated by the Triad of Europe, Japan and North America. They also question its political implications and suggest that far from being powerless as the theory implies, the state can still make a difference. As they argue, in this less than completely globalized economy, there are still opportunities for the development of governance mechanisms at the level of the international economy that neither undermine national governments, nor hinder the creation of national strategies for international control. In other words the world of 'markets' remains susceptible to conscious intervention. To this extent, the world economy is not out of control: politics, politicians and the people – in other words the state under conditions of democracy – can make a difference.[4]

A third line of radical attack has not been to question the reality of globalization so much as to point to its appalling human consequences. In a world where the market is 'unbound' – they argue – where there is in effect no alternative to the market, capitalism has assumed an increasingly aggressive posture: and this has led to the most extreme forms of inequality and economic polarization (Altvater and Mahnkopf 1997; also Hurrell and Woods 1995; and Saurin 1996). Nor is this accidental: nor can it be overcome without challenging the foundations of the system itself. Furthermore, if global economic integration has generated what one critic has rather mildly termed 'underconsumptionist tendencies', it has tended to do so not only within capitalist countries but also across them (Palan 1993). This is why the gap between the have and have-not nations has tended to increase rather than decrease in an era of global capitalism. According to one study, in an unregulated capitalist world economy, the outcome has been that those countries and regions which already possessed abundant resources and power have remained powerful and prosperous, while those that did not have become poorer and even more dependent than before (Sayer and Walker 1992).

Finally, many radical critics have wondered whether or not some of the advocates of globalization have tended to underestimate the anarchic and competitive character of the world capitalist system. Though accepting the more general thesis about global interdependence, many on the left do not accept the liberal corollary that we have moved beyond the age of conflict. And though war in the more traditional sense is highly unlikely, this does not rule out intense competition at the other levels. Realist by inclination, radicals have noted several areas in the world today where antagonism rather than co-operation is the norm. America's intense rivalry with France over trade, Germany's attempt to exercise economic hegemony over Europe at the expense of the United Kingdom, and the United States' more recent drive to open up the markets of Asia-Pacific, all point to a slightly less benign view of economic reality than that suggested by the 'globalists' (Petras and Morley 1997).

Capitalist contradictions

Perhaps the most serious difference however between radicals and their more orthodox peers concerns the long-term stability of world capitalism. Though few but the most orthodox economists would subscribe to a simple theory of global economic equilibrium, there is an underlying assumption among most non-Marxists that even though the international economic system might go through periodic booms and busts, these movements are either functional to the system overall (Schumpeter recall once talked of 'creative destruction') or can easily be resolved.[5] Naturally enough radicals do not share this sense of optimism. Nor in one sense can they given their opposition to the *status quo*. The problem for the left of course is that they have too often cried wolf before to be taken seriously now. However, with the onset of the Asian economic crisis it at last seems as if their prediction of economic doom has finally turned out to be true; and inevitably they have drawn some comfort from the fact that the Asia-Pacific miracle so-called has turned into a nightmare – one that has even prompted *The Economist* to ask whether the world as a whole is on the cusp of a new slump.[6]

But long before the collapse of capitalist optimism in Asia, radicals had already begun to articulate a theory of crisis. Basically, this consisted of a number of distinct arguments.

The first part was in essence an updated version of Hobson mediated via Keynes and restated in different forms by radical economists like Sweezy and Magdoff: and what this amounted to in effect was a belief that there was a fundamental contradiction between the world economy's capacity to produce, and the people's ability to consume. In other words, there existed what Marx had frequently referred to in his work as a systemic tendency to overproduction – one which he thought could not be overcome as long as capitalism continued to exist. Though long consigned to the proverbial dustbin of history, this particular theory has enjoyed something of a revival over the past few years, and not just among radicals but also more mainstream economists concerned that the great boom of the 1990s could easily be followed by the great crash of the early twenty-first century. Indeed, the thesis itself has been given an enormous boost with the publication of the evocatively sub-titled study by Wiliam Greider, *The Manic Logic of Global Capitalism*. Though Greider's underlying argument is not designed to support revolutionary conclusions, the fact that his study evokes the ghost of Marx (and has become an instant best-seller) would suggest that what one radical reviewer has called this 'powerful and disturbing book' has touched a very raw nerve among more orthodox analysts (Greider 1997).

Greider's pessimism however is not just based upon a general argument about the overproductive character of modern capitalism. It also flows from a more detailed analysis and awareness of the increasingly integrated and highly open character of the international economy, which allows billions to be moved, or lost, in a matter of hours; and where events in one country or set of countries are very rapidly felt around the world in a domino process that once set in train becomes very difficult to stop. A good example of this was provided by what happened in Hong Kong in late 1997. Here a 25 per cent fall on the Hong Kong Stock Exchange quickly led to a major decline in share prices around the world. In the same way, the meltdown in Indonesia has had a profoundly depressing effect upon the rest of Asia, while the financial crisis in Japan has sent seismic shocks right across the Pacific to the United States. And so it will go on according to radicals until governments either decide to reflate the world economy – which they are scared to do politically – or there is the crash predicted by Greider.

The argument that the system might well be spinning out of control is further supported in radical analysis by the argument that we are now living in an era where finance rather than industry – and finance capital rather than productive capital – have assumed the dominant role in the world economy.[7] While there may not be anything especially 'radical' about this particular empirical observation, there is about some of the conclusions which radical theorists tend to draw from it. First, in their view, the preponderance of finance effectively means that capitalism today has little or no interest in supporting industrial policies that sustain full employment. This therefore means that the system overall is now less able to fulfil at least one basic human right: the right to work. More generally, the overwhelming power of finance capital introduces enormous instability into the system as those with money either seek speculative gain with little concern about the political consequences of their actions, or move their money at very high speed if and when conditions change. What makes the situation all the more volatile of course is that there are no national or international means for controlling these various movements and flows. Consequently, a very dangerous and apparently unbridgeable gap has opened up between those institutions that are supposed to manage the world economic system in the general interest and the specific interests of the banks, the large pension funds and the insurance companies.

Finally, the tendency towards crisis in the post-Cold War epoch has been reinforced, it has been argued, by the end of the Cold War itself. Though not all radicals adhere to the argument that the Cold War was good for capitalism (there was a powerful current of thought which suggested the opposite) there are those who maintain that even though the superpower conflict was costly these costs were more than offset by the benefits. By the same token, while there has been obvious economic benefits accruing from the termination of the Cold War, its ending has created major problems for the West as a whole. First, governments in key capitalist countries like the USA and the UK no longer have military spending as a way of pump priming their economies (Markusen and Yudken 1992). Second, there are the unforeseen but really quite huge costs involved for Germany caused by reunification – costs that have transformed Germany from being a boom economy into one of the great under-performing economies of Europe. Third, though the end of the Cold War has been followed by what most radicals see as a temporary boom in the USA, its passing has fundamentally weakened America's capacity to act abroad. And without American leadership, the international order in general and the world capitalist system in particular are bound to suffer. Working on the good realist assumption that American power was an essential element in the post-war reconstruction of international capitalism, a number of radicals believe that now that the Cold War is over and America can no longer exercise its hegemony so effectively, the world system is likely to become a good deal less stable (McCormick 1995). Difficult times lie ahead for the last remaining 'superpower without a mission' (Cox 1995).

Hegemonic still? The United States

This brings us quite logically to the question of the United States: the source of most radical distaste during the Cold War, and the cause of much intellectual anguish since, it has now seen off the only power in the world capable of limiting its reach. Though less vilified in the 1990s than it was previously, the USA nonetheless continues to fascinate radicals in ways which no other nation does. The reasons for this are clear. No other country is as powerful, dynamic or as 'exceptional' as the United States of America. Indeed, according to one 'European' analyst, even American radicals and Marxists are more interesting and 'have been more intellectually productive and innovative' than their comrades across the Atlantic since the late 1960s! (Therborn 1996).

Three issues have been of greatest interest to radical critics: one concerns the use of American power; another, the nature of American foreign policy in the post-Cold War era; and the third America's position within the larger international system. Let us deal briefly with each.

The question about American power has been an especially problematic one for the left in the post-Cold War period. Naturally enough, most (but by no means all) radicals opposed American intervention against Iraq in 1991. However, since then, many have found themselves in the somewhat paradoxical position of attacking the United States not for being too interventionist, but for not being interventionist enough. The issue which led to this rather odd state of affairs was of course the war in ex-Yugoslavia. Here the left found itself caught between a rock and a hard place. On the one hand, being radicals they were deeply suspicious of any American involvement on the continent of Europe. On the other hand, it was palpably clear that if the USA did not get involved, the genocide in Bosnia would continue. There was no easy squaring of this particular circle. Some, therefore, decided to stick to their ideological guns and opposed any American role (Petras and Vieux 1996). Others, however, bit the political bullet and urged Washington on. Indeed, one of the greatest ironies of this particular tragedy was that many radicals who had earlier criticized the United States for having intervened in the Gulf because of oil, now pilloried the USA for not intervening in the Balkans because there was no oil. Moreover, having been the strongest critics of the American military before Bosnia, some on the left at least now became the most bellicose advocates of tough military action against the Serbs.

If radicals seemed to have had serious problems in dealing with USA power in the post-Cold War world, they appear to have had none at all in attacking America's self-proclaimed goal of promoting democracy. To be fair, they did not oppose the United States because they were against democracy as such, but rather because they thought that its championing of the policy was either a sham or, more obviously, a device designed to obscure America's economic objectives in the larger capitalist system. Chomsky in fact has even argued that the USA has actually deterred democracy,[8] while Furedi in his broadside has attacked all Western talk of making the world a better place as little more than a cover for neo-colonialism (Furedi 1994). Others have been slightly less harsh, or at least more subtle. This is certainly true of the important work undertaken by Gills and Robinson in their analysis of the Third World. In an attempt to move the argument forward, both have proposed the thesis that certain forms of 'low intensity democracy' have had an important role to play in both containing popular protest while legitimizing painful economic reforms being advocated by Washington (Gills *et al.* 1993; Robinson 1996). Robinson indeed has put forward a whole historical argument concerning the complex interplay between social change and elite rule in Latin America. Deploying the much used and admired Gramsci, he argues that by the 1980s it had become clear to the dominant group that the old repressive methods were no longer workable in an age of globalization; and supported by the USA, they therefore replaced coercive means of social control with consensual ones. Though the policy carried certain risks, in the end it achieved precisely what it had been designed to do: namely, to secure political stability in a period of social upheaval caused by Latin America's more complete integration into the world capitalist system.

The third and final 'great debate' has turned around the hoary old problem as to whether or not the United States is, ever has been, or will be, in decline. Regarded by many in the IR profession today as a non-issue (though this was not the view between the Vietnam War and the end of the Cold War) it continues to inform a large part of the modern radical discussion about the USA. Some like Bernstein and Adler (1995) are in little doubt that the United

States is in decline – and has been so since the late 1960s. Others like Stephen Gill assert that the 'declinist' thesis is quite false (1986, 1990). Clearly there is no consensus on the issue, and it would be misleading to suggest that there was one. Yet whereas radicals before the collapse of the USSR were more inclined to believe that the United States was on the way down, since 1991 they have tended (along with nearly everybody else) to assume that there is still a good head of steam left in the engine of the American capitalist machine. US success in the Cold War, its easy victory over Iraq, the financial crisis in Japan, Europe's inability to resolve the situation in ex-Yugoslavia and the economic boom in the USA after 1992, have in fact convinced many that American power is still something to be reckoned with. Indeed, according to one study written by a Latin American with impeccable left-wing credentials, Marxists have to face up to the unpalatable fact that the United States is not only *not* in decline, but can actually look forward to the future with enormous self-confidence. The prophets of (relative) doom like Paul Kennedy may know their history according to Valladao; however, they are in his view a century or two adrift; and if historical analogies must be drawn then it should be with Rome in triumph after its victory over Carthage, not with Britain in the post-war period, or Spain in the sixteenth century. The twenty-first century will be American (Valladao 1996).

Changing the world

The issue of American power leads finally to the question of political renewal on the left. The two are obviously connected. After all, if America is in decline as some on the left believe, the political possibilities for radicals would seem to be bright. If, on the other hand, we can look forward to continued American hegemony, then capitalism by implication must be secure: and if capital is secure, then the possibility of radical breakthrough is highly unlikely.

This in turn raises the even larger problem of what radicals or Marxists are supposed to do in a world where on the one hand the 'socialist alternative' seems to have failed, and where on the other the market, in spite of its manifest contradictions, looks like 'it's the only game in town'. The intellectual left has responded to this dilemma in a number of ways. Two deserve special mention here.

The first has been to accept that for the time being there may in fact be no alternative to the market, and the only thing one can do, therefore, is develop strategies that seek to build areas of opposition and resistance within the larger interstices of 'civil society' – either at the national or global level (Held 1997). With this in mind, no doubt, many on the left have endorsed campaigns to extend the realm of democracy or increase the degree of information available to the public at large. In Britain a good deal of radical energy has also been expended on supporting constitutional change, while in the United States radical activists have been involved in an as yet unsuccessful effort to develop a comprehensive health system. The left have also engaged in numerous other campaigns covering a range of questions, from women's rights and trade union recognition, right through to the increasingly popular issue of the environment – on which there is now a vast academic literature. Indeed, one of the more interesting developments over the past few years has been the marked rise in a radical discourse on major environmental questions. One might even be tempted to suggest that the struggle to save 'mother earth' from what some now see as impending environmental catastrophe has taken over from the equally influential movement ten years previously to prevent the collapse of the world into nuclear war.

The second way in which the left has responded to the current situation has been to explore ways and means by which the dynamics of globalization can either be slowed down or even arrested entirely – a perspective explored with typical intellectual sensitivity by Robert Cox. According to Cox, there is no reason for despair insofar as the dynamics of globalization are bound to throw up various forms of resistance around the world. This will come from many layers impacted by the internationalization of production, including groups outside of the production process proper. Resistance to global capitalism however is also bound to involve workers themselves who have been placed under unremitting pressure by the logic of a global capitalism constantly seeking to weaken the position of organized labour (Cox with Sinclair 1996: 191–208). According to radical critics, moreover, the proletarian genie is not just a figment of some rabid left-wing imagination. In country after country – from South Korea to France, from Germany to the United States itself – workers have begun to take action to resist attempts to make them mere robots in a world without frontiers, where capital owes no loyalty – except of course to its shareholders.[9] They may not yet have united, but at last the workers are beginning to act.

However, as Cox would be the first to admit, resistance to globalization is not exactly the same thing as a positive or coherent strategy, and until there is such a strategy, there will always remain what he calls 'a vacuum to be filled – a challenge to critical thinking on the left'. And at the heart of this challenge 'is the question of the motive force for change' (Cox with Sinclair 1996: 192). For if the working class is not the universal class described by Marx, and the vision of a new society has been besmirched by the experience of the USSR, then there is little possibility of major political transformation. Furthermore, even if the world is in crisis, or in what Hobsbawm prefers to call a 'state of social breakdown', without a vision of a different society, nothing can fundamentally change (1994: 459). This presents radicals with a major problem. For however sound their analysis, if the world remains the same (or even gets worse) they will simply be left standing where they have been for a very long time: on the sidelines of history. In this sense their greatest challenge perhaps is not so much intellectual as political; and until they can provide a coherent answer to the question of what it is they are for rather than what it is they are against, they will remain what they have been, in effect, for more years than they would care to admit – well-informed rebels without a political cause.

Notes

1   According to Anthony Giddens, 'globalization is almost worth not naming now: it is less a phenomenon, it is simply the way we live. You can forget the word globalization: it is what we are' (cited in John Lloyd, 'Interview: Anthony Giddens', *New Statesman*, 10 January 1997).

2   For a materialist though not necessarily orthodox Marxist account of the long history of capitalist economic interdependence see Braudel (1973, 1982, 1984) and Germain (1996).

3   In her radical critique of the view that states are now powerless to make policy because of globalization, Linda Weiss (1997) even talks about 'the enhanced importance of state power in the new international environment'. The Canadian Marxist, Leo Panitch (1994), is another radical who disputes the notion that globalization has rendered national politics meaningless.

4   According to the blurb on the back of one noted study on the new 'borderless world', 'nation states are dinosaurs waiting to die ... [they] have lost their ability to control exchange rates and protect their currencies ... they no longer generate real economic activity ... the fate of nation states are increasingly determined by choices made elsewhere' (Ohmae 1996).

5   In an attack on what he identified as a 'Marxist vision' of a world economic crash, the American economist, Lester Thurow (1997), argued that elected governments could and would in the end act to prevent the destruction of 'both the economic system and democracy itself'.

6   See 'Will the World Slump?', *The Economist*, 15 November 1997, pp.17–18.

7   One well-established Marxist has argued that the era of 'financial expansion represents the "autumn" of a prevailing capitalist order as it slowly gives way to a new order' (Arrighi 1994; see also Altvater 1997).

8   Chomsky's discussion of democracy and America's role in supporting it in the post-war period is somewhat more nuanced than the actual title of his book – *Deterring Democracy* – would suggest. See, in particular, 'The Decline of the Democratic Ideal', ibid., pp.331–50.

9   See 'Global Economy, Local Mayhem', *The Economist*, 18 January 1997, pp.15–16.

Bibliography

Altvater, E. (1997) 'Financial Crises on the Threshold of the 21st Century', in L. Panitch and C. Leys (eds), *Socialist Register, 1997*, London: Merlin Press, pp.48–74.

Altvater, E. and Mahnkopf, B. (1997) 'The World Market Unbound', *Review of International Political Economy*, 4, 3, Autumn: 448–71.

Arrighi, G. (1994) *The Long Twentieth Century*, London: Verso.

Baran, P. (1957) *The Political Economy of Growth*, New York: Monthly Review Press.

Bernstein, M. and Adler, D. (eds) (1995) *Understanding American Economic Decline*, Cambridge: Cambridge University Press.

Braudel, F. (1973) *Capitalism and Material Life, 1400–1800*, New York: Harper & Row.

—— (1982) *The Wheels of Commerce*, New York: Harper & Row.

—— (1984) *The Perspective of the World*, London: Collins/Fontana Press.

Burnham, P. (1997) 'Globalisation: States, Markets and Class Relations', *Historical Materialism*, 1, 1: 150–60.

Callinicos, A. (1982) *Is There a Future for Marxism?*, Basingstoke: Macmillan.

Chomsky, N. (1992) *Deterring Democracy*, New York: Vintage.

—— (1994) *World Orders: Old and New*, London: Pluto.

Cox, M. (1995) *US Foreign Policy After the Cold War*, London: The Royal Institute of International Affairs.

—— (ed.) (1998) *Rethinking the Soviet Collapse*, London: Cassell Academic.

Cox, R. (1981) 'Social Forces, States and World Orders', *Millennium*, 10, 2: 126–55.

—— (1983) 'Gramsci, Hegemony and International Relations', *Millennium*, 12, 2: 162–75.

Cox, R. with Sinclair, T. (1996) *Approaches to World Order*, Cambridge: Cambridge University Press.

Davidson, J. and Lord Rees-Mogg, W. (1993) *The Great Reckoning*, New York: Touchstone.

Denitch, B. (1990) *The End of the Cold War*, London: Verso.

Ellman, M. (1993) 'Multiple Causes of the Collapse', *RFE/RL Research Report*, 2, 23, 4 June.

Ellman, M. and Kontorovich, V. (eds) (1992) *The Disintegration of the Soviet Economic System*, London: Routledge.

Frank, A. (1969) *Capitalism and Underdevelopment in Latin America*, New York: Monthly Review Press.

Frank, A. and Gills, B. (eds) (1993) *The World System: Five Hundred Years or Five Thousand?*, London: Routledge.

Furedi, F. (1994) *The New Ideology of Imperialism*, London: Pluto Press.

Gamble, A. (1999) 'Marxism after Communism', in M. Cox, K. Booth and T. Dunne (eds), *The Interregnum: Controversies in World Politics 1989–1999*, Cambridge: Cambridge University Press, pp.127–44.

Germain, R. (1996) 'The Worlds of Finance: A Braudelian Perspective on IPE', *European Journal of International Relations*, 2, 2: 201–30.

Gill, S. (1986) 'American Hegemony: Its Limits and Prospects in the Reagan Era', *Millennium*, 15: 311–39.

—— (1990) *American Hegemony and the Trilateral Commission*, Cambridge: Cambridge University Press.

Gills, B., Rocamora, J. and Wilson, R. (eds) (1993) *Low Intensity Democracy*, London: Pluto Press.

Gray, J. (1998) *False Dawn*, London: Granta Books.

Greider, W. (1997) *One World, Ready Or Not: The Manic Logic of Global Capitalism*, New York: Simon & Schuster.

Halliday, F. (1993) *The Making of the Second Cold War*, London: Verso.

—— (1994) *Rethinking International Relations*, Basingstoke: Macmillan.

—— (1995) 'The End of the Cold War and International Relations', in K. Booth and S. Smith (eds), *International Relations Theory Today*, University Park: Pennsylvania State University Press, pp.38–61.

Held, D. (1997) *Democracy and the Global Order*, Cambridge: Cambridge University Press.

Hirst, P. and Thompson, G. (1996) *Globalization in Question*, Oxford: Polity Press.

Hobsbawm, E. (1994) *The Age of Extremes: A History of the World, 1914–1991*, New York: Pantheon.

Hoffmann, S. (1995) 'Democracy and Society', *World Policy Journal*, XII, 1: 35–9.

Hurrell, A. and Woods, N. (1995) 'Globalisation and Inequality', *Millennium*, 24, 3: 447–70.

Markusen, A. and Yudken, J. (1992) *Dismantling The Cold War Economy*, New York: Basic Books.

McCormick, T. (1995) *America's Half-Century*, Baltimore, MD: The Johns Hopkins University Press.

Ohmae, K. (1996) *The End of the Nation State*, New York: HarperCollins.

Palan, R. (1993) *Underconsumptionism and Widening Income Inequalities: the Dynamics of Globalization*, Newcastle: Newcastle Discussion Papers in Politics, September.

Panitch, L. (1994) 'Globalization and the State', in R. Miliband and L. Panitch (eds), *Socialist Register, 1994*, London: Merlin Press, pp.60–93.

Petras, J. and Morley, M. (1997) 'US–French Relations in the New World Order', unpublished manuscript.

Petras, J. and Vieux, S. (1996) 'Bosnia and the Revival of US Hegemony', *New Left Review*, 218, July–August: 3–25.

Robinson, W. (1996) *Promoting Polyarchy*, Cambridge: Cambridge University Press.

Saurin, J. (1996) 'Globalisation, Poverty, and the Promises of Modernity', *Millennium*, 25, 3: 657–80.

Sayer, A. and Walker, R. (1992) *The New Social Economy*, Oxford: Blackwell.

Schlesinger, A. (1997) 'Has Democracy A Future?', *Foreign Affairs*, 76, 5, September–October.

Stephanson, A. (1998) 'Rethinking Cold War History', *Review of International Studies*, 24, 1: 119–24.

Therborn, G. (1996) 'Dialectics of Modernity', *New Left Review*, 215, January–February: 59–81.

Thomas, K. (1997) 'Myth Breaker', *Guardian*, London, 10 July, p.16.

Thurow, L. (1992) *Head To Head*, New York: William Morrow.

—— (1997) 'The Revolution is Upon Us', *The Atlantic Monthly*, March: 97–100.

Ticktin, H. (1992) *The Origins of the Crisis in the USSR*, Armonk, NY: Sharpe.

Valladao, A. (1996) *The Twenty First Century Will Be American*, London: Verso.

van der Pijl, K. (1993) 'Soviet Socialism and Passive Revolution', in S. Gill (ed.), *Gramsci, Historical Materialism and International Relations*, Cambridge: Cambridge University Press, pp.237–58.

Wallerstein, I. (ed.) (1979) *The Capitalist World-Economy*, Cambridge: Cambridge University Press.

—— (1996) 'The Inter-state Structure of the Modern World-system', in S. Smith, K. Booth and M. Zalewski (eds), *International Theory: Positivism and Beyond*, Cambridge: Cambridge University Press.

Walt, S. (1998) 'International Relations: One World, Many Theories', *Foreign Policy*, 110, Spring: 29–46.

Weiss, L. (1997) 'Globalization and the Myth of the Powerless State', *New Left Review*, 225, September–October: 3–27.

Wood, E. and Foster, J. (eds) (1997) *In Defense of History: Marxism and the Postmodern Agenda*, New York: Monthly Review Press.

4 The pertinence of imperialism

Fred Halliday

The conjuncture of 2000

The twenty-first century opened amidst a flurry of optimism about the prospects for global capitalism. From the continuing growth of the US economy, through enthusiasm for e-commerce to new perspectives on break-throughs in biology and medicine, the prospects for human fulfilment and emancipation were, it was claimed, unlimited. Yet over this prospect of opti-mism there hung at least three major shadows, ones that darkened not only the headlines of the press but also the horizons of those who gathered, in Washington, London or Davos, to contemplate, and manage, the new millen-nium. One was the failure of the WTO conference in Seattle: the sight of a major conference on world trade having been forced to disperse amidst acri-mony and chaos underlined the limits of current global management – reflecting the conflicts between representatives of states within the conference, as well as the protests of those on the streets without. A second shadow was the state of the world's financial system. Outgoing IMF managing director Camdessus warned of complacency in the face of new tensions while pessimism surrounded the world's newest currency the euro: launched a year before as a rival to the dollar, it had lost a third of its value by the year's end. Third, and most seriously, there was the shadow of global inequality, a topic conveniently suppressed in the 1990s amidst much market-babble, but now recognised – by the World Bank and the United Nations Development Programme (UNDP) among others – as a central, increasingly dangerous, feature of globalisation.

The onset of the new capitalist millennium was, therefore, confronted with a deep challenge: not that, as a century before, of organised movements of the oppressed, on class and national grounds, against a system of global hegemony, nor, for the time being at least, that of imminent inter-state conflict. One contrast in substance and mood between the world at 1900 and that at 2000 was the markedly greater prominence a century earlier of a belief in conscious, collective, human agency and of the possibilities of purposive political action. The optimism of 2000 rested more on assertions about the progress of science or the workings of the market – agency had, conveniently, been dissolved, but not resolved. Yet, from above, in the worryings of Davos man about Seattle people, or in the widespread, and globally diffused, protests at the impact of globalisation, the new age was being placed in question.

The changes brought about by globalisation and the conflicts it evidently generated underline the relevance of placing these processes in their historical and contemporary context, i.e. the expansion of capitalism. By any measure – trade, investment, global reach of companies – capitalism has continued more and more to draw the world into its ambit. 2000 opened with a rush to global mergers. Capitalism has expanded not only through the penetration of markets, but through a range of policies designed to limit the resistance of other societies – trade liberalisation, privatisation, the removal of subsidies, 'compliance'. Four major historical processes have, in the past two decades, been collapsed into one: first, the completion of that subjugation of the pre-capitalist world which was begun five centuries before and which has now brought the remotest desert, forest and mountain village into the ambit of market relations; second, the destruction of that bloc of states that had, in a world-wide but ultimately failed campaign, sought to extract themselves from the world market; third, the intensification of technological change linked to capitalist expansion, which, by its very self-consuming rapidity, serves to reinforce oligarchic domination; fourth, the transition from a capitalism of rival national economies, a Keynesian-directed capitalism, to one in which states ensure the conditions for a free flow of goods and finance, while preventing the free flow of labour. Never has the link, boldly asserted by Marx and Engels in 1848, between capitalist domination and technological change, and between all of these and state policies, been as evident as is the third industrial revolution and the information revolution of the 1990s and beyond.

Two absent terms: capitalism, imperialism

To state this may be said to state the obvious, but it is not, because of the absence, or suppression, within orthodox discussion of the two analytic terms central to the analysis of this process. The first is capitalism itself: the term 'capitalism', the concept (never actually used by Marx) that seeks to denote the character of contemporary socio-economic relations, is one of which orthodox social science, and international relations, avoid speaking. It is as if the central motor of this phenomenon is too complex, or too sacred, for social science to utter its name: this, more than any other discursive denial, constitutes the ideology of social science, globalisation studies included, today. That this process is conducted for profit, with the aim of both subjugating and incorporating, is the central dynamic, and secret, of the modern epoch. The epiphenomenon of capitalist modernity – the introduction of new technologies, mergers, the erosion of 'outmoded' working practices, in the UK demutualisation – have here their explanation. International political economy has much to say on the manifestations of this process – structures of production and finance, the behaviour of firms: less on the socio-economic system underpinning this, capitalism itself. The study of globalisation, and indeed of contemporary world politics, is, first and foremost, the study of contemporary capitalism. Indeed, paraphrasing Horkheimer,[1] one may say: those who do not want to talk about capitalism, should not talk about international relations, or globalisation.

The other term, central but suppressed, is that of imperialism. Imperialism has, at best, had a half-life in the study of international relations. If the subject of the expansion of European, and later US and Japanese, control of subordinated states was accepted as a legitimate object of *historical* analysis, other branches of the social sciences – economics, sociology, politics and international relations – tended to avoid the topic. IR has recognised the importance of structures of power and inequality, but these have been treated as self-standing entities, sepa-rate from, or at best contingently related to, the world market and the global organisation of production. Yet this neglect within orthodox social science was countered by a vigorous, and sustained, debate on imperialism within historical materialism, where imperialism is seen as constituting the exploitative and global character of capitalist expansion, deriving primarily from economic factors, but reinforced by political, legal and cultural forms (Kemp 1967; Owen and Sutcliffe 1972; Brewer 1980). It was, famously, 'the highest stage of capitalism' – the Russian *novishii etap* being equally possible to render as 'newest' or 'most modern'. This has been evident from the early 1900s onwards: indeed no concept originating within historical materialism has had such resonance in the twentieth century, the impact ranging far outside conventional Marxist or socialist circles, to include much of third world nationalism, and indeed Islamic fundamentalism as well.

This impact has, however, seemed to falter in the 1990s, a victim on the one hand of the collapse of the state system that proclaimed itself to be 'anti-imperi-alist', and on the other of the prevalence of 'globalisation' as a characterisation for those processes that were previously seen as denoted by imperialism. The term has indeed virtually disappeared from the intellectual map: a brief survey of international relations journals, and of publications of the left, shows a radi-cally reduced interest in the topic. One exception, in a work of sustained historical and theoretical quality, has been Giovanni Arrighi (1991). Significantly, however, many other Marxist writers no longer regard it as a central part of their analysis.[2] Denial of the concept has been accompanied by fragmentation of theme: thus one can detect a range of issues that would, historically, have been encompassed within the discussion of imperialism that are now discussed as separate, possibly autonomous, topics: migration, environmental degradation, indigenous peoples, income inequality, gender and development, not to mention globalisation itself.

Current theoretical fashion also militates against recognition of the centrality of imperialism. Thus constructivism, a transposition to international relations of concepts of role and identity long abandoned in sociology, is little concerned with *objective* structures of power and domination. Contemporary political theory, with its validation of community, identity and nation at the expense of universal and rational criteria, has a *moral* position on imperialism, and 'Eurocentrism':

but this is not matched by any substantive analysis of the mechanisms of imperial power. Within post-positivist studies, there is much discussion of 'post-colonialism', but this is taken more as a cultural construct, and has displaced the analysis of 'post-colonial society' of a materialist kind pioneered in the 1960s (Alavi 1964). Similarly the critique of orientalism, pioneered by Edward Said, has displaced the far more cogent materialist work, of writers such as Anouar Abdel-Malek and Maxime Rodinson, that preceded it. In regard to resistance, contemporary literature is not without its invocations of the alternative, but this is too often either a romantic invocation of marginality – eco-feminism in India, Commandante Marcos in Chiapas, a simplification of Seattle – or a vague and ahistorical claim about growing anti-systemic social movements (Arrighi *et al.* 1989). Much of the literature on Seattle in particular reinforced this – neglecting the reality that it was as much *inter-state* conflicts within the conference as *movement-state* conflict without that determined the outcome.

As for globalisation itself, this too has served to obscure the central concepts and analytic claims of the imperialism literature. This displacement reflects at once a political and a theoretical conjuncture, but, arguably, one that has impoverished contemporary debate, just as it debilitates attempts to confront, resist and, potentially, turn to emancipatory advantage contemporary globalisation. The argument that follows offers, in summary form, some reflections on this intellectual challenge, reformulating some classical tenets of historical materialism on imperialism and examining how far these may be, and may not be, relevant to the contemporary world. The conjuncture of 2000, embodying both the end of the Cold War and its global political significance, and the spread of globalisation, provide occasion for this. They offer at once an opportunity to revisit earlier debates on capitalist expansion, and to identify the weaknesses and historical limitation of the classical arguments.

Imperialism and capitalist expansion: the five classical themes

Imperialism was not, it is often argued, one of the themes with which the founders of historical materialism concerned themselves: Marx and Engels had, famously, an ambivalent and, in retrospect, less than consistent position of opposition to European political and military expansion; at the same time their broad assumption, only partly qualified in later writings on semi-peripheral states such as Ireland and Russia, was that capitalism would create an increasingly unified world (see Shanin 1983). The bases for the supersession of capitalism lay in the diffusion of its social relations and productive forces, and the generation, on a world scale, of the contradictions inherent in that development. It was left to later Marxists, not least Lenin and Trotsky, to formulate what was to become the leitmotif of twentieth-century analysis of imperialism and anti-imperialism alike, the theory of combined and uneven development, one that recognised the explosive character of a growing hierarchy of wealth and power within an increasingly unified capitalist world (Rosenberg 1996).

Yet, in two respects, this reading of the writings of Marx and Engels is misleading. It is this very analysis of the diffusion of the capitalist mode of production that provides, in the 2000s, as in the 1850s, the basis for any discussion of the contemporary world – the use of the term 'Eurocentric' confuses an ideological Eurocentrism, ascribing primacy to European culture and values, with a scientific or historical Eurocentrism, which, quite rightly, ascribes the primary dynamic the creation of the capitalist world-system to western Europe and, later, the USA. On the other hand, the very limitation of the concept of 'imperialism' to relations between more- and less-developed countries, or what are today called 'north–south relations', obscures the other, analytically and historically anterior, dimension of the character and contradictions of developed capitalism itself: for Marx the term 'imperialism' meant initially that militarisation and expansionism of developed capitalist states, starting with France in the 1850s. This imperialism led to the later subjugation of Asia, Africa and Latin America in the latter part of the nineteenth century.

Imperialism *began* within the more developed capitalist states themselves: the study of imperialism involves therefore the location of 'north–south' relations within this dual context, the global expansion of capitalism on the one hand, the political and military expansion of developed capitalist states and their inter-state rivalry on the other. Freed of the distraction of the Cold War, a strategic conflict in which capitalism confronted its authoritarian socialist other, the conjuncture of 2000 returns the focus to the level of conflict *between* capitalist states, in economic and military terms: these are the themes to which Marx and Engels directed attention.

Within twentieth-century historical materialism we can identify two broad periods in which the subject of imperialism was addressed: the two decades after 1900, in the writings of Lenin, Luxemburg, Hilferding, Kautsky and other Marxist writers; the two decades from the 1950s, in the work of such authors as Paul Baran, Andre Gunder Frank, Harry Magdoff and Bill Warren. These two high points of discussion on imperialism corresponded to the two central themes in Marx and Engels themselves: the focus of the 1900–20 period was primarily on intra-capitalist relations, and above all the causes of World War I; the focus of the second was primarily on 'north–south' relations, variously framed in terms of surplus appropriation, dependency and underdevelopment. Yet in neither case was there an exact, exclusive, focus: the literature of the early twentieth century contained within it, notably in studies of colonial exploitation and the agrarian question, and in the work of Rosa Luxemburg, analysis of transformation *within* subordinated countries, the second generation of literature related exploitation of the south to the broader dynamic of monopoly capitalism, to the militarisation of Western society in the Cold War epoch, and to the harnessing of third world exploitation and intervention to the conflict with the Soviet Union in the Cold War. Both phases of the analysis of imperialism aspired, therefore, to a global, developed and underdeveloped, combined and uneven, analysis of the dynamics of imperialism.

At the risk of simplification, it is possible to extract from this literature, treated as a whole, five broad themes, which can be regarded as constituting the historical materialist argument on imperialism:

1   The inexorable expansion of capitalism as a socio-economic system on a world scale.
2   The necessarily competitive, expansionist and warlike character of developed capitalist states.
3   The unequal character of capitalist expansion, and the reproduction on a world scale of socio-economic inequalities.
4   The creation on a world scale of structures of inequality or power and wealth not only in the economic, but in the social, political, legal and cultural spheres.
5   The generation, through the very process of capitalist expansion, of movements of resistance, of anti-imperialism.

Summary as they may be, these constitute a set of basic arguments that run through the historical materialist literature, from the 1840s to the 1970s, and which stand in marked contrast to other more orthodox social science accounts. Above all, they locate the diffusion of imperialism within the context of the global expansion of capitalism.

Taken as a whole, this historical materialist characterisation of the international system was subjected to several, reiterated, critiques (Warren 1981). In the first place, the relationship established between the economic requirements of capitalism and the formal, colonial, subjugation of the non-European world was presented as unfounded. The greatest flow of British capital went not to colonies but to semi-developed states, Argentina and the United States. The economic theory of causation – variously presented as due to surplus capital, the need for raw materials and/or labour power, or the need for markets – was challenged as misrepresenting the pattern of capital export in the high imperial period, or as overstating the contribution of the colonial world to European economic growth.[3] This highlighted not so much the weakness of the historical materialist theory as its unduly limited scope: for whatever the combination of reasons that led to the 'new imperialism' of 1870–1914, the overall pattern of European expansion, from the 1490s onwards, was intricately related to the economic needs of a developing and expanding Europe. This is the strength of the explanatory claim made by 'world-systems theory'. The conceptual underpinnings of Wallerstein's world-systems theory may be subject to critique: the earlier period of expansion, up to the early eighteenth century, was a precursor of capitalism but was in its internal socio-economic and political formation pre-capitalist. Wallerstein's central insight, on the historical continuity and progressive expansion of the European economic and political system over five centuries, is nonetheless most relevant.

Recent scholarship has indeed established the centrality of capitalism in what had hitherto been regarded as the least capitalist of imperial activities, new world slavery: as Robin Blackburn (1997) has shown, slavery not only served a central role in generating profits in the eighteenth century but in the very formalisation of exploitation and labour management presaged later forms of workplace, and penitentiary, subordination. A second criticism concerned the centrality of colonies, i.e. of formal political control: construed in this sense, domination was not central to the stability of developed capitalism. Yet this too understated the force of the historical materialist argument: for while formal control was never the exclusive form of imperial domination – as evident in regard to such countries as Argentina or Mexico before 1914 – the integration of these states, and of later newly independent countries, was one subordinated to the developed capitalist countries.

More substantial were the critiques of the standard Leninist position articulated *from within* Marxism itself. In the first period this critique was most associated with Kautsky (1970), who questioned the second of the major theses identified above, namely the necessity of conflict between developed capitalist states. While abruptly contradicted by the outbreak of World War I a few weeks after he had written his analysis, Kautsky nonetheless pointed to an important weakness of the central Leninist argument: the necessary relation between developed capitalism and war. The latter part of the twentieth century was to show that the relation was more flexible and contingent than Lenin, seizing on the opportunity of 1914, had envisaged. The most cogent critique of the later literature was provided by those who argued, against dependency theory, that capitalism *was* within a hierarchical system capable of development in the third world: cautiously argued by Cardoso (1972) in his theory of 'dependent development', and more robustly in Warren (1980) in his 'imperialism, pioneer of capitalism', this reasserted the original insight of Marx into the global impact of capitalism, and excoriated the romanticisation of nationalism and pre-capitalist society that had underlain the dependency literature. For Warren, in particular, the analysis of imperialism required a return to the classical Marxist tradition of analysing the expansion of capitalism: hence in addition to the works of Marx and Engels themselves, Warren distinguished between a later, underconsumptionist, Lenin of *Imperialism* (1916), and the earlier more scientific *Development of Capitalism in Russia* (1900).

The theory in retrospect

Note has already been taken of the five central theses that constitute the historical materialist argument. It is now possible, in an equally schematic manner, to assess how far, from the vantage point of the analysis of the contemporary world, these theses are valid. If there is much to challenge orthodox and atemporal formulations, it is also possible to see in which respects the classical tradition remains relevant.

1   That the expansion of capitalism has been the defining characteristic of modern history needs little discussion here. Long obscured by the prevalence of inter-state conflict in its colonial, intra-European and Cold War

forms, it is now clearer that the process of nineteenth-century capitalist expansion under conditions of broad inter-state collaboration has now been recuperated by the globalisation of the late twentieth century. At the same time, the combination of dynamism and inequality which was marked in the height of the colonial period, up to 1914, has been replicated even more dramatically today. That capitalism unites *and simultaneously* divides the world is the central truth of our times.

2   The thesis on war between developed capitalist states, and more generally of the warlike character of such states, would appear to have received strong support from the development of the twentieth century. In addition to two world wars, there has been a history of repeated intervention in third world states in the post-1945 epoch. The theory received, it was argued, further support from the conduct of advanced capitalist states during the Cold War: here military expenditure served not only an international function, of pressure on the communist world, one that ultimately contributed to the collapse of the USSR, but also as a means of boosting profits and employment within the developed capitalist states. This was the theory known, variously, as 'military Keynesianism' and the 'permanent arms economy'. In the late twentieth century, Cold War military expenditure served, within an under-consumptionist perspective, the purposes which colonial expansion had served in the latter part of the nineteenth century. While constrained from major inter-state wars, the major capitalist states did engage during the Cold War in a series of wars with radical third world movements.

Contemporary reassessment nevertheless suggests a modification of this argument. The pattern of inter-capitalist war that characterised the first part of the twentieth century expressed not a permanent, but a conjunctural, and contingent, tendency within advanced capitalism: the resort to war, and the militarisation of society accompanying it, served the interests of political and economic power in that period. It was not autonomous of the prevailing political and economic formation of capitalism, but was dependent or contingent on it: yet that capitalism itself did not remain permanently in the condition in which World Wars I and II were generated. This is, however, distinct from arguing that it was a necessary, recurrent, feature of capitalism in general. The argument for a contingent relationship of capitalism to war suggests, also however, that arguments on the necessarily pacific nature of capitalism are also unfounded: much as these may have appealed to the earlier sociologists in the 1840s, or to theorists of interdependence and the democratic peace in the 1980s and 1990s, such assertions of a necessary relation between capitalism and peace are as untenable as their counterparts. As with authoritarian political regimes, racial segregation, the gendered division of labour or formal colonial rule, arguments as to the *necessary* interrelation of capitalism with specific forms of political and social order are shown, in retrospect, to be limited. Capitalism is neither necessarily pacific nor necessarily warlike, any more than it is necessarily authoritarian or democratic.

3   The evidence of the past decades contradicts much of dependency theory
     but reinforces the argument on the growth of global inequality and the
     reproduction of an oligarchic economic system. Dependency theory had
     argued not only that the 'south' or the 'periphery' was subjected to the
     'north' but that this subjection involved greater and greater impoverishment.
     This was the basis of the theory of the 'development of underdevelopment'
     espoused by Gunder Frank. Developments over the past three decades have
     demonstrated the falsity of this approach and the validity, in this respect, of
     the criticisms of Warren, Cardoso and others: industrialisation, and
     economic growth in general, have been possible in a range of peripheral
     countries and on a scale that dependency theory did not envisage. At the
     same time the very incorporation of third world economies into global capi-
     talism has led to a massive increase in the flow of capital, through foreign
     direct investment, into the third world – from $50 billion in 1990, to $150
     billion in 1997, this figure being amplified by further flows of private capital,
     in the form of bank loans and portfolio investment. Capitalism has, in this
     respect, fulfilled part of its promise, in pursuit of its very global spread.
         The character of this globalisation has, however, belied any prospect of a
     universal spread of prosperity. In five central respects this economic change
     has confirmed the oligarchic character of the globalisation process: first, the
     increased economic levels of third world countries have not prevented a
     growing inequality in world income;[4] second, the incorporation of peripheral
     and semi-peripheral societies has come about through the reproduction of
     capitalist class relations within these countries such that the gap between
     indigenous rulers and the mass of the population has widened; third, in one
     group of recently incorporated societies, the former communist countries of
     eastern Europe and the USSR, capitalist penetration has been accompanied
     by massive absolute *falls* in living standards – on average 40 per cent; fourth, to
     a degree far greater than in the early twentieth-century imperialism, the flow
     of capital has been under conditions of instability and mobility that have only
     confirmed the vulnerability of third world states, and, by extension, of the
     international financial system; fifth, in a dimension earlier writers were only
     dimly conscious of, and which state socialism in its own manner compounded,
     capitalism has come to threaten the very environmental balance of the planet,
     creating in so doing an imbalance of environmental concern and protection
     between north and south that mirrors the global hierarchy as a whole.

4   The historical materialist focus on the mechanisms and institutions of capi-
     talist domination has received striking confirmation from developments in
     recent decades: the instruments of global economic management – IMF,
     World Bank, WTO and Group of 7 – have represented the interests of hege-
     monic capital, promoting the global spread of free market capitalism even as
     they seek to manage it and, in the face of instabilities, lessen the tensions. The
     study of what in orthodox IR is benignly termed 'international institutions'
     analyses the political mechanisms put in place at the international level for

the management of this capitalist world. Equally, the processes of economic integration found in Europe and Latin America – EU, Mercosur, NAFTA – correspond to forms of integration of capitalist economies the better to promote shared interests.

This process of political and economic integration has been accompanied by the globalisation of a culture that is itself an instrument of subordination: the diffusion of information under the control of an oligopoly of communications firms, and the diffusion of a life style that is associated with the dominant US power, serve to reinforce that cultural domination, and that definition of the expectations of legitimate social and political action, that are central to the maintenance of any hegemonic system. Cultural hegemony allows for diversity, but one construed in corporatist, nativist and essentialist terms: it does not permit the articulation of an alternative hegemonic culture that would threaten to unstick the ideological glue that permeates the system. The site of conflict is, moreover, less that between 'Western' and 'non-Western' values as it is one revolving around *different interpretations of what is now a global set of values, originating historically in the West*: the challenge to hegemony has come in terms of such concepts as equality, independence, revolution, rights. A study of the works of figures generally associated with the 'revolt against the West' will show that their core ideological concepts were part of a radical, anti-hegemonic but universal discourse. This is as true of Gandhi, Fanon and Khomeini as it is of Mao Tse-tung, José Marti or Gamal Abd al-Nasir, let alone Che Guevara or Nelson Mandela.

5   The fate of anti-imperialism, and of what are termed 'anti-systemic' movements, presents a dual challenge to the historical materialist tradition. On the one hand, the twentieth century witnessed great and persistent struggles against imperialism and capitalism, vindicating the view that the spread of capitalism would generate mass revolt, be this in the semi-peripheral but independent states – Russia, China, Cuba, Iran – or in countries formerly controlled by imperialism. For much of the century it appeared as if, in their combined and growing impact, these challenges would weaken the global capitalist system. Even when this challenge had been contained, it appeared that they could in various ways hold out against the world market: such a challenge took both revolutionary – communist – and reformist – NIEO (new international economic order) – forms. Yet neither of these challenges was sustained: reformist programmes of the 1970s, summarised in the NIEO, evaporated after rhetorical resistance, while the bloc of state-controlled economies succumbed in the 1980s and 1990s to reincorporation. The greatest challenge to the modern world capitalist system since around 1500 had failed.

This crisis of anti-imperialism was, however, matched by another development, namely the deformation of anti-imperialism itself. Anti-imperialism had classically involved a coalition of forces, a combination of socialist and Marxist parties on the one hand, with nationalist and national liberation movements on the other: the management of that coalition, and the shifting balance of forces within it, had constituted one of the enduring political tensions of the twentieth century. It had involved both a set of shared, universalist, goals and a belief in a potential historical alternative. Until the 1970s, however, the different components of that movement had espoused certain common goals – independence from Western capitalist domination, mass-based revolt, and a programme of secular modernisation: the claim of anti-imperialism was, indeed, not that it rejected the goals of capitalist modernity – democracy, economic development, equality of men and women, secularism – but rather that it was able the better to fulfil the modernist programme that capitalism, for all its claims, could not.[5] Increasingly, however, from the 1970s anti-imperialism came to comprise not only groups with such modernist programmes but other, more various, components: that ambivalence towards modernity that was always latent within nationalism came to the fore in movements of religious fundamentalism, a politics of ethnic identity, valorisations of nature and other, irrational, forms. This was true equally in the developed and in the third worlds. At the same time, an increasing part of the remaining traditional anti-imperialist movement came to be dominated by forms of authoritarian politics that represented the worst of the traditional left – Sendero Luminoso in Peru, the PKK in Turkey. At a time when liberal trends in capitalism showed themselves more flexible towards democratisation and human rights, anti-imperialism came to represent a coalition of the romantic and the authoritarian. This was incapable of sustaining a consistent resistance to prevailing forms of capitalism or of offering an alternative that was visibly superior to the programme inherent in the more democratic capitalist states.

The challenge which this posed was, therefore, the reconceptualisation of resistance to, and supercession of, imperialism itself: as within societies, so on a world scale, there developed a tension long present in the conflicts of modernity between a reformist approach, that sought to realise the democratic and economic potential of capitalist modernity, by bringing it under greater democratic control, and one that sought to reject it entirely. The very opening up of capitalist politics to discourses of rights and of democratisation in the 1980s and 1990s, coupled to the removal of Cold War justifications for authoritarian rule, provided a new political space in which to oppose prevailing forms of political and economic power.[6] The failure of revolutionary anti-imperialism in its classic form was tied to its espousal of a teleological history, of the possibility of struggle in the name of a transition to post-capitalism, both desirable and sustainable, that proved to be invalid. Equally, it was associated with political dictatorships that proved incapable of democratic, popular, evolution. In its more recent form, latent as it was with promises of deliverance through authoritarian rule, and associated increasingly with anti-modernist confusion, such anti-imperialism itself inhibited the emergence of an alternative, emancipatory and realistic, contestation: facilely aligning with a range of regimes whose practice was even more remote from the emancipatory agenda than their opponents, many anti-imperialists found themselves acting, in the spirit of a long discredited stagist view of history, as apologists for semi-peripheral dictatorship.

One of the most telling challenges for any theory of imperialism, both in regard to the analysis of contemporary global structures and of alternatives to them, is to offer an understanding of the place and character of alternative forces. This is as necessary to rebut the hegemonic triumphalism of the epoch as it is to learn from the catastrophic simplifications of the century past: between mawkish indulgence of globalisation, and a vapid idealisation of alternative forces, there needs to be a space which identifies those, within movements, civil contexts, the media, the intelligentsia, and, in their individual and combined form, states that can form the basis for such a challenge. Any such conception that abandons the principles of democracy, and the more advanced conceptions of rights which contemporary liberalism has espoused, or which seeks to displace rather than transform states, is misdirected. A radical alternative to globalisation can only transcend the structures of inequality in the world today if it builds, in material and ideological form, on the best that its opponent has created.

Contemporary challenges

The critique which has already been levelled at the classical Leninist theory of imperialism, by historical event and intellectual reassessment alike, should underline the dangers of any fideist reassertion of orthodox verities. Imperialism, in the sense that Lenin understood it, was not the highest stage of capitalism, nor was developed capitalism necessarily tied to war. The forces of resistance generated by imperialism were not fated, by some immanent logic, to overwhelm the capitalist states. Nor have all those who have opposed imperialism represented an alternative that is, on political or ethical grounds, preferable to imperialism itself. The intellectual challenge facing critical analysis of international relations now is not to revive a 'correct' theory: it is of a rather different kind, and may be divided into four broad themes.

In the first place, there is a need to grasp the *historicity* of the contemporary phase of world capitalism, its relation to earlier phases in this century, and before, and the limits which may be inherent in its current phase. Contemporary world capitalism is evidently able to avoid war between developed capitalist states and rests increasingly on mechanisms of financial globalisation. The analytic challenge is to identify what it is that is specific to this phase, without lapsing into eternal and themselves ahistorical projections, about post-modernity, globalisation, or the end of inter-state conflict. Equally it involves assessing the dynamic of the contemporary world, and the potential for alternatives that it is creating, without reinventing those teleologies on which much earlier materialist and anti-imperialist writing implicitly relied.

Second, we need not just an analysis of the international state system but of that which underlies, and has long underlain, it, namely the international *social* system, a global sociology not of overventilated generalisations about globalisation, but of the contemporary reproduction of class, wealth and power on a world scale. To do this involves both a locating of different social forces on the world map, but equally their relation to particular structures of economic and political power, be they in terms of production circuits, financial structures or mechanisms of distribution. Several candidates for such a global sociology already exist: dependency theory, world-systems theory, various elaborations of 'hegemony' (Rupert 1995; Bromley 1993; Cox and Sinclair 1996) and 'postimperialism', the last a theory about the creation of a new transnational capitalist elite that incorporates third world economies into those of the developed world (Becker *et al.* 1987). Any such sociology needs to combine awareness of the increasingly integrated character of capitalist elites, and, at the same time, the reproduction and intensification of overall income disparities, and of new inter-bloc conflict.

Third, we need to assess and rethink something that was central to the classical analysis of domestic and international society, namely mechanisms of domination. At the moment we have vague intimations of military, political, economic and cultural power, as well as of the role of law – international, but also citizenship law – as an instrument for global control. We have very little sense of how ideologies – of nationalism, identity, religious affiliation – and means of communication fit into the global system of domination. How central, for example, is the US domination of global culture and news diffusion to the reproduction of its system of political control? How far since 1989 are systems of military domination linked to those of economic control?

Finally, we need to assess, in the light of materialist and rational criteria, the potential for alternatives in the contemporary world. A mere rallying of disparate self-proclaimed anti-imperialist forces is hardly sufficient, leaving aside the fact that these have no directing centre. The breaking down of the barrier between Marxist and 'reformist' critics of capitalism evident since the 1970s in the domestic field needs to be replicated on the international plane. Any policy of critique has to be linked both to the potential for improving on what already exists and on the identification of social forces capable of realising such a critique. Central to any such project is the need for democratic control of the forces that are, ideologically, presented as objective and beyond social control – markets, technological change, scientific advance. There is room here for some neo-Warrenite scepticism about what passes as credible anti-imperialism today. One shudders, for example, to think what the more hard-headed of the socialist tradition of the twentieth century would have thought if they had seen that the last great global mass event of the twentieth century would be the motley agglomeration on the streets of Seattle.

Conclusion: the pertinence of imperialism

If understood in terms of the five themes identified above, imperialism is not just a possible, but a necessary, part of any comprehension of the contemporary world. Shorn of teleology and of dehistoricised extrapolation, the classical literature can contribute to a framework for understanding the dynamics of contemporary capitalism, in rebutting both the vapidities of neoliberal orthodoxy and disembodied globalisation alike. Equally, imperialism, along with other

Marxist concepts, can challenge prevailing 'alternative' approaches within the study of society and international relations, be they 'post-colonialism' or idealisms of constructivism and its ilk. Above all, it can provide the basis of what any theory of imperialism entails, which is that of a critique of political realities: the task, common to both developed and developing countries, is that of bringing the processes of contemporary capitalism under democratic control, and of realising the emancipatory potential within advanced and subordinated capitalism alike. There are many things in the contemporary world that would have surprised, and challenged, Marx and his immediate associates: the reproduction of capitalist inequality on a world scale, and the masking of this process by appeals to science, inevitability or even culture, would not.

Notes

1   'Those who do not want to talk about capitalism should not talk about fascism.'
2   For example, in *Marxism and Social Science*, edited by Andrew Gamble, David Marsh and Tony Tant (1999), there is no entry on imperialism.
3   Patrick O'Brien (1990) has argued that imperial investment, by lowering investment rates at home, weakened Britain *vis-à-vis* its competitors.
4   UNCTAD (United Nations Conference on Trade and Development) figures indicate that in the quarter century from 1965 to 1990 the share of world income owned by the richest 20 per cent of the world's population rose from 69 per cent to 83 per cent. Average per capita income in the richest 20 per cent was thirty-one times higher than in the poorest 20 per cent in 1965, sixty times higher in 1990 (*The Economist*, 20 September 1997).
5   A classic version of this was the Trotskyist theory of permanent revolution: in essence, this stated that capitalism could not, under contemporary conditions, fulfil the 'tasks' of modernity and that these could only be realised under socialism. These 'tasks' included national independence, industrialisation, land reform, democracy, cultural development (see Löwy 1981).
6   For a powerful critique of militarism in the Latin American left, see Castañeda (1994).

Bibliography

Alavi, H. (1964) 'The Post-Colonial State', *Socialist Register*.
Arrighi, G. (1991) 'World Income Inequalities and the Future of Socialism', *New Left Review*, 189, September–October.
Arrighi, G., Hopkins, Terrence and Wallerstein, Immanuel (1989) *Anti-System Movements*, London: Verso.
Becker, D., Frieden, J., Schatz, S. and Sklar, R. (1987) *Postimperialism: International Capitalism and Development in the Late Twentieth Century*, Boulder, CO: L. Rienner.
Blackburn, R. (1997) *The Making of New World Slavery*, London: Verso.
Brewer, A. (1980) *Marxist Theories of Imperialism: A Critical Survey*, London: Routledge & Kegan Paul.
Bromley, S. (1993) *American Hegemony and World Oil*, Cambridge: Polity Press.
Cardoso, F. (1972) 'Dependent Capitalist Development in Latin America', *New Left Review*, 74, July–August.
Castañeda, J. (1994) *Utopia Unarmed*, New York: Vintage Books.

Cox, R. and Sinclair, T. (1996) *Approaches to World Order*, Cambridge: Cambridge University Press.

Gamble, A., Marsh, D. and Tant, T. (eds) (1999) *Marxism and Social Science*, Basingstoke: Macmillan.

Kautsky, K. (1970) 'Ultra-Imperialism', *New Left Review*, 59, January–February.

Kemp, T. (1967) *Theories of Imperialism*, London: Dennis Dobson.

Löwy, M. (1981) *The Politics of Combined and Uneven Development*, London: Verso.

O'Brien, P. (1990) 'The Imperial Component in the Decline of the British Economy before 1914', in M. Mann (ed.), *The Rise and Decline of the Nation State*, Oxford: Blackwell.

Owen, R. and Sutcliffe, B. (eds) (1972) *Studies in the Theory of Imperialism*, London: Longman.

Rosenberg, J. (1996) 'Isaac Deutscher and the Lost History of International Relations', *New Left Review*, 215, January–February.

Rupert, M. (1995) *Producing Hegemony*, Cambridge: Cambridge University Press.

Shanin, T. (1983) *Late Marx and the Russian Road*, London: Routledge & Kegan Paul.

Warren, B. (1980) *Imperialism. Pioneer of Capitalism*, London: Verso.

5 A flexible Marxism for flexible times

Globalization and historical materialism

Mark Laffey and Kathryn Dean[1]

How is the revolutionary subject to be tensed and spaced out, centered and decentered, sober and drunk, German and French, at one and the same time?

(Eagleton 1988: ix)

a friend told me recently that the late Chris Hani of South Africa's Communist Party once laughingly informed her that he had been too busy working on revolution to read *Das Kapital*...

(Lam 1996: 263, n.4)

'Workers of the World _____!'

(Hitchcock 1996: 71)

We are living in a Marxist moment. The internationalization of capital, so central to the rhetoric and reality of globalization, has prompted a renewed interest in historical materialism. This interest takes the form of a return to economistic Marxism, as the continuing necessity of Marxism is justified in terms of its superior capacity to analyse capitalism. This economism arises from the conceptualization of capitalism as an 'economy', rather than as a complete way of life, the purpose of historical materialism being the study of this 'economy' (e.g. Gamble 1999: 142–4). This return to economistic historical materialism diminishes Marxism's critical potential. This is because, first, it reproduces the economistic logic of capitalism itself. Second, it ignores, or treats as epiphenomenal, the matter of subjectivity. This neglect of subjectivity is a neglect of the question of agency (e.g. Castree 1995a: 269). Third, it risks blindness to the truly radical character of globalization as a multiplicity of processes, which set the capitalist economizing logic against myriad cultural differences. An understanding of this new conjuncture demands an expansion of Marxist horizons beyond European parochialism (e.g. Chakrabarty 1996: 55). In short, the critical power of historical materialism is undercut by its economism, which results in the neglect of subjectivity, and an inability to theorize the issues of identity and difference foregrounded by globalization.

A Marxism adequate for the twenty-first century must correct these deficiencies if it is to provide the means to articulate new visions of possible futures and ways to achieve them (e.g. Smith 1996). It must, to paraphrase Raymond Williams (1989), provide resources of hope. In this chapter, we argue that a Marxism adequate to a moment in which the putative subject of Marxism has never been more 'decentered' and 'spaced out' (Eagleton 1988: ix) cannot emerge out of a return to an economistic historical materialism. 'As an imperfect name for a differential and uneven process of transition from an international economy to an imaginary unified global economy "globalisation" is a flexible concept for flexible times ...' (Herod *et al.* 1998: 2). What we need is a flexible Marxism for flexible times. Minimally, this requires plausible accounts of subjectivity and the economy. We find resources for such a reworking of historical materialism in the disputed legacy of Louis Althusser. In attempting to transcend the simple analysis of causality implied in the base/superstructure metaphor, Althusser provides the theoretical raw materials for eliminating economism and for strengthening the critical dimension of historical materialism. He also offers Marxists a non-reductive way of understanding cultural diversity, and of the ways in which capitalism itself may serve to intensify, rather than eliminate, such diversity.

The chapter is organized as follows. First, we chart the return to historical materialism in the context of globalization and show how that return works against historical materialism's claim to be a critical theory. Second, we trace this return to a particular understanding of Western Marxism, of Althusser and his influence, and argue that this understanding is mistaken. On the contrary, addressing the lacunae evident in the return to Marxism with respect to its account of subjectivity and the economy requires a return to Althusser and his legacies in contemporary social and political thought. Ours is not a post-Marxist position but the defence of a Marxism different from that of the emergent orthodoxy. Third, we offer a re-reading of Althusser's work, showing where and how it opens up issues and questions closed down or ignored in more recent scholarship and offers ways forward. In a short conclusion, we reflect on the broader implications of our argument for the politics of theory and the making of new worlds.

Globalization and the return of *which* Marxism?

The collapse of really existing socialism in the Soviet Union and Eastern Europe and the continuing rhetoric and reality of globalization have together breathed new life into historical materialism. Globalization is good for historical materialism. No longer caught in the middle of Cold War ideological and superpower struggle and faced with the seeming triumph of capital in achieving for the first time a truly global reach (Smith 1997), the relevance of Marxism to our historical moment is widely asserted. Against efforts to link Marxism to the failed Soviet and East European regimes, thereby to consign all three to the dustbin of history, the demise of really existing socialism is transformed instead into the liberation of historical materialism. Thus Fredric Jameson asserts that 'it does not seem to make much sense to talk about the bankruptcy of Marxism, when Marxism is precisely the science and the study of just that capitalism whose global triumph is affirmed in talk of Marxism's demise' (1991a: 255). Historical materialism and capitalism are on this view bound tightly together: Marxism is defined by its 'allegiance to a specific complex of problems, whose formulations are always in movement and in historic rearrangement and restructuration, along with their object of study', capitalism itself (Jameson 1996: 19). So long as we have capitalism, then, we must have Marxism.

While we accept that Marxism is, above all, the critical science of capitalism, we want to reject, in the name of a truly critical theory, the reduction of that science to political economy. We want to reject the assumption that the persistence of capitalism implies 'business as usual', if that assumption means a return to an unreconstructed economism. Such an assumption 'is complacent and hopelessly inadequate' (Sayer 1995: 13).[2] It is hopelessly inadequate in that it fails to take seriously, not only the real historicity of capitalism itself – the different modes in which it appears under different spatio-temporal conditions (Albritton 1991) – but also the persistence of non-capitalist forms of life and the likelihood of the emergence, out of the latter, of forms of resistance not reducible to the European categories which are Marxism's legacy (e.g. Jameson and Miyoshi 1998; Lowe and Lloyd 1997a).

This raises the question: which Marxism? Historical materialism has always been a diverse tradition of theory and practice. There is no such thing as Marxism, there are only Marxisms: 'as a category "Marxism" is, in fact, no better than a gnomic vulgarity' (Castree 1995b: 1163; Carver 1998). The existence of multiple Marxisms forces us to choose among them. In making our choice, we need to be sensitive to the contextual character of all theorizing and to correct for specific contextual effects that may render our theory misleading when directed towards changing and context-specific objects of study. Marxisms are unavoidably shaped by the circumstances of their production, and incorporate specific features of the world in which Marxist theorists are situated. This is itself a Marxian point to which Marxists are sometimes insufficiently attentive. They are also sometimes insufficiently attentive to the historicity of capitalist forms of life mentioned above. As capitalism itself changes in some key respects (as in, for instance, changes in means and objects of production as traced by Albritton 1991), so, too, must our theorizing change. We cannot simply recycle past historical materialisms and assume they will be adequate to our historical moment and to capitalism in our time (Sivanandran 1998/9: 7–8). Moreover, if we understand historical materialism as a critical theory, then we must look for a Marxism that is attentive to questions of subjectivity and agency. In their neglect of such questions, economistic conceptions of capital are both cognitively inadequate and politically impoverishing; they impoverish the political imagination and induce pessimism and feelings of hopelessness (Gibson-Graham 1996: 251–65 and passim). The answers to our two questions thus converge: questions of conceptual and theoretical adequacy are directly relevant to questions of political agency. The kind of Marxism we embrace now will shape our capacity to remake our futures (Jameson 2000). As we will show, the form of the most recent return to historical materialism undermines its claim to be a critical theory.

The return to Marxism in the context of globalization takes a variety of forms, as the other contributions to this volume demonstrate. But in its most prominent and widely praised articulations, it has two distinguishing features. First, Marxism is defined as an economism: it provides a 'crucial set of concepts' for understanding the capitalist mode of production (Gamble 1999: 142–3). This is the only defensible conception of historical materialism now. Other features of the Marxist heritage such as the labour theory of value – Marxism's 'microfoundations' (142) – are simply implausible, as is the claim to be a total science of society. In the end, argues Gamble, 'if the primacy of the economic is lost, then Marxism loses its distinctiveness and its value in social theory' (143). This particular conception of historical materialism has recently been celebrated in the reception of Robert Brenner's analysis of the world economy (see also Rosenberg 1994).[3]

This economism renders invisible the theoretical problem of agency. It either assumes the emergency of the appropriate transformative agency, i.e. the homogeneous and revolutionary proletariat, or it retreats into silence on this matter. Unfortunately, even the most sophisticated accounts of capitalism will take us no further forward if they are not accompanied by an understanding of those conditions needed to engender the extraordinary capacities needed for such agency. If we are not to reproduce the authoritarianism of vanguardism, we need to consider the question of capacities at the level of subjectivity or individuation, rather than at that of class. This is not to claim that the concept of class is redundant, but to argue that better accounts of class – accounts which do not merely impose the category on an empirical world on the basis of an examination of the logic of capitalism – require an examination of subjectivity.[4]

The valorization of an economistic conception of class is accompanied by the vigorous rejection of identity politics, i.e. of politics embodying claims to 'recognition' rather than 'redistribution'. The assertion of class involves giving priority to the emancipatory project of socialism over other forms of oppression such as race or gender (Wood 1995: chap. 9).[5] Not only are these forms of identity held to be less politically important than that of class, but the politics of identity and subjectivity is linked directly to postmodernism and liberal individualism (e.g. Wood 1986).

Defining Marxism as an economism means that 'conflicts that fall "outside" the development of class consciousness are politically subordinate, or constitute "false consciousness": antagonisms articulated, for example, around gender or race, are seen as effects of [or as secondary to] a more fundamental contradiction' (Lowe and Lloyd 1997b: 13). But in the context of a putatively global capitalism, this serves to marginalize struggles that do not take class forms. As numerous scholars have documented, the struggles engendered by capitalist relations of production, particularly in the colonial and postcolonial world, most often take cultural forms that are incompatible with European-style proletarianization (ibid.). A Marxism flexible enough to grasp these conflicts and to do so in a materialist and politically progressive manner cannot be built on a Marxist foundation that expresses only a Western and European conception of modernity.

This point is of more general significance. Globalization raises in acute fashion a set of issues located – at least from the point of view of the return to historical materialism – squarely within the superstructure. If we accept that globalization involves the revitalization of capitalism's attempt to colonize the world, we must at the same time resist: (a) conceptualizing that attempt in 'economistic' terms; and (b) assuming that that colonization is bound to be complete and successful. This is a crucial political task if historical materialists are to meet the challenge of arming, organizing, and speaking to and for an increasingly polyglot, feminized and internally differentiated global proletariat.

For many both inside and outside the West, the assertion that capitalism is a form of domination more fundamental than, say, race or gender, and thus that the privileged agent of anti-capitalist struggle is a unified class subject (e.g. Wood 1995: chap. 9; but see Eagleton 1988: vii), is experienced not as liberating but as an imposition and a denial of other forms of subjectivity. Advancing such apparently economistic forms of political agency risks the temptation of inflicting a political violence intended to reduce otherness to sameness.[6] If 'liberating humanity for its own development is to open up the production of difference, even to open up a terrain for contestation within and among differences', as Harvey (1995: 15) suggests, economism is not the way to liberation. Fortunately, economism is not the only mode of historical materialism available to us.

In order to address these questions, we cannot simply return to being historical materialists in the same old economistic way. Globalization itself forces us to engage with a set of issues central to Western Marxism, namely, the so-called superstructural issues. More accurately, a critical understanding of globalization demands that we distance ourselves from economistic theorizing by rejecting altogether the 'very simple' base/superstructure model on which it is grounded.

Significantly, the return to historical materialism has also been articulated through explicit rejections of Althusser and his works, which are criticized as overly structuralist, thereby erasing agency, as Stalinist, and as having opened the way to the excesses of post-structuralism and postmodernism (e.g. Cox with Sinclair 1996: 94–5, 176, 404–5; Wood 1995: 7–9 and passim). These criticisms are the theoretical equivalent of shooting the messenger who brings bad news, since, as Althusser points out, it is capitalism itself which seeks the transformation of subjects into 'bearers of structures'.[7] However, he does not assume the total success of such capitalist projects, as will be seen. To the contrary, his account of causality in complex social formations forbids such assumptions. It is because Althusser is attentive to such matters that his work is rich in the theoretical resources for thinking the complexity, fragmentation and contradiction of our 'flexible times'. Against much conventional wisdom, we argue that the resources for addressing the issues we have raised above are to be found in the work of Althusser and his legacies.

Rescuing Althusser from his critics

Arguing for the continuing relevance of Althusser's work to the contemporary analysis of globalization and the articulation of a different, flexible Marxism is no easy task. Across the social sciences, Althusser is almost universally reviled.[8] Indeed, rejection of Althusser serves as a touchstone for some of the more prominent schools of thought in the analysis of contemporary world politics and globalization: in the writings of virtually all neo-Gramscian scholars, for example, 'the specter of Althusserian structural Marxism is raised again ...' (Drainville 1994: 108). In a familiar logic of self and other, a particular reading of Althusser and of structural Marxism more generally serves to define each of these projects. Recent calls for the reinvigoration of historical materialism, both in relation to globalization and more generally,[9] take for granted a particular reading of the Althusserian moment and of its broader context, Western Marxism.

According to Perry Anderson, who popularized the term, Western Marxism was a formation that over-emphasized secondary issues such as ideology, philosophy, politics and culture and consequently gave insufficient attention to political economy. This was a Marxism that ignored the base and instead 'came to concentrate overwhelmingly on study of superstructures' (Anderson 1976: 75). This superstructural fixation, the product of a political defeat, resulted in

> a remarkable range of reflections on different aspects of the culture of modern capitalism. But these were never integrated into a consistent theory of its economic development, typically remaining at a somewhat detached and specialised angle to the broader movement of society: taxable with a certain idealism, from the standpoint of a more classical Marxism.
>
> (Anderson 1998: 72)

Accordingly, Anderson lauds Fredric Jameson's account of postmodernism as the 'most complete consummation' of Western Marxism because it grounds the 'cultural logic' of capital in Ernest Mandel's account of Late Capitalism (Anderson 1998: 72; Jameson 1991b; Mandel 1975). In contrast to the sophisticated dead-end represented by Western Marxism, the way forward for a historical materialist account of globalization, it appears, is by way of a return to the classical statements of political economy and, in particular, the analysis of imperialism (Anderson 1976: 94 and passim; Bromley 1999; Rosenberg 1996; cf. Harvey 1995: 5).

Anderson's argument both misunderstands and understates the real achievements of Western Marxism and its contributions to historical materialism, and in particular to political economy. Western Marxism is not only a Marxism of the superstructures. Considerable effort by Althusser and others went into trying to rethink or overcome the base/superstructure dichotomy (Althusser 1984a, 1990a, 1990b).[10] This puts in question the organizing device of Anderson's narrative. Seeing the contributions of Western Marxism as primarily contributions to the analysis of superstructures misconstrues the relations between Althusser's de-centring of economic determinism and the analysis of other 'levels' such as the political or the ideological.

Moreover, Anderson's argument, in common with others who have sought to define themselves against Althusser, depends on a highly questionable reading of Althusser's project. That reading has a number of characteristic features, none of which is sustainable. First, Althusser's work is deemed to be in league with, a product of, or liable to culminate in Stalinism. But this reading, which depends on drawing a more or less direct line from political to theoretical practice, is contradicted both by the explicitly anti-Stalinist nature of Althusser's interventions and by his sustained criticism of just the kind of reduction of theoretical practice to political practice that the charge assumes (Sprinker 1987: 177–9). Althusser's insistence on the need for Marxists to write 'a true historical study of the conditions and forms of … consciousness' (1990a: 105) follows from his analysis of Stalinism, as do also his notes on the requirements for such a study in his essays on socialist humanism and the ideological state apparatuses (ISAs) (Althusser 1984a).

Second, Althusser is accused of offering a functionalist account of both ideology and the state, an account that, whatever its other features, works to undermine the possibility of change, whether revolutionary or otherwise. Here too the criticism relies on misreading Althusser's work. His essay on the ISAs is a functional, not functionalist, account of capitalism's conditions of reproduction, one which focuses on the capitalist need to reproduce subjectivities adequate to the reproduction of capitalism itself (Lock 1988; cf. Panitch 1996: 87 on functions and functionalism). However, careful readers of 'Contradiction and Overdetermination' will understand that such reproduction cannot be guaranteed but is inherently open to dysfunctionality and subversion for reasons to be explored below. Indeed, the ISAs are 'multiple', 'distinct', and 'relatively autonomous' sites of 'the clashes between the capitalist class struggle and the proletarian class struggle' (Althusser 1984a: 23; Sprinker 1987: 194). Althusser's account of the ISAs is not an invitation to defeatism and despair but rather a call to arms (Sprinker 1987: 229).[11]

Third, and most damaging for any work that claims to be a critical theory, Althusser's historical materialism is accused of being a structuralism, with no place for human agency. This charge, now so widespread as to have become dogma, is the lynchpin of Anderson's rejection of Althusser and is also central to Wood's criticisms (Anderson 1983: 39; Wood 1995: chap. 2). However, as Althusser himself noted, in an unusually direct statement of capitalism's deviancy, it is capitalism that effects (or attempts to effect) this outcome (see Althusser 1990d: 237–8). Understanding this 'terrible practical reduction' is a prerequisite for an understanding of the (absence of) potential for heroic transformative collective agency. In any case, Althusser's development of the materialist dialectic involves the reconceptualization of the structure/agency dichotomy as practice. This broader framework of Althusser's needs to be kept in mind when reading the ISAs essay, as must his insistence on the distinction between subjects 'of' and 'in' history. The point is not to eliminate subjectivity or agency, but to understand the historicity of forms of subjectivity and agency.

We have argued that the different understanding of agency and of its conditions of possibility afforded by Althusser's work is of considerable significance in the context of globalization. But it is also worth noting the tremendous fruitfulness of these ideas in contemporary social theory and in particular its more materialist strands (e.g. Callari *et al,.* 1995). From this point of view, then, the works of Althusser, and of Western Marxism more generally, should be seen not as a deviation produced by a political defeat, but as a necessary attempt to account for that political defeat in terms of the inadequacies of economism. These works are 'a threshold behind which we cannot allow ourselves to fall' (Hall 1985: 97).[12]

Re-reading Althusser

As we have argued above, the new historical materialism, in common with other positions within the field, emerges partly in response to a specific reading of Althusser, one that we contest. In seeking to reassert the significance of his work for how we understand globalization, then, part of what is at stake is 'reading for the best Althusser' (paraphrasing Johnson 1982). It is to that task that we now turn. We focus first on Althusser's reworking of the base–superstructure metaphor, and, second, his notes on the need for a theory of capitalism and subjectivity.

Beyond the base–superstructure metaphor: or, the materialist dialectic

As noted above, Althusser introduces complexity into Marxist theorizing in the first instance by insisting on: (a) an inclusive, rather than exclusive, concept of mode of production (i.e. by conceptualizing it as a total mode of life rather than as an 'economy'); and (b) the distinction between mode of production and social formation. A social formation is composed of more than one form of life. Moreover, it is social formations that we find in real, as opposed to theorized, life. Beyond these crucial conceptual distinctions, Althusser rejects the simple model of causality implied in the base–superstructure, in ways that will be discussed below.

The capitalist mode of production in its 'pure' form is one marked by economism, which is what marks it off from all other modes of production. It must seek the instantiation of an expressive totality whose constitutive levels are subsumed under the law of value. It must try to ensure that the 'base' will get the 'superstructure' that its flourishing demands; that evenness – in the sense of smoothly functioning supportive practices in the different levels – rather than unevenness will pertain. However, for Althusser – who, again, was not a functionalist – this is impossible. Because of the character of causality in social wholes, capitalism would be bound to generate 'unevenness' rather than 'expressiveness' even in the mythical case of an actually existing pure capitalist mode of production. Here unevenness refers to the coexistence of different, possibly contradictory, logics within a unity. So, we can infer that whereas the logic of capitalism is a colonizing logic, the separation of dedicated levels of practices allows of the (at least temporary) escape from that logic. Resistance to (or drift away from) commodification is possible, at least in the short term, and in relation to certain kinds of practices carried on at extra-economic levels. Capitalism must seek to domesticate those differences by subsuming them under the law of value, that is, by ensuring that they function to reproduce capital. One task for a critical theory, then, is to identify and encourage the flourishing of differences which are anti- and/or non-capitalist (see Gibson-Graham 1996), even as it recognizes that capitalism has shown a remarkable ability to, as it were, 'respect' non-capitalist social forms while also exploiting them (Lowe and Lloyd 1997b: 15). It cannot be assumed that difference will emerge in one homogeneous anti-capitalist form as a proletarian collective actor and indeed this is not the case. Such an assumption is informed by a simplistic idea of one, clear-cut, system-destroying contradiction between 'capital' and 'labour'. The materialist dialectic warns us of the foolishness of expecting such a beautifully simple negation of the negation.

The concept of totality or social whole directs us towards an expanded conception of mode of production; one which incorporates an internal relations model of causality involving claims about the mutual constitutedness of 'base' and 'superstructure'. Moreover, Althusser reminds us that modes of production are not to be found in their pure form; instead, what we find are social formations. This distinction between mode of production and social formation is vital if we are to take into account the possible causal weight of 'survivals' (of non-capitalist practices) in a globalizing world (Marx 1981: 172; Althusser 1990a: esp. 106). From this point of view, capitalism's economizing project is threatened from two directions: from its own contradictory character (which is not merely the 'simple contradiction' between capital and labour); and from the persistence of pre- or non-capitalist 'survivals' in social formations. If we assume the successful institutionalization of capitalism's economistic dynamic, we will be guilty of the very functionalism with which Althusser has been charged, and against which he himself theorizes. In short, neither mode of production nor social formation functions as the base–superstructure metaphor suggests. It is not enough, then, to complete Marx's account of the capitalist 'base' through a similarly rigorous and comprehensive account of the 'superstructure'. But this is precisely what Anderson's endorsement of Jameson's account of postmodernism implies (1998: 72). The new historical materialism, insofar as it assumes that phenomenological forms can be derived from property relations (e.g. Tetschke 1998), betrays a similar 'base-and-superstructure' logic. We must abandon this disabling metaphor completely and replace it with a framework of concepts capable of capturing the complexity of causality in social wholes.[13]

Althusser's contribution to the development of a flexible Marxism builds on his conceptual reworking of the dialectic, in 'On the Materialist Dialectic', so as to exclude both idealism (voluntarism) and mechanical materialism (determinism or economism). These binaries are the result of abstracting elements from the social whole (or totality) and reifying the resulting abstractions. Idealism and materialism are abstractions from a totality of human practices that, being human, are necessarily composed of both ideal and material elements. It logically follows that the 'economy' is also necessarily composed of ideal and material elements. To conflate the economic and the material is to risk the danger of naturalizing capitalist practices that privilege the economic. Capitalism seeks a world in which the economic 'determines' all human practices. It is this culturally novel phenomenon that the base–superstructure seeks to explain, but in a manner which stays uncritically close to its object of study. In contrast to this very simple, or even simplistic, explanatory device, the dialectic involves understanding a mode of differentiation involving the spatio-temporal fragmentation of an original unity into elements that are internally related or mutually constitutive. It is this fragmentation of the mutually constitutive that produces contradictions. Understanding the resulting contradictory totality requires conceptual development beyond the binaries characteristic of liberal social theory; hence Althusser's rejection of the 'inversion' metaphor which remains within a binarized theoretical world, and hence also his stress on the concept of practice. Whereas the base–superstructure metaphor encourages us to think in terms of an external model of causality, the materialist dialectic involves the conceptualization of necessary elements or levels of the social whole as internal relations among practices (see also Ollman 1976, 1993).

By its very nature the base–superstructure metaphor takes on the character of a binary opposition and pushes towards analytic rather than dialectical thought. That is to say, it pushes us towards liberal, rather than historical materialist, modes of thought. What it reveals most clearly is the economism – that is, the political attempt to instantiate economic determinism – that is the identifying characteristic of capitalism. At the same time, however, the metaphor conceals the historico-culturally unprecedented – that is, the culturally deviant – nature of this economism. It distorts by naturalizing the historico-cultural. Expressed in Althusserian terms, economism is a concept in theoretical ideology, in the sense that it expresses the common sense of capitalist culture by representing a constitutive element of capitalist practices in naturalistic, rather than critical, mode (Althusser and Balibar 1970: chap. 4; Althusser 1990b). In doing so, it risks contributing to, not the transformation, but (at worst) the reproduction, or, at best, the reform, of existing social relations. We need to be clear that economism is a capitalist political project, rather than a universal fact of human life. Moreover, it has required state-led cultural transformation for its relative success (cf. Corrigan and Sayer 1985). But, beyond that, the survival of capitalism has required state-led action to save capitalism from itself, or from economism. In addition, as Althusser enables us to understand, even where apparently completed, there will emerge contradictory practices that may become the basis for the subversion of that economism. A brief word about Althusser's controversial conceptual borrowing from psychoanalysis will be of use at this point.

Contradiction and overdetermination

In seeking an account of causality that would be adequate to the particular complexity of a contradictory totality such as capitalism, Althusser turned to psychoanalysis, in which he found the source of his major theoretical innovation, namely, the concept of overdetermination. Unfortunately he failed to theorize his borrowing, thereby leaving his readers in some confusion, if not outright rejection.[14] There is not the space here to go into this matter in any detail. However, the point needs to be made quite forcefully that overdetermination does not mean merely a plurality of causes, as some noted commentators on Althusser have suggested (e.g. Callinicos 1976, 1993). In contrast to multi-causality, which suggests a multiplicity of externally related causal factors, overdetermination involves a complex causal process within a totality of contradictorily and internally related parts. What attracts Althusser to Freud's concept of overdetermination is its fruitfulness in terms of capturing a complex process of causality which functions in a contradictory social whole, composed of a multiplicity of distinct, but internally related and mutually constitutive, practices having a tendency – because of their spatio-temporal separation within complex social formations – to drift apart (see Marx 1951: 383, for the conception of contradiction intended here). What this means is that the economy, all by itself, cannot produce out of its own resources its means of reproduction; neither can the political or the ideological. The economy, all by itself, cannot determine anything and even to speak in this way is to speak nonsense. Determination suggests a simple linear mode of causality between externally related entities. While this mode of causality will be found in localized domains within social wholes, it cannot pertain at the level of the social whole itself, as the base–super-structure metaphor would lead us to believe (Jameson 1981: 25). It is because the world is overdetermined, rather than determined, that the future is open rather than closed, or, as Balibar puts it, overdetermination 'is the very form assumed by the *singularity* of history' (Balibar 1996: 108).

This radical and fruitful reconceptualization of causality is one which acknowledges the necessary diversity of human life while at the same time enabling us to identify forms of diversity that are likely to be dysfunctional – in an emancipatory way – for capitalism. Diversity arises within capitalism itself from a peculiar kind of fragmentation of internally related levels of practices that enables these practices to develop (at least in the short term) 'as if' they were autonomous, hence relative autonomy. Relative autonomy is a condition that emerges out of the spatio-temporal separation of necessary practices; it is a social logic arising from the coexistence of necessity and contradiction. The concept of relative autonomy enables the theorization of the causal effects and political possibilities inhering in the simultaneous connectedness and separation (real interdependence and apparent independence) characteristic of relations between the different 'levels' of practices – political, ideological, economic – in capitalist social formations. It therefore enables the theorization of transforma-tive agency as a potential, and of difference, rather than homogeneity, as a necessary attribute of capitalism.

For Althusser, the social whole as 'pure' mode of production can exist only as a 'logical' or thought object. In the empirical world, the unevenness to be expected from 'pure' social wholes is intensified in the form of social formations. We have Althusser's analysis of the Russian and later the Soviet social formation as an illustration of this situation (Althusser 1990a: 19). Althusser's use of this example is intended to achieve several aims at once. First, it provides an illustration of the particularly contradictory dynamic of a social formation, as opposed to a mode of production. Second, it is an account of a fundamental destructuration (i.e. the dissolution of a functional relationship between levels) that throws up the possibility of historical change. Third, it constitutes a warning about the theoretical wrong-headedness and political dangers of economism. In the case of Stalinism, an economistic analysis dictated a revolutionary programme of privileging the transformation of production relations on the assumption that necessary, i.e. socialist or radically democratic, 'superstructural' changes would follow.[15] Here, failure to pay specific attention to the cultural sphere resulted in the subversion of the communist project as the causal weight of 'survivals' counteracted that of socialist ownership of means of production. Expressed otherwise, subjects constituted by feudal social relations, i.e. peasants, were susceptible to and supportive of a personalized form of political power.[16]

The denaturalizing of subjectivity undertaken by Althusser in his ISAs essay centres on his reconceptualization of ideology as a necessary element of all human life.[17] What the reductive Marxist stance ignores is the fact that humans are such as to need ideological constitution; in fact there is no human in the absence of ideology in this sense. Hence the much misunderstood claim that ideology 'has no history' (Althusser 1984a: 33). Ideology in this sense is what Marx refers to as a 'rational abstraction' in that it refers to a universal property of human life (Marx 1973b: 85). We are creatures of culture, therefore of ideology (Althusser 1984b: 154, n.2). Ideologies so defined are the conjoining of socio-cultural force and meaning in that they consist in a nexus of social relations and practices having the power to constitute humans as subjects possessing historico-culturally specific dispositions, skills, and aptitudes. Ideological practices are those that constitute the natural 'to-be-humanized' being as a specific kind of subject (Althusser 1984b). It is the historico-cultural specificity of forms of subjectivity that in turn produces the capacity for specific kinds of activity. Forms of action (practices) are culturally given. In turn, the necessary diversity and contradictory relationship of practices in capitalist social formations is the source of new non- or anti-capitalist practices. For Althusser, it is the function of the state to ensure that such practices do not emerge or flourish as it is the function of 'science' or critical theory to aid the denaturalization of capitalist ideology so as to aid socialist transformation.

Because subjectivity is historico-cultural rather than natural, and because social wholes are marked by overdetermination rather than determination, economism is bound to be inadequate as an account of the social, and of the way in which fundamental transformation is effected. As we saw above, failure to attend to the cultural tasks of subject reconstitution contributed to the Soviet failure to move towards the radical democracy to be expected from a socialist revolution: Stalinism was the outcome of an economistic analysis that was blind to the importance of subjectivity. Similarly, responses to Stalinism such as existentialist Marxism and the socialist Marxism of Khruschev repeated the error by assuming the existence of the right kind of subjectivity (Althusser 1990c). For this reason, failure was bound to ensue since neither yielded an understanding of the historico-cultural specificity of forms of subjectivity and therefore of capacities for specific kinds of action. In short, taking subjectivity for granted is bound to result in the subversion of the revolutionary project. This is the message that Althusser sought to communicate to his fellow Communists in mid twentieth-century France. It is a message that needs to be heard by those who advocate a return to classical Marxism, particularly in light of the issues raised by globalization. Models of class struggle and proletarian formation that assume the only 'real' struggles are those that take class forms or which involve trade unionism simply miss the diversity of the forms taken by anti-capitalist struggle in the context of globalization and cut Marxists off from them. This is not to say that classical Marxism is 'dead' – far from it – but to insist on the fruitfulness of re-reading its texts once again, through the lens offered by Althusser's advances. A return to classical forms of historical materialism now runs the risk of participating in the reproduction of the very economism carried forward by a seemingly global capitalism.

As Resch (1992: chap. 4) shows, the structural Marxist research programme initiated by Althusser has developed a variety of tools – concepts, theories and methods – by which to carry out analysis of subjectivity. Fortunately, we do not need to start from scratch. Prominent in this literature is the work of feminist scholars influenced by Althusser who, in good Marxist fashion, have been busily engaging with the best bourgeois scholarship on subjectivity and in effect taking it away from its non-Marxist origins.[18] This work is particularly significant: in a sense, it rescues the concept of subjectivity for historical materialism. It also mounts a direct challenge to those who see struggles – whether in theory or out of it – organized around gender and other forms of identity politics as necessarily inferior to the more fundamental matter of class or as operating in opposition to it. But examples of the creative elaboration of Althusser's re-reading of historical materialism in order better to understand and explain the non-proletarian nature of the cultural struggles engendered by capitalist globalization are rapidly proliferating elsewhere as well, offering a rich basis on which to build a flexible Marxism for flexible times.

Globalization after Althusser: the politics of theory

If the global horizon of really existing capitalism is indeed the harbinger of a renewed Marxist project, we cannot avoid the question: which Marxism? This is not only a matter of explanatory power and critical insight. It is also and fundamentally a question of politics. By its very nature, globalization raises a set of questions about how we theorize the economy and subjectivity. The significance of Althusser's work for the development of a flexible Marxism is that it enables us to address these questions in a distinctively Marxist way and in terms that strengthen the claims of historical materialism to be a genuinely critical theory. It offers hope of generating a critical theory that is attentive to the quite proper concerns of political economy without at the same time being blind to the importance and relatively autonomous causal power of difference. This will be a historical materialism that proceeds neither by reducing difference to political economy nor by rejecting its significance altogether. In contrast, dominant elements in the recent return to historical materialism do both. The way forward, then, is arm in arm with Althusser, not without him.

Any attempt to organize an anti-capitalist movement out of numerous particularistic struggles, many of which refuse even to concede that capitalism is the problem, will require discussion of

> the relations between commonality/difference, the particularity of the one and the universalism of the other. And it is at that point that socialism as an alternative vision of how society will work, social relations unfold, human potentialities be realised, itself becomes the focus of conceptual work.
>
> (Harvey 1995: 15)

Without denying the necessity of making connections between intellectual work and broader social struggles, 'the creation of a diverse Marxian intellectual culture is an important political act in itself, with far-reaching consequences ... the development of new and creative directions in Marxian theory is of fundamental importance as we confront the new world order' (Callari *et al.* 1995: 4). In seeking to discipline historical materialism by excluding some Marxisms at the outset, we are also likely to initiate a set of practices that will inform and shape the futures we collectively make. Most importantly, those futures will reflect this denial of difference. In attempting to deny that Marxism is and ought to be a plural subject, we run the risk of producing a future in which it will be that much more difficult to retrieve the kind of pluralism that Harvey, among others, identifies as integral to socialism. Nor can these matters be left until 'after the revolution', or whatever comes to stand in for it. As Cynthia Enloe (1989: 59–60) notes, similar issues, of identity and difference, emerged in the Indochinese Communist Party during the 1920s and 1930s with respect to the status of women. In the interests of solidarity and the movement, the women suppressed these questions. Decades later, when the Party finally took power, women were absent from its leadership. The masculinization of public life in post-independence Vietnam and the willingness of the state to offer the bodies of young women as a commodity to the agents of international capital such as Nike is in part a by-product of this suppression of difference.

As we consider how to rebuild a Marxist project after the Cold War and in the face of globalization, it is worth reflecting on the experience of the Indochinese Communist Party. In this chapter, we have emphasized a set of issues that revolve around difference, both within Marxism and outside it, and tried to link those issues to the question of the production of the revolutionary subject. Conceptions of Marxism as an economism, we suggested, are not well equipped to deal with such issues. With Andrew Gamble, we agree that historical materialism offers a powerful and incisive critique of capitalism. But 'if Marxism cannot help us imagine radical alternatives to the current world system, then perhaps it must be willing to abandon its claims to revolutionary praxis ... to abolish itself as a theory of the future' (Makdisi *et al.* 1996b: 12). Globalization, both as a project and as a new reality of world politics, forces us to engage critically with the plausibility of historical materialism as an explanatory account of the world, with the limits of its political imagination, and thus with its adequacy as a political project. This returns us directly to Andrew Sayer's (1995) and J.K. Gibson-Graham's (1996) otherwise very different doubts about historical materialism as an account of capitalism and points beyond them to David Harvey's (1995: 15) call for a socialist avant-garde capable of articulating together the differences that divide us. A Marxism capable of measuring up to that task, we suggest, must grapple with a set of questions the contours of which we have only begun to sketch here. The contested legacies of Louis Althusser are not an obstacle but a necessary aid in that struggle to build a flexible Marxism for flexible times.

Notes

1 Earlier versions of this chapter were presented at the Trans-Atlantic Workshop on Historical Materialism and Globalisation, University of Warwick, 16–17 April 1999 and the Annual Meeting of the International Studies Association, Los Angeles, 14–18 March 2000. Thanks to Tarak Barkawi, Claire Cutler, and Jutta Weldes for comments, and to Tarak for the phrase 'living in a Marxist moment'.

2 Postone (1993) offers an excellent critique, grounded in Marx's own work, of economistic Marxisms.

3 For example, 'Marx's enterprise has certainly found its successor'; Editor's Introduction to Brenner (1998: v).

4 The attempts of 'analytical Marxism' to provide appropriate microfoundations for economism results in a kind of Marxism without Marx. See, for example, Carver and Thomas (1995) and Weldes (1989).

5 See Fraser (1995) for an account of the relations between recognition and redistribution.

6 It is in this context that Chakrabarty asks:

> Do Marx's categories allow us to trace the marks of that which must of necessity remain unenclosed by these categories themselves? In other words, are there ways of engaging with the problem of [the] 'universality' of capital that do not commit us to a bloodless liberal pluralism that only subsumes all difference(s) within the Same?
>
> (1996: 58–9)

7

> If you do not submit the individual concrete determinations of proletarians and capitalists, their 'liberty' or their personality to a theoretical 'reduction', then you will understand nothing of the terrible practical 'reduction' to which the capitalist production relation submits individuals, treating them only as bearers of economic functions and nothing else.
>
> (Althusser 1990d: 238)

8

For some – a-political literary deconstructionists – he is too faithful to Marxism and, consequently, unworthy of a place in the theoretical adventure playground that is post-structuralism at its worst. For others – the post-Althusserians – he is to be praised for having prepared for their own 'post-Marxist' paradigms. If, for the Nietzschean avant-garde, he is the Marxist Same, for humanist Marxism he is the Stalinist Other. As far as some anglophone Marxists are concerned, on the other hand, he is simply all-too-French.

(Elliott 1987: 327)

Obviously, there is not one Althusser but many, just as there is not one Marx (Carver 1998).

9 For example, the British journal *Historical Materialism: Research in Critical Marxist Theory* in its notes for contributors states: '*Historical Materialism* welcomes contributions from all in sympathy with its aims of revitalising, debating and extending *classical* Marxism as a political project and theoretical tradition' (No.6, Summer 2000 inside back cover; emphasis added). See also Rosenberg (1994); Wood (1995); cf. Makdisi *et al.* (1996a).

10 As a result,

Many Marxists have accepted the need to reformulate the distinction between base and superstructure outlined in classical Marxist theory even if they would not accept Althusser's own approach to the problem of defining 'structures in dominance' that are determining 'in the last instance'.

(Jackson 1992: 46, n.6)

11 As Sprinker argues,

Althusser's aim ... was not to deny historical agency as such, but to demolish the claims of voluntarism. Althusser never doubted that there are subjects or historical agents, men and women who make their own history, but he insisted from the first that for Marxism the other half of that oft-quoted sentence from the Eighteenth Brumaire is decisive: they don't make it just as they please, but out of circumstances encountered and given from the past. It is not, therefore, any species-specific capacity of human nature (Sartre's praxis, for example) that produces historical subjects, but the forces and circumstances of the given social whole.

(1987: 230)

Significantly, his position is not so far from the position of E.P. Thompson whose work Wood claims is so superior to that of Althusser (Wood 1995: 68).

12 Recent work on globalization and culture informed by this different reading of Althusser – such as Aihwa Ong's analyses of 'flexible citizenship' (1999) – is testament to the continuing power of the modes of analysis his historical materialism makes possible.

13 In attempting this replacement, Althusser was consciously following Gramsci although he was also departing from Gramsci so as to eliminate what he saw as idealist/voluntarist (historicist or Hegelian) tendencies in Gramsci's work; see Althusser in Althusser and Balibar (1970: chap. 5).

14 Levine (1981: 272), for example, finds 'irremediable obscurities' in Althusser's account of overdetermination whereas Resch (1992: chap. 1) finds the concept to be a fruitfully supple source of understanding of the complex diversity and structural unity of social formations.

15 This insight was not new at the time of Althusser's writing. Its importance for Althusser marks a continuity between his work and Gramsci's, but note also Althusser's silence on Trotsky's important work on this question.
16 Marx's (1973a) analysis of 'Bonapartism' is relevant here.
17 As numerous scholars have noted, Althusser's usage of the term 'ideology' was highly idiosyncratic and infelicitous, not least because it leads to confusion between his argument and more usual efforts to comprehend the relations between meaning and power (e.g. Thompson 1990: chap. 1, esp. pp.70ff.).
18 For example, Hennessy has recently developed a powerful 'materialist feminist' critique of post-structuralist conceptions of subjectivity (1993, 1996).

Bibliography

Albritton, Robert (1991) *A Japanese Reconstruction of Marxist Theory*, London: Macmillan.
Althusser, Louis (1984a) 'Ideology and Ideological State Apparatuses', in *Essays on Ideology*, London: Verso.
—— (1984b) 'Freud and Lacan', in *Essays on Ideology*, London: Verso.
—— (1990a) 'Contradiction and Overdetermination', in *For Marx*, London: Verso.
—— (1990b) 'On the Materialist Dialectic', in *For Marx*, London: Verso.
—— (1990c) 'Marxism and Humanism', in *For Marx*, London: Verso.
—— (1990d) *Philosophy and the Spontaneous Philosophy of the Scientists and Other Essays*, G. Elliott (ed.), London: Verso.
Althusser, Louis and Balibar, Etienne (1970) *Reading Capital*, trans. Ben Brewster, London: New Left Books.
Anderson, Perry (1976) *Considerations on Western Marxism*, London: Verso.
—— (1983) *In the Tracks of Historical Materialism*, London: Verso.
—— (1998) *The Origins of Postmodernity*, London: Verso.
Balibar, Etienne (1996) *The Philosophy of Marx*, trans. Chris Turner, London: Verso.
Brenner, Robert (1998) 'The Economics of Global Turbulence', *New Left Review*, 229.
Bromley, Simon (1999) 'Marxism and Globalisation', in Andrew Gamble, David Marsh and Tony Tant (eds), *Marxism and Social Science*, London: Macmillan, pp.280–301.
Callari, Antonio, Cullenberg, Stephen and Biewener, Carole (eds) (1995) *Marxism in the Postmodern Age: Confronting the New World Order*, New York: Guilford Press.
Callinicos, Alex (1976) *Althusser's Marxism*, London: Pluto Press.
—— (1993) 'What is Living and What is Dead in Althusser's Marxism?', in E. Ann Kaplan and Michael Sprinker (eds), *The Althusserian Legacy*, London: Verso.
Carver, Terrell (1998) *The Postmodern Marx*, Manchester: Manchester University Press.
Carver, Terrell and Thomas, Paul (eds) (1995) *Rational Choice Marxism*, University Park, PA: The Pennsylvania University Press.
Castree, Noel (1995a) 'On Theory's Subject and Subject's Theory: Harvey, Capital, and the Limits to Classical Marxism', *Environment and Planning A*, 27: 269–97.
—— (1995b) 'A Review Essay: The Lonely Hour of the Last Word: Marx, Althusser, and the Critical Critics', *Environment and Planning A*, 27: 1163–78.
Chakrabarty, Dipesh (1996) 'Marx After Marxism: History, Subalternity, and Difference', in S. Makdisi, C. Casarino and R.E. Karl (eds), *Marxism Beyond Marxism*, New York: Routledge, pp.55–70.
Corrigan, Philip and Sayer, Derek (1985) *The Great Arch*, Oxford: Blackwell.
Cox, Robert, with Sinclair, Timothy J. (1996) *Approaches to World Order*, Cambridge: Cambridge University Press.

Drainville, Andre (1994) 'International Political Economy in the Age of Open Marxism', *Review of International Political Economy*, 1 (1): 105–32.

Eagleton, Terry (1988) 'Foreword', in Kristin Ross, *The Emergence of Social Space: Rimbaud and the Paris Commune*, Minneapolis, MN: University of Minnesota Press.

Elliott, Gregory (1987) *Althusser: The Detour of Theory*, London: Verso.

Enloe, Cynthia (1989) *Bananas, Beaches and Bases*, Berkeley, CA: University of California Press.

Fraser, Nancy (1995) 'From Redistribution to Recognition? Dilemmas of Justice in a "Post-Socialist" Age', *New Left Review*, 212: 68–93.

Gamble, Andrew (1999) 'Marxism after Communism: Beyond Realism and Historicism', *Review of International Studies*, 25 (Special Issue): 127–44.

Gibson-Graham, J.K. (1996) *The End of Capitalism (As We Knew It): A Feminist Critique of Political Economy*, Oxford: Blackwell.

Hall, Stuart (1985) 'Signification, Representation, Ideology: Althusser and the Post-Structuralist Debates', *Critical Studies in Mass Communication*, 2 (2): 91–114.

Harvey, David (1995) 'Globalization in Question', *Rethinking Marxism*, 8 (4): 1–17.

Hennessy, Rosemary (1993) *Materialist Feminism and the Politics of Discourse*, New York: Routledge.

—— (1996) 'Queer Theory, Left Politics', in Saree Makdisi, Cesare Casarino and Rebecca E. Karl (eds), *Marxism Beyond Marxism*, New York: Routledge, pp.214–42.

Herod, Andrew, O Tuathail, Gearoid and Roberts, Susan M. (1998) *An Unruly World? Globalization, Governance and Geography*, London: Routledge.

Hitchcock, Peter (1996) 'Workers of the World _____!', in Saree Makdisi, Cesare Casarino and Rebecca E. Karl (eds), *Marxism Beyond Marxism*, New York: Routledge, pp.71–88.

Jackson, Peter (1992) *Maps of Meaning: An Introduction to Cultural Geography*, New York: Routledge.

Jameson, Fredric (1981) *The Political Unconscious: Narrative as a Socially Symbolic Act*, Ithaca, NY: Cornell University Press.

—— (1991a) 'Conversations on the New World Order', in Robin Blackburn (ed.), *After the Fall: The Failure of Communism and the Future of Socialism*, London: Verso, pp.255–68.

—— (1991b) *Postmodernism, or the Cultural Logic of Late Capitalism*, Durham, NC: Duke University Press.

—— (1996) 'Actually Existing Marxism', in Saree Makdisi, Cesare Casarino and Rebecca E. Karl (eds), *Marxism Beyond Marxism*, New York: Routledge, pp.14–54.

—— (2000) 'Globalization and Strategy', *New Left Review*, 4: 49–68.

Jameson, Fredric and Miyoshi, Masao (eds) (1998) *The Cultures of Globalization*, Durham, NC: Duke University Press.

Johnson, Richard (1982) 'Reading for the Best Marx: History-writing and Historical Abstraction', in Richard Johnson, Gregor McLennan, Bill Schwartz and David Sutton (eds), *Making Histories: Studies in History Writing and Politics*, Minneapolis, MN: University of Minnesota Press.

Lam, Maivan Clech (1996) 'A Resistance Role for Marxism in the Belly of the Beast', in Saree Makdisi, Cesare Casarino and Rebecca E. Karl (eds), *Marxism Beyond Marxism*, New York: Routledge, pp. 255–64.

Levine, Andrew (1981) 'Althusser's Marxism', *Economy and Society*, 10 (3): 243–83.

Lock, Grahame (1988) 'Louis Althusser and G.A. Cohen: A Confrontation', *Economy and Society*, 17 (4): 499–507.

Lowe, Lisa and Lloyd, David (eds) (1997a) *The Politics of Culture in the Shadow of Capital*, Durham, NC: Duke University Press.

—— (1997b) 'Introduction', in Lisa Lowe and David Lloyd (eds), *The Politics of Culture in the Shadow of Capital*, Durham, NC: Duke University Press, pp.1–32.

Makdisi, Saree, Casarino, Cesare and Karl, Rebecca E. (eds) (1996a) *Marxism Beyond Marxism*, New York: Routledge.

—— (1996b) 'Introduction: Marxism, Communism, and History: A Reintroduction', in Saree Makdisi, Cesare Casarino and Rebecca E. Karl (eds), *Marxism Beyond Marxism*, New York: Routledge, pp.1–13.

Mandel, Ernest (1975) *Late Capitalism*, rev. edn, New York: New Left Books.

Marx, Karl (1951) *Theories of Surplus Value: A Selection from the Volumes Published as Theorien über den Mehnert*, ed. Karl Kautsky, taken from Marx's preliminary ms. for *Capital 4*, trans. G.A. Bonner and Emile Burns, London: Lawrence & Wishart.

—— (1973a) *Surveys from Exile: Political Writings, vol. 2*, ed. David Fernbach, London: Allen Lane.

—— (1973b) *Grundrisse: Foundations of the Critique of Political Economy*, trans. M. Nicolaus, Harmondsworth: Penguin.

—— (1981) *Capital: A Critique of Political Economy*, trans. David Fernbach, Harmondsworth: Penguin.

Ollman, Bertell (1976) *Alienation: Marx's Conception of Man in Capitalist Society*, 2nd edn, Cambridge: Cambridge University Press.

—— (1999) *Dialectical Investigations*, London: Routledge.

Ong, Aihwa (1987) *Spirits of Resistance and Capitalist Discipline: Factory Women in Malaysia*, Albany, NY: SUNY Press.

—— (1999) *Flexible Citizenship: The Cultural Logics of Transnationality*, Durham, NC: Duke University Press.

Panitch, Leo (1996) 'Rethinking the Role of the State', in James H. Mittelman (ed.), *Globalization: Critical Reflections*, Boulder, CO: Lynne Rienner Press, pp.83–116.

Postone, Moise (1993) *Time, Labor and Social Domination: A Reinterpretation of Marx's Critical Theory*, Cambridge: Cambridge University Press.

Resch, Robert Paul (1992) *Althusser and the Renewal of Marxist Social Theory*, Berkeley, CA: University of California Press.

Rosenberg, Justin (1994) *The Empire of Civil Society: A Critique of the Realist Theory of International Relations*, London: Verso.

—— (1996) 'Isaac Deutscher and the Lost History of International Relations', *New Left Review*, 215: 3–15.

Sayer, Andrew (1995) *Radical Political Economy: A Critique*, Oxford: Blackwell.

Sivanandran, A. (1998/9) 'Globalism and the Left', *Race and Class*, 40 (2/3): 5–19.

Smith, Hazel (1996) 'The Silence of the Academics: International Social Theory, Historical Materialism and Political Values', *Review of International Studies*, 22 (2): 191–212.

Smith, Paul (1997) *Millennial Dreams: Contemporary Culture and Capital in the North*, London: Verso.

Sprinker, Michael (1987) *Imaginary Relations: Aesthetics and Ideology in the Theory of Historical Materialism*, London: Verso.

Tetschke, Benno (1998) 'Geopolitical Relations in the European Middle Ages: History and Theory', *International Organization*, 52 (2): 325–58.

Thompson, John B. (1990) *Ideology and Modern Culture*, Stanford, CA: Stanford University Press.

Weldes, Jutta (1989) 'Marxism and Methodological Individualism: A Critique', *Theory and Society*, 18 (3): 353–86.

Williams, Raymond (1989) *Resources of Hope*, London: Verso.

Wood, Ellen Meiksins (1986) *The Retreat From Class: A New 'True' Socialism*, London: Verso.

—— (1995) *Democracy Against Capitalism: Renewing Historical Materialism*, Cambridge: Cambridge University Press.

Part II

Historical materialism as a theory of globalization

6 Class struggle, states and global circuits of capital

Peter Burnham

There are two significant methodological sins commonly committed by those claiming to offer a Marxist approach to international relations. The first is to assume that Marx's work can only be rendered intelligible for an international relations audience through a reading of Lenin (and less frequently through Stalin and Mao). This results in the adoption of a quite uncritical statist world-view rooted in a determinist, structuralist methodology far removed from Marx's rich critique of classical political economy. If the first sin plunges Marx into Parsonian structural-functionalism, the second reduces Marxism to the status of empiricist sociology with the plaintive cry, what about the workers? In the hands of 'Marxist sociologists' and neo-Gramscian international relations theorists, 'class' is all too easily detached from the social relations of production, becoming just another 'interest' in a methodology characterised by Weberian factor analysis.

To remedy these ills it is necessary to return to the central works of Marx to clarify the concepts 'class', 'capital' and 'state'. This is the only basis on which Marx's approach to international relations can be recovered. The interpretation developed in this chapter emphasises the centrality of class struggle and sees the state as an aspect of the social relations of production. As I shall outline, this approach has a long history in Western Marxism and has most recently been articulated under the banner of 'open Marxism'. The chapter therefore begins by discussing the fundamentals of 'open Marxism', drawing particular attention to the concepts of 'class', 'labour' and 'struggle'. This provides the background for discussing how a class struggle theory of the state can be developed from Marx's account of the transition from feudalism to capitalism. By way of conclusion the chapter highlights how Marx's discussion of the circulation of capital provides a basis for analysing recent developments in the global political economy.

Towards an 'open' interpretation of Marx

The call for the development of 'open Marxism' is a response to the crisis of theory produced by the various forms of deterministic 'closed Marxism', which dominated radical discourse following the articulation of the state ideology Marxism-Leninism.[1] The attempt to break away from the reductionist dogmatism of Marxist structural-functionalism while avoiding the complementary error of humanistic subjectivism has a long tradition in Marxist thought.[2] Consistent with the 'open', critical tradition is the work produced by, among others, Luxemburg, Korsch, Bloch, Rubin, Pashukanis, Rosdolsky, the Italian tradition of 'autonomist' Marxism and more recently by contributors to debates on value and the state held in the early years of the Conference of Socialist Economists (CSE).[3]

This particular approach to Marxism is 'open' in three main respects. First, its rejection of all forms of determinism is based on reasserting the centrality of class struggle. Class, in this view, is not to be understood in sociological fashion as a static, descriptive term applied to groups of individuals sharing common experiences or life-chances or workplace relations. Rather it is recognised that the separation of labour from the means of production, and thereby the existence of private property, indicates that we are all born into a class society. The class relation between capital and labour is already present, already presupposed, the moment the possessor of money and the possessor of labour power confront each other as buyer and seller (Marx 1978: 114). As Clarke (1978: 42) clarifies, it is the concept of class relations as being analytically prior to the political, economic and ideological forms taken by those relations (even though class relations have no existence independently of those forms) that makes it possible for a Marxist analysis to conceptualise the complexity of the relations between the economic and the political, and their interconnections as complementary forms of the fundamental class relation, without abandoning the theory for a pragmatic pluralism. Class relations, in this sense, are of course antagonistic relations. Class struggle therefore lies at the heart of Marx's account of accumulation as capital must not only extract surplus from labour daily in the production process but must also ensure the successful reproduction of the total social circuit of capital through its three principal forms. This calls for constant 'intervention' from state managers and for the establishment of various forms of international regimes and institutions. If the circuit of capital is understood in terms of struggle and potential crisis then determinism of all kinds is rejected. Struggle, as Holloway (1991: 71) points out, by definition is uncertain and leaves outcomes open. In essence this version of Marxism, based on an understanding of the complexities of the rotation of capital, focuses on resistance to the imposition of work and thereby points to the fragility of capitalism as a system of class domination.

Second, this interpretation of Marxism is anchored in the methodological approach of form-analysis. Rather than understanding form in terms of species (the form of something more basic which lies behind the appearance), the 'open' tradition sees form as a mode of existence – something exists only in and through the forms it takes (Bonefeld *et al.* 1992: xv). Hence Marx's advance over the classical political economists who mistook the bourgeois form of social production for eternal, natural relations of production, thereby failing to see the specificity of the value-form and consequently of the commodity-form, the money-form and the productive-form. The importance of this distinction is not only that it sensitises us to the fluidity of social relations but more fundamentally it breaks with the old appearance/essence distinction which has long bedevilled

Marxism. Money capital and commodity capital do not, for instance, denote branches of business that are independent and separate from one another. Rather they are simply particular functional forms of industrial capital, 'modes of existence of the various functional forms that industrial capital constantly assumes and discards within the circulation sphere' (Marx 1978: 136). Capital, as self-valorising value, should be understood as 'movement', as a circulatory process, not as a static thing or structure (Marx 1978: 185). Likewise, it is unnecessary to remain fixed in statist fashion to ideas of the enduring nature of the nation-state. Instead our focus is on the changing character of the form of the 'political' in relation to the circuit of capital. Form-analysis also presents an alternative to the deterministic base/superstructure image of Marxism. In this 'hard structural determinist' reading, exemplified by one-dimensional Soviet Marxism-Leninism, the 'economic base' determines the 'political superstructure', thus rendering redundant any serious analysis. Although Engels later tried to soften this approach by introducing the notion of 'determinant in the last instance', this has done little to dissuade structuralist Marxists (and technological determinists) from the view that 'the economy' should be awarded primacy when studying social formations. The state in this model is seen as epiphenomenal, its existence reducible to the 'economic base' and changes in state policy are understood as merely reflecting altered economic relations. The notion of 'relative autonomy' has done little to correct this 'reductionist' reading of Marx. Open Marxism interprets the base/superstructure metaphor as a provisional level of abstraction useful only for very limited analytical purposes (Sklar 1988: 9). Monocausal economism is thereby replaced with the dialectical notion that social relations of production only exist in the form of economic, legal and political relations. It is not simply a case of arguing in Weberian fashion that each of these relations exercise reciprocal and causative influence. Rather, Marx is at pains to stress that antagonistic class relations are always manifest in economic, political and legal forms. In this way 'economics' rests as firmly on 'politics' and 'law' as vice versa (Wood 1981). The fundamental error of determinist schools is that they understand the *social* relations of production in terms of technical economic relations, thereby replicating the fetishism that Marx's critique of classical political economy sought to dispel.

Finally, open Marxism breaks with mainstream international relations theory by rejecting methodologies based on positivism. The error of positivistic orthodoxy, Marx outlines in the *Grundrisse*, is that it simply brings outward appearances into an external relationship with one another, 'the crudity and lack of comprehension lies precisely in that organically coherent factors are brought into a haphazard relation with one another, i.e. into a purely speculative connection' (Marx 1986a: 26). Unlike non-dialectical research which begins with an isolated unit and attempts to reconstruct the whole by establishing external connections, dialectical research starts with the whole and then searches for the substantive abstraction which constitutes social phenomena as interconnected, complex forms different from, but united in, each other (Bonefeld 1993: 21; Ollman 1993: 12–17; Rosdolsky 1977). Notions of externality and structure are replaced by the dialectical categories of process and contradictory internal relationship. While non-dialectical methodologies in social science are based on abstract, ahistorical principles used simply to reorder everyday observable events, Marx begins by noting that capitalist society is an historically specific form of the social production process in general. Like all its forerunners capitalist production proceeds under certain material conditions, which are also expressed as specific social relations that individuals enter into in the process of reproducing their life. The key therefore to understanding the character of social relations within capitalism, and thereby the inner connection between apparently disparate phenomena, lies in tracing how definite social relations between men assume the fantastic form of relations between things. This task requires a critical theory, not a methodology which asserts that all knowledge must only be based on the observable. Hence, for Marx, diverse phenomena such as the state and the economy do not exist as externally related entities but as moments of the class relation from which they are constituted (Bonefeld 1992: 100).

In opposition therefore to most international relations theory, the open Marxist tradition understands the 'state' as an aspect of a wider and more fundamental set of social relations based on the separation of labour from the conditions of production. The state should not be seen as 'autonomous' or as 'determined' by a supposed 'economic base'. Rather, the starting point is that provided by Evgeny Pashukanis (1978: 139) who poses the question,

> why does class rule not remain what it is, the factual subjugation of one section of the population by the other? Why does it assume the form of official state rule, or – which is the same thing – why does the machinery of state coercion not come into being as the private machinery of the ruling class?; why does it detach itself from the ruling class and take on the form of an impersonal apparatus of public power, separate from society?

Similarly in relation to the market, why do goods and services take the form of commodities? Why do the products of labour confront each other as commodities? The chief originality of Marx's work is that he completes classical political economy's analysis of value and its magnitude and goes on to reformulate the basis of social science by asking 'why this content has assumed that particular form' (Marx 1976: 174).

Class struggle and the state

Applying the dialectical method to the study of the state involves first specifying, on a very general level, the relationship between labour and political domination. Marx is emphatic that the most significant distinguishing feature of each social formation is not so much how the bulk of the labour of production is done, but how the dominant propertied classes controlling the conditions of production ensure the extraction of the surplus which makes their dominance possible (De Ste. Croix 1981: 52). Marx's most direct exposition of this point is in *Capital Volume 3* (1981: 927), where he writes:

The specific economic form in which unpaid surplus labour is pumped out of the direct producers determines the relationship of domination and servitude, as this grows directly out of production itself and reacts back on it in turn as a determinant. On this is based the entire configuration of the economic community arising from the actual relations of production, and hence also its specific political form. It is in each case the direct relationship of the owners of the conditions of production to the immediate producers ... in which we find the innermost secret, the hidden basis of the entire social edifice, and hence also the political form of the relationship of sovereignty and dependence, in short the specific form of state in each case.

The 'state' understood as 'politically organised subjection' (Abrams 1988) charged with the enforcement of rule, empowered to exercise force to safeguard the relations which constitute the social order, is to be understood as the 'moment of coercion' without which no class society can exist. The originality of Marx's work is that he understands the 'political' as a form constituted by the antagonistic relationship between the direct producers and the owners of production (Holloway and Picciotto 1977; Holloway 1995). In this way he provides not a functionalist but a class struggle theory of the state. Objectivist readings of Marx couched in terms of forces and relations of production, impending cataclysmic crisis and growing class consciousness, are supplanted by an approach which sees the future as essentially open, to be realised in struggle with no predetermined lines of development.

This reformulation seeks to reinstate exploitation (not consciousness or common awareness) as the hallmark of class. As De Ste. Croix (1981: 43) points out, 'class (essentially a relationship) is the collective social expression of the fact of exploitation, the way in which exploitation is embodied in a social structure'. Exploitation, as the appropriation of part of the product of the labour of others, can take a number of forms. For instance, surplus can be extracted through the exploitation of wage labour or it can be obtained from unfree labour (chattel slaves, serfs or debt bondsmen). While classes are identified by their position in the whole system of social production (above all according to their degree of ownership or control of the conditions of production), class struggle is the inevitable process of domination and resistance which results from the exploitation of labour. As De Ste. Croix (1981: 44, 57) explains, it may not necessarily involve collective action by a class as such, and it may or may not include activity on a political plane. To see class struggle simply in terms of class consciousness and active political conflict is to lose the meaning ascribed to it by Marx in the *Communist Manifesto*, and more importantly, leads to the vacuous conclusion that it is absent from most capitalist societies today. By placing exploitation at the heart of class it is possible to arrive at a more subtle conclusion. The ruling class is engaged in a permanent struggle which calls forth continuous resistance. Even slaves who are kept in irons and are driven with a whip can conduct some kind of passive resistance, if only by quiet sabotage and breaking a tool or two (De Ste. Croix 1981: 66). In contemporary capitalism, struggles to resist the imposition of

labour take a variety of forms: from unofficial workplace disputes to official industrial stoppages; from community action to one-day demonstrations; and from
simple lack of cooperation at work to absenteeism, illness and sabotage.

In summary, Marx argues that our first task is to focus on the relationship
between the direct producers and the owners of production to ascertain how the
ruling class secures the extraction of surplus value. The particular form and
mode in which the connection between workers and means of production is
effected is what distinguishes the various economic epochs of the social structure
(Marx 1978: 120). On this basis it is possible to introduce consideration of the
state, since, as Clarke (1983: 118) clarifies,

> the state does not *constitute* the social relations of production, it is essentially
> a *regulative* agency, whose analysis, therefore, presupposes the analysis of the
> social relations of which the state is regulative. The analysis of the capitalist
> state conceptually presupposes the analysis of capital and of the reproduc-
> tion of capitalist relations of production, despite the fact that in reality, of
> course, the state is itself a moment of the process of reproduction.

The character of the capitalist state, and by implication the international state
system, is therefore to be analysed against the background of the contradictions
inherent in the development and reproduction of the capitalist mode of production. Marx lays the basis for this analysis in his historical studies of the transition
from feudalism to capitalism.

Marx's account of the rise of the modern state is set in the context of the
social struggles which accompanied the overthrow of feudal relations of property
and production.[4] In his reading, the character of old civil (feudal) society was
directly political. An individual's position within an estate determined his/her
political relation, that is, his/her separation and exclusion from other components of society. As clarified in *Capital Volume One* (1976: 170),

> here, instead of the independent man, we find everyone dependent – serfs
> and lords, vassals and suzerains, laymen and clerics. Personal dependence
> characterises the social relations of material production as much as it does
> the other spheres of life based on that production.

In these circumstances different subdivisions of trade and industry are the property
of different corporations; court dignities and jurisdiction are the property of
particular estates; and the various provinces the property of individual princes.
Hence, in the Middle Ages we find serfs, feudal estates, merchant and trade guilds,
and corporations of scholars, with each sphere (property, trade, society, man)
directly political – 'every private sphere has a political character or is a political
sphere; that is, politics is a characteristic of the private spheres too' (1975a: 32).

This discussion of the identity of civil and political society in feudalism has
important ramifications for theorising the emergence of the capitalist state form.
Marx saw the identity of the civil and political estates as the expression of the

identity of civil and political society. Within each individual principality, the princedom was a particular estate – 'their estate was their state' (1975a: 72) – which had certain privileges but which was correspondingly restricted by the privileges of the other estates. As Marx summarises, 'they did not become political estates because they participated in legislation; on the contrary, they participated in legislation because they were political estates' (1975a: 73). To this can be added the significant rider that the relation of estates to the Empire was merely a treaty relationship of various states with nationality, 'their legislative activity, their voting of taxes for the Empire, was only a particular expression of their general political significance and effectiveness' (1975a: 72).

Thus within feudal social relations, although the Holy Roman Emperor and the Pope stood at the apex, the structure was not a continuous hierarchy but rather sovereignty was parcellised and acts of force were not centrally orchestrated or rooted in a general system of right (Kay and Mott 1982: 80–4). In the feudal corvee, force was applied directly to serfs as producers, compelling them to produce rent for the lord. This force was particular, applied to each serf separately, in contrast to the compulsion to work in capitalism which operates through an impersonal labour market. 'Relations therefore were not mediated through a central authority, but were made directly at all points … feudal relations of production were immediately relations of power' (Kay and Mott 1982: 82). By contrast capitalist relations take place through the apparent exchange of equivalents. Labour and capital meet in the 'exclusive realm of Freedom, Equality, Property and Bentham' (Marx 1976: 280), brought together by a contract whose very nature expels all immediate political content. As Kay and Mott (1982: 83) make clear, a crucial presupposition of modern contract is that both parties are deprived of the right to act violently in defence of their own interests, with the consequence that, 'in a society of equivalents relating to each other through contract, politics is abstracted out of the relations of production, and order becomes the task of a specialised body – the state'. In this way, the state as the particularised embodiment of rule, and the replacement of privilege by equivalence, are part of the same process, since 'citizens' only face each other through the medium of the state which is 'equidistant' from them. In short, 'the abstraction of the state as such belongs only to modern times. The abstraction of the political state is a modern product' (Marx 1975a: 32).

The emergence of the capitalist state form was neither an automatic response to the development of world trade, nor simply a matter of the peaceful transfer of power from one class to another. Capitalist relations of production were established through the struggles of the peasantry and the nascent middle class who sought freedom from the dependencies of the Middle Ages. The long-run history of the decline of feudalism in England, for example, shows that although the crises of feudalism began in the thirteenth century it was not until the mid seventeenth century that the abolition of feudal tenures facilitated capital accumulation and the consolidation of property which formed the basis for the eighteenth-century Whig oligarchy (Corrigan and Sayer 1985: 82; Hilton 1978). In this period feudal social relations came under increased pressure as rural depopulation aggravated struggles over feudal rents between the land-owning class and the peasantry. In the second half of the fourteenth century, falling feudal rents intensified the crisis of feudalism as competition between lords and heightened demands on peasants from ecclesiastical estates resulted in increased pressure for an enlarged surplus product. The success of the English manorial peasantries in resisting this pressure was reflected juridically in the virtual disappearance of servile villeinage which allowed the retention of surplus on peasant holdings, a degree of social differentiation and prosperity among the peasant community, and a slow reorientation towards small-scale commodity production for domestic and international markets (Hilton 1973 and 1978; Dobb 1946). The response of the threatened ruling class, in this instance the nobility, was the absolutist state, summarised by Anderson (1974: 18) as 'a redeployed and recharged apparatus of feudal domination – designed to clamp the peasant masses back into their traditional social position, despite and against the gains they had won by the commutation of dues'. However, the struggles of the nascent bourgeoisie transformed the absolutist state from an apparatus for the defence of aristocratic property and privilege, into an institution whose concentration of power facilitated the changes required by the nascent mercantile and manufacturing classes in the phase of 'primitive accumulation'.

In the first draft of *The Civil War in France*, Marx (1986b: 483–4) recognises that

> the centralised state machinery which, with its ubiquitous and complicated military, bureaucratic, clerical and judiciary organs, entoils (enmeshes) the living civil society like a boa constrictor, was first forged in the days of absolute monarchy as a weapon of nascent middle-class society in its struggle of emancipation from feudalism.

The seignorial privileges of the medieval lords and clergy were transformed into the attribute of a unitary state power, displacing the feudal dignitaries by salaried state officials, and transferring arms from medieval retainers of the landlords to a standing army. Nevertheless, the development of bourgeois society remained clogged by 'all manner of medieval rubbish, seignorial rights, local privileges, municipal and guild monopolies and provincial constitutions' (Marx 1986b: 328). In France the gigantic broom of the French Revolution of the eighteenth century swept away these relics, while in England, although historians dispute points of subtlety concerning the English Civil War, there is little question that between 1660 and 1700, the independent power of the Crown was broken, never to be regained. Corrigan and Sayer (1985: 79) interpret this period as 'a watershed in the long making of the "State" as an impersonal body, a transcendent object representing "society", the Leviathan theorised by Hobbes in these years as "Mortall God" '. Between these dates we can trace the birth of the Treasury, the Board of Trade, and the restructured Secretary of State's departments. Also, the introduction of Common Law providing stability and liberty for property ownership. Correspondingly, legislation against non-Parliamentary taxation was confirmed in 1660, financially subordinating the Crown to Parliament. Finally, the Navigation

Acts of 1661 enabled the creation of the closed colonial system, providing for the subordination of the colonies to Parliament (Corrigan and Sayer 1985: 83).[5]

The historic change in the form of the state occurred gradually as political revolutions overthrew sovereign power (which constituted the political state as a matter of general concern), and fundamental class struggles, which were both prompted by and were expressions of changing social relations of production, 'necessarily smashed all estates, corporations, guilds, and privileges, since they were all manifestations of the separation of the people from the community' (Marx 1975b: 166; Clarke 1988). These struggles simultaneously abolished the direct political character of civil society while creating the modern state. Gradually relations within civil society were transformed from the 'motley feudal ties' characterised by 'the most heavenly ecstasies of religious fervour ... and chivalrous enthusiasm' (Marx and Engels 1976: 487), to the crass materialism of modern private property relations subject to the rule of money and law, and the egotistical struggle of each against all. Marx is emphatic:

> the *establishment of the political state* and the dissolution of civil society into independent *individuals* – whose relations with one another depend on law, just as the relations of men in the system of estates and guilds depended on privilege – is accomplished by *one and the same act.*
>
> (1975b: 167)

The 'abstraction' or 'particularisation' of the modern state sets limits to its powers (Clarke 1988: 127–8). The state merely gives form to the social relations whose substance is determined in civil society, so that the state 'has to confine itself to a formal and negative activity, for where civil life and its labour begin, there the power of the administration ends' (Marx 1975c: 198). The formal and regulatory activity par excellence of the state is to uphold the basis of the new social relations which comprise the framework of civil society.

Therein for Marx, the capitalist state is 'based on the contradiction between public and private life, on the contradiction between general interests and private interests' (1975d: 46). By upholding the rule of law and money, the state maintains the formal discipline of the market, and thereby mediates the contradiction between the expression of general and particular interests. This discipline must necessarily be imposed in an 'independent form' which is divorced from private interests: 'Just because individuals seek only their particular interest, which for them does not coincide with their common interest, the latter is asserted as an interest "alien" to them, and "independent" of them ... in the form of the state' (Marx 1975d: 46–7; Clarke 1988).

From the 'state', to national states in the global economy

It has proved remarkably difficult to develop a critical Marxist theory of the international state system which avoids the crudities and absurdities of

Marxism-Leninism base/superstructure dogma.[6] A major problem has turned on reconciling a view of 'the state' primarily defined relative to a domestic class structure, with the fact that the state is a component of an international state system (Barker 1978; Picciotto 1991; Callinicos 1992). As Picciotto (1991: 217) has pointed out, this tendency has been greater in Marxist than non-Marxist writing, since the Marxist emphasis on the class nature of the state has made it necessary to discuss the state in relation to society, and it has become convenient to assume a correlation between the society and the classes within it and the state within that society.

This difficulty however is more apparent than real and is a product of conflating levels of analysis. The capitalist state form is not derived from a 'domestic' analysis, to which 'external' determinants are then appended *a posteriori*. As indicated above, the capitalist form of the state is derived from an analysis of the class struggles which undermined feudal social relations. When turning to analyse contemporary global relations it is fundamental to switch our focus and level of abstraction from 'the state' (capitalist state form) to particular national states and more broadly to the political management of the global circuits of capital (Holloway 1995). In so doing we are confronted with the following paradox. While from its earliest stages capitalist accumulation has proceeded on a global level, national states have developed on the basis of the principle of territoriality of jurisdiction. The fragmentation of the 'political' into national states, which from their very inception comprise an international system, has developed in an uneven fashion alongside the internationalisation of capital. As Picciotto (1991: 217) further clarifies, the transition from the personal sovereign to an abstract sovereignty of public authorities over a defined territory was a key element in the development of the capitalist international system, since it provided a multifarious framework which permitted and facilitated the global circulation of commodities and capital. The 'capitalist state' thus originated in the context of an international system of states establishing a framework for the generalisation of commodity production based (initially) on petty commodity production and a world market.

This view which locates the development of the capitalist state in the establishment and maintenance of generalised commodity production, offers a distinctive way of understanding the emergence of the global political economy. Whereas world-systems theorists similarly emphasise the absolute dependence of the world economy on the state system, in taking a global perspective it is neither necessary nor helpful to start from the market. As Picciotto (1991) again outlines, in Wallerstein's schema it is the world market and the consequent international division of labour that allocated a particular role to each region, from which flowed the relationship of exploitation and hence the form of the state. However, it was not trade that transformed production relations, but the contradictions of feudal and post-feudal production relations that led to transformations both of the world market and the form of the state (Brenner 1977; Rosenberg 1994). By viewing national states as political nodes in the global flow of capital, it is possible to avoid both the Smithian bias introduced by focusing uncritically on the market and the mistakes of orthodox IPE (international political economy) which treat state and market as independent variables.

In this light, class relations do not impinge on the state, they do not exist in 'domestic' society and make their presence felt by influencing the state which operates in the international realm. Rather the state itself is a form of the class relation which constitutes global capitalist relations. These relations appear, for example, as British relations on the world market. Yet as Marx clarifies in *The Civil War in France*, struggles between states are to be understood, at a more abstract level, as struggles between capital and labour which assume more and more the character of the national power of capital over labour. The notion of 'integration' into the global economy does not imply that a state could choose not to be integrated. A political strategy of 'national economic autonomy' has always been, in an absolute sense, impossible. Policy is not made in the absence of the global economy. It is made within an international context as each state is a participant in the global economy. Such a perspective does not mean that national policies are of secondary importance. Rather, it locates them within a context in which these policies exist and through which they develop. National states exist as political 'nodes' or 'moments' in the global flow of capital and their development is therefore part of the antagonistic and crisis-ridden development of capitalist society. The state itself cannot resolve the global crisis of capital. It can, however, enhance its position in the hierarchy of the price system by increasing the efficiency of capitalist exploitation operating within its boundaries (Bonefeld *et al.* 1995).

A conceptualisation of capitalism in terms of the aggregation of national economies makes it impossible to understand the constraints imposed on national states which derive from their role as political managers of global circuits of capital. Unless one conceptualises the global mode of existence of the labour/capital relation, then balance of payments problems, pressure on currency, exchange rate fluctuations, and problems of public debt can only be understood as impinging on individual states through external forces (Bonefeld 1993). The open Marxist approach suggests that the apparent solidity of the 'state' masks its existence as a contradictory form of global social relationship. The state is not only an institution but a form-process, an active process of forming social relations and therefore class struggles channelling them into non-class forms – citizens' rights, international human rights – which promote the disorganisation of labour (Holloway 1991: 75–6). The key to comprehending capitalist society is that it is a global social system based on the imposition of work through the commodity-form (Cleaver 1979: 71–86). The reproduction of bourgeois social relations at all levels (from the overseer, to the managing director, state managers, international agencies, and alliances between states) rests upon the ability of capital (in all its forms and guises) to harness and contain the power of labour within the bounds of the commodity-form. The struggles which ensue over the imposition of work, the regulation of consumption through the commodification of labour time as money and the confinement of the production of use values within the bounds of profitability produce constant instability and crisis. It is the everyday struggles in and against the dominance of the commodity-form which are manifest as 'national' economic crises or balance of payments problems or speculative pressure on currency. Thus Marx's approach to international relations does not reject the 'state' as a category but rather sees relations between national states in terms of the antagonistic social relationships which constitute states as political moments of the global composition of class relations.[7]

The political 'management' of global circuits of capital

A number of implications flow from the view that states should be conceptualised as political nodes in the global flow of capital. The first relates directly to current debates on whether capitalism has entered a new stage characterised by globalisation. If we theorise the class relation as a global social relationship and national states as political nodes active in the reproduction of global circuits of capital, then 'globalisation' loses some of its mystique. States are not to be thought of as 'thing-like' institutions losing power to the market. Rather, in a context characterised by the intensive and extensive development of the global circuits, state managers have been able to reorganise their core activities using market processes to 'depoliticise' the management of difficult aspects of public policy (Burnham 1999). It should be no surprise that a global system resting on an antagonistic social relationship will be subject to dynamic change as both state and market actors seek to remove what they perceive to be blockages in the flow of capital. In essence, state managers are above all circuit managers. 'Globalisation' presents serious problems for approaches based on national conceptions of capitalism and for those frameworks that insist on regarding 'states' and 'markets' as fundamentally opposed forms of social organisation. However, for the open Marxist tradition 'globalisation' simply represents a deepening of existing circuits and a broadening of the 'political', as regulative agencies (both public and private) beyond the national state are drawn into the complex process of 'managing' the rotation of capital. To develop this point further it is necessary to grasp Marx's discussion of the total circulation process of capital.

In *Capital Volume 1*, Marx introduces the 'general formula of capital'. Capital in its most general form is defined as value that expands itself, 'the value originally advanced, therefore, not only remains intact while in circulation, but increases its magnitude, adds to itself a surplus-value, or is valorised. And this movement converts it into capital' (1976: 252). While passing through the sphere of circulation (as money-capital and commodity-capital) there can be a redistribution of value but its magnitude cannot be increased. Hence Marx identifies the commodity which when purchased can be used in production to create new value -- labour power. In *Capital Volume 2* Marx continues this discussion emphasizing that capital, as self-valorizing value, is a movement, a circulatory process that passes through a sequence of transformations, a series of metamorphoses that form so many phases or stages of a total process (1978: 132). Two of the phases, or forms of capital, belong to the circulation sphere (money-capital and commodity-capital), one to the sphere of production (productive capital). As Marx summarises, the capital that assumes these forms in the course of its total circuit, discards them again and fulfils in each of them its appropriate function, is *industrial capital* – industrial here in the sense that it encompasses any branch of production that is pursued on a capitalist basis.

(1978: 133)

In Marx's basic representation of the circuit:

$$M - C\,(LP+MP) \ldots P \ldots C' - M'(M+m)$$

M is money capital; C is commodity capital (here composed of labour power and means of production); the dots indicate that the circulation process is interrupted; P is productive capital; C' again is commodity capital (now the bearer of a capital value which has been valorised, enriched with surplus value) and M' is again money capital (composed of M, the capital value, and m, the new value, surplus value, realised in money form).

The total social circuit in effect consists of three phases:

- The circuit of money capital, $M - C \ldots P \ldots C' - M'$, where the initial and concluding form of the process is that of money capital.
- The circuit of productive capital, $P \ldots C' - M' - C \ldots P\,(P')$, in which surplus value is created and thereby expanded accumulation becomes possible. It is here that we see the 'real metamorphosis of capital, as opposed to the merely formal metamorphoses of the circulation sphere' (1978: 132).
- The circuit of commodity capital, $C' - M' - C \ldots P \ldots C'\,(C'')$, in which the starting point is commodity capital, the product of a previous production process, already enriched with surplus value.

For our purposes there are two important points which emerge from this very brief overview of the circulation of capital. First, the determining purpose, the driving motive common to all three circuits, is the valorisation of value, the basis of which is the exploitation of labour power. Each particular circuit presupposes the others and although in reality each individual industrial capital is involved in all three at the same time, the circuit is a constant process of interruption as capital clothes itself in its different stages, alternately assuming them and casting them aside (Marx 1978: 109). Hence, capital is simultaneously present and spatially coexistent in its various phases or modes of existence. If however a breakdown occurs in one part of the circuit, the whole process may be brought to a standstill. The cycle of accumulation therefore is fraught with the possibility of crisis at every stage. As Marx indicates:

every delay in the succession brings the coexistence into disarray, every delay in one stage causes a greater or lesser delay in the entire circuit, not only that of the portion of the capital that is delayed, but also that of the entire individual capital.

(1978: 183)

Since the circuitry of modern capitalism is both intensive and extensive (in terms of the interpenetration of capitals and the global domination of this mode of production) the potential for interruption and crisis is immense. Each of the three phases of the total circuit is prone to disruption (in a multitude of ways ranging from financial crisis to industrial unrest and lack of effective demand experienced as 'overproduction'). At the most basic level the circulation of capital is undermined by any process which potentially reunites labour with the means of production and subsistence. This understanding of capitalism points to the permanence of crisis and the necessity for crisis management at both national and international levels. Every crisis in the international system of course has its own particular line of development. However, by focusing on the circuits of capital we are able to analyse the social form of crisis thereby relating the particular to the general. Finally, this framework establishes a clear break with realist state-centrism and with crude Leninist 'state as capitalist trust' theories. As political nodes in the global flow of capital, states are essentially regulative agencies implicated in its reproduction but unable to control this reproduction or represent unambiguously the interests of 'national capital'. In brief, state managers seek to remove barriers to the accumulation of capital, which flows in and through their territories. The fundamental tasks of state managers (from welfare to the management of money, labour and trade etc.) therefore relate directly to ensuring the successful rotation of capital both nationally and internationally. However, as noted above, the difficulties of containing conflict and enhancing the accumulation of capital have led to a more diverse process of circuit management involving a range of actors, agencies and regimes seeking to regulate aspects of the metamorphosis of capital.

It may not be fashionable to suggest that texts produced in mid-Victorian Britain are the key to understanding the politics of the global economy in the twenty-first century. However, Marx's theory of capitalist society rooted in the concepts of value, surplus value, capital and class offers a powerful alternative to bourgeois social science which, in his day and ours, seems to offer

> nothing more than a didactic and more or less doctrinaire translation of the everyday notions of the actual agents of production ... [corresponding] to the self-interest of the dominant classes, since it preaches the natural necessity and perpetual justification of their sources of income and erects this into a dogma.
>
> (Marx 1981: 969)

Notes

1   The term 'open Marxism' was first used in this way by Mandel and Agnoli 1980, and has since been systematically developed by Bonefeld *et al.* 1992; and Holloway 1991, 1995. See also Burnham 1994; Clarke 1988, 1991.
2   For an overview see Anderson 1980.
3   See Bonefeld *et al.* 1992, Introduction; and Holloway and Picciotto 1977. On autonomous Marxism see Witheford 1994; Cleaver 1979; and Negri 1991. On the CSE see the journal *Capital and Class*.
4   Also see Burnham 1995a and 1995b.

5   For further details see Corrigan and Sayer 1985; Elton 1974; Loades 1977; Hoskins 1977; Turner 1980; and the various contributors to Hilton 1978.
6   See for instance the early attempts by Kubalkova and Cruickshank 1980; and Thorndike 1978. More recent work includes Linklater 1996; and Rosenberg 1994. For an overview see Smith 1996. On neo-Gramscian IPE, see Cox 1987; and Gill and Law 1988.
7   Also see Holloway 1995.

Bibliography

Abrams, P. (1988) 'Notes on the Difficulty of Studying the State', *Journal of Historical Sociology*, I, I.

Anderson, P. (1974) *Lineages of the Absolutist State*, London: Verso.

—— (1980) *Arguments Within English Marxism*, London: Verso.

Barker, C. (1978) 'A Note on the Theory of Capitalist States', *Capital and Class*, 4: 118–26.

Bonefeld, W. (1992) 'Social Constitution and the Form of the Capitalist State', in W. Bonefeld, R. Gunn and K. Psychopedis (eds), *Open Marxism*, Volume 1, London: Pluto.

—— (1993) *The Recomposition of the British State during the 1980s*, London: Dartmouth.

Bonefeld, W., Brown, A. and Burnham, P. (1995) *A Major Crisis*, Aldershot: Dartmouth.

Bonefeld, W., Gunn, R. and Psychopedis, K. (eds) (1992) *Open Marxism*, Volume 1, London: Pluto.

Brenner, R. (1977) 'The Origins of Capitalist Development', *New Left Review*, 104: 25–92.

Burnham, P. (1994) 'Open Marxism and Vulgar International Political Economy', *Review of International Political Economy*, 1, 2: 221–31.

—— (1995a) 'State and Market in International Political Economy: Towards a Marxian Alternative', *Studies in Marxism*, 2: 135–59.

—— (1995b) 'Capital, Crisis and the International State System', in W. Bonefeld and J. Holloway (eds), *Global Capital, National State and the Politics of Money*, London: Macmillan.

—— (1999) 'The Politics of Economic Management in the 1990s', *New Political Economy*, 4, 1: 37–54.

Callinicos, A. (1992) 'Capitalism and the State System: A Reply to Nigel Harris', *International Socialism*, 54.

Clarke, S. (1977) 'Marxism, Sociology and Poulantzas' Theory of the State', *Capital and Class*, 2.

—— (1978) 'Capital, Fractions of Capital and the State', *Capital and Class*, 5: 32–77.

—— (1983) 'State, Class Struggle and the Reproduction of Capital', *Kapitalistate*, 10/11.

—— (1988) *Keynesianism, Monetarism and the Crisis of the State*, Aldershot: Edward Elgar.

—— (ed.) (1991) *The State Debate*, London: Macmillan.

Cleaver, H. (1979) *Reading Capital Politically*, Hemel Hempstead: Harvester.

Corrigan, P. and Sayer, D. (1985) *The Great Arch*, Oxford: Blackwell.

Cox, R. (1987) *Production, Power and World Order*, New York: Columbia University Press.

De Ste. Croix, G.E.M. (1981) *The Class Struggle in the Ancient Greek World*, London: Duckworth.

Dobb, M. (1946) *Studies in the Development of Capitalism*, London: Routledge.

Elton, G. (1974) *England Under the Tudors*, London: Methuen.

Gill, S. and Law, D. (1988) *The Global Political Economy*, Hemel Hempstead: Harvester.

Hilton, R. (1973) *Bond Men Made Free*, London: Methuen.

—— (1978) 'Introduction' and 'Capitalism – What's in a Name?', in R. Hilton (ed.), *The Transition From Feudalism to Capitalism*, London: Verso.

—— (ed.) (1978) *The Transition From Feudalism to Capitalism*, London: Verso.

Holloway, J. (1991) 'In the Beginning was the Scream', *Common Sense*, 11: 73.

—— (1995) 'Global Capital and the National State', in W. Bonefeld and J. Holloway (eds), *Global Capital, National State and the Politics of Money*, London: Macmillan.

Holloway, J. and Picciotto, S. (1977) 'Capital, Crisis and the State', *Capital and Class*, 2: 76–101.

Hoskins, W. (1977) *The Making of the English Landscape*, London: Hodder & Stoughton.

Kay, G. and Mott, J. (1982) *Political Order and the Law of Labour*, London: Macmillan.

Kubalkova, V. and Cruickshank, A. (1980) *Marxism-Leninism and Theory of International Relations*, London: Routledge & Kegan Paul.

Lenin, V.I. (1917) *The State and Revolution*, Moscow: Progress.

Linklater, A. (1996) 'Marxism', in S. Burchill and A. Linklater (with R. Devetak, M. Paterson and J. True), *Theories of International Relations*, London: Macmillan.

Loades, D. (1977) *Politics and the Nation 1450–1660*, London: Fontana.

Mandel, E. and Agnoli, J. (1980) *Offener Marxismus*, Frankfurt: Campus Verlag.

Marx, K. (1975a) 'Contribution to the Critique of Hegel's Philosophy of Law', in K. Marx and F. Engels, *Collected Works (MECW)*, Volume 3, London: Lawrence & Wishart.

—— (1975b) 'On the Jewish Question', in K. Marx and F. Engels, *Collected Works (MECW)*, Volume 3, London: Lawrence & Wishart.

—— (1975c) 'Critical Marginal Notes on the Article by a Prussian', in K. Marx and F. Engels, *Collected Works (MECW)*, Volume 3, London: Lawrence and Wishart.

—— (1975d) *The German Ideology (MECW)*, Volume 5, London: Lawrence & Wishart.

—— (1976) *Capital Volume 1*, Harmondsworth: Penguin.

—— (1978) *Capital Volume 2*, Harmondsworth: Penguin.

—— (1981) *Capital Volume 3*, Harmondsworth: Penguin.

—— (1986a) *The Grundrisse (MECW)*, Volume 28, London: Lawrence & Wishart.

—— (1986b) *The Civil War in France (MECW)*, Volume 22, London: Lawrence & Wishart.

Marx, K. and Engels, F. (1976) *The Communist Manifesto (MECW)*, Volume 6, London: Lawrence & Wishart.

Murray, P. (1988) *Marx's Theory of Scientific Knowledge*, London: Humanities Press.

Negri, A. (1991) *Marx Beyond Marx*, London: Pluto.

Ollman, B. (1993) *Dialectical Investigations*, London: Routledge.

Pashukanis, E. (1978) *Law and Marxism*, London: Pluto.

Picciotto, S. (1991) 'The Internationalisation of Capital and the International State System', in S. Clarke (ed.), *The State Debate*, London: Macmillan.

Rosdolsky, R. (1977) *The Making of Marx's Capital*, London: Pluto.

Rosenberg, J. (1994) *The Empire of Civil Society*, London: Verso.

Sklar, M. (1988) *The Corporate Reconstruction of American Capitalism, 1890–1916*, Cambridge: Cambridge University Press.

Smith, H. (1996) 'The Silence of the Academics: International Social Theory, Historical Materialism and Political Values', *Review of International Studies*, 22, 2.

Thorndike, T. (1978) 'The Revolutionary Approach: the Marxist Perspective', in T. Taylor (ed.), *Approaches and Theory in International Relations*, London: Longman.

Turner, M. (1980) *English Parliamentary Enclosure*, Folkestone: Dawson.

Wallerstein, I. (1984) *The Politics of the World-Economy*, Cambridge: Cambridge University Press.

Witheford, N. (1994) 'Autonomist Marxism and the Information Society', *Capital and Class*, 52.

Wood, E. Meiksins (1981) 'The Separation of the Economic and the Political in Capitalism', *New Left Review*, 127: 66–95.

7 Historical materialism and the emancipation of labour

Kees van der Pijl

My argument in this chapter is that historical materialism, as a synthesis between idealism and (naturalistic) materialism, only in our own era is becoming an organic, rather than 'artificial', 'willed', mode of social consciousness. The socialist labour movement, as a movement of manual workers committed to overturning the rule of capital, certainly was Marxist in name and inspiration. However, in hindsight, it must be considered a preliminary phenomenon – the left wing of the bourgeois democratic movement against clerical-monarchical rule rather than the main force of something new. For the greater part of the period between Marx's lifetime and today, what passed for historical materialism was actually naturalistic materialism, the idea that everything including ideas is a manifestation of physical forces ('matter'). The Marxism of the Second International as well as Soviet Marxism, to name only the main currents, are illustrative here.

It took until well into the twentieth century before mental and manual labour achieved the degree of integration, and the common form as wage labour for capital, on which the assimilation of historical materialism is premised. Today, the objective conditions for an understanding of society's creative capacity to shape its own destiny are becoming reality; just as the globalisation of the discipline of capital is bringing to light the limits of society's present course.

Naturalistic materialism emerged (in sixteenth- and early seventeenth-century Western Europe) when the emancipation of manual labour intersected with the transformation of contemplative philosophy into experimental natural science. Materialism indeed may be considered the organic perspective arising out of the initial encounter between emancipating physical labour and practical philosophy – in industry. The idea that everything social and political derives from the transformation of nature will come most naturally to people engaged in this process themselves.

Idealism, on the other hand, which holds that all aspects of reality derive their substance, meaning, and tendency from mental forces ('spirit'), would be more akin to those engaged in intellectual functions – in church and state, or any other context in which, usually by reference to some legitimating principle, a unit of social cohesion has to be 'managed' and 'planned'. In other words, for those whose encounter with social forces striving for emancipation poses problems of a managerial nature from which the element of a shared experience, as in the case of natural science and labour in industry, is absent.

Of course, elaborating either materialism or idealism into theoretical systems was always the work of intellectuals. But as Gramsci notes (1971: 389), while idealist tendencies in Marxism were the work mainly of 'pure' intellectuals, materialism has been strongest among intellectuals 'more markedly dedicated to practical activity and therefore more closely linked ... to the great popular masses'. Only when the managerial perspective merges with the productive one in what Sohn-Rethel (1973) calls 'social synthesis', and mental and manual labour are reunified into the 'collective worker' as a result of the socialisation of labour (Marx's *Vergesellschaftung*), the social setting for the assimilation of historical materialism really crystallised. Let us trace the main outlines of this history, beginning with the origins of modern naturalistic materialism and its relation to the emancipation of labour.

Natural science and the emancipation of manual labour

Materialism as such was already formulated in the abstract by the Greeks of Antiquity. Thus Democritus, in Bertrand Russell's rendition (1961: 89), maintained that 'the soul was composed of atoms, and thought was a physical process. There was no purpose in the universe; there were only atoms governed by mechanical laws.'

However, throughout Greek-Hellenistic civilisation, civic life was still entirely divorced from physical labour. Its social ideal was contemplation, which was primarily ethical and aesthetical – the quest for the good and the beautiful. Labour was the slaves' predicament. 'Thinking' therefore stood in a relation of straight antinomy to 'work'. This remained so until the rise of Christianity in the Roman Empire, when in the early monasteries, religious men and women began to earn their own living with manual labour after the eastern example. In the course of the European Middle Ages, there emerged an organic, corporatist concept of society in which a mutual dependence of knowledge and labour replaced their dualistic opposition.

This new concept of society, which is associated with Thomas Aquinas (†1274), arose in conjunction with the guild organisation of trades and crafts. The guilds over the next few centuries became the vehicles for advancing the interests of their members in the context of municipal government. The process of social emancipation of manual labour now becomes irreversible, and the world of work begins to be reflected on in a critique of the 'non-productive' idleness of the feudal upper classes. In the humanist utopias of Thomas More (†1535), Campanella (†1639), and Johannes Andreae (†1654), the ethical ideal is projected on the world of productive activity, interpreted as the opposite of the frivolities of the feudal rulers and their greed for wealth (Meeus 1989: 44–5).

At this juncture, a paradigmatic shift of perspective occurred when Galileo (†1642), in the attempt to verify the revolutionary hypotheses of Copernicus about the orbits of the planets, began to use self-made instruments, such as the telescope, in an active mode of research that involved observation and experiment. 'Labour', physical effort, now was made part of thinking, leaving behind purely contemplative thought. 'The classical hierarchy of *vita contemplativa* and *vita activa* thus was overturned, but also the hierarchy within the *vita activa*, in which language and being active (*praxis*) had towered high over vulgar bodily labour' (Meeus 1989: 48). The new pragmatic activism, which reoriented thought towards the practical improvement of human life, was generalised into a materialist doctrine by Francis Bacon (†1626).

Thomas Hobbes, who was Bacon's assistant before he went to Florence to see Galileo, systematised Bacon's materialism. In the process, however, he demarcated it sharply from the realm of the metaphysical; he also argued, obsessed as he was with civil disturbance, that speculation about metaphysical questions was politically seditious.

> The Light of humane minds is Perspicuous Words, but by exact definitions first snuffed, and purged from ambiguity; *Reason* is the *pace*; Encrease of *Science*, the *way*; and the Benefit of man-kind, *the end*. And on the contrary, Metaphors, and senslesse and ambiguous words, are like *ignes fatui*; and reasoning upon them, is wandering amongst innumerable absurdities; and their end, contention, and sedition, or contempt.
>
> (Hobbes 1968: 116–17)

According to Engels, Hobbes 'sacrificed the physical movement to the mechanical and the mathematical; geometry is proclaimed as the chief science' (*MEW* 22: 293). Applied science left metaphysics alone and adopted an agnostic perspective. As a result, it was possible that highly religious men such as Isaac Newton could apply the new-found principles of inquiry of the material world without reservation – also because it was actively encouraged from above. This happened through the Royal Society set up after the Restoration (and of which Newton and Boyle were members), in order to improve agriculture, manufacture, navigation, medicine, etc., and also through the Anglican church. Sprat, the bishop of Rochester, subscribed even to the goal of 'liberation of humanity from the clusters of misconceptions' – on one condition: that God and the soul would remain exempt from scientific inquiry (Trevelyan 1961: 289–90). Locke, too, settled for agnosticism when he stated that it is not man's concern to know everything, but to know those things that matter to his practical life (quoted in Meeus 1989: 49). Thus scientific endeavour became organically related to labour while its materialist assumptions were politically neutralised.

The class of manual labourers that was formed in the industrial revolution developed a consciousness of itself on the terrain prepared by the *Magna Carta* and Locke – a tradition of native liberty, guild loyalty, and self-regulation against the encroaching state. It shared the practical materialism of the philosophers and inventors, but did not find in materialism a ready doctrine that would further orient its emancipation politically. In the 1790s, following the revolution in France, 'the ambiguities of Locke seem[ed] to fall into two halves, one Burke, the other Paine' (Thompson 1968: 100). Yet the democratic radicalism of the Painite variety, too, placed self-regulation before everything else and was closer to the manufacturing bourgeois than to the worker (ibid.: 104).

Materialism accordingly did not become a revolutionary doctrine in England – also because the early separation from the church of Rome and subsequent protestantism reduced the clerical-conservative aspect of state power. Skilled machinists were taught by adult education courses and widely read professional magazines; at London University (established in 1827), science figured prominently in the curriculum, while theology, in contrast to Oxford and Cambridge, was not taught at all (Trevelyan 1961: 524-5). However, the pervasive Lockean tradition with its separation of state and society, politics and economics, militated against broadening the synthesis of applied science and manual labour. Craft workers' struggles against machine production and the backlash produced in England by the French Revolution combined to push the working class on the defensive. 'The twenty-five years after 1795 may be seen as the years of a long counter-revolution, and in consequence the Radical movement remained largely working-class in character, with an advanced democratic populism as its theory' (Thompson 1968: 888).

This balance of forces allowed the British manufacturing bourgeoisie to impose, within the broader liberal setting, a harsh regime on the workers. Bentham, Ure and others, writing in the 1820s and 1830s, developed theories centring on *discipline* as they elaborated patterns of labour organisation grafted on the subordination of man to machine. But discipline was not a state task; it fell to the factory-owner himself, whose tasks accordingly required him to be 'a man of Napoleonic nerve and ambition' (Ure quoted in Meeus 1989: 126).

In France on the other hand, the unity between state and church (while demarcating itself from Rome under Richelieu) did retain the original feudal-clerical nexus. Here the state found itself in the position of a collective social subject, driving forward the social development which in England proceeded, after 1688, by legal rather than executive state support. Certainly the transformation towards an experimental, empirical natural science took place in France, too. But an understanding like the one between the Anglican Church and the new natural science here was impossible because of the tight imbrication of state power, the feudal order and the religious monopoly of the Gallican Church. Therefore the new thinking in France retained a claim to universality, exemplified in the rationalism of Descartes (†1650); while simultaneously containing the practical-empirical aspects of the thinking of his English contemporaries, Bacon and Hobbes.

In the system of Descartes, the rational mind is sharply distinguished from the material world. Instead of relegating the moment of rationality to the practical world of experience, as happened in England, rationality is universalised into a comprehensive category. Materialism (the mechanical operation of forces in space, including the human body) in the mirror of this comprehensive rationality equally pertains to all aspects of life. In England, the technical rationality of the engineer and the material world of production were joined in the industrial revolution; in France, the world of production presents itself as a concern of the state. As Lefebvre argues (1976: 29), the French state and its *raison d'Etat*, shaped in the seventeenth century under the Cardinals and Louis XIV, and philosophical rationalism, mutually conditioned each other. Typically, Descartes held that by applying the new natural science, the craftsman's knowledge would become a *public* possession, too (Meeus 1989: 49).

The emancipation of labour in eighteenth-century France required that the workers be liberated from the guilds, which had become obstacles to further development. They 'confined labor, production and sale of commodities to licensed corporations with their own internal monopoly of training, goods and services' (Schama 1990: 85). French materialism offered a programme including this liberation along with the liberation of all other aspects of life. Thus Holbach, one of the most explicit materialists, in 1770 wrote that

> the source of many evils visiting mankind everywhere must be sought in the misconceptions and the religious imaginations. The gods emerged out of the ignorance about natural causes. ... No less dangerous are the prejudices that have turned people blind to their governments. The real foundations of rule were entirely unknown to the peoples.
>
> (Holbach 1971: 72–3)

In the same spirit, Voltaire in 1776 published a critique of religion, *La Bible enfin expliquée*, a signal subject also for later materialists.

François Quesnay (†1774), one of the contributors to the *Encyclopédie* (which among other things made the guilds' craft secrets public), offered a materialist economic doctrine distinguishing between productive (essentially, agricultural) and non-productive activity. Physiocrat economics was premised on *laissez-faire*, and advocated a free labour market against the mercantilism of Colbert and the feudal world of the guilds on which it was grafted. Turgot, one of the Physiocrats, as minister of Louis XVI on the eve of the Revolution, in vain attempted to dissolve the guilds and eliminate feudal labour duties.

However, in the French Revolution, the workers' interest had not yet differentiated itself from that of the bourgeoisie. The doctrine of the Rights of Man tended to appeal to all citizens belonging to the 'productive classes' as well as to the radicalised aristocrats of whom Holbach was a representative. Indeed the political culture of France until recent times has remained deeply bourgeois – characterised by individuality and subjectivity, as well as by a pervasive, atheist materialism. As in England, the French working class and the democratic movement at large developed their basic orientation before Marxism could make an impact. The fact that 'industry' in France long retained a typical craft and small workshop association, with the strong state the dominant, constraining social force, favoured Proudhon's anti-authoritarian socialism and anarchism among the workers (Abendroth 1972: 34–5).

By its effective confiscation of society, the French state towered over this (petty) bourgeois universe as collective rationality incarnate. The Cartesian articulation between rationalism and materialism was embodied in the engineer-state theorised by Saint-Simon (Therborn 1980: 117–18). While the Anglo-Saxon empirical tradition and its Lockean universe spread throughout the English-speaking world along with its expansion as a capitalist heartland, the rational engineer-state model evolved into the norm for those societies which resisted peripheralisation by state-led industrialisation. In these societies, progressive theorising tended to evolve within the matrix set by the French example. That is, rationalism relating to or even identified with the state (actual or future); and anti-clerical materialism animating a modern, 'developmental' view of the world. But this type of thinking, rationalist and materialist, occurred in a more backward social setting precluding the type of synthesis achieved in France, let alone the synthesis between idealism and materialism wrought by Marx.

Under these conditions, the moment of 'rationality' becomes an entirely idealist construction. As Gramsci notes (1971: 115–16), 'What is practice for the fundamental class becomes "rationality" and speculation for its intellectuals' – Kant, Hegel, Croce, or Pitirim Sorokin. On the other hand, materialism emerges as its counterpoint, equally radical but in unproductive antinomy to it. Thus in Germany, materialism emerged in the 1830s with a burst of analyses of religion in the spirit of Holbach and Voltaire – Strauss's *Life of Jesus*, Bruno Bauer's *Critique of the Synoptic Gospels*, and Ludwig Feuerbach's *Essence of Christianity* (see Therborn 1973: 7). These men, too, were progressive intellectuals but without a mass following. The industrial revolution picked up seriously only after unification, in the 1870s. And as Kuczynski writes (1949: 137), it was made from above, by the state, while the different modern classes (bourgeoisie and workers) 'dangled at the tail of this development, instead of driving it forward'.

Feuerbach did develop naturalistic materialism further, though. Thus he provided democratic militants with a compelling doctrine that seemed to point beyond the 'critical' confusion of tongues among Hegelians. A theology student drawn into radical political clubs during his studies of Hegel and natural science, Feuerbach's work on Christianity is not just a political tract. It is a scholarly treatise on how ideas emerge from the material foundations of life. Thinking in Feuerbach's view is merely the highest form of a general principle in nature, that of *reflection*. Not unlike fire reflects the qualities of wood as it burns, mental images reflect the qualities of their object (Biedermann 1986: 39–40). Applied to religion, the belief in God is argued to be the (unconscious) exteriorisation of the essence of man, a reflective enlargement of primitive self-consciousness (Feuerbach 1971: 76).

This was the materialism that was adopted by the progressive classes, both bourgeoisie and workers, in early nineteenth-century Germany. Further to the east, not only the bourgeoisie was lacking; states were often incompetent in carrying out a comparable revolution from above. This turned the democratic intellectuals into champions of capitalist industrialisation. First an industrial society had to emerge, before, on its foundations, a more just order could be erected. Certainly Marxism now had become an ideological force, but it was paradoxically adopted as a 'doctrine of modernisation' (e.g. in Lenin's attacks on the Narodnik populists). Indeed in Russia, as Gramsci noted in an article of 1917,

> Marx's *Capital* was more the book of the bourgeoisie than of the proletariat. It stood as the critical demonstration of how events should follow a predetermined course: how in Russia a bourgeoisie had to develop, and a capitalist era had to open, with the setting-up of a Western-type of civilization, before the proletariat could even think in terms of its own revolt, its own class demands, its own revolution.
>
> (Gramsci 1977: 34)

Marx of course developed his historical materialism as a critique of Feuerbach, both in the famous 'Theses' and, with Engels, in other works. Historical materialism is defined primarily in opposition to the naturalistic materialism of Hobbes, Holbach, and Feuerbach. Since, as I have indicated already, the mainstream Marxist labour movements have all tended to confuse the two, let me briefly sum up the differences, in particular on the issue of epistemology, the theory of knowledge ('where do ideas come from?').

Marxist versus materialist epistemology

In his critique of Feuerbach's theory of religion, Marx argues that the particular, historical society in which people live constitutes the source of religious projections; not some naturalistic 'essence' of man. This goes to the heart of the difference between the physicalist epistemology of naturalistic materialism and the social-historical one of Marx and Engels. In the words of the Dutch Marxist, Anton Pannekoek, 'the fundamental tenet of materialism that the spiritual is determined by the material world, means something completely different in the two doctrines'.

> To bourgeois materialism it means that ideas are the product of the brain, to be explained from the structure and the transformations of brain matter, and hence, ultimately, from the dynamics of the atoms in the brain. To historical materialism, it means that the ideas of man are determined by social circumstances; society is the environment which through his senses impresses itself on him.
>
> (Pannekoek n.d.: 25)

People never face nature as happens in a physics laboratory (and since Heisenberg we know that even there they don't passively 'face' it). Primitive man, when confronted, say, with lightning, at the same time experiences a supernatural phenomenon which is part of a social construction of reality. When we deal with electricity today, it is likewise part of a broader social and economic reality, including a life-style aspect which in its magical connotations is surprisingly close to man's myth-enclosed past. At any rate, a whole set of social arrangements is folded into the electric power that reaches the individual. The 'economies' which support each of the steps by which electricity reaches energy consumers, are likewise implicated in the socket they plug into (I intentionally use terms from Bohm 1983 such as enfolding and implication, which in my view are part of an epistemology akin to historical materialism but derived from modern physics). Society is nature transformed by labour, and in modern society, we have no other way of confronting nature than in its social forms. Therefore, as Ilyenkov writes (1982: 127), 'socio-historical properties of things very often merge in the eyes of the individual with their natural properties, while transitory properties of things and of man himself begin to seem eternal properties bound with the very essence of things'.

From the different relationships between the material and the spiritual, different concepts of science are derived as well. Along with the development of tools, people train their physical and mental capacities in order to respond adequately to their environment. Science, the chief product of thinking, thus becomes a productive force in its own right, but of course always as part of an entire configuration of social arrangements, collective beliefs, and conventions – never in a straight, unmediated confrontation with nature. To quote Pannekoek again,

> Historical materialism considers the work of science, its concepts, contents, laws and forces of nature principally as creations of the spiritual labour of man, even if they owe their emergence to nature. Bourgeois materialism, on the contrary, considers all this (seen from the scientific viewpoint) as elements of nature itself, which are merely discovered and brought to light by science.
>
> (Pannekoek n.d.: 26)

Historical materialism therefore cannot be applied in a positivistic way, which assumes that the mind registers, by reflection or otherwise, what nature holds up to it. Both knowledge and 'material reality' are part of a comprehensive process of interactive movement; the stage of positive knowledge of a fixed reality external to the 'observer' according to historical materialism simply cannot be reached.

The persistence of materialism in the labour movement

As indicated above, when Marxism became available as a doctrine for the labour movement, the English (including English-speaking North American etc.), French, and some smaller national democratic movements already had largely developed their basic outlook. But even in Germany during Marx's lifetime, the budding labour movement almost by necessity placed its hopes on what the state could offer it; notably the tendency represented by Lassalle. Because the late-industrialising contender state historically constitutes itself as the architect of social development, substituting for autonomous social forces, these forces in turn tend to see their own fate through the prism of state intervention (Marx in his *Critique of the Gotha Programme* made sufficiently clear what he thought of this strategy, but he paradoxically was a lone voice in the movement claiming to follow him).

After Marx's death, it fell on Friedrich Engels to explain Marx's often difficult and certainly incomplete intellectual legacy to a new generation of labour leaders. The rapidly growing workers' parties and trade unions faced the task of developing a trained cadre who could handle the day-to-day problems of the industrial workers as well as place their struggles in historical perspective, and they turned to Engels for guidance. Against the backdrop of a veritable 'second industrial revolution' in Germany, interacting with spectacular advances in natural science, Engels tended to emphasise the materialist side of Marx to the point of subordinating the second element, dialectics (to which I will turn presently). In his notes and editorial approach to the later volumes of *Capital* he saw to press, or in the *Anti-Dühring* (a popularised, didactic polemic intended to provide an overview of historical materialism), Engels tended to consider dialectics as an aspect of objective, material reality, reflected in the human mind as dialectical thinking. Also, his interpretation of some of the new mathematics and natural science in formal-dialectical terms (penetration of opposites, transformation of quantity into quality, etc.), while unsuccessful and often tried as a thought experiment only, was received as codified Marxism (van Erp 1982: 80–1).

The labour leaders, involved in the same social development but also keen on simplification and concerned to offer the workers a doctrine close to their direct experiences, in their correspondence with Engels encouraged this naturalistic-materialist tendency. Mehring and Kautsky in Germany, Plechanov in Russia, and Labriola in Italy, all corresponded with Engels (Anderson 1978: 16), and his letters in the 1890s (more particularly those to Bloch, Schmidt and Borgius – see Engels 1972) indeed contain such famous statements as those on 'economic causation in the final instance' later elaborated on by Althusser.

Thus, pressed on the one hand by leaders concerned with practical organisational tasks, and in the setting of an industrial revolution deeply affecting a hitherto landed society, Engels in his concern to codify critical theory into doctrine tended to present a materialism more positive, objective, and obeying a compulsive logic, than anything Marx (and he himself in an earlier phase) had ever contemplated. However, as Avineri has argued (1968: 144):

> considering only the objective side of historical development and not its subjective elements, is open to all of Marx's criticism in his *Theses on Feuerbach*. ... Such a view ultimately sees in man and in human will only an object of external circumstances and, *mutatis mutandis*, of political manipulation.

For Labriola, this verdict is perhaps not justified (Gramsci contrasts him in this respect with Plekhanov, see Gramsci 1971: 386–7). But Kautsky's influence on German and European Marxism (he was the editor of Marx's *Theories of Surplus Value* and the author of a series of authoritative works, e.g. on agriculture) is plainly in the naturalistic-materialist tradition. Even before he shifted to a centrist political stand around 1910, Kautsky's thinking assumed an automatic process of (economic) transformation, in which the party was admonished to wait for events to come about (G. Fülberth in Kautsky 1972: xix). Kautsky actually rejects Bernstein's claim that there is a contradiction between Engels's last letters and the main body of Marxism. As evidence he (Kautsky) refers to the revised, 1894, edition of the *Anti-Dühring*. There Engels says that the root causes of all social changes and political transformations are to be found not in ideas or philosophy, but in the economy (see Kautsky 1974: 535–6).

This line of argument was also followed by the Marxist labour movement in Russia. Plekhanov's *Fundamental Problems of Marxism* of 1908 (which incidentally was inspired by Labriola but also includes a critique of the latter's 'idealist distortions') built straight on Feuerbach. It claimed that Marx and Engels 'completed' Feuerbach's materialism (Plekhanov 1969: 31; cf. Gramsci's judgement of Plekhanov as a 'vulgar materialist', 1971: 387). Lenin's *Materialism and Empirio-Criticism*, written also in 1908, placed Plekhanov, Engels, Feuerbach and Joseph Dietzgen in a single tradition (*Coll. Works* 14: 27). Although Lenin after the shock of August 1914 turned to the study of Hegel that led to the 'Philosophical Notebooks' and inspired works like his *Imperialism*, and all subsequent writings (cf. Löwy 1981: 72), the 1908 tract became the foundation Soviet Marxist orthodoxy. Actually it was only the translation and propagation abroad of *Materialism and Empirio-Criticism* in 1927 that prompted Pannekoek to write his critique, *Lenin as a Philosopher*.

In this booklet, Pannekoek demonstrates that Lenin, in his angry polemic against the founders and followers of neo-positivism (Mach and others), did not so much defend Marxism, but the materialism of Feuerbach (Pannekoek n.d.: 8, 65). As a trained physicist and professor of astronomy, Pannekoek easily demonstrated that Lenin in his argument with the new natural scientists had strayed far beyond his competence, confusing key concepts such as matter, energy, nature, and so on. One might indeed say that the pre-World War I generation of labour leaders which rose to prominence as Marxism spread further to the East (for all their differences, Lenin, Hilferding, Luxemburg, Trotsky, Preobrazhensky, and Bukharin – see Anderson 1978: 17) were equally influenced by modern industrial society and the new natural science that accompanied it. As a consequence they entrenched in a materialism (and a corollary positivistic scientism) which turns Marxism into a footnote to bourgeois economics.

This has remained the dominant tendency in Soviet and Western Marxism. Ernest Mandel in Belgium, considered by many the paramount representative of contemporary Marxism during his lifetime, most obviously pursued this line of analysis (1962, 1972). Louis Althusser (1965, 1974 – incidentally the French translator of Feuerbach) in turn developed a variety of Marxism which, its sometimes original language notwithstanding, is basically a rehash of the anti-utopian, positivistic, and naturalistic-materialist version of the Marxism of the 2nd and 3rd Internationals. Dialectics is absent from this interpretation, alienation considered a concept belonging to a youthful Marx still under the spell of pre-Marxist ideology.

My argument, which can only be formulated as a hypothesis here, would be that by its influence in academic circles, Althusserianism contributed to the restorative self-definition of the students as a separate class of intellectual workers in a way demarcating them from the workers with whom they rubbed shoulders in the May movement. However, dialectics, alienation/fetishism, etc., while legacies of idealist philosophy, are key components of Marxism. While in isolation, e.g. as managerial doctrine, contemporary idealism may generate such theoretical perspectives as systems theory (cf. van der Pijl 1998: chap. 5), in combination with a concept of class struggle and materialism it, on the contrary, can unify the perspectives of mental and manual workers, just as the original Marxism synthesises and transcends idealism with materialism.

Marxist versus idealist dialectics

Idealism, too, can be traced to Ancient Greek philosophy. Thus Anaxagoras maintained that mind, spirit, is the source of all motion, and governs all forms of life; it is 'infinite and self-ruled, and is mixed with nothing'. All other substances, however, are composites of opposites (hot/cold, white/black, etc. – Russell 1961: 80). Later Greek philosophers complained that Anaxagoras did not make clear *how* the mind moves, or relates to the world of opposites. Socrates, one of the critics, became famous for his view that ideas advance through question and answer, as we know through the dialogues recorded by Plato – *dialectics*.

In Chinese philosophy, notably in the neo-Confucianist synthesis wrought by Zhu Xi in the twelfth century, there is a comparable doctrine of mutually penetrating opposites in elementary matter, *qi*; which is also subject to a higher spiritual principle, *li*. Significantly, this version of Confucianism, which was hegemonic in the prosperous era from the fourteenth to the mid seventeenth centuries, was also the basis of the famous examination system by which Chinese state officials were selected (Bor *et al.* 1995: 145; cf. Giles 1915: 335–7).

In the European Enlightenment the problematic surfaced again when Immanuel Kant sought to synthesise the rigid separation between mind and matter made by Descartes and other rationalists, and the scepticism of Hume, with whom the mind was reduced to a rather untrustworthy registration device of sense experience. In the *Critique of Pure Reason* Kant argued in the rationalist tradition that the mind at birth is equipped with transcendent, pure reason (knowledge which exists without having been experienced, hence 'transcendent'). This reason allows experiences to be categorised. But partly conceding the sceptical counterargument, Kant held that reason cannot cover all aspects of reality, since reality ultimately remains beyond its reach as an object – a *thing-in-itself* (1975: 84ff.).

As Alfred Sohn-Rethel has argued (1973: 30), Kant's philosophy of knowledge is the first instance of a *theory of social synthesis*, that is, a theory in which all separate (mental) activities and elements of experience are understood as elements in an organically developing, functioning totality. Kant defined 'system' as an evolving totality, the 'unity of manifold knowledge under an idea' (1975: 839–40). This is the foundation for systems theory, the preeminent form of contemporary idealism. But as Sohn-Rethel rightly emphasises, the synthesis here still serves as the basis for the *separation* of mental from manual labour. Management theory as well as Weberian sociology are grafted on Kant's notion of how the mind processes the facts of experience into purposeful rationality. But management theory adds cybernetic regulation to Kant's idea of organic development, in that control serves to feed back experience into the process. 'Management endeavors to make purpose the equivalent of teleology, and thereby subordinate teleology to the experience regulated by purpose', Grundstein writes (1981: xix).

The limits of the intellect in Kant's perspective become apparent when it ventures into the realm of abstract totalities of thought, beyond what can be experienced – questions regarding the beginning and end of time, freedom versus determination, etc. When reason tries to answer questions like these, it stumbles on contradictions it cannot solve, 'antinomies' (ibid.: 463ff.). Yet Kant in one respect made a great stride towards historical materialism, at least if we follow Lucio Colletti, who argues (1973: 118) that Kant

> maintains the distinction between *real* conditions and *logical* conditions; so that, having recognized that thought is a *totality*, he considers it (precisely because the totality is only of *thought*) to be only *one* element or one part of the process of reality.

In other words, subjective idealism as such allows for the independent development of a reality beyond its control. Management theory in the same way acknowledges the fact that the reality it must direct obeys a logic of its own, hence the need for regulation; but at the same time it proceeds on the assumption of 'the fundament of human regulativeness' (Grundstein 1981: 1). It thus constructs an image of the relation between mental labour and manual labour based on the latter's surrendering its autonomy.

In the thinking of Hegel, Kant's perspective of (subjective) 'pure reason' guiding a reality ultimately beyond its grasp is transcended by placing historical, creative humanity at the centre of an evolving totality. For Hegel, the limitation of the grasp of the mind to what can be experienced is unacceptable. In his thinking, reality is entirely subsumed under the 'mind', indeed a *World Spirit* acting through, and realised in, the restless pursuit of knowledge by historical mankind. Marx appreciated the fact that Hegel conceived of history as the *result of a labour process* – even though this labour process was still one-sidedly conceived as a process of mental labour. The greatness of Hegel's *Phenomenology* and its end-results – the dialectics of negativity as the dynamic and generative principle – therefore comes down to Hegel's conception of the self-education of man as a process, the objectification as juxtaposition, as exteriorisation and suspension of this exteriorisation; that he, therefore, grasps the essence of *labour* and understands the objective human being ... as a result of its *own labour.*

Marx wrote in the 'Economic-Philosophical Manuscripts' of 1844.

> Hegel adopts the viewpoint of modern national economists. He grasps *labour* as the *essence*, as the self-affirming essence of the human being; he only sees the positive side of labour, not its negative side. Labour is the *actualisation* [*Fürsichwerden*] of the human being within the *exteriorisation*, or the *exteriorised* human being. [But] the only labour which Hegel knows and recognises is *abstract, spiritual* labour.
>
> (*MEW Ergänz.Bd.* 1: 574)

For Hegel, the fact that the mind runs into contradiction when it tries to answer the great existential questions of ultimate reality does not mean that reality is unknowable, on the contrary. That which lies at the other end of what is perceived by the senses according to Hegel is also a product of thought – what else could it be?

'These very things, which are supposed to stand on the other extreme beyond our thought, are themselves things of the mind ... the so-called thing-in-itself is only a mental figment of empty abstraction', he says in the *Science of Logic* (which I quote here from the excerpts in Lenin 1973: 83). Contradiction to Hegel is not a borderland of thought where we should not venture, but the essence of being. '*All things are in themselves contradictory*', Hegel writes. Contradiction should be recognised as the essence of things, from which their rationality can be grasped in the context of a comprehensive conceptual system.

> Compared to it, identity is merely the determination of the simply immediate, the dead being; [contradiction] however is the *source of all movement and liveliness*; only insofar as something contains a contradiction within itself, *it moves, has drive and activity.*
>
> (Lenin 1973: 128–9, emphases by Lenin)

Hegel's aim was to transcend the Cartesian dualism of mind and matter, and show that everything obeys an objective rationality which is eventually realised in human civilisation, the World Spirit concretised. 'What is rational, is real, and what is real, is rational' (Hegel 1972: 11; cf. Kojève 1968: 44). Hegel rehabilitates the principle of dialectics as a principle of development (rather than something out of bounds for rational thought). Consciousness 'progresses from the first unmediated confrontation between itself and the object, to absolute knowledge', he writes (Lenin's excerpt, 1973: 88). However, this process is largely predetermined. 'History' is like a systemic, organic process of growth, its final shape programmed by the DNA contained in the primordial 'World Spirit'. 'Reason governs the world, and history accordingly must have run its course rationally', he states in the *Philosophy of History* (1961: 48–9), the posthumous lectures in which he traces the course of rational freedom from ancient China to the Europe of his days.

The historical materialist concept of dialectics has taken this Hegelian interpretation of a 'system' evolving historically through the sustained human effort to transcend contradiction. However, it has added a 'materialist' counterpoint by interpreting this system as an open-ended succession of types of human society each structured around a particular labour process. Marxist dialectics thus includes: *first*, the argument that humanity does not face nature in contemplation, but practically, in the social labour process, and thus creates its own 'material' conditions of existence. This relates to the 'enfolding' of material nature in society referred to above. The epistemological inference here is, again, that there can be no static, positive knowledge of a fixed reality external to the 'observer' because subject and object are part of an evolving totality. Therefore, as the 11th Thesis on Feuerbach holds, unlike philosophers *interpreting* the world differently, people should set themselves the task of changing it; not as a moral imperative, but because that is how they relate to the world anyway.

Second, the assumption of the materiality of contradiction, i.e. the conflicting social forces involved in the development of society. The basic contradiction between humanity and nature (which mankind is part of *and* separate from) socially evolves through class struggles. With increasing social control over the forces of nature, the need to keep exploited classes in a state close to nature is lessened, their horizon widened, and emancipation may advance accordingly. Class struggles in historical materialism mediate all causation or determination – there is no way in which abstractions such as the 'economic' or the 'political' can operate but through people's active involvement (however motivated) in these struggles.

Third, while the world-view of every ruling class claims universality for itself, in practice it covers a reality riven by social conflict. Every society tends to produce a particular, historically determined and hence transitory idealisation of itself, from which the real contradictions are argued away. This was how Marx approached Hegel's theory of the state (supposedly the embodiment of the general interest), but also the theories of political economy of Smith, Ricardo and their followers, who tended to analyse capitalism as a basically harmonious, self-equilibrating market system composed of free, equal and equally self-interested individuals. But as Marx writes, under the surface, 'in the depths, entirely different processes go on, in which this apparent individual equality and liberty disappear' (1973: 247).

Historical materialism and collective labour

The conditions under which Marxism was originally formulated included its author's philosophical training and participation in the main debates in

Germany, as well as his political activity in the progressive Rhineland; his exile in France with its rich political tradition including socialism; and finally, his studies of political economy in the country of the industrial revolution, England. This has been noted often enough. Above, I have indicated why the actual labour movement, if it adhered to an explicit philosophical position at all, more often adopted naturalistic materialism than Marx's historical materialism because manual labour in combination with experimental natural science was conducive to that perspective. On the other hand, classical German idealism also developed concepts of labour, but then, *mental* labour – with Kant, in what would turn out to be a managerial perspective, and in Hegel, a historical one, be it history within a rationalist construction.

Therefore, if historical materialism is the synthesis between these two traditions, we may assume that the reunification of mental and manual labour constitutes a crucial condition of historical materialism becoming an organic mode of thinking for those striving for the emancipation of labour from the discipline of capital. Sohn-Rethel's theory of 'social synthesis' is particularly apposite here.

The twentieth century is the century of the spread, along with capital itself, of a technocratic-managerial class of paid functionaries, the 'cadres' (Duménil and Lévy 1998). This class of cadres, as I have argued elsewhere (1998: chap. 5), arises in the process of capitalist socialisation, or *Vergesellschaftung*. By this concept, Marx means that the social labour process turns the elements of production (raw nature, human beings, tools, and knowledge) into collective, social arrangements which in turn structure and renovate the labour process itself. The division between mental and manual labour *and their necessary reunification* is one form of socialisation, and the parcellisation of tasks in both domains (always aimed at reunifying them under the discipline of capital) has progressed dramatically in the century now being closed. Work no longer requires the integral mobilisation of the capacities of design and execution; it becomes social in the sense of partial – shared with present and past social labour (Marx 1973: 832). *Vergesellschaftung*, then, includes:

> The conscious technical utilisation of science, the planned exploitation of the earth, the economisation of all means of production by their use as means of production of combined, social labour, the devouring of all peoples in the net of the world market and with it, the international nature of the capitalist regime.
>
> (*MEW* 23: 790)

The element of alienation, the 'exteriorisation of the human being in labour' (implying loss of autonomy) that Marx speaks of in the Economic-Philosophical Manuscripts referred to earlier, is inherent in the form of free exchange and creates the need for a cadre acting to impose the discipline of capital. The *collective worker* of which Marx speaks, in fact is riven by class-like antagonisms required by disciplinary subordination under the 'alien' force of private capital.

In the 1920 and 1930s, the gradual rise of a cadre of qualified technicians, managers, and clerical personnel led to a qualitative change in the organisation of large-scale industry and advanced capitalist society, captured by the notion of the 'managerial revolution'. In the New Deal by which the United States responded to the deflationary crisis of the late 1920s, early 1930s, managerialism and the large corporation capable of making economic concessions to the workers on account of rising productivity indeed seemed to triumph over the more classical pattern of owner-manager capitalism. However, the scientific management from which the managers derive their power is premised on the strict separation of mental and manual labour. Nevertheless, the fact that managers, too, are employees of capital, 'proletarianised' so to speak (even if, usually, very comfortably so), creates a totally new situation. Sohn-Rethel says of this transformation that 'this tendential identity of form between manual and intellectual labour clearly is a development of tremendous impact ... [it consti-tutes] the hidden source and focus of articulation of the transformation process in which contemporary society finds itself' (1973: 21).

Indeed we may say that from this moment on, all political development revolves around the question how the mutual relation between the cadres and the workers will develop in the context of class struggles elicited by the imposi-tion of the discipline of capital on society – in prosperity and in crisis, in peace and war. The significance of the students' and workers' movements culminating in 'May 68' in my view is that in this episode, for the first time, the themes of alienation, the collective worker, and the role of autonomy in overturning the discipline of capital and the state gained widespread popular resonance.

All idealisms represent, albeit in a distorted way, a real state of affairs and hence cannot simply be rejected and discarded, as the naturalistic materialists do. Thus the World Spirit of Hegel is recognised by Marx as something which indeed 'transcends living individuality and buries it under itself ...'. What Hegel expresses is a 'real idealism of capital, in which a derivative becomes the original and unfolds its own law of motion' (H. Reichelt, preface to Hegel 1972: xliii, xxx). Today's neoliberal dogma, which keeps society on its course of planetary disaster, is the contemporary form of such a World Spirit. 'Globalisation' accord-ingly is not just a mirage. It is an idealisation of the global discipline of capital; something which has come about after a protracted series of defeats for those resisting that discipline, not because God, human nature or History prescribe it. Indeed in Gramsci's words, 'what the idealists call "spirit" is not a point of departure but a point of arrival, it is the ensemble of superstructures moving towards concrete and objectively universal unification and it is not a unitary presupposition' (1971: 446).

The dialectical critique contained in historical materialism confronts all self-idealisations by contrasting them with the real contradictions – as in today's globalised world, the exhaustive effects of the discipline of capital on society and the biosphere. In the process, critical theory gravitates into a field of force where it encounters social forces actually resisting this exhaustive discipline. Of course in the final analysis it then depends on the quality and timeliness of the argument and the political talent of all involved whether theory under those conditions can become an integral part of the forces of resistance and social transformation. However, history itself, as the sum total of social struggles through which humanity's metabolism with nature evolves, inevitably renders obsolete any rigid doctrine, entrenched political posture, or fixed utopia. As Engels wrote in this connection,

> all that is real in the sphere of human history becomes irrational in the process of time, and is therefore irrational by its very destination ... and everything which is rational in the minds of men is destined to become real, however much it may contradict existing apparent reality.
>
> (Engels quoted in Stedman Jones 1973: 19–20)

Bibliography

Abendroth, W. (1972) *Sociale geschiedenis van de Europese arbeidersbeweging*, trans. P. Bimmel, Nijmegen: SUN [1965].

Althusser, L. (1965) *Pour Marx*, Paris: Maspero.

—— (1974) *Antwoord aan John Lewis*, trans. T. Volger, Nijmegen: SUN.

Anderson, P. (1978) *Over het westers marxisme*, trans. H. van der Kooy, Amsterdam: Van Gennep [1976].

Avineri, S. (1968) *The Social and Political Thought of Karl Marx*, Cambridge: Cambridge University Press.

Biedermann, G. (1986) *Ludwig Andreas Feuerbach*, Köln: Pahl-Rugenstein.

Bohm, D. (1983) *Wholeness and the Implicate Order*, London and New York: Ark Books [1980].

Bor, J., Petersma, E. and Kingma, J. (eds) (1995) *De verbeelding van het denken. Geïllustreerde geschiedenis van de westerse en oosterse filosofie*, Amsterdam and Antwerpen: Contact.

Colletti, L. (1973) *Marxism and Hegel*, trans. L. Garner, London: NLB [1969].

Duménil, G. and Lévy, D. (1998) *Au-dela du capitalisme?*, Paris: Presses universitaires françaises.

Engels, F. (1972) 'Vier brieven over de materialistische geschiedsopvatting', *Te Elfder Ure*, 19(3/4): 117–29.

Erp, H. van (1982) *Het kapitaal tussen illusie en werkelijkheid. Dialektiek en histories realisme bij Marx*, Nijmegen: SUN.

Feuerbach, L. (1971) 'Religion als Selbstentfremdung des Menschen' [from *Das Wesen des Christentums*, 1841], in K. Lenk (ed.), *Ideologie. Ideologie und Wissenssoziologie*, Neuwied and Berlin: Luchterhand [5th edn, 1961].

Giles, H.A. (1915) *Confucianism and its Rivals* [Hibbert Lectures 1914], London: Williams & Norgate.

Gramsci, A. (1971) *Selections from the Prison Notebooks*, Q. Hoare and G.N. Smith (eds), New York: International Publishers.

—— (1977) *Selections from Political Writings 1910–1920*, Q. Hoare (ed.), New York: International Publishers.

Grundstein, N.D. (1981) *The Managerial Kant: The Kant Critiques and the Managerial Order*, Cleveland, OH: Case Western Reserve University Press.

Hegel, G.W.F. (1961) *Vorlesungen über die Philosophie der Geschichte*, Stuttgart: Reclam [1837].

146   *Kees van der Pijl*

—— (1972) *Grundlinien der Philosophie des Rechts*, intro. by H. Reichelt, Frankfurt: Ullstein [1821].

Hobbes, T. (1968) *Leviathan*, intro. C.B. Macpherson, Harmondsworth: Penguin [1651].

Holbach, P.T. de (1971) 'Die Funktion religiöser Vorstellungen' [from *Système de la nature*, etc., 1770], in K. Lenk (ed.), *Ideologie. Ideologie und Wissenssoziologie*, Neuwied and Berlin: Luchterhand [5th edn, 1961].

Ilyenkov, E.V. (1982) *The Dialectics of the Abstract and the Concrete in Marx's 'Capital'*, trans. S. Syrovatkin, Moscow: Progress [1960].

Kant, I. (1975) *Kritik der reinen Vernunft*, Stuttgart: Reclam [1781].

Kautsky, K. (1972) *Der Weg zur Macht*, ed. and intro. by G. Fülberth, Frankfurt/M: Europäische Verlagsanstalt [1909].

—— (1974) 'Bernsteins kritiek op de methode van het marxisme', trans. J.F. Ankersmit [1901] *Te Elfder Ure*, 21(3): 525–53.

Kojève, A. (1968) *Introduction à la lecture de Hegel*, Paris: Gallimard [1947].

Kuczynski, J. (1949) *Die Geschichte der Lage der Arbeider in Deutschland. Band I: 1800 bis 1932*, Berlin: Freie Gewerkschaft.

Lefebvre, H. (1976) *Théorie marxiste de l'Etat de Hegel à Mao*, vol. II of *De l'Etat*, Paris: Ed. Générales 10/18.

Lenin, V.I. *Collected Works*, Moscow: Progress (1960–5).

—— (1973) *Philosophische Hefte*, Vol. 38 of *Werke* Edition, Berlin: Dietz.

Löwy, M. (1981) *The Politics of Combined and Uneven Development*, London: Verso.

Mandel, E. (1962) *Traité d'économie marxiste*, Paris: Ed. Générales 10/18, 4 vols.

—— (1972) *Der Spätkapitalismus. Versuch einer marxistischen Erklärung*, Frankfurt: Suhrkamp.

Marx, K. (1973) *Grundrisse*, Pelican/NLB edn, Intro. and trans. M. Nicolaus, Harmondsworth: Penguin.

Meeus, M. (1989) *Wat betekent arbeid? Over het ontstaan van de westerse arbeidsmoraal*, Assen: Van Gorcum.

MEW: Marx–Engels Werke, Berlin: Dietz (1960–73).

Pannekoek, A. (n.d.) *Lenin als filosoof*, Amsterdam: De Vlam [1938].

Pijl, K. van der (1998) *Transnational Classes and International Relations*, London and New York: Routledge.

Plekhanov, G.V. (1969) *Fundamental Problems of Marxism*, J.S. Allen (ed.), New York: International Publishers [1908].

Russell, B. (1961) *History of Western Philosophy*, London: Allen & Unwin [2nd edn, 1946].

Schama, S. (1990) *Citizens: A Chronicle of the French Revolution*, New York: Vintage.

Sohn-Rethel, A. (1973) 'Technische Intelligenz zwischen Kapitalismus und Sozialismus', in R. Vahrenkamp (ed.), *Technologie und Kapital*, Frankfurt: Suhrkamp.

Stedman Jones, G. (1973) 'Engels and the End of Classical German Philosophy', *New Left Review*, 79: 17–36.

Therborn, G. (1973) 'The Working Class and the Birth of Marxism', *New Left Review*, 79: 3–15.

—— (1980) *Science, Class and Society: On the Formation of Sociology and Historical Materialism*, London: Verso.

Thompson, E.P. (1968) *The Making of the English Working Class*, Harmondsworth: Penguin [1963].

Trevelyan, G.M. (1961) *Sociale geschiedenis van Engeland*, trans. G.D.J. Blok, Utrecht and Antwerpen: Aula [1944].

8 Making sense of the international system

The promises and pitfalls of contemporary Marxist theories of international relations

Hannes Lacher

Introduction

Marxism is dead – or so we have been told many times since the fall of the Berlin Wall. The gravediggers of Marxism are many, alone the corpse will not lay still. Indeed, over the last few years, there has been a proliferation of works which purport to renew the Marxist project, sometimes in purely theoretical terms, but often with explicitly political intentions which may become increasingly attractive as transnational economic integration proceeds apace and continues to produce global social inequalities.

One aspect of social life which has received particular attention by those trying to resuscitate Marxism is the international system. The theorization of international relations has, of course, long been regarded as a decisive lacuna of Marxist scholarship, and conceptual advance on this issue can rightfully be regarded as critical to its future appeal. So far, these efforts have not been noted by the systematizers and disciplinarians of IR (international relations) and IPE (international political economy). In the USA, at least, Marxism (which so far, in the form of 'world-systems theory', had been present in the academic discourse under the label of 'globalism' or 'structuralism') seems to have lost its status as a serious and influential perspective in the usual triadic representations of the discipline, having been replaced by 'constructivism'.

The purpose of this chapter is to bring into focus the conceptual and theoretical innovations which have been made, over the last decade, by Marxists in their attempts to come to terms with the international system. I will concentrate on the work of Mark Rupert, Justin Rosenberg and Peter Burnham, though others have contributed significantly to this emerging perspective.[1] In order to better understand their contribution and the distinctiveness of their approach (which, while far from being homogeneous, is marked by important commonalities), I will first review the development of Marxist thinking on the international system. It will be shown that the central question asked by Marxists about international relations has changed significantly over time: the classical theorists of imperialism and their successors were concerned with explaining the effects of changes in capitalist production on the conduct of the international affairs of states whose existence as separate political units was taken for granted; by contrast, the question that has emerged as central in recent years is how the existence of an interstate system in the capitalist epoch can be explained in the first place.

The second part of this chapter will look at the answers given by Rupert, Rosenberg and Burnham. These authors draw on the results of the Marxist debate over the nature of the capitalist state which emerged in the 1970s and 1980s, which have given rise to a 'form-theoretical' reformulation of the Marxist understanding of the state. I will argue that while this more general reconstruction of historical materialism does indeed provide the starting point for a Marxist theory of the international, it suffers from the implicit assumption that the capitalist state exists in the singular; it cannot simply be applied to the international system in the way proposed by the theorists under consideration. Indeed, I will argue that their work does not, in the end, provide a satisfactory answer to the question they pose; at best, they offer a partial determination of the modern international system as a social form of capitalist society.

The third part will then sketch out an alternative interpretation of international relations in the capitalist epoch. I will suggest that the interstate-ness of capitalist political space cannot be explained by reference to the nature of capitalism or the 'laws' or 'logic' of capital. Instead, it should be seen as a 'historical legacy' from pre-capitalist history which continues to structure social relations into the present period. To be sure, capitalist 'geopolitics' (for want of a better generic term) is very different from absolutist or feudal geopolitics; but that the totality of capitalist social relations is structured politically by a geopolitical system is not inherent in capitalism itself. This implies that we cannot simply 'apply' Marxism to international relations; we also have to ask some fundamental questions about the way in which the modern interstate system shapes and configures the existence, reproduction and the forms of competition of capital.

Marxism and international relations: heritages and trajectories

To the authors of the *Communist Manifesto*, the relations between states were of little interest. In particular, Marx and Engels seemed to agree with their liberal contemporaries that the importance of war in social life had declined since the Vienna Congress. This tendency, Marx and Engels suggested, was the result of the development of capitalism: 'The national differences and antagonisms between peoples are daily more and more vanishing, owing to the development of the bourgeoisie, to freedom of commerce, to the world-market, to uniformity in the mode of production' (Marx and Engels 1998: 36). This perspective does not, however, imply the obsolescence of sovereignty as such; sovereign states remain the guarantors of private property and the means of sustaining capitalist class relations. But the more the 'universal interdependence of nations' developed, the more would the conflicts between states be overshadowed by the struggles between the antagonistic classes of global capitalist society.[2]

This perspective became increasingly problematic as war re-emerged as a regular form of interaction between capitalist states, and as these states were able to muster the support of their 'nations' in these wars during the last third of the nineteenth century. While Marx and (especially) Engels recognized the growing importance of interstate conflict and nationalism, and indeed made them the topic of a large number of their journalistic writings, they did not integrate them into their theory of capitalist global society (Linklater 1996: 124–5). Only when the prospect of a general war between developed capitalist states became real in the age of imperialism did Marxists take up the challenge of theorizing international relations.

The classical Marxist theorists of imperialism suggested that even while capitalism became global and brought about international interdependence, it also became increasingly marked by the division of global capital into rival national blocs. As a consequence of a supposedly inevitable tendency towards the centralization and concentration of capital, competition was all but eliminated within state boundaries, while states themselves became agents in the advancement of their national monopolies in the world market. Thus, according to Bukharin (1972: 80), the internationalization of the economy and of capital was accompanied by the 'nationalization' of capital interests. The notion of a new relationship between state and capital, as a result of the emergence of monopoly capitalism, was also taken up by Lenin. The change in the character of capitalism was taken to account for the difference in the dynamics of international relations compared to the period of 'competitive capitalism' in which Marx wrote. It forced capitalist states to divide the world in the interest of their national capitals (Lenin 1973: 88–92).

Questions of war and international relations thus emerged at the centre of Marxist theories of imperialism. But the depth of the questions asked about international relations was limited. Crucially, while the (changing) content and function of the capitalist state was subjected to more sustained analysis than it had received from Marx and Engels, the nation-state as a social form was taken as given. Anthony Brewer (1990: 122) therefore correctly points out that Lenin's 'crucial failing' is his 'failure adequately to theorise the place of the nation state in the world economy'.

The traditional Marxist understanding of the state – which was decisively shaped by the debate on imperialism – has over time been recognized, not least by Marxists themselves, as one of the main problems of historical materialism. But it was only with the emergence of structural Marxism of Althusser and Poulantzas that a decisive break with the Leninist orthodoxy was achieved – though at a high price to be paid in the form of structural instead of economic determinism (Carnoy 1984: chap. 4). Ironically, the almost simultaneous attempt by Immanuel Wallerstein to theorize the modern interstate system as part of a larger capitalist world-system preserved the Leninist conceptualization of the state while adding a structuralist component as well. But for all its shortcomings, world-systems theory finally posed the question why the boundaries of the state and the world economy did not coincide in capitalism.

According to Wallerstein, the dissolution of the universal empire of the European Middle Ages was the precondition for the emergence of a capitalist world economy, allowing capitalists to make use of political differences. The interstate system is therefore the necessary and logical form of politics under capitalism. Indeed, Chris Chase-Dunn argues that 'the interstate system of unequally powerful and competing states is the political body of capitalism'. Capitalism can only exist in this form and needs to reproduce the 'division of sovereignty in the core'; capitalist competition in turn serves to reproduce the interstate system and geopolitical competition (Chase-Dunn 1991: 107 and 150).

World-systems theory has been surpassed in influence, at least in IR and IPE, by Robert W. Cox's historicist materialism of world orders during the 1980s, which reacted not least against the structuralism and economism of Wallerstein. But it should be noted that the research problematique developed by Cox, which focuses on the specific 'historical structures' of capitalism rather than on the mode of production, remains limited as a social theory precisely by its failure to engage with the fundamental institutional structure of capitalist modernity (rather than their historical variations).

Simon Bromley is therefore right to argue that

> the neo-Gramscians have singularly failed to develop a theoretical, as opposed to descriptive, specification of the principal structures of the international system. For no amount of discussion of such themes as 'hegemony', 'historic blocs' and 'transnational capital' adds up to a theory of the modern states system or of the world market.
>
> (Bromley 1995: 232)

In this respect Cox has gone back behind world-systems theory, which had at least posed the theoretical problem of the interstate system as an historically specific social form of modernity, however much its solutions (and the way in which it arrived at them) were found wanting.

But Cox's strong reaction against both economism and structuralism was shared by numerous Marxist approaches during the late 1970s and the 1980s, whose focus increasingly became the capitalist state, though they also entailed a more general rejection of the base/superstructure model.[3] E.P. Thompson's critique of Althusser and Poulantzas was crucial for initiating the search for alternative foundations of a non-economistic historical materialism framework. The 'political Marxism' of Ellen Meiksins Wood and Robert Brenner, the 'open Marxism' of Werner Bonefeld *et al.*, as well as the work of Derek Sayer, represent different (and often complementary) conceptualizations which have overcome the base/superstructure model without succumbing to structuralism (Wood 1991 and 1995; Brenner 1986 and 1989; Bonefeld *et al.* 1992; Sayer 1989).

These approaches emphasize the specifically capitalist nature of the separation of politics and economics, thus pointing to the 'paradox' that it was *only* the capitalist state which might be called autonomous. In fact, this autonomy is entailed in the concept of capital itself, which presupposes the insulation of an economic realm within which surplus appropriation takes place by economic means, by the control over things rather than people. The state is thus to be regarded as the institutional centre of the residual sphere of public authority, from which a crucial dimension of power, the power to appropriate surplus, had been abstracted and privatized.

The capitalist state, in this perspective, is not capitalist because it responds to the directives of the bourgeoisie, but because its very form of existence, as the locus of the abstractly political relations of domination, marks it out as part and parcel of a society in which exploitative powers have been separated from the political sphere. The capitalist state is thus the political form of existence of capitalist class relations which reproduces the capital relation by reproducing its own autonomy, as well as that of 'the economy'.

'Open Marxism' and the international system[4]

While these arguments may provide the basis for a non-reductionist Marxism, the question that needs to be asked is whether they also yield a satisfactory theory of international relations. It is noticeable, for instance, that the Marxist state debate was led overwhelmingly in terms which seemed to suggest that capitalist society was organized politically in the form of a single capitalist state.[5] It thus failed to engage with the question which has marred Marxism from its very origins, namely why it is that the capitalist state exists only as part of a system of states, and thus why capitalist politics assumes a 'geopolitical' form.

This question has been posed most insistently to Marxists by Fred Halliday. According to Halliday, Marxism 'begs the question of why, if there is a world economy in which class interests operate transnationally, there is a need for states at all. What, in other words, is the specificity and effectivity of distinct states within a single economic totality?' (Halliday 1994: 91). The state debate of the last twenty-five years certainly allows us to understand why capitalism needs and entails statehood; but does it explain why the totality of capitalist social relations is fractured politically along territorial/national lines – and hence the existence of distinct states?

This question becomes critical when we turn to the Marxist theories of international relations which emerged over the last decade. The work of Mark Rupert, Peter Burnham, and Justin Rosenberg, among others, draws heavily on the state debate (and on the more general attempts to overcome the base/superstructure model). In particular they take the crucial argument underlying these debates, i.e. that the separation of politics and economics is historically specific to capitalism, to provide the key to the understanding not just of the capitalist state, but of the modern international system of sovereign states as well. This international system is thus decoded as a particular form of existence of capital as a social relation.

Burnham: national state, global accumulation and capitalism-in-general

Peter Burnham explicitly situates his conceptualization of the international system in the context of the 'capital relation approach' developed by Holloway, Picciotto, Clarke, Bonefeld and others (see the chapters in Clarke 1991). The key question of this approach is not how the political 'superstructure' is determined by the economic 'base', but what kind of social relationship gives rise to the separation of political and economic realms which appear to be autonomous and to follow some endogenous logic (Burnham 1991: 87, 1994: 228; Holloway and Picciotto 1991: 112).

The historical foundation of this separation, it is argued, is the emergence of capitalist production relations, which are marked by the privatization of the power to extract surplus, thus leaving the state to organize the general conditions of accumulation and exploitation. In that sense, the autonomy of the state is only apparent, as it is premised upon the reproduction of the capital relation.

At the same time, this capitalist state is quite independent from the directives or interests of capitalist pressure groups. As capital can only exist in the form of numerous and competing individual capitals, it cannot impose a particular strategy of accumulation on the state; on the contrary, capital relies on the state to define and organize the 'general will' of capital, by continually imposing the market as the form through which not only capital and labour, but also individual capitals among themselves, relate to each other. The state does so mainly through the impersonal means of the law, property rights and money. The state, in short, 'must seek to maintain the rule of the market' and to secure the general conditions for capital accumulation (Burnham 1990: 180).[6] In fact, the state is the only possible social form for the organization of the 'general interest' in capitalism. Burnham thus rejects even sophisticated attempts to ground the state and its changing role in the economy in terms of the social formation of hegemonic coalitions, as the state cannot simply be the condensation of private interests.

The state, for Burnham, is a crucial social form of capitalist society; it does not stand in a zero-sum relationship with the market, as the globalization thesis suggests, but has an internal connection with this other fundamental form of the capital relation. Moreover, capitalist society has always been a world society, and in that sense, Burnham suggests, we should follow Marx in seeing 'capitalism as a single social system in which state power is allocated between territorial entities' (Burnham 1994: 229). The implication is that competition between individual capitals is complemented by competition between national states which aim to secure the reproduction of 'their' capitals in the world market. The consequent 'inter-imperialist rivalry' between national states is limited, however, by their common interest in maintaining global capitalism and accumulation. Competition and cooperation are complementary strategies of states, though realism and liberalism have absolutized one to the detriment of the other.

For Burnham, then, nation-states 'have a similar relation of conflict and collaboration as individual capitals'; this follows from his argument that the 'role of the capitalist state is to express the "general interest" of capital. However, the national form of the state implies that the state can only constitute this "general interest" on a national basis' (Burnham 1990: 185). But the question *why* '[n]ational states ... are the political form of capitalist social relations' is not answered – or even posed – by Burnham. If the state is regarded as 'capital-in-general', then clearly the derivation of the territorial or national form of the state needs an explication which can tell us *why* capital-in-general is territorially fragmented and thus only partial. Capital is a global social relation and capitalist society a world society; so why is the general interest of capital realized and operationalized at the level of territorial segments of this world society? Surely to answer the question 'what kind of society exists in the form of differentiated political and economic realms?' can only lead us to conceptualize 'the state' as a capitalist relation of production; it does not, however, allow us to derive the territorially fragmented character of 'the political'. That the capitalist state does not exist in the singular but as one among many is thus not directly given by the capital relation.

Rupert: capitalist international relations as second order alienation

The same conceptual problem is apparent in Mark Rupert's characterization of international politics as 'a kind of second order alienation' (1995: 33). In capitalism, Rupert argues, the products of human labour take on the semblance of autonomy from its producers; they confront them as the objectified form of their productive powers, as 'alien and hostile forces' which appear to have a life of their own. The relationship between these objects seems to be regulated by their inherent qualities, rather than by the social relationships between their creators, and are thus able to present themselves as objective facts to which social life has to adapt. Positivist theories of social science take these facts as their starting point and never penetrate to the social relations which underlie them, thereby dehistoricizing and fetishizing the social order of a given period.

Rupert, by contrast, argues that the power which the objects of human labour have achieved over social life has its roots in the private appropriation of the products of individual labour. This privatization, moreover, implies a differentiation of political and economic forms of power; these spheres consequently seem to be related externally rather than internally. But the form of the abstract political state is just as much an expression of the alienated relations between individuals mediated by things as the market.

> The modern political state developed within and is integral to a political-economic system of class rule – a state–society complex in which property is assigned to the private sphere as a primordial individual right, and hence is exempted from ongoing political dialogue in the public sphere.
>
> (Rupert 1995: 24)

The public sphere of political action organized within the state is thus an impoverished realm premised upon the relinquishing of a substantial part of societal self-determination and its subordination to the market.

The 'modern state' thus has its foundation in the capital relation. Rupert is adamant, however, that this cannot be taken to imply that the role of the state and its relationship to the market is fixed. Drawing on Marx and Gramsci, he suggests that the 'structured separations of state–society and politics–economics in capitalist social formations' can be bridged through the agency of a 'historic bloc' (Rupert 1995: 29). These formally separated realms periodically achieve a transient unity (or more precisely a temporary functional correspondence) as they are brought into a purposive relationship, which allows for the pursuit of specific strategies of accumulation for which social hegemony has been secured. In this way, the potentially contradictory relationship between these realms is articulated in a functional whole, though the underlying dynamics of capitalist society prevent these structural 'fixes' from becoming permanent. Rupert here relies heavily on the notion of hegemonic class coalitions imparting a particular social purpose onto the state, thereby shaping the way in which the state seeks to secure the reproduction and stability of capitalism as a whole. His theorization of the capitalist state is in this respect less prone to the functionalism of Burnham's understanding of the role of the capitalist state. But is Rupert better able to provide an explanation of the national form of the capitalist state than Burnham?

Rupert argues that

> insofar as the formal separations of state and society, of public and private, of the political and economic aspects of life, are integral to the historical reality of capitalism, we may say that capitalism and its manifold relations of alienation are the necessary context within which the historical construction of sovereign states – understood in the modern sense as functionally specialized administrative-coercive, 'political', organizations – becomes possible.
>
> (1995: 32–3)

But again, this only allows us to understand the abstract character of the capitalist state, not its territorial shape, which Rupert does not problematize. He suggests that 'national and international should be construed as two aspects of an internally related whole, a whole which is in some sense capitalist and alienated' (1995: 32). But why capitalist politics should take this spatially differentiated form is left open. At most, Rupert's approach can explain why the territorially bounded sovereign state took the form of an abstracted realm of the political and became the organizational centre of political action in capitalist society – itself a huge advance over the Weberian fetishization of the state. But this perspective cannot explain why the abstract state has to be (and historically took shape as) a territorial state in the first place. To characterize the relations between such abstract states in terms of alienation certainly helps us to understand the dynamics of international relations – what it is that is contested in this geopolitical form – but it does not provide an explication of the fact that global capitalism is organized politically through the medium of a system of national states.

Rosenberg: sovereignty and the 'empire of civil society'

Implicit in Rupert's and Burnham's untheorized assumption that the capitalist state is a national state is a particular understanding of the emergence of the capitalist mode of production. Rupert notes in this vein that 'the system of states ... emerged historically along with capitalist production' (1995: 33). This, of course, is a perspective that is widely accepted, notwithstanding the many alternative theorizations of exactly how this process took place. It points to the 'long sixteenth century' with its rising long-distance trade, increasing commodity production, the rise of the middle classes and the emergence and consolidation of the 'modern' state which controls the means of violence in a territorially circumscribed area, best exemplified in the absolutist state. Justin Rosenberg, by contrast, argues that neither was the early modern world economy capitalist in nature, nor was the absolutist state a capitalist state (Rosenberg 1994: 42, 92, 123 and 135ff). For him, the rise of capitalism dates from the late eighteenth century, and it was in this period that the sovereign state emerged.

Even more explicitly than Rupert, Rosenberg equates the abstractedness of the political in capitalism with state sovereignty. In fact, he suggests that we define sovereignty 'as the social form of the state in a society where political power is divided between public and private spheres' (1994: 129). Cutting through familiar debates in IR as to whether increasing economic interdependence implies the demise of state, this allows us to see that the consolidation of sovereignty and the creation of the capitalist world market were coeval. Both were made possible by the abstraction of 'the political' from production and exchange. This process simultaneously allows for the creation of a homogeneous political space in which formally equal citizens relate directly to the state, and independent wielders of political authority become subsumed under state authority; and for the 'porousness' of the boundaries of these states for the private activities of economic subjects (1994: 131). 'The possibility of an international economy', Rosenberg concludes, 'is thus structurally interdependent with the possibility of a sovereign states-system' (1994: 87–8).

This argument, however, is apt only to establish the compatibility of the territorial or national state with the global existence of capitalist class relations and a world market; it does not establish why capitalism politically exists or, indeed, needs to exist in the form of an interstate system. Indeed, this fact does not seem worth explaining to Rosenberg. Noting that a world state has never existed he concedes that anarchy, as a generic attribute of the relations between independent states, is not limited to a particular historical epoch. He insists, however, that this attribute does not tell us much about the dynamics of specific international systems. Hence, the task facing IR is precisely to develop a theory of *capitalist* anarchy (Rosenberg 1994: 139).

Yet this is already conceding too much to Realism. Feudalism, for instance, would be ill understood if described as 'anarchic' (cf. Fischer 1992; Hall and Kratochwil 1993; Lacher 1998). In fact, Rosenberg himself introduces a more concrete, and rather different, historical perspective when he argues that capitalism involved the 'historical shift from empire to states-system' (1994: 155). But surely this process took place before the eighteenth century, and thus, on the basis of Rosenberg's own argument, before the rise of capitalist social relations. Rosenberg seems to acknowledge as much when he elsewhere distinguishes the process of state-formation in the early modern period, involving the centralization and bureaucratization of political authority, from the capitalist transformation of the state, the latter 'lagging some way behind' the former (1994: 130). Rosenberg here accepts that the differentiation between internal and external that was the consequence of state formation preceded the capitalist separation of politics and economics – without drawing the theoretical implications.

The problem which surfaces here is a more general one with Rosenberg's argument: while he succinctly contrasts pre-capitalist and capitalist societies and their structural characteristics, he does not provide a dynamic historical account of the rise of capitalism and its relationship to state formation. His argument thus remains often schematic – photographic, in a sense – especially with respect to the timing of the crucial steps of the transition to capitalism, and thus to the social forms and structural dynamics which different social orders entail.

It is hard, then, to completely follow Rosenberg's conclusion that '[b]ehind the contemporary world of independent equal states stands the expropriation of the direct producer' (1994: 172). Rosenberg, like Rupert and Burnham, conflates the abstracted character of capitalist politics, which derives from the privatization of the power to extract surplus, with the sovereignty of the capitalist state. But the sovereignty of political rule in capitalism does not necessarily entail its national boundedness. Once we clearly recognize the distinctiveness of the process whereby internal and external structures became differentiated from the separation of politics and economics, it becomes necessary to pose the question of the capitalist character of the state and the interstate system in different terms. No longer can we derive the national state and the interstate system from the capital relation and take them to be the straightforward 'geopolitical expression of a wider social totality' (1994: 55). We have to first ask why the capitalist system does have a geopolitical expression at all. If state-formation and the supersession of universal empire have their origins in a social logic which precedes the rise of capitalism, as Rosenberg himself suggests in places, then we have to find a way of conceptualizing the totality of capitalist social relations in ways which allow for the recognition that not every organizational or institutional form of our epoch was itself brought into existence by capitalism.

The challenge of territoriality

The Marxist theories of international relations surveyed above ultimately fail to meet the challenge, set out by Halliday, to explain the 'specificity and effectivity of distinct states within a single economic totality'. They take the territorial boundedness of the capitalist state as given and proceed to ground the interstate system in essentially the same conceptual operations in which the Marxist state debate sought to derive *the* capitalist state. In this way, the theoretical problem why capitalist political space is territorially fragmented disappears from view.

But unlike their predecessors, Rupert, Rosenberg and Burnham cannot afford to ignore this problem because it is thrown up by the very changes in Marxist theory designed to overcome the base/superstructure model and the pitfalls of economic determinism. For the Marxist theorists of imperialism, for instance, it was still possible to sidestep the problem of multiple capitalist polities, assuming as they did that certain states were capitalist because they were directed by the bourgeoisie; states, in other words, were capitalist by virtue of the actions of capitalists on them. At least within their own framework, states could be taken as given, however unsatisfactory this remains from the perspective of a critical social theory of international relations.

However, once we begin to define the capitalist character of the 'state' at the much higher level of abstraction, which marks the Marxist state debate, this becomes plainly impossible. The question why the capitalist state embodies only a territorially circumscribed subset of the capitalist relations of domination becomes unavoidable. For nothing in the argument that capitalism entails the abstraction of political from economic power leads to the conclusion that political power needs to be organized by multiple and competing centres of territorially organized sovereignty.

Is the theoretical impossibility to show that the same historical process which leads to the separation of politics and economics (i.e. the expropriation of the direct producers) also entails the emergence of system of sovereign states, a real problem? In any case, is it not a well-established fact that the modern state and the capitalist economy arose in tandem, as at least Burnham and Rupert seem to agree? In this case, it might be argued that the problem is simply one with Marxism itself, and with its tendency to overextend the explanatory powers of the concept of capital. After all, other – non-Marxist – approaches, most notably John Ruggie's work on the medieval-to-modern transition, have shown how the separation of the political and the economic and the differentiation of the internal and the external are part of the rise of modernity. By not taking both of them to be expressions of the transition to capitalism, but as autonomous structures following independent logics of modernization, these approaches seem able to avoid the theoretical conundrums which face Marxist theories of the international system.

But are they? It may be argued that Ruggie's suggestion that modernity is characterized by the differentiation of politics and economics, as well as of the domestic and international realms, becomes rather circular when he goes on to explain the emergence of modernity in terms which presuppose the very autonomy of the spheres which he sees as the product of the process of modernization. Ruggie's theory of the transition is based on the interaction between already autonomous spheres which become increasingly differentiated

– a quantitative process of rising 'dynamic density' (Ruggie 1993: 152–60, 169). It does not, however, provide an account of the qualitative rupture that dissolved feudalism's organic unity of politics and economics.

It is here that it becomes useful to return to Marxism, or at least to the non-deterministic Marxism developed since the late 1970s. But rather than trying to derive a capitalist interstate system from the same theoretical foundations which in the earlier debates had yielded only 'the state', we have to pursue a more historical path to understanding the geopolitical structure of capitalist political space. On this path, we can follow some of the most creative attempts to explicate the rise of capitalism in non-economistic and non-circular terms, the 'political Marxism' of Robert Brenner and Ellen Meiksins Wood. This approach explains the demise of feudalism as a result of the internal contradictions of a society in which political privileges, laws, monopolies not only constituted relations of personal domination, but simultaneously formed the socially decisive relations of surplus expropriation. Pre-capitalist property was thus 'politically constituted' and it is in the struggles between the aristocracy and the peasantry but also, and equally importantly, between the members of the nobility itself, over their relations of domination and dependence, that the dynamics of feudalism as well as the reasons for the demise of feudalism can be found (Brenner 1986; Wood 1991).

Ruggie, of course, also argues that 'basic structure of property rights ... characterizes an entire social formation', including its international system (Ruggie 1983: 282); but whereas property appears as merely regulative of a basically autonomous economic structure operating in Ruggie's account, property (or 'social property relations') should be understood as constitutive of historically a very different system of production, distribution and surplus appropriation, as well as sovereignty. Most importantly, however, Brenner recognizes that property in feudalism is very different from property in capitalism, in that it is not the control of things, but the control over people that confers access to surplus in feudalism.

On the basis of this argument, Brenner suggests that the demise of feudalism was not generally followed by the rise of capitalism. In fact, the societies in which the 'modern state' is usually taken to have emerged, the absolutist societies of France, Spain and Prussia, were not capitalist at all. Their social structure continued to be marked by the centrality of political forms of surplus appropriation. The difference was that in absolutism the state itself became the main locus of 'politically constituted property', while in feudalism it had been distributed among individual lords (Brenner 1985; Wood 1991).[7]

This argument also provides the basis for Rosenberg's claim that the world economy of the early modern period was not a capitalist world economy, but remained based on the age-old exploitation of price differentials between segmented markets. But even if there was, *pace* Ruggie and the majority of historical sociologists (but see Skocpol 1979: 55), no separation of politics and economics in absolutist Europe, there certainly emerged, *pace* Rosenberg, a system of sovereign states and with it the differentiation of internal and external spheres. It is thus *not* the late eighteenth-century structural shift from personal-ized relations of domination to a system of impersonal relations mediated by things, 'which explains why the units are no longer empires but bordered, sovereign states' (Rosenberg 1994: 146).

We may gain a better understanding of absolutism if we differentiate between feudalism's parcellized personal domination and absolutism's generalized personal dominion (Gerstenberger 1990). The latter was articulated precisely as a claim to sovereignty over the inhabitants of a particular territory by rulers who regarded their state as patrimony. Clearly, absolutist sovereignty was fundamen-tally different from capitalist sovereignty based on 'general impersonal rule', and only the capitalist abstraction of political power from surplus appropriation allowed for the consolidation of sovereignty beyond what was possible in abso-lutism where legal privileges and corporate or regional particularism remained necessarily pervasive.

Yet the continental European capitalist transition of the late eighteenth (or, more likely, early nineteenth) century took place within these territorialized states, and within a system of sovereign states.[8] It reproduced the boundaries of particular states and the boundedness of political communities. Crucially, then, that capitalism came to exist politically in the form of an international system for reasons not directly given by the nature of capital. In this sense, capitalism's political space need not be organized by exclusive territoriality. The differentia-tion of internal and external spheres arose from the dynamics of political accumulation since the late feudal period, and thus within a social context from which capitalism was absent.

This argument raises two broad sets of questions in the context of the attempt to develop a historical materialist theory of international relations: first, what were the consequences of the capitalist reconstitution of society for the dynamic of the international system? And, second, what are the implications for the capitalist 'logic of process', for the way in which capital operates and for the fundamental laws of motion and contradictions of capitalism?

1   Just as the capitalist territorial state is different from the absolutist territorial state, so is the capitalist international system marked by a dynamic funda-mentally distinct from absolutist geopolitics. Modernity in international relations cannot, as Ruggie (1993) suggests, be defined in terms of territori-ality, as this obscures the nineteenth-century transformation of the social relations of sovereignty, and hence of the changes in the content of what is contested between territorial states. Territoriality became exclusive with respect to political space only, while the privatization of appropriative power allowed for the organization of surplus extraction across boundaries through the productive employment of contractually secured labour. While the social realm of the sovereign authority of a state was thereby restricted it also became dependent on the successful reproduction of 'its' capitals in the world economy. As a consequence, the old problematique of sovereignty, i.e. the assertion and rejection of claims to universal empire and the securing of

the territorial integrity of a state's polity, society and economy, was supplanted by a new problematique which has increasingly dominated the discourse of sovereignty ever since: the ability of states to shape their societies' destiny in the face of world economic interdependence (Diner 1993: 38ff.).

2   The first question could still be answered within the parameters of the Marxist theories (especially Rosenberg's) reviewed above. But to point to the ways in which the interstate system has become part and parcel of capitalist modernity is only one side of the story. In addition, we have to ask how the exclusive territoriality of political authority in turn structures the existence of capital. Capital is a social relation as well as a process of self-valorization, and in both these dimensions, it is profoundly 'configured' by the fact that the spatial organization of the capitalist polity does not correspond to the space of the world economy and world society based on the capital relation.

Of course, much of Marxist (and non-Marxist) reflection on the global political economy is focused on the tensions between global accumulation and territorial sovereignty; but only by explicitly problematizing the international character of capitalist politics can we gain theoretical leverage on this issue. Marx, for instance, constructed his theory of capital precisely by abstracting from the multiplicity of capitalist states and suggesting that in order to understand the process of capital accumulation 'in its integrity ... we must treat the whole world of trade as one nation and assume that capitalist production is established everywhere and has taken possession of every branch of industry' (Marx 1977: 727). Trying to understand capitalist society's concrete existence, however, we have to reintroduce the interstate system, without assuming that capital operates globally in the same way, whether political space is fractured territorially or not.

It is thus necessary to ask in what way the 'logic of process' of the capitalist mode of production became structured by the fact that its political space is fractured by sovereign territoriality; how this shapes the nature of competition between individual capitals; how the fragmentation of the capitalist polity structures the relations between classes domestically and internationally; how the world market is regulated by territorial authority and what the dynamics for the restructuration of the relationship between states and the world market are; and in what way the operation of the law of value is modified in the world market context by the fact that the circulation of capital is mediated by national currencies.

Instead of systematically answering these questions, I will here limit myself to suggesting that the starting point has to be the recognition that 'the international' is deeply problematic to the individual state seeking to maintain the ability of the capitals located or rooted within its boundaries to successfully extract surplus value and to accumulate. The fact that the state cannot control the conditions under which 'its' capitals have to reproduce themselves (and thus allow the state to reproduce itself in turn) entails a very different role of the state in the international and domestic contexts. Whereas the state domestically stands apart from the competition between individual capitals, and seeks to regulate the economy through universal forms of governance like the rule of law and money, in the international sphere it is or can itself be a competitor seeking to promote the interests of its capitals with political and economic means.

Internationally, individual states can use their political power to structure international competition in ways which benefit 'their' capitals to the detriment of the capitals of other states. They can use their borders and currencies to mediate the competition between the multitude of individual capitals. Thus, the world market is not simply a system of individual capitals competing with each other economically, but it is a system in which states are parties in the competition for world market shares rather than guarantors of the market as such. In that sense, it may be argued that the domestic separation of politics and economics, which constitutes the modern interstate system and the world market society, is 'unthinkable in the sphere of world society' (Diner 1993). Political and economic forms of power mesh in the international politics of capitalist states in a way, which goes beyond the state interventionism known from the domestic sphere, which fundamentally reproduces the separateness of politics and economics.

Conclusions

I have argued that the interstate-ness of capitalist political space cannot be derived from the nature of the capital relation. Instead, it should be regarded as a 'historical legacy' from pre-capitalist historical development. This is not to advocate a methodological pluralism that posits the autonomy of different social structures, each supposedly following endogenous logics. Such an approach would be fundamentally ahistorical as it ignores the very historicity of the separation of politics and economics, which the 'radicalized ontology' of contemporary Marxism correctly emphasizes. We have to start from historical totalities rather than transhistorical interacting structures that produce history as they interact.

The relevant historical totality to the conceptualization of the system of sovereign territorial states is capitalism. But while theoretical analysis shows that capitalism can no more exist without a state than it can exist without a market, it cannot explain the existence of multiple capitalist states. For this, we have to turn to a historical analysis of the way in which capitalism emerged; such analysis can draw on the innovations of Marxist theory over the last twenty-five years, but we cannot apply Marxist state theory to the international system in the more direct way suggested by Rosenberg, Burnham and Rupert.

Taking the international character of global capitalism to be a contingent aspect of capitalism raises the question of how to theorize capitalism as a totality. While Marxist theorists of IR have posited the need to start from the consideration of social totalities, they have spent little time on explicating their understanding of this concept, nor have they engaged with its troubled history in Marxist theory from Lukács to Althusser and beyond (Jay 1984). I have argued that not all social forms of really existing capitalism are necessarily or in all respects the emanations of the capital relation, as the Lukácsian concept of 'expressive totality' suggests. In this sense, rather than simply taking them to be internal to capitalism, certain institutions should be theorized as *internalized*. This avoids both the Weberian pluralism of ontologically irreducible structures, and the Marxist tendency to reduce everything, including the interstate system, to a necessary expression of the capital relation.

So the argument about the pre-capitalist origins of the state-system should not be taken to imply that international politics in the nineteenth and twentieth centuries represents a logic which is still absolutist, lagging behind a more modern economy. The interstate system is capitalist, because it has become capitalist in the process of the totalization of capitalism – in other words, in the process of capitalism becoming a totality (a totality, moreover, which inherently produces difference and contradictions). But while the international system has become internalized it has simultaneously structured and configured the way in which capital operates: it has fundamentally shaped both the process of capital accumulation as well as the social conditions under which the capital relation was reproduced.

This leads to a final critical point. For the new Marxist theories of IR/IPE, taking national states and the world market to be necessary institutionalizations of the separated capitalist spheres of politics and economics, the question of globalization can be resolved without empirical inquiry and theoretical contortions: as long as there is capitalism, there will be national sovereignty. But this argument foreshortens a necessary debate to which historical materialism could contribute much. It does so on the basis of its confusion of the capitalist state form with its concrete territorial institutionalization. Other forms of capitalist statehood may be possible, like the transnational state suggested elsewhere in this volume by William Robinson.

Whether or not such a process of transnational state-formation is actually taking place is an open question; it is neither a foregone conclusion nor an impossibility within the framework of capitalist modernity. Moreover, even if the national state has become so entrenched that no transnational state can emerge, this may pose a contradiction to capitalist reproduction (and of individual states) in a world where the existence of capital has become global rather than international. From this perspective, the real issue may not be whether globalization undermines territorial sovereignty, but whether the continuing reproduction of territoriality prevents the emergence of a political framework that would allow for further global economic integration.

Notes

1 Other contributions include Boyle 1994; Bromley 1995, 1996 and 1999; Siegelberg 1994. For references on Rupert, Rosenberg and Burnham, see below.
2 As Linklater (1996) points out, Marx and Engels thought of the form of class struggle as national; the goal, however, was the transformation of the global society constituted by capitalist production relations.
3 Many of the most important contributions to this debate were published in the journal *Capital & Class* and collected in Clarke 1991; cf. Carnoy 1984 and Holloway and Picciotto 1978.

4   The term 'open Marxism' is used by Burnham to characterize his own approach, drawing on the closely related work of Bonefeld *et al.* (1992); it is here applied to Rosenberg and Rupert as well, who share substantial aspects of Burnham's 'open Marxism'.

5   Cf. Barker 1991: 204: 'One might get the impression from [Holloway and Picciotto] as from a mass of other Marxist writings on the state, that capitalism has but one state. Where it is acknowledged that the beast is numerous, the implications of that very concrete fact are not developed at all.'

6   Cf. Burnham 1991: 89:

> The state as an aspect of the social relations of production must be seen as [*sic*!] one remove from the interests of particular capital since the form of the state dictates that its role is to address the contradictory foundations of accumulation in the guise of meeting the interests of capital-in-general.

7   This summary passes over the crucial role of capitalist development in England emphasized by political Marxists; for a more comprehensive treatment, see Lacher 1998.

8   For a more detailed account of the role of absolutist international relations in the transition to capitalism, and on the subsequent transformation of the international system itself, see Lacher (2003).

Bibliography

Barker, C. (1991) 'A Note on the Theory of the Capitalist States', in Simon Clarke (ed.), *The State Debate*, London: Macmillan, pp.204–13.

Bonefeld, W., Gunn, R. and Psychopedis, K. (1992) *Open Marxism*, Vol. 1, London: Pluto Press.

Boyle, C. (1994) 'Imagining the World Market: IPE and the Task of Social Theory', *Millennium*, 23 (2): 351–63.

Brenner, R. (1985) 'The Agrarian Roots of European Capitalism', in T.H. Aston and C.H.E. Philpin (eds), *The Brenner Debate: Agrarian Class Structure and Economic Development in Pre-Industrial Europe*, Cambridge: Cambridge University Press, pp.213–329.

—— (1986) 'The Social Basis of Economic Development', in J. Roemer (ed.), *Analytical Marxism*, Cambridge: Cambridge University Press.

—— (1989) 'Bourgeois Revolution and Transition to Capitalism', in A. Beier, D. Cannadine and J. Rosenheim (eds), *The First Modern Society*, Cambridge: Cambridge University Press, pp.271–304.

Brewer, A. (1990) *Marxist Theories of Imperialism: A Critical Survey*, 2nd edn, London: Routledge.

Bromley, S. (1995) 'Rethinking International Political Economy', in J. Macmillan and A. Linklater (eds), *Boundaries in Question*, London: Pinter Publishers, pp.228–43.

—— (1996) 'Globalization?', *Radical Philosophy*, 80, Nov./Dec.: 2–5.

—— (1999) 'Marxism and Globalisation', in A. Gamble, D. Marsh and T. Tant (eds), *Marxism and Social Science*, Chicago, IL: University of Illinois Press, pp.280–301.

Bukharin, N. (1972) *Imperialism and World Economy*, London: Merlin.

Burnham, P. (1990) *The Political Economy of Postwar Reconstruction*, London: Macmillan.

—— (1991) 'Neo-Gramscian Hegemony and the International Order', *Capital & Class*, 45 (Autumn): 73–93.

—— (1994) 'Open Marxism and Vulgar International Political Economy', *Review of International Political Economy*, 1 (2): 221–32.

Carnoy, M. (1984) *The State and Political Theory*, Princeton, NJ: Princeton University Press.

Chase-Dunn, C. (1991) *Global Formation: Structures of the World Economy*, Oxford: Blackwell.

Clarke, S. (ed.) (1991) *The State Debate*, London: Macmillan.

Cox, R. (1987) *Production, Power, and World Order*, New York: Columbia University Press.

Diner, D. (1993) 'Imperialismus und Universalismus: Versuch einer Begriffsgeschichte', in D. Diner (ed.), *Weltordnungen: Über Geschichte und Wirkung von Recht und Macht*, Frankfurt: Fischer, pp.17–60.

Fischer, M. (1992) 'Feudal Europe, 800–1300: Communal Discourse and Conflictual Practices', *International Organization*, 46 (3): 426–66.

Gerstenberger, H. (1990) *Die subjektlose Gewalt. Theorie der Entstehung buergerlicher Staatsgewalt*, Bd. 1, Muenster: Westfaelisches Dampfboot.

Hall, R. and Kratochwil, F. (1993) 'Medieval Tales: Neorealist "Science" and the Abuse of History', *International Organization*, 47 (3): 479–91.

Halliday, F. (1994) *Rethinking International Relations*, Basingstoke: Macmillan.

Holloway, J. and Picciotto, S. (eds) (1978) *State and Capital: A Marxist Debate*, London: Edward Arnold.

—— (1991) 'Capital, Crisis and the State', in S. Clarke (ed.), *The State Debate*, London: Macmillan, pp.109–41.

Jay, M. (1984) *Marxism and Totality*, Berkeley, CA: University of California Press.

Lacher, H. (1998) 'The Doubtful Modernity of the Westphalian System: Absolutist and Capitalist Sovereignty', paper presented at the 39th International Studies Association Conference, Minneapolis, 17–21 March 1998.

—— (2003) *The International Relations of Modernity: Capitalism, Territoriality and Globalization*, London: Routledge.

Lenin, V. (1973): *Imperialism*, Peking: Foreign Languages Press.

Linklater, A. (1996) 'Marxism', in S. Burchill *et al.*, *Theories of International Relations*, New York: St Martin's Press, pp.119–43.

Marx, K. (1977) *Capital: A Critique of Political Economy, Vol. 1*, trans. Ben Fowkes, New York: Vintage Press.

Marx, K. and Engels, F. (1998) *The Communist Manifesto*, New York: Monthly Review Press.

Picciotto, S. (1991) 'The Internationalisation of Capital and the International System', in S. Clarke (ed.), *The State Debate*, London: Macmillan, pp.214–24.

Rosenberg, J. (1994) 'The International Imagination: IR Theory and "Classic Social Analysis"', *Millennium*, 23 (1): 85–108.

Ruggie, J. (1983) 'Continuity and Transformation in the World Polity: Toward a Neo-realist Synthesis', *World Politics*, 35 (1): 261–85.

—— (1993) 'Territoriality and Beyond: Problematizing Modernity in International Relations', *International Organization*, 47 (1): 139–74.

Rupert, M. (1995) *Producing Hegemony*, Cambridge: Cambridge University Press.

Sayer, D. (1989) *The Violence of Abstraction*, Oxford: Blackwell.

Siegelberg, J. (1994) *Kapitalismus und Krieg: Eine Theorie des Krieges in der Weltgesellschaft*, Münster: LIT Verlag.

Skocpol, T. (1979) *States and Social Revolutions*, Cambridge: Cambridge University Press.

Thomson, J. (1995) 'State Sovereignty in International Relations', *International Studies Quarterly*, 39 (95): 213–33.

Wood, E. (1991) *The Pristine Culture of Capitalism*, London: Verso.

—— (1995) *Democracy Against Capitalism: Renewing Historical Materialism*, Cambridge: Cambridge University Press.

9 The dialectic of globalisation

A critique of Social Constructivism

Benno Teschke and Christian Heine

Introduction

Two contemporary international relations (IR) orthodoxies – Social Constructivism and Neo-Weberian Historical Sociology (NWHS) – converge in their rejection of historical materialism and their adoption of parts of Max Weber's philosophy of social science for theorising international politics. Both argue that Marxism's natural-scientific epistemology stipulates rules for the construction of universally valid deductive-nomological laws that govern social phenomena in an objective fashion. It thus fails to make sense of the inter-subjective and conscious construction of variable rules and norms that are constitutive of international forms of conflict and co-operation (Ruggie 1998: 30). Constructivism and NWHS suggest furthermore that historical materialism's irremediable economic functionalism has little to offer for conceptualising the role of the state and inter-state relations in the overall development and repro-duction of the modern system of states and, *a fortiori*, international institutional change (Spruyt 1994; Weiss and Hobson 1995; Hobson 1997, 1998). This rejec-tion of historical materialism in contemporary mainstream IR theory reflects a broader consensus in the social sciences that tends to disqualify Marxist contri-butions on grounds of their inherent techno-determinism, mono-causal class reductionism, historicist and teleological tendencies (Giddens 1987, [1981] 1995; Mann 1986, 1993; Habermas 1984: 144). It is suggested, in contrast, that Constructivism and NWHS offer viable alternatives to the perceived strictures of Marxism by embracing a much wider array of methodologies – research strate-gies designed to express a pluralist, if not eclectic, stance.[1]

This chapter re-examines the nature of Marx's thought and argues that the subsumption of its formal structure under the deductive-nomological protocols of the natural sciences disfigures his dialectically informed philosophy. We suggest in turn that Constructivism and NWHS rely on a selective reading of Weber and have failed to address the limits and contradictions of his philosophy of science. This failure undermines the theoretical basis and substantive empir-ical claims of both approaches. In contrast, we claim that Marx's philosophy provides a coherent approach for conceptualising the nexus between conscious agency and institutions on the one hand, and the nexus between political authority and economic forces on the other. His dialectical philosophy also provides a good framework for theorising international change. Employing this dialectical approach, we trace the origins and nature of globalisation and its effect on state–economy relations, understanding it as the outcome of the long economic downturn that has governed the capitalist world economy since the 1970s.

The chapter is divided into three main sections. The first section sets out Constructivism's central theoretical assumptions, specifies some of its recurring objections against Marx, and introduces one important constructivist approach to globalisation. The second section re-examines core features of dialectical thought with specific regard to its understanding of reality, history and conscious agency. These are contrasted with central Weberian positions. On this basis, the third section seeks to show how a dialectically controlled interpretation of globalisation can provide a viable alternative to both constructivist as well as orthodox international political economy (IPE) stances on globalisation. We argue that a dialectical reading of the current state of the world political economy can arbitrate between one-sided politicist and economistic versions of globalisation, while explaining important consciousness-mediated similarities and variations in state–society responses to the contemporary restructuring of international capitalism.

Constructivism against Marx

Core elements of Constructivism

The core constructivist claim is that historically varying forms of conflict and co-operation are predicated upon inter-subjectively constructed institutions. These institutions lay down the 'rules of the game' for international politics (Ruggie 1998; Kratochwil 1989; Wendt 1999).[2] Constitutive rules provide systems of meaning that act as frames of reference for collectively binding and norm-governed action. The very possibility of successful international institution-building rests on collective acts of intentionality, that shape converging fundamental norms and values among participating actors. Shared norms and values point to successful processes of communicative agreement that constitute the *differentia specifica* of the social world. It follows that social scientists – including IR scholars – have to seek interpretive, not observational, access to their object-domain, since their area of research is not objectively given, but pre-constituted by consciousness-driven and communicatively mediated processes of the collective construction of social reality. Interpretive access to the social world also implies the direct involvement of the social sciences in the maintenance and modification of rules and norms. The term 'epistemic communities' captures this phenomenon.

As a result, IR seeks to understand the *Wertrationalität* (rationality of ends), not the *Zweckrationalität* (instrumental rationality) embodied in international institutions. History is then conceived in terms of a rational reconstruction of a sequence of historically diverse international institutions, which are bound up with underlying value communities. These value communities not only guide the social and political purpose of institutions, but also provide their necessary legitimacy. Hence political authority derives from stable and consensual communities of value. These constitute the basic units of identity. The constructivist research agenda is then defined by identifying value-based legitimate institutions and by theorising their transformations, predicated on changes of value-communities. As a rule, these changes are themselves regarded as norm-governed in so far as they are set in motion by cognitive processes of critique, argumentation, persuasion, and social learning within and between epistemic communities.

Constructivism's critique of historical materialism

To date, Constructivism has failed to produce a systematic critique of historical materialism in general and of Marx-inspired IR literature in particular. Rather, it has tended to trivialise or caricature Marxist theorems in fleeting remarks, while simultaneously incorporating many of their best insights into its core theoretical repertoire. Through this strategy of 'denial or appropriation', Constructivism has thus largely succeeded to re-invent itself as the main IR rival paradigm to Rationalism (Realism and Liberalism) in a silent process of semantic repackaging.[3] Nonetheless, three recurring core criticisms can be identified, revolving around historical materialism's epistemological status, its theoretical focus, and its philosophical legacy.

John Ruggie claims that Marxist thought, like the positivism of the Austrian Theoretical School (marginal utility theory), 'sought to reduce problems of social action and social order to material interests, and [...] embraced naturalistic monism, that is, the idea that the natural sciences embody the only valid model of science to which the social sciences should [...] aspire' (Ruggie 1998: 30). Marxism is thus irredeemably tied to a positivist and naturalist view of social science, seeking to establish a single transhistorical covering law.

Alexander Wendt argues that Marxism has failed to understand the relational character of social and political phenomena, including capitalism (Wendt 1999: 94–5).[4] His distinction between the forces of production, understood as brute material forces, and the economic system-defining relations of production, understood as rules premised on shared ideas, leads him to reject Marxist 'materialist' definitions of capitalism in favour of a cultural/ideational conceptualisation. Two possible conclusions can be drawn from Wendt's observation. Constructivists could redefine the concept of capitalism by theorising the 'discursive conditions that constitute capitalist relations of production' as an ideational and, by implication, non-coercive phenomenon (Wendt 1999: 136).[5] Alternatively, they could challenge the idea that Marxism defines capitalism materialistically as Wendt asserts, instead recovering the relational-dialectical character of the term 'relations of production', and coercive origins and ongoing contradictory history of capitalism as a hierarchical system of exploitation. This is what we shall try to do in the following sections.

Friedrich Kratochwil, finally, remains sceptical of Marx's philosophical legacy, claiming that it is inextricably bound up with an optimistic and teleological philosophy of consciousness premised on the idea that Reason and history will come eventually into accord with each other. The charge is that even in its secu-larised version Marxism cannot divest itself from the pseudo-religious certainties of the 'last twitches of Enlightenment ideology' (Kratochwil 1997: 440). While there is, of course, textual evidence – ranging from Marx himself to Lukács – for claiming that Marxism embraces such a philosophy of history by replacing Hegel's Spirit with the victorious march of respective progressive and ever more universal classes, this interpretation does not do justice to the state of the current Marxist debate. Alternative readings of Marx are available.

To conclude, in the constructivist universe Marxism is equated with the stan-dards of a naturalist science, attacked as a reductionist-economic theory, and dismissed as a teleological philosophy. Before we attempt to rectify this interpre-tation, we want to introduce an exemplary constructivist reading of globalisation. Thereafter, we can advance an alternative account of globalisation on the basis of a different reading of Marx's epistemology.

Putting Constructivism to the historical test: Ruggie on globalisation

Ruggie's core argument centres around domestic state–society relations that generate what he calls 'social purpose' expressing an underlying normative consensus on the nature of national relations between authority and the market. He claims that this notion can shed light on the actual content of historically divers international regimes. 'Power and legitimate social purpose become fused to project political authority into the international system' (Ruggie 1998: 65).

Two fundamental problems organise his research: first, to identify the 'gener-ative grammar' of international political authority; second, to explain the occurrence of regime change not exclusively with reference to variations in power capacities (as Neorealism and Hegemonic Stability Theory (HST)), but in terms of the covariance in the fusion of power and 'social purpose' (Ruggie 1998: 64–5). For example, while the decline of British power and the subse-quent collapse of international order expressed fundamental divergences in the state–society relations of the system's constitutive units, the decline of US power did not imply the breakdown of international order due to the cross-national persistence of shared 'social purpose'. Given that 'social purpose' is held constant, adaptations to the new post-1973 international situation do not reflect fundamental power-based discontinuity (either the rise of protectionism or the return to classical liberalism), but reveal norm-governed as opposed to norm-transformative regime changes. The transformation of 'embedded liber-alism' is henceforth dependent on the 'inter-subjective' re-evaluation of welfare/capitalist state–society relations in the face of the resurgent 'ethos of liberalism'. Therewith Ruggie claims to have made the case not only against

HST and Neorealism, but also against neoliberal institutionalism providing the rationale for adopting a Weberian hermeneutical framework, which focuses on intersubjectivity and shared meanings. Let us now turn to his argument on globalisation.

In spite of the decline of US hegemony, 'embedded liberalism' persisted after the collapse of Bretton Woods, because 'social purpose' was held constant across the major industrialised states (Ruggie 1998: 65). Moving on to the 1990s, Ruggie (1995, 1997) sketched a new situation. Divergences in 'social purpose' became more pronounced among the three dominant economic blocks: the pluralist US market economy, the social market economy of Continental Europe, and the corporatist market economy of Japan, while globalisation meant the (re-)disembedding of the world economy from political control. A commitment to international multilateralism remains real, though weak, because competing national policies struggle for stability at home and success abroad. A period of turmoil and disarray is forecast. Theoretically, the assumption of growing divergences of 'social purpose' must lead Ruggie to conclude that norm-transformation, not norm-governance, drives current regime transformation. What, then, transforms these norms?

In Ruggie's scheme, globalisation is a result of the confluence of the success of GATT (and other international regimes), which made national boundaries redundant as expressions of the jurisdictional reach of national economies; and of a series of private sector institutional transformations. These are listed as the liberalisation of international markets in finance, goods, and services, as well as a shift in the patterns of international production from a division of labour among national economies to an international division of labour at the level of firms (multilateral corporations operating within transnational strategic alliances). These developments render traditional public policy goals – controlled economic growth, full employment and social stability – obsolete.

Like Goethe's Sorcerer's Apprentice, who could not control the forces that he unleashed, international post-war regime-imposed liberalisation turns out to be no longer compatible with domestic social compacts. But why is it that post-war liberalisation was compatible with domestic social compacts, while post-Bretton Woods liberalisation was not? The simple answer that Ruggie overlooks is that the latter failed to deliver the goods. Capitalism, for reasons stated later, entered a period of long economic downturn. Under conditions of negative economic growth and intensified domestic re-distributional conflicts, domestic social compacts were re-structured while states struggled to enhance their competitiveness. In other words, the domestic and multilateral institutional mechanisms of the 'Golden Capitalist Age' entered into a period of contradiction with changing economic fundamentals. While Ruggie wastes little time on these macro-economic changes, he concludes that

> The post-war trade regime was intended to achieve and maintain a sustainable balance between the internal and external policy objectives of governments, in keeping with the embedded liberalism compromise. It was

not designed to re-structure domestic institutional arrangements. Yet, domestic re-structuring is what the trade policy agenda increasingly has come to be about. Highly politicised trade policy disputes and potential instability in trade relations appeared to be the virtually inevitable consequence of successful liberalisation.

(Ruggie 1995: 516)

While this is a highly acute observation, it is not quite clear why these developments have to be theorised on the basis of changing epistemic communities. As a rule, a huge hiatus yawns between Ruggie's abstractly articulated basic methodological assumptions – norm-governance, change through social learning, etc. – and his thick descriptions of socio-economic developments. In Ruggie's idiom, what happened is this: the success of the constitutive rules of GATT had the unintended consequence of destroying the post-war social compact based on welfarism as well as GATT itself. New constitutive rules (WTO) and domestic 'social purposes' (neoliberalism) were devised in reaction to liberalisation/globalisation. In other words, a change in socio-economic reality preceded changes in the norms and rules of value communities. National and international regimes are trying to catch up with forces beyond their immediate control. However, why present turmoil is due to 'epistemic disarray in the community of scholars and policy analysts' rather than to economic crisis and the end of the era of sustained system-wide growth that generates nationally sharply diverging policy prescriptions, is hard to see (Ruggie 1995: 526, also 1997).

To conclude, the invocation of Weberian methodological precepts is unable to provide an explanation, as opposed to a mere description, of regime changes because within Ruggie's epistemic account material outcomes can only be derived from a prior cognitive shift in the relevant value communities. Theoretically, outcomes are always intentional and projected back onto an assumed prior alteration of value consensus. However, Ruggie's admission that neoliberalism/globalisation is an unintended consequence of the success of GATT jars with Constructivism's fundamental premise of collective intentionality. This minor logical problem aside, the central constructivist problem is that cognitive shifts have no apparent external referent, but recursively 'invent' the new socio-material reality out of themselves. The reasons for the 'resurgent ethos of liberalism' that drove globalisation in the 1980s and 1990s remain unidentified. In essence, Ruggie wants to explain changes in international economic regimes without economics and changes in international political regimes without politics by smuggling in the formal categories of convergence or divergence in 'social purpose'. However, an aggregate notion like 'social purpose' obscures the social processes and political mechanisms at work that generate conflict and compromise, crisis and successful institutionalisation among individuals, classes, and nations, as it remains silent on the repressive processes that ensure conventionality qua agreement. In other words, there is no extra-ideational explanation of changes in value communities – changes, according to our argument, that react to developments outside the explanatory reach of interpretive methodologies.

Karl Marx: elements of dialectical thinking

This section sets out and defends Marx's dialectical understanding of reality, history and agency. Our argument is that contrary to the constructivist claim, shared by NWHS and orthodox IPE, Marx's thought is not only non-naturalistic, non-reductionist and non-teleological, but in principle better able to critically understand international economic and political change. On the basis of the following re-examination of core elements of dialectical thinking, we will be in a position to advance an alternative theoretically controlled and empirically informed interpretation of globalisation.

Reality: human praxis and historical societalisation

What constitutes social reality? According to Marx, social reality is constituted by a contradictory ensemble of social relations that forms a historically specific *Vergesellschaftungszusammenhang* (context of societalisation) between nature and society. All human phenomena are related to this context. Hence, it must be clearly distinguished from Weber's 'vast chaotic stream' that can be ordered through subjective value-positions (Weber [1904] 1949: 84 and 111). It is also incompatible with the constructivist notion of reality as an inter-subjectively agreed convention, and with the positivist (naturalist) concept of one objective reality whose covering law can be disclosed through 'trial and error'. The Marxian epistemological principles that capture the nexus between society and nature are Hegelian in origin. However, Marx rejects Hegel's objective idealism as well as Feuerbach's objective materialism in favour of a philosophy of historical praxis (subjective materialism) (Heine and Teschke 1996, 1997; Neufeld 1995; Krombach 1997).

Marx argues that through the transformative power of conscious human praxis, both nature as 'man's inorganic body' and human nature are constantly reconstituted. Through this dynamic metabolism, nature is socially transformed into products, being into becoming, timeless essences into contradictory processes. Man is simultaneously the subject and the object of the socio-historical process. However, the triangle man–nature–society is of necessity contradictory. These contradictions are universal and transhistorical, yet appear historically in ever renewed, but definite, manifestations. History, as Hegel stressed, is the resolution of contradictions that interpret themselves (Hegel 1991). Dialectical thinking reflects this contradictory, dynamic, and transformative character of social reality and interferes critically into its reproduction. It avoids therefore the formulation of transhistorical invariants understood as objective laws and a de-politicised notion of conventionality based on learning and the fiction of open debate, and elevates contradictions to the logical status of the driving principle behind historical development.

Yet, in spite of this transitory character of history as process, *vergesellschaftete* reality is for Marx itself ordered and structured *per se*, before we impose our cognitive categories on it. Behind the infinite immediacy of subjective experiences, he assumes a temporarily institutionalised and spatially delineated core to reality. We claim that this core, as we will argue in the following section, is defined by historically variable social property relations, constituting the nodal point of intersection between nature, man, and society.

The assumption of an ordered structure of reality diverges not only from Weber's idea of infinite chaos, it is potentially able to reveal Weber's position as representative of the cognitive condition of modernity (see Weber [1919] 1946a and [1919] 1946b). For Marx's notion of the capital relation, institutionalised in capitalist social property relations, contains not only an account of individuation, it also entails an account of why social reality appears as a universe of discrete things. First, individuation results from the making of abstract labour, that is, the transformation of property-possessing, economically independent, but politically dependent labour into disowned, legally and politically free, but economically dependent wage labour. This transformation captures the essence of the transition from feudalism to capitalism. The new capitalist property regime creates the real illusion of civil society as an aggregate of contractual relations between isolated individuals.[6] At the same time, the state appears as the Hegelian ethical sphere of public interest now separated from the sphere of private needs constitutive of civil society and the market. Human beings are at once citoyens and bourgeois. Second, the transformation of labour into a commodity that can be bought and sold on the market turns human beings and their produce into abstract things (reification and alienation), while money organises exchange abstractly as the universal equivalent. The primary form of modern inter-subjectivity is thus constituted by money as the pervasive medium of extra-communicative power. Hence, the 'fetishism of commodities', that reflects 'personal independence based upon dependence mediated by things', constitutes the fundamental cognitive experience of capitalist modernity (Marx [1867] 1976: 163–77; Marx [1857–8] 1993: 158). Third, the historical completion of the market as a universal based on generalised commodification leads to a form of society in which not only individuals, but also their value-positions and interests, are atomised and competing.

As a result, the modern incoherence of experience can be explained as reflecting precisely the hieroglyphic character of the capitalist object-world that appears to the naked eye as an inchoate and endless aggregate of discrete entities, individual acts, or preferences. Hegel's 'bad infinity' (*'schlechte Unendlichkeit'*) is Weber's 'vast chaotic stream'. While Enlightenment philosophy recognises the atomised nature of modernity, Marx unveils its unifying theme. The reified nature of the world of objects assumes a reality – a 'second nature' – independent of our own volition and intelligibility. While this world is indeed a world of our own making, it confronts us as something alien, external, and unfathomable. Thus, through a Marxist dialectical approach, we can theorise and demystify institutions that are central to modernity: individuation, the fiction (*Realabstraktion*) of the 'self-regulating' market, civil society as the sphere of private freedom, and the modern state as the sphere of collective reason. This reveals the link between competing private interests, irreconcilable value-positions and Max Weber's acceptance and promotion of scientific pluralism (Weber [1919] 1946b).

In this sense, Weber's theory runs two risks. First, his value pluralism exemplifies the fragmented experience of the modern abstract 'I' and the wider antinomies of bourgeois thought and culture: the Kantian distinction between noumena (transcendental things-in-themselves) and phenomena, the separation between facts and values, the opposition between free will and necessity, form and content, and subject and object (Weber [1904] 1949: 81). Second, Weber's causal pluralism reflects the apparent differentiation of the world into multiple petrified spheres, which 'follow their own laws' and interact only externally (Weber [1904] 1949: 70). But does the recognition of the fragmented world, both normatively as well as causally, entail necessarily the call for pluralist theories?

History: 'laws', contradictions, agency

Weber's theory of history falls into two irreconciled parts: history as the chaotic aggregate of subjectively intended individual acts (methodological individualism), battles with history as a universal process of rationalisation, locking individuals increasingly into iron institutional structures (Weber [1904–5] 1992: 181; Weber [1922] 1968). For Marx, in contrast, history is the resolution of contradictory and competing strategies of reproduction that are bound up with historically institutionalised social property relations and may or may not alter the institutional set-up. Action and structure are dynamically mediated.

From this angle, history has no pre-defined telos, yet it is inherently teleological in so far as each human act is willed and conscious, that is, it strives towards the realisation of a purpose. Yet, purposeful acts are embedded in wider forms of collective action, whose nature is governed for Marx primarily by the proprietary relation of individuals to the means of production. Men enter *nolens volens* determinate relations of production and operate within them. However, the stress on class relations on the basis of unequal access to and property of the means of production is not an axiom, but merely a research hypothesis whose validity must be corroborated in concrete research. Writing history is thus not a manipulative exercise of fitting facts into the Procrustean bed of a transcendental philosophy of history (Marx [1845] 1994a: 112).

Let us now spell out why social property relations define the core structure of society. Historically, access to property and the means of reproduction is politically established. Politically constituted regimes institutionalise time-bound balances of class forces by fixing social property settlements that set the parameters for purposeful, bounded, but antagonistic forms of social action on both sides of the labour process.[7] For example, under capitalism, as a rule, propertyless direct producers are compelled to sell their labour power on a labour market to make a living. Equally, capitalists are compelled to maintain themselves in business through competitive re-investment in the means of production or other measures of cost-cutting (shedding of labour) according to the 'invisible' working of the price-mechanism. The logic of collective action works differently under feudal property relations. Here, direct producers are in possession of the means of production. Hence, lords are forced to invest in the means of coercion to guarantee the extra-economic exploitation of a dependent peasantry while simultaneously maintaining themselves militarily over and against rival lords. Equally, peasants are compelled to produce the totality of their produce on their plots and to resist lordly exactions (Brenner 1986; Teschke 1998). In a word, property-mediated relations of exploitation impose limits on the spectrum of action and thought. While the contradictory strategies of reproduction on both sides of the labour-process do not exhaust the complex of consciousness-formation, a theory of the latter cannot dispense with recognising the former. Dominant forms of bounded action (consciousness) know an external referent.

Yet while politically constituted regimes (property regimes, authority-relations) institutionalise social conflicts in time and space, setting the time-bound and norm-mediated absolute limits for contradictory strategies of reproduction, these institutions may turn themselves into the object of contestation during periods of general crisis. Rule-maintenance and rule-negotiation – violent or not – are actively played out processes. The resolution of social conflicts in times of crisis, mediated by a given balance of class forces, is however logically indeterminate, though not wholly contingent, and thus guarantees the non-unilinear, non-inevitabilistic, and open-ended character of history as a process with no fixed terminus (Brenner 1985).[8] Still, the resolution of contradictions is retrospectively intelligible through historical research. Historical development is thus neither the circular, contentless, and recursive re-enaction of structures through agency and vice versa (Giddens 1984), nor the result of a 'messy' process of complex interaction, nor a necessitous succession of stages, driven by the mechanic contradictions between the development of the forces of production and relations of production. It is the result of agency-driven qualitative transformations of social relations.[9] These give rise to new forms of bounded agency. Consequently, the course of history cannot be deduced or even predicted from de-subjectified economic 'iron laws', which govern human beings in a determinist and automatic fashion behind their backs. While any specific property regime sets indeed definite parameters for human activity, this determination is never absolute.

Why does this matter? Simply put, while there are 'laws' in history – defined by prevailing property relations – there can be no laws of history. Law-like generalisations only apply to spatio-temporal contexts. Therefore, Weber's naturalistic characterisation of Marx's notion of law – and Ruggie's uncritical adoption of Weber's position – as expressing objective and universal validity is misguided (Weber [1904] 1949: 68–76 and 86–7; clearly demonstrated in Kocka [1966] 1985: 136–40).

Thus a hermeneutical or psychological understanding of the meaning or motivation (*mentalité*) on the side of individuals, groups, or classes does not provide an exhaustive explanation (Adorno [1969] 1976: 14). The capitalist profit motive cannot be tautologically derived from an ascetic ethics of work, 'market rationality', or a naturalised homo oeconomicus. Rather, an entire structure of meanings and motivations (interests or preferences) is 'objectively' imposed upon human beings by extra-subjective socio-material relations. Social relations of production and exploitation define entire strategies of action and modes of consciousness, provided the actor wants to survive and be recognised by society. In this sense, ideational phenomena are amenable to theorisation in so far as they express and try to come to terms with a social 'essence' hidden from view. From this perspective, Weber's views of history can be qualified, both with respect to his claim of necessarily plural and indeterminate ultimate value-positions adopted by researchers, as well as with respect to the chaotic appearance of reality itself.

The diversity of phenomena does not simply 'reveal' a core structure (the logic of capital), but is mediated by it and lends it a definite form. Phenomena cannot be reduced to capital, nor can capital be dissolved in appearances. Yet capital does not exist in the singular, but is politically mediated in a system of states with their own distinct, but not fully independent, historical trajectories. Thus the concrete analysis of capitalist societies must understand how the pressures exerted by capital are broken and deflected through the conscious actions of classes within and between capitalist societies.[10] Hence, politics and geopolitics, among other 'moments', enter immediately the determination of the course and nature of capitalist societies. Yet this does not imply the plea for a series of incommensurable national *Sonderwege* (special paths), since capitalism – in a historically sequenced form which is itself co-constitutive of their relative uniqueness brought about in a pattern of geographically combined yet socially uneven development – is common to all of them. The logic of process has to replace the logic of structure. Historical variations among capitalist societies can be controlled by, but not reduced to, their identical core structure. In this sense, historical research has to establish this unity-in-diversity. However, there is no unmediated access to the facts without and ideas within (Krombach 1997). The crucial question is how we can best control this process of interpretation that is, of necessity, always a process of abstraction, even for archival workers. This is the task of metatheory. This is the task of dialectic.

Theorising globalisation

This outline of dialectical elements will now help us to set out an alternative explanation of globalisation that transcends the insufficiencies of constructivist accounts. To recapitulate, Ruggie theorised the end of 'embedded liberalism' in terms of epistemic disarray subsequent to divergences in national 'social purposes' as a result of successful liberalisation. We criticised this account because it treated 'social purpose' as a domestic black box, failed to relate globalisation to capitalist crisis, and underspecified the fundamental relation between states and markets under capitalism. However, the wider debate on globalisation is precisely defined by an attempt to understand the changing configuration of this relation. A widely held 'strong' version on globalisation suggests that greater openness in matters of trade, finance, services, and investment as well as the flexible transnational operations of footloose corporations drastically reduce the macro-economic steering capacity of the state in unprecedented ways (Ohmae [1990] 1999; Reich 1991; Horsman and Marshall 1994; compare Hirst and

Thompson 1996). The assumption is that a globally integrated world economy exerts identical pressure on policy choices in different national contexts, imposing a similarity, if not uniformity, in public policy outcomes. In extremis, these developments amount to a self-cancellation of the state as a meaningful economic entity itself and the rise of a borderless world.

Furthermore, the standard liberal explanation tends to start with a description of a series of private sector economic and technological innovations and/or the observation of a quantitative increase in global transaction flows (sometimes described as the independent variable), followed by an assessment of their effects on state capacities (the dependent variable).[11] Problems of causality are here compounded by problems of evaluation. First, causality is inherently functional, going from the economic to the political. Second, globalisation is conceived as a zero-sum relation between states and markets: Keynesianism is equated with a strong state, while neoliberalism stands for a weak state. Third, uniformity in outcomes is proposed.

In contrast to the constructivist and liberal accounts sketched above, our core argument is that globalisation refers to a conscious re-structuring of state-society and inter-state relations in response to the onset of the long economic downturn during the 1970s. Globalisation is neither a techno-economically induced, nor a purely politically driven, phenomenon, but the result of a dialectical, that is class-contested and consciously mediated, re-formulation of private and public strategies of reproduction under conditions of long-term negative growth.[12] We argue that capitalist state power has not undergone a quantifiable reduction, but a qualitative shift in purpose, which may be broadly defined as a shift from the welfare state to the competition state (*Wettbewerbsstaat*). This thesis is premised on the assumption that success and failure in the market are never exclusively determined by the market, but depend always on the political conditions of capital-accumulation. However, while it is suggestive to argue that the world market constitutes today a *Sachzwang* (objective compulsion) (Altvater and Mahnkopf 1997), this compulsion was politically assisted, remains politically regulated, and is potentially politically reversible. Furthermore, while the state's main function today is to directly support the competitiveness of its firms on a world-wide scale, important national divergences in public policy responses to globalisation are discernible (Streeck 1998). Thus, states are not the victims or losers of globalisation, but have both *nolens volens* facilitated and eventually benefited from the internationalisation of capital. If anything is withering away today, it is not the state as such, but rather its democratic legitimacy.

In order to support our argument, we will first have to restate the basic relation between the economic and the political under capitalism. In a second step, we will provide an account of the origins of globalisation as an outcome of the international profitability crisis. In a third step, we will set out divergences in state responses to the long downturn of the world-economy, that validate our dialectical claim that while globalisation entails a historically unprecedented shrinkage of policy choices, states constitute still the main relays for the reproduction of capitalism.

The fundamental relation between the economic and the political under capitalism

The core premise of a historical materialist approach to globalisation is that the differentiation between the economic and the political is unique to capitalism.[13] In pre-capitalist societies, the economic remains always embedded in social, cultural, or political processes that regulate production, exchange, distribution, and consumption.[14] The process of the disembedding of the market from socio-political norms allows in principle for economic self-regulation through the 'invisible hand' of the price-setting market. This is correctly observed, but inadequately theorised, in Polanyi's work on *The Great Transformation* (Polanyi [1944] 1957).

Marx characterises this transformation as a shift from forms of 'extra-economic compulsion' under pre-capitalist social property relations to forms of economic exploitation instituted in the capital relation, theorised by the law of value (Marx [1867] 1976). Capitalism refers to a form of society predicated on the separation of the direct producers from their means of reproduction – the making of 'free' labour – so that generalised market-dependency translates into the disembedding of economic processes of production and exchange from direct political power. Henceforth, dispossessed and commodified direct producers are economically forced to make a living by entering into private economic contracts without direct political interference, as capitalists are compelled to compete in the market to maximise profits. Inter-capitalist competition necessitates specialisation and the out-pricing of competitors, predicated on product-innovation and the reduction of production costs. Cost cutting results either in the lowering of wages, the intensification of labour, or the replacement of labour by dint of technological rationalisation, based on competitive re-investment. A theory of technological innovation, leading to productivity gains and general growth, is thus built into capitalism itself. At the same time, profit-maximisation and inter-capitalist competition generate also a territorially expansive tendency towards the opening up of markets via trade.

Furthermore, a theory of the modern state is built into capitalist social property relations. Generalised market dependency, displacing pre-capitalist forms of direct political exploitation, allows for the pooling of political power in a sovereign state abstracted from civil society. The conflict-ridden and geopolitically mediated generalisation of the capital-relation allows for the conceptual and historical differentiation between an un-coercive 'economic economy' and a 'political state', monopolising the means of violence in a specific territory.[15] Henceforth, the state's minimal aims are to enforce private contracts and to defend private property internally and externally so as to keep the private profit-accumulation cycle intact. Capitalism thus understood allows us to conceptualise the structural and institutional differentiation between state and economy/civil society as an internal relation. In other words, this separation of the economic and the political is unique to capitalism as a totality. On this basis, changes in the configuration between the economic and the political within capitalist societies never transcend this structural differentiation, but are always changes internal to capitalism.

These changes generate crisis. Crisis is built into the capitalist accumulation cycle in so far as capital–labour relations contain, as a rule, a structural conflict of interests and as inter-capitalist rivalry, both nationally and internationally, tends to drive profit margins down. The state is thus permanently involved in the mediation and resolution of domestic and international social and economic crises through political regulation, economic intervention, diplomatic accommodation and war (Mayer 1971). However, the conflict-resolving power of the state depends primarily on those institutions that express and reproduce the capital–labour compromise, while being structurally limited by its fiscal dependency on the capital circuit. Therefore, the crisis-ridden historical development of capitalism remains central for an explanation of variations of state–economy relations and inter-state relations. In a very real sense, therefore, capitalist markets remain at a certain level of abstraction always de-politicised as long as the self-regulation of the market through the price mechanism is not fundamentally challenged. In other words, there can be no re-embedding of the economic into the political, only greater or lesser degrees of political management. Historically diverse capitalist state–society relations – the classical liberal, the corporatist, the interventionist-welfare, and the neoliberal state – simply represent variations in the degree of re-politicisation and de-politicisation (but no re-embedding) of the economy in what are essentially capitalist totalities.

It follows that we cannot adopt a Weber-inspired multi-causal approach towards the external and contingent interaction between institutionally separated spheres that display their endogenous logics (configuration analysis/types of state–society relations), as orthodox IPE and NWHS tend to do.[16] The orthodox Weber-informed view of a zero-sum relation between states and markets rests on an erroneous dichotomy.[17] It imparts a false sense of institutional identity and operative autonomy to what are preconceived as two discrete entities displaying competing collective wills. A reified power-based logic of bureaucratic rationality is here opposed to an independent profit-based logic of economic rationality. We suggest therefore that a dialectical philosophy of internal relations provides the necessary epistemological rationale for understanding the changing domestic and international relations between states and markets.

The origins of globalisation as a result of capitalist crisis

The post-war historical compromise in the advanced capitalist world between labour and capital was designed and internationally successfully institutionalised during a period of US hegemony, unprecedented and sustained economic growth, and system-competition between East and West. 'Embedded liberalism' and welfare programmes were predicated on the post-war boom.

However, between 1965 and 1973, that is before the onset of the oil shocks, a series of world-economic crisis symptoms interlocked (Brenner 1998: 93–234). At the core of the onset of crisis was an uneven but system-wide aggregate fall in the rate of profit predicated on falling rates of productivity in the G-7 countries. According to Robert Brenner, this profit-squeeze cannot be attributed to vertical class conflicts and excessive wage-growth but results from intensified international inter-capitalist competition, exerting downward pressure on prices due to over-capacity and over-production and a failure of re-adjustment at the level of the firm (Brenner 1998). Falling profits translated into decreasing levels of investments and rising unemployment. Intense pressure on the welfare state, due to a falling rate of tax returns, accelerating inflation, skyrocketing interest rates, and drastic rises in public debts, led to a downwards spiral in overall economic performance that challenged the viability of the post-war compromise.

Governments first responded by trying to sustain the welfare compromise by re-mobilising formerly successful Keynesian policies of demand-led counter-cyclical macro-economic management during the 1970s to stimulate growth. Yet the expansion of credit, while preventing the slide of a series of recessions (1970–71, 1974–75, 1979–82) into a full-blown depression, also impeded and delayed market exit by under-performing firms so as to prolong the profitability crisis that remained fundamentally determined by over-production and over-capacity. The net effect was a massive surge of public debts that failed to jump start economies and to reinvigorate growth. For example, the US military public spending programme of the early 1980s and general tax cuts, through a combination of high interest rates and a massive dollar revaluation (Reaganomics), proved a massive disaster for the US economy. Mitterrand's return to public planning was severely punished by international capital markets. Under conditions of system-wide negative economic growth and the failure of export-led recovery through a series of competitive currency devaluations, Keynesianism failed.

Within this context of economic downturn and political crisis, major shifts in private economic strategies for restoring the conditions of successful capitalist accumulation eroded the post-war model. Falling rates of profit made re-investment into production less attractive. Capital, in its liquid money form, was increasingly diverted into financial markets that promised higher short-term rates of return. Thus, the first step associated with globalisation implied the de-regulation of international money markets (O'Brien 1992). Simultaneously, capital interests pushed for the liberalisation and widening of markets for goods and services, pressed for a re-definition of industrial relations, the flexibilisation of labour markets, tax cuts and the reduction of indirect labour costs, while intensifying the re-structuration of intra-firm organisation of production in a transnational direction. Rationalisation involved the shedding and/or intensification of labour, as well as the introduction of new technologies. Business policies aimed for the general reduction of production costs and the loosening of the structural dependence by firms on 'business-unfriendly' national policy-contexts. In extremis, big firms used threats of investment strikes, capital flight and the dislocation of their sites of production.

This catalogue of business strategies set the parameters for public policy options and gradually de-legitimised the corporatist triangle between government, employers, and unions (Streeck 1998). It followed a massive system-wide shift in the balance of class forces in favour of capital, assisted by growing levels of unemployment that undermined labour's structural bargaining power. However, in spite of the success of the employers' offensive, the global profitability crisis persisted.[18] The accumulation of crisis symptoms inaugurated a critical historical conjuncture, composed of a period of transition (1965–79/82) and a period of neoliberal consolidation (1979/82–2000). Yet, while states faced the same economic crisis symptoms across the board, variations in state responses are discernible that vitiate the fashionable thesis of the end of the sovereign state.

General crisis: the dialectic of converging business strategies and diverging state responses

The logic of the market set absolute limits to private strategies for re-establishing the conditions of successful capital accumulation. A falling average rate of profit prompted similar private sector strategies in the advanced capitalist world. Variations within these limits do not refute the general objective of regaining profitability. The new situation came to be characterised by the persistence of economic crisis and a general diversification, intensification, and internationalisation of private strategies of capital accumulation: globalisation unbound. Yet the uneven spread of crisis, non-synchronous national and sectoral business cycles, nationally diverging balances of class forces, and historically different institutional contexts of industrial relations, translated into palpable divergences in political management strategies that do not follow an exclusive economic rationality (Weiss 1999). These state variations reflect consciously adopted public policies that call for a dialectical theorisation.

While in the 1980s monetarism (tight money, fiscal austerity, balanced budgets) became the watchword of the day in states that were most severely challenged by negative growth and public debts, it neither meant the end of the state, nor the system-wide and chronologically simultaneous adoption of identical public policies. With the parameters for public policy choices set by the general economic downturn, governments devised diverse counter-strategies of state-supported macro-economic management. This diversity is evidenced in the respective configuration of the components of national-economic policy matrices that determine macro-economic regulation, including fiscal and monetary policy, industrial relations, social security and education systems, as well as industrial and sectoral policy. The new situation is characterised by diversity-in-identity.

In the early 1980s, the 'German model' that was traditionally based on export-led growth, currency undervaluation, consensual corporatism, high-skilled labour, anti-inflationary and tight monetary policies, high taxes and a relatively strong commitment to welfarism did not immediately follow the path of radical liberalisation. Rather, the CDU/FDP coalition, while profiting from the record US budget deficit and a strong dollar, pursued a policy of modest macro-economic deficit spending and gradual state-supervised privatisation to counter economic recession combined with an active policy of wage moderation while continuing to subsidise exports. In the mid-1980s, after the Plaza Accord between the USA, Germany and Japan, Germany managed to avoid recession in spite of DM revaluation due to productivity increases, wage concessions, and the rationalisation of industries as a result of an active 'national-economic' industrial policy. However, unemployment rose to unprecedented levels. With the onset of unification, the full turn towards neoliberalism was postponed once again. Deficit spending, easy money, extra levies on taxes and state-controlled privatisation in the East led to a short-lived boom, the massive long-term accumulation of public debts, and inflationary pressure that has become the policy-restraining legacy left to the incoming SPD/Grüne government. The current policy follows a peculiarly contradictory path. On the one hand, Germany is committed to the implementation of austerity programmes, combined with tax reform, tight money and flexibilisation of labour markets, broadly in line with neoliberal prescriptions.[19] On the other hand, continuing financial transfers to the New Länder and a strategy for European regionalisation and enlargement run directly counter to the strong globalisation thesis that equates neoliberalism with the loss of state capacity.[20] Contrary to the globalisation thesis of a retreating state, the German state acts as the main circuit of transmission between domestic capital interests and regional and international institutions.

After the failure of the greatest Keynesian experiment in American history under Reagan and the accumulation of the highest US deficit ever, successive US governments made it their political objective to devalue the dollar and to re-establish the competitiveness of American commodities. The state adopted a neoliberal strategy of leaving the economy to market forces to re-establish competitiveness the hard way, since it was structurally unable to do anything else. From the mid-1980s onwards, the USA witnessed massive industrial shakeouts, rising unemployment, the intensified flexibilisation of labour markets, a downward spiral in wages, and the creation of a massive low-wage sector. Austerity programmes translated into tight money, corporate tax cuts, balanced budgets, and the declining growth of welfare spending. The creation of a regional free trade area (NAFTA) offered additional opportunities for relocating labour-intensive low-cost production sites abroad, while driving the American workforce into submission. In spite of an attempt by the incoming Clinton administration to revive public spending, Congress rebuffed even this modest trial of Keynesian demand-management (Brenner 1998: 194).

While the current US boom seems to vitiate any notion of capitalist crisis, huge economic imbalances have accumulated that carry all the signs of a bubble economy.[21] From the mid-1990s consumer debts have reached unprecedented levels since consumers buy on the back of spiralling stock market values.[22] However, stock markets have over-valued real increases in company profits by about three times. Consequently, the current account deficit approaches 5 per cent of US GDP while net foreign debts stand at over $2,000 billion (Atkinson 2000). Sooner or later the dollar will have to de-value punctuated by a series of interest rate rises that will throttle growth and may lead to a massive depreciation in stocks. Even if the US trajectory approximates the neoliberal model, we still have to note that neoliberalism is a conscious state policy that is not to be confused with the self-cancellation of the state. The more active side of the US neoliberal state is clearly displayed in its fiscal and monetary policies and its unilateral attempts to dominate the agenda of multilateral institutions (WTO, IMF, World Bank Group), while holding the UN hostage to its unpaid debts.

Turning to Asia, Japanese state–economy relations present another structural variant over and against the Anglo-American and European models, constituting perhaps the strongest case against the 'strong' globalisation thesis (Murphy 2000). The Japanese political economy is characterised by distinctive corporate structures and strategic alliances between state, banks, and sectoral business interests. However, as in the German case, the Japanese state promotes export-led growth through currency under-valuations and continuous re-investment into the domestic innovation cycle. High levels of savings and restrictions on foreign investment assist this process. During the 1980s, in an effort to make Japanese production cost-effective, the state actively encouraged Japanese firms to move labour-intensive production sites abroad, while providing incentives to concentrate high-tech production facilities at home (Weiss 1997: 21–2). The strategy was recently updated in that MITI embarked upon a programme of relocating the entire production of older generations of produce in order to ensure domestic 'high engineering' (Ehrke 1997). However, after the Plaza Accord in 1985, the Japanese state tried to stem declining exports after the yen revaluation by providing ultra-easy money. Yet the expected investment boom failed to materialise, throwing the economy into a long and deep recession in 1991–5. In spite of this economic under-performance, the state failed to embrace neoliberal standard measures (de-regulation, privatisation), while trying to revive the economy through a mixed strategy of major public spending programmes and decreases in interest rates. After the Reverse Plaza Accord in 1995 and the ensuing devaluation of the currency, massive rounds of public spending had to be counterbalanced by major tax increases.[23] While unemployment rose within limits, wage growth was drastically reduced.[24] Overall, the Japanese state did not succumb to neoliberal prescriptions, but is constantly required to re-structure its capacities to ensure international economic competitiveness.

In sum, the state has not seen its competencies and steering-power reduced. Rather, what has occurred during the course of the last twenty years is a structural incapacity by democratically legitimated collective actors to harness the power of the state to any other purposes than those in the interest of capital. The reason for this is that capitalism entered a prolonged period of crisis and states are structurally tied to the power of capital. This does not imply the mutual cancelling out of state capacities, but their re-structuration and mobilisation for the establishment of competitive advantages in favour of domestic and international capital.

Conclusion

This chapter has challenged Constructivism's objections to historical materialism on three counts. It rejects the notion that Marx embraces a naturalist deductive-nomological form of science, an economic reductionist theory of society, and a teleological philosophy of history. We have furthermore argued that Constructivism's theoretical programme is in itself deficient and ill equipped to theorise international political and economic change. A re-examination of the dialectical nature of Marxian thought provided an alternative starting point for thinking about the state/economy nexus, international relations in general and about globalisation in particular. We made three substantive claims. First, the origins of globalisation are rooted in the crisis of the capitalist world economy beginning in the 1970s. Second, the power of capitalist states has not been reduced. Rather, it has been transformed in favour of reconstructing the national and international conditions of growth and capital accumulation under massive, if unevenly successful, pressure from respective capitalist classes. While the conjunctural re-configuration of the relation between states and markets cannot be dissociated from the long economic downturn, we do not witness the end of the state and the rise of a borderless world, but a temporally and regionally uneven redefinition of state functions in the direction of the competition state. Third, although the capitalist crisis imposed identical pressures on states, variations in state responses can be explained with regard to differences in the structural bargaining power of social forces in nationally diverging institutional contexts.

Notes

1 Constructivism draws on an increasingly heterogeneous array of literatures. While the more proximate impulses came from the work of Berger and Luckmann 1966; Giddens 1984; Searle 1995; and the later Habermas 1984 and 1987, its classical roots are now associated with Max Weber, Emile Durkheim, and even Karl Marx himself. Cf. Kratochwil 1996: 217; Onuf 1989; Wendt 1992, 1999; Ruggie 1998.
2 Following Adler's classification our outline of Constructivism refers to its 'modernist' camp (Adler 1997).
3 Kratochwil 1997: 437. Katzenstein, Keohane and Krasner distinguish today only between Rationalism and Constructivism (Katzenstein *et al.* 1999: 6).
4 Similarly, by misappropriating the work of Robert Brenner, Ruggie also claims that capitalism is essentially a constitutive rule (Ruggie 1998: 23).
5 How Wendt can repeatedly invoke the master–slave dialectic to exemplify the nature of 'constitutive relationships' without acknowledging its centrality for Hegelian Marxism is quite an achievement (Wendt 1999: 25).
6 Kratochwil concedes as much, but argues that law and formal organisations 'are analytically independent of the issue of ownership of the means of production' (Kratochwil 1993: 78). However is law also independent from the institutionalisation of class conflicts between capital and labour, pre-structured by property?
7 The nature of the political can be based on class, religion, gender, race, kinship. In principle, however, the political is constitutive of social production, appropriation, re-distribution, and consumption.
8 Let us note that Marx foresaw the resolution of class struggle in either 'a revolutionary re-constitution of society at large, or in the common ruin of the contending classes' (Marx [1848] 1994b: 159).

9 On Marx's ill-fated 1859 Preface cf. Printz 1969.
10 For the relation between the classical tradition of Geopolitik and Marxism compare Teschke 2001.
11 Cf. the contributions in Keohane and Milner 1996 and Strange 1996. On the 'dependent and independent variable' syndrome cf. Keohane and Milner 1996: 3–5 and Frieden and Rogowski 1996: 26–8.
12 For a techo-economic account cf. Castells 1996–8, for a politicist account cf. Weiss 1997: 23 and 1999.
13 The idea of a differentiation between the political and the economic under capitalism has been argued, by Wood 1981; Brenner 1986; Rosenberg 1994; Boyle 1994; Burnham 1994; Bromley 1995 and 1999.
14 The implications of this insight for IR are drawn out in Teschke 1998.
15 However, multiple state territories are not a function of capitalism, but a legacy of pre-capitalist territory-formation (compare Teschke 2002: 30–38)
16 Mann 1986, 1993; Hobson 1997, 1998. An entire discipline (IPE) is based on the assumption that the modern international system is constituted by a complex layer-cake of 'ontologically' separate but interrelated structures that follow their own independent logic. See Strange 1996: 26. 'State and market, whatever their respective origins, have independent existences, have logics of their own, and interact with one another' (Gilpin 1987: 10).
17 Strange 1996 argues for the retreat of the state, while Mann 1997 argues for the rise and rise of the nation-state.
18 Brenner suggests that manufacturing accepted lower rates of return because fixed capital sunk in plant and machinery posed a structural disincentive to swiftly change lines, preventing a rapid re-adjustment through massive industrial shakeouts. Insufficient exit and increased entry through intensified international competition blocked the creative destruction of capital, generating a series of recessions and prolonging the economic downturn (Brenner 1998).
19 OECD Observer, No. 214, Oct./Nov. 1998. See http://www.oecd.org/publications/observer/214/e-toc htm.
20 OECD Economic Surveys, Germany, Nov. 1999.
21 OECD Observer, No. 217/18, Summer 1999. See http://www.oecd.org/publicaions/observer/217/e-toc htm.
22 OECD Economic Surveys, United States, May 1999.
23 OECD Observer, No. 219, Dec. 1999. See http://www.oecd.org/publications/observer/219/e-toc htm.
24 OECD Economic Surveys, Japan, Nov. 1999.

Bibliography

Adler, E. (1997) 'Seizing the Middle Ground: Constructivism in World Politics', *European Journal of International Relations*, 3 (3): 319–63.
Adorno, T. W. ([1969] 1976) 'Introduction', in T.W. Adorno, Hans Albert *et al.*, *The Positivist Dispute in German Sociology*, trans. G. Adey and D. Frisby, London: Heinemann, pp.1–67.
Altvater, E. and Mahnkopf, B. (1997) 'The World Market Unbound', *Review of International Political Economy*, 4 (3): 448–71.
Atkinson, M. (2000) 'Dollar Beware', *Guardian*, 18 January 2000.
Berger, P. and Luckmann, T. (1966) *The Social Construction of Reality*, Garden City, NY: Doubleday.
Boyle, C. (1994) 'Imagining the World Market: IPE and the Task of Social Theory', *Millennium*, 23 (2): 351–63.

Kratochwil, F. (1989) *Rules, Norms, and Decisions*, Cambridge: Cambridge University Press.

—— (1993) 'Contract and Regimes: Do Issue Specificity and Variations of Formality Matter?', in V. Rittberger and P. Mayer (eds), *Regime Theory and International Relations*, Oxford: Clarendon Press and New York: Oxford University Press, pp.73–93.

—— (1996) 'Is the Ship of Culture at Sea or Returning?', in Y. Lapid and F. Kratochwil (eds), *The Return of Culture and Identity in IR Theory*, Boulder, CO and London: Lynne Rienner Publishers, pp.201–22.

—— (1997) 'Awakening or Somnambulation?', *Millennium*, 26 (2): 437–42.

Krombach, H. (1997) 'Dialectic as the Philosophical Science of Socio-Historical Relations', *Millennium*, 26 (2): 417–36.

Mann, M. (1986) *The Sources of Social Power*, Volume I, Cambridge: Cambridge University Press.

—— (1993) *The Sources of Social Power*, Volume II, Cambridge: Cambridge University Press.

—— (1997) 'Has Globalization Ended the Rise and Rise of the Nation-State?', *Review of International Political Economy*, 4 (3): 472–96.

Marx, K. ([1867] 1976) *Capital: A Critique of Political Economy*, Volume I, trans. B. Fowkes, London: Penguin.

—— ([1857–8] 1993) *Grundrisse: Foundations of the Critique of Political Economy*, trans. M. Nicolaus, London: Penguin.

—— ([1845] 1994a) 'The German Ideology, Part I', in L. Simon (ed.), *Karl Marx: Selected Writings*, Indianapolis, IN: Hackett, pp.102–56.

—— ([1848] 1994b) 'The Communist Manifesto', in L. Simon (ed.), *Karl Marx: Selected Writings*, Indianapolis, IN: Hackett, pp.158–86.

Mayer, A. (1971) *Dynamics of Counterrevolution in Europe, 1870–1956*, New York: Harper & Row.

Murphy, T. (2000) 'Japan's Economic Crisis', *New Left Review*, II, 1: 25–52.

Neufeld, M. (1995) *The Restructuring of International Relations Theory*, Cambridge: Cambridge University Press.

O'Brien, R. (1992) *Global Financial Integration: The End of Geography*, London: Pinter Publishers.

Ohmae, K. ([1990] 1999) *The Borderless World*, New York: Harper Business.

Onuf, N. (1989) *World of Our Making*, Columbia, SC: University of South Carolina.

Polanyi, K. ([1944] 1957) *The Great Transformation*, Boston, MA: Beacon Press.

Printz, A. (1969) 'Background and Ulterior Motives of Marx's Preface of 1859', *Journal of the History of Ideas*, 30 (3): 437–50.

Reich, R. (1991) *The Work of Nations*, New York: Knopf.

Rosenberg, J. (1994) *The Empire of Civil Society*, London: Verso.

Ruggie, J. (1995) 'At Home Abroad, Abroad at Home: International Liberalisation and Domestic Stability in the World Economy', *Millennium*, 24 (3): 507–26.

—— (1997) 'Globalisierung und der gesellschaftliche Kompromiß des sozial regulierten Liberalismus: Das Ende einer Ära?', in W. Fricke (ed.), *Jahrbuch Arbeit und Technik: Globalisierung und institutionelle Reform*, Bonn: Dietz Verlag, pp.369–82.

—— (1998) *Constructing the World Polity*, London: Routledge.

Searle, J. (1995) *The Construction of Social Reality*, New York: Free Press.

Spruyt, H. (1994) *The Sovereign State and Its Competitors*, Princeton, NJ: Princeton University Press.

Strange, S. (1996), *The Retreat of the State*, Cambridge and New York: Cambridge University Press.

Brenner, R. (1985) 'The Agrarian Roots of European Capitalism', in T.H. Aston and C. Philpin (eds), *The Brenner Debate*, Cambridge: Cambridge University Press, pp.213–32?.

—— (1986) 'The Social Basis of Economic Development', in J. Roemer (ed.), *Analı Marxism*, Cambridge: Cambridge University Press, pp.23–53.

—— (1998) 'The Economics of Global Turbulence: A Special Report on the Wc Economy, 1950–98', *New Left Review*, 229: 1–265.

Bromley, S. (1995) 'Rethinking International Political Economy', in A. Linklater and MacMillan (eds), *Boundaries in Question*, London: Pinter, pp.228–43.

—— (1999) 'Marxism and Globalisation', in A. Gamble, D. Marsh and T. Tant (edᵢ *Marxism and Social Science*, London: Macmillan, pp.280–301.

Burnham, P. (1994) 'Open Marxism and Vulgar International Political Economy', *Revieⱳ of International Political Economy*, 1 (2): 221–31.

Castells, M. (1996–8) *The Information Age: Economy, Society and Culture*, Volumes I–III, Oxford: Blackwell.

Ehrke, M. (1997) 'Japans Antwort auf die wirtschaftliche Globalisierung', in W. Fricke (ed.), *Jahrbuch Arbeit und Technik: Globalisierung und institutionelle Reform*, Bonn: Dietz Verlag, pp.406–14.

Frieden, J. and Rogowski, R. (1996) 'The Impact of the International Economy on National Policies: An Analytical Overview', in R. Keohane and H. Milner (eds), *Internationalization and Domestic Politics*, Cambridge: Cambridge University Press, pp.25–47.

Giddens, A. (1984) *The Constitution of Society: Outline of the Theory of Structuration*, Cambridge: Polity Press.

—— (1987) *The Nation-State and Violence: Volume Two of A Contemporary Critique of Historical Materialism*, Cambridge and Oxford: Polity Press.

—— ([1981] 1995) *A Contemporary Critique of Historical Materialism*, London: Macmillan.

Gilpin, R. (1987) *The Political Economy of International Relations*, Princeton, NJ: Princeton University Press.

Habermas, J. (1984) *The Theory of Communicative Action. Volume 1: Reason and the Rationalization of Society*, trans. T. McCarthy, Boston, MA: Beacon Press.

—— (1987) *The Theory of Communicative Action. Volume 2: Lifeworld and System: A Critique of Functionalist Reason*, trans. T. McCarthy, Boston, MA: Beacon Press.

Hegel, G.W.F. (1991) *The Philosophy of History*, trans. J. Sibree, Buffalo, NY: Prometheus.

Heine, C. and Teschke, B. (1996) 'Sleeping Beauty and the Dialectical Awakening: On the Potential of Dialectic for International Relations', *Millennium*, 25 (2): 399–423.

—— (1997) 'On Dialectic and International Relations: A Reply to Our Critics', *Millennium*, 26 (2): 455–70.

Hirst, P. and Thompson, G. (1996) *Globalization in Question*, Cambridge: Polity Press.

Hobson, J. (1997) *The Wealth of States*, Cambridge: Cambridge University Press.

—— (1998) 'The Historical Sociology of the State and the State of Historical Sociology in International Relations', *Review of International Political Economy*, 5 (2): 284–320.

Horsman, M. and Marshall, A. (1994) *After the Nation-State*, London: HarperCollins.

Katzenstein, P., Keohane, R. and Krasner, S. (1999) 'International Organization and the Study of World Politics', in P. Katzenstein, R. Keohane and S. Krasner (eds), *Exploration and Contestation in the Study of World Politics*, Cambridge, MA/London: MIT Press, pp.5–45.

Keohane, R. and Milner, H. (eds) (1996) *Internationalization and Domestic Politics*, Cambridge: Cambridge University Press.

Kocka, J. ([1966] 1985) 'The Social Sciences between Dogmatism and Decisionism: A Comparison between Karl Marx and Max Weber', in R. Antonio and R. Glassman (eds), *A Weber–Marx Dialogue*, Lawrence, KS: University Press of Kansas.

Streeck, W. (1998) 'Industrielle Beziehungen in einer internationalisierten Wirtschaft', in U. Beck (ed.), *Politik der Globalisierung*, Frankfurt/Main: Suhrkamp.

Teschke, B. (1998) 'Geopolitical Relations in the European Middle Ages: History and Theory', *International Organization*, 52 (2): 325–58.

—— (2001) 'Geopolitik', in W.F. Haug (ed.) *Historisch-Kritisches Wörterbuch des Marxismus*, vol. 5, Hamburg: Argument-Verlag, pp.322–34.

—— (2002) 'Theorizing the Westphalian System of States: International Relations from Absolutism to Capitalism', *European Journal of International Relations*, 8(1): 5–48.

Weber, Max ([1919] 1946a) 'Politics as a Vocation', in H.H. Gerth and C. Wright Mills (eds), *From Max Weber: Essays in Sociology*, London: Routledge & Kegan Paul, pp.77–128.

—— ([1919] 1946b) 'Science as a Vocation', in H.H. Gerth and C. Wright Mills (eds), *From Max Weber: Essays in Sociology*, London: Routledge & Kegan Paul, pp.129–56.

—— ([1904] 1949) 'Objectivity in Social Science and Social Policy', in E. Shils and H. Finch (eds), *The Methodology of the Social Sciences: Max Weber*, Glencoe, IL: Free Press, pp.49–112.

—— ([1922] 1968) *Economy and Society: An Outline of Interpretive Sociology*, in G. Roth and C. Wittich (eds), Berkeley/Los Angeles, CA and London: University of California Press.

—— ([1904–5] 1992) *The Protestant Ethic and the Spirit of Capitalism*, translated T. Parsons, London/New York: Routledge.

Weiss, L. (1997) 'Globalization and the Myth of the Powerless State', *New Left Review*, 225: 3–27.

—— (1999) 'Globalization and National Governance: Antinomies or Interdependence?', *Review of International Studies*, 25: 59–88.

Weiss, L. and Hobson, J. (1995) *States and Economic Development: A Comparative Historical Analysis*, Cambridge and Oxford: Polity Press.

Wendt, A. (1992) 'Anarchy is What States Make of It: the Social Construction of Power Politics', *International Organization*, 46 (2): 391–425.

—— (1999) *Social Theory of International Politics*, Cambridge and New York: Cambridge University Press.

Wood, E.M. (1981) 'The Separation of the Economic and the Political in Capitalism', *New Left Review*, 124: 66–95.

Part III

Historical materialism and the politics of globalization

10 The class politics of globalisation[1]

Alejandro Colás

The objective of Marxist theory is to explain the past and present of human societies in order to illuminate future possibilities for human emancipation. This basic principle – most eloquently captured in Marx's eleventh thesis on Feuerbach, 'The philosophers have only interpreted the world in various ways; the point is to change it' – is arguably the distinguishing feature of Marxism as a social theory. With the possible exception of feminism, no other modern social theory has explicitly aimed to bridge the gap between theory and practice, between social-scientific analysis and political action, in the way that Marxism has over the past century and a half. One category privileged by Marxism in this endeavour is that of 'class'. Although Marx and Engels dedicated a comparatively small amount of their work to the elucidation of this concept, it is indisputably one of the pivotal notions in the Marxist understanding of society, history and socio-historical change. More importantly, it is the one category upon which the Marxist project of socialist transformation hinges (Wood 1986).

Taking these two basic assumptions as a given (that Marxist theory is about socialist transformation and that this aim is premised on class politics), the rest of the chapter proposes, first, to evaluate the place of an historical materialist understanding of 'class' in the debates on globalisation and second, to identify the potential social and political sources of a reinvigorated socialist internationalism in the new century. In essence, my argument is that the current phase of international capitalist accumulation ('globalisation') continues to produce social and political cleavages both among and within specific states and societies. These cleavages take on a class form, in the Marxist sense, and can therefore be seen simultaneously as cause and consequence of the processes associated with globalisation. In other words, 'globalisation' is treated here as expressive of the class antagonisms inherent in capitalism, and as such, representative of yet another site of struggle between those who seek to reproduce the existing international capitalist order and those who aim to transform it in the direction of a genuinely democratic, i.e. socialist, international society.

I start from the premise that the idea of globalisation has no independent explanatory power, and that it describes a process of intensified socio-economic and political integration across the world which is derivative of other concepts (capitalism, the system of states, technology, international organisation). From an historical materialist perspective, the processes associated with globalisation should be seen as stemming from transformations in the global reproduction of capitalism. In other words, a Marxist account of globalisation should aim to explain this process with reference to capitalist development: as a consequence, rather than a cause, of changes in the world-wide articulation of capitalism.

Bearing this initial assumption in mind, I suggest that historical materialist analyses of the interaction between class and globalisation throw up two different, though by no means incompatible, results. On the one hand, the perspectives that privilege class as an *agent* (or subject) of globalisation tend to emphasise the hegemonic role of international or transnational *ruling classes* in the unfolding of this process. Thus, authors associated with the so-called 'neo-Gramscian' school of International Relations (IR), and those concerned with the theorisation of 'postimperialism', understand globalisation as a product of strategies devised by transnational 'historic blocs' or the 'corporate international bourgeoisie' in their collective management of the global capitalist economy.[2] On the other hand, those interpretations that focus upon class as an *object* of globalisation are inclined towards an analysis of the impact of this process upon *exploited classes*, be these industrial workers, peasants or agricultural day-labourers. From the classic accounts of the 'new international division of labour' to the more recent considerations on globalisation and 'flexible accumulation', these views highlight the diversification of capitalist relations of production and the concomitant fragmentation of working-class politics arising out of capitalist globalisation (Fröbel *et al.* 1980).

The argument presented here is critical of both these perspectives. It seeks to emphasise the necessary interaction between the objective and subjective dimensions of class in the process of globalisation. In so doing, it suggests that the phenomena associated with globalisation should be explained with reference to the protracted national and international struggles between capital and labour. These antagonisms, which have arguably always been fought out at the intersection of the domestic and the international, in turn feed back into the ongoing dynamic of class-formation and class-mobilisation on a global scale. Thus, the class politics of globalisation is presented here as a process where the domestic opposition between capital and labour is simultaneously resolved and reproduced at an inter-state level; as a process whereby the very policies and strategies developed by capitalists and workers in response to globalisation, themselves throw up new expressions of international class antagonisms.[3]

This understanding of the class politics of globalisation will be elucidated first through a critique of the neo-Gramscian and postimperialist accounts of capitalist globalisation by claiming that their tendency to reify ruling-class agency obscures the centrality of class struggle – both domestic and international – in the configuration of hegemonic 'historic blocs'. Next, I consider those theorists of globalisation that identify in this process a fragmentation and, ultimately, the conceptual extinction of the two antagonistic classes which

Marx and Engels claimed defined capitalist society: bourgeois and proletarians. In criticising these perspectives, it will be argued that they conflate these abstract class categories with their concrete expression in actual social relations; or put differently: that they confuse what are *contingent* expressions of capitalist social relations with the defining *structural* relation of capitalism – the capital/labour relation. Once such a distinction (between abstract/concrete or structural/contingent) is respected, I maintain, it is all but impossible to do away with the two-class model when analysing global capitalism. Finally, the latter point will be qualified by suggesting that far from representing the triumph of the 'pristine culture of capitalism', actually existing global capitalism is still a domain where the overarching logic of capitalist exploitation is imbued, and in some cases forcibly articulated with non-capitalist social hierarchies associated with production, ethnicity, sex, and indeed political authority.[4] Contrary to the predominant view of globalisation as a *homogenising* process, I shall argue – with reference primarily to relations of exploitation – that it is actually reinforcing many of the *divisive* structures and institutions of the international system such as state sovereignty, uneven development, military power and ethnic and religious chauvinisms.

The consequences of all this for socialist strategy are briefly considered at the end of the chapter. To anticipate, my main contention is that the class antagonisms produced by capitalist globalisation can only be successfully harnessed to the project of socialist transformation by making explicit the connection between the abstract, universal nature of capitalist exploitation and its concrete manifestation in particular socio-historical settings. Analyses of globalisation which, by seeing classes as either the hapless victims of this process or the commanding agent of its unfolding, privilege one or the other view of global capitalism, run the risk of obviating the dynamic nature of the system and missing the crucial link between its abstract and concrete expressions. It follows from this that socialist transformation is unlikely to be spurred on by globalisation until an internationalist socialist movement is capable of translating our everyday experiences of alienation and exploitation – both within and without the workplace – into collective action against capitalism at the global level.

Before proceeding into a fuller exposition of these arguments, a qualification and a definition are in order. The qualification is that little of what follows is premised on an *empirical* account of the global constellation of classes under capitalism. Such an empirical analysis would undoubtedly be necessary in order to strengthen the claims made in this chapter, but I proceed unashamedly from the abstract to the concrete; assuming that Marxists must abstract out a problematic before we determine how this is or is not concretised in actual social relations. Second, and following on from this, the next section will offer a brief – and necessarily schematic – excursus into Marxist conceptions of class. Here, I shall define the way in which 'class' is employed in the rest of the chapter – a usage closest to that expounded by E.P. Thompson in his various writings on the subject (Thompson 1963, 1978a, 1978b).

The Marxist category of class

Although the term 'class' had been commonplace in social and political thought long before Marx and Engels first employed it, there is little doubt that it acquired a distinctive meaning in their writings (see Bottomore 1991; Labica and Bensussan 1982). The two central innovations which Marx and Engels brought to bear upon the concept were its historicisation and its association to conflicting social interests. Class divisions had, according to Marx and Engels, been a characteristic of human societies throughout history. The advent of capitalism, however, brought about a specific form of social differentiation: that of modern classes defined through their proprietary relation to the means of production. Furthermore, inherent to these new set of productive relations was the necessary clash of interests between the two major classes – bourgeois and proletarians. This double reworking of the idea of classes within modern civil society was formulated most clearly in the *Communist Manifesto*. Here Marx and Engels remind us that 'The history of all hitherto existing society is the history of class struggles' and that 'In the earlier epochs of history, we find almost everywhere a complicated arrangement of society into various orders, a manifold gradation of social rank' (1967: 80). Modern capitalist society, however, marked a break with previous forms of social gradation:

> The modern bourgeois society that has sprouted from the ruins of feudal society has not done away with class antagonisms. It has but established new classes, new conditions of oppression, new forms of struggle in place of the old ones.
>
> Our epoch, the epoch of the bourgeoisie, possesses, however, this distinctive feature: it has simplified class antagonisms. Society as a whole is more and more splitting up into two great hostile camps, into two great classes directly facing each other: Bourgeoisie and Proletariat.
>
> (Marx and Engels 1967: 80)

The distinction between these two classes and their respective interests has remained axiomatic to the Marxist understanding of capitalism. Yet this elegant expression of class conflict in modern society begs at least two kinds of question relevant to our discussion of globalisation: first, where do the other classes which have shaped the modern world (peasants, slaves, share-croppers, petty bourgeois, lumpenproletarians, landowners and so forth) fit in?; second, how important is class consciousness to the definition of class? Both these questions have from the outset been at the heart of Marxist debates on class.

An initial appraisal of Marx and Engels's definition of classes under capitalism reinforces the view espoused in the *Communist Manifesto*: the dynamics of bourgeois society lead to the absorption of all existing classes into either one of the two antagonistic camps, bourgeois or proletarians. Marx's major investigations of capitalist society (the three volumes of *Capital*, *Theories of Surplus-Value* and the *Grundrisse*) bear this view out, as does Engels's work on the subject, *The Condition of the English Working-Class*.[5] At an abstract level, therefore, there is no sustained theorisation by Marx or Engels of the way in which pre-capitalist classes are integrated into and survive under the capitalist mode of production.

It is only when we turn to Marx's historical and political writings that social classes other than the bourgeoisie and the proletariat find a role in the unfolding of capitalist modernity. Terms like 'lumpenproletariat', 'finance aristocracy' and 'petty-bourgeoisie' are used in Marx's journalism on France and England to decipher the political developments in these two countries (see Elster 1986: esp. chap. 6). Perhaps more notorious is Marx's discussion of the peasantry in *The Eighteenth Brumaire of Louis Bonaparte*. Here, Marx identifies a 'vast mass' of small-holding peasants as '[t]he most numerous class of French society'. They share similar conditions of life and a common mode of production, '[b]ut without entering into manifold relations with one another' (Marx 1977: 105). The upshot of this situation was clear for Marx:

> In so far as millions of families live under economic conditions of existence that separate their mode of life, their interests and their culture from those of other classes, and put them into hostile opposition to the latter, they form a class. In so far as there is merely a local interconnection among these smallholding peasants, and the identity of their interests begets no community, no national bond and no political organization among them, they do not form a class.
>
> (Marx 1977: 106)

This celebrated passage opens up the second key problem of the Marxist approach to class, namely that of class consciousness. For while Marx and Engels clearly identified class under capitalism with a collective position *vis-à-vis* the means of production, they also implied that the existence of a class was conditional upon its capacity to forge cultural and political means of self-representation. The classic formulation of this duality in the Marxist understanding of class was presented in *The Poverty of Philosophy* where Marx distinguishes between *class-in-itself* and *class-for-itself*. Referring to the early history of English working-class combinations, Marx asserts that

> Economic conditions had transformed the mass of the people of the country into workers. The combination of capital has created for this mass a common situation, common interests. This mass is thus already a class as against capital, but not yet for itself. In the struggle, for which we have noted only a few phases, this mass becomes united, and constitutes itself as a class for itself. The interests it defends become class interests. But the struggle of class against class is a political struggle.
>
> (Marx n.d.: 166)

These, therefore, are the ambiguities which Marxist commentators on class have had to deal with. On the one hand, Marx and Engels forcefully argued that class was objectively determined under capitalism through the exploitative relationship between the proprietors of the means of production and those who owned nothing but their labour-power. Moreover, these two classes would gradually draw into their ranks the class remnants of previous modes of production: landowners, peasants, artisans and petty traders. On the other hand, some of Marx's writings suggest that class becomes subjectively defined through consciousness, and that furthermore, the 'residual' classes like the peasantry had a significant role to play in an understanding of modern capitalist society, particularly in its international articulation.[6]

The way out of this false impasse is simply to reject this artificial duality. Like the associated dichotomies of Marxist thought (base and superstructure, agency and structure, theory and practice) the objective and subjective views of class should not be seen as mutually exclusive, nor put in opposition to each other. Rather, they should be understood in relational terms as constituting different expressions of a single phenomenon which arises out of concrete historical processes. In other words, classes emerge within the context of objective social structures such as the capitalist mode of production; but in order to explain the socio-historical dynamics of any society we must also account for the collective agency of individuals that reproduce these very structures.

One of the strongest formulations of this view of class lies in E.P. Thompson's historical elaborations of class formation, most notably in his seminal *The Making of the English Working-Class*. It is in his polemical *The Poverty of Theory*, however, that Thompson defines class most succinctly:

> Classes arise because men and women, in determinative productive relations, identify their antagonistic interests, and come to struggle, to think and to value in class ways: thus the process of class formation is a process of self-making, although under conditions which are 'given'.
>
> (Thompson 1978a: 9)

Clearly, Thompson's interpretation of class represents one among several other approaches to the subject within the Marxist tradition – both classical and contemporary. Moreover, his conception of class has been subjected to searching critiques from some of the foremost Marxist theorists of our time (compare Anderson 1983; Katznelson and Zolberg 1986; Kaye and McClelland 1990). Yet neither of these considerations fundamentally undermines the validity of adopting Thompson's understanding of class for the purposes of this chapter. Although a full analysis of the writings on class produced by Lenin, Lukács, Kautsky, Gramsci or Luxemburg, and the more recent reformulations of the concept by 'analytical Marxists', would undoubtedly provide a more comprehensive picture of Marxist debates on the subject, such an undertaking is beyond the scope and expertise of this chapter. As regards the contemporary critiques, their broad acceptance of Thompson's key premises would suggest a greater consensus than might at first appear. Even Perry Anderson's famous and characteristically pointed attack of Thompson's excessively 'voluntarist and subjectivist definition of class' can be said to rest more on a difference in emphasis over what exactly it means to '[t]hink, to struggle and to act in class ways' than on a substantive disagreement about the objective determination of classes within specific social structures such as capitalism.[7] In short, the basic tenet of the Thompsonian understanding of class – that class emerges out of historically determined relations of production which generate an antagonism of interests and values between different social groups – appears as the most suitable starting-point for a Marxist interpretation of class and globalisation.

Class as an agent of globalisation

Allowing for the imprecision and analytical superficiality of the term,[8] globalisation can be said to refer to at least four contemporary phenomena:

1   The alleged exponential increase over the past thirty years in cross-border financial, trade and capital flows in relation to total output (within OECD economies, at least).
2   The accompanying retreat of state intervention into and/or regulation of these flows.
3   The increasing transfer of responsibilities previously allocated to national states onto multilateral agencies or international organisations in the management of the world's (socio-economic and political) affairs – what is often defined as 'global governance'.
4   The growing homogenisation of political, economic and cultural norms and practices across significant sectors of the world population.

To their credit, from the 1970s onwards many Marxist and *Marxisant* scholars pioneered the recognition and analysis of all or part of these new developments in international relations. Furthermore, they did so by deliberately employing notions of class in an intellectual climate that was actively hostile to the deployment of this category. This section critically evaluates two such approaches – 'postimperialism' and neo-Gramscian 'transnational historical materialism' – with a view to delineating my own perspective on class and globalisation in contrast to theirs.

In essence, the two approaches under review sought to explain developments in the global political economy since the 1970s with reference to the international self-organisation of the capitalist ruling class. Though separated in time by almost twenty years and in method by their different conceptions of Marxism, the theory of postimperialism and neo-Gramscian transnational historical materialism shared a common analytical concern with the new institutions of global capitalism such as multinational corporations, multilateral agencies and transnational pressure groups. Moreover, in explaining the rise and development of these new phenomena, the theorists attached to both these 'schools' emphasised the central role of transnational ruling-class coalitions in sustaining the global material and ideological domination of capital.

I shall shortly raise two interconnected shortcomings of both these analyses of class and globalisation. Before doing so, however, it is important to highlight some of the differences between the two approaches, thereby further elucidating their contributions. Moreover, it should be borne in mind that some of the writings considered do not explicitly couch their analyses in terms of globalisation as such – I have assumed that their problematic could reasonably be framed within the contemporary debates on the subject.[9]

In the first place, while theorists of postimperialism were more narrowly concerned with the role of multinational corporations in capitalist development and the attendant transformation in class relations, the neo-Gramscians expressly underline the threefold interaction between production, political institutions and ideology in the construction of historical 'world orders'. Thus, for Becker and Sklar, '[Postimperialism] begins with the observation that global corporations function to promote the integration of diverse national interests on a new transnational basis' (1987: 6). Out of this process there emerged a novel configuration of international class forces, where imperialist domination from the metropole was superseded by a new coalition of interests between, on the one hand, a national 'managerial bourgeoisie' comprising private managers and public functionaries in the less developed countries, and, on the other hand, a transnational 'corporate bourgeoisie' attached to the major multinational corporations from the advanced capitalist states. This partnership was sustained primarily through the harmony of interests arising out of the local managerial bourgeoisie's need for foreign direct investment and the corporate bourgeoisie's willingness to accept conditions imposed by the host administration – what Sklar dubbed the 'corporate doctrine of domicile' (1987: 29).[10] All this resulted in the emergence of a 'worldwide corporate and managerial bourgeoisie as a class in formation that now comprises three overlapping entities ["corporate bourgeoisie", "managerial bourgeoisie" and the "corporate international bourgeoisie" – a composite of the latter two]' (1987: 31).

Though the neo-Gramscian approach was also concerned with the process of transnational class formation, its major theorists sought to escape a reductionist explanation of this phenomenon. For the neo-Gramscians transnational class formation was the outcome of processes far more complex than the simple convergence of interests between multinational corporations and specific fractions of the third world bourgeoisie. In fact, transnational historical materialism has to date paid little attention to the articulation of class relations outside OECD countries and has focused instead on the class alliances forged in the heartlands of capitalism. Thus, Kees van der Pijl's path-breaking work *The Making of an Atlantic Ruling Class* (1984), his more recent *Transnational Classes and International Relations* (1998a), and Stephen Gill's (1990) study on the Trilateral Commission aimed to demonstrate the existence of an institutionalised international ruling class within the advanced capitalist states: what one could inelegantly call an 'international bourgeoisie-for-itself'.

The strategy deployed by the neo-Gramscians in this endeavour has varied considerably. At one extreme, van der Pijl's early work made little reference to the Gramscian categories later developed by his 'Italian School' colleagues, and focused instead on the more orthodox Marxist analysis of class fractions in the history of trans-Atlantic ruling-class coalitions from 1917 to 1971. Taking his cue from the second and third volumes of Marx's *Capital*, van der Pijl (1984) argued that, at different periods during this century, distinctive fractions of an Atlantic ruling class could be identified with two different conceptions of capital: money-capital and productive-capital. While the fraction emanating from the former tended towards a liberal internationalist view of the Atlantic economy – one geared towards the generation of profits through the circulation of *money* capital and therefore pre-disposed towards US hegemony in an open international economy – the latter fraction was associated with continental industrial capitalism and therefore more inclined towards nationally based, demand-side policies aimed at extracting surplus-value through the valorisation of *productive* capital. At the other end of the neo-Gramscian spectrum Robert W. Cox expanded both the geographical and conceptual reach of transnational historical materialism by embracing notions of 'world order' and 'state power'. Though insisting on its emergence out of concrete 'social relations of production', Cox argued that class was articulated internationally through the medium of a hegemonic world order (e.g. *Pax Britannica* or *Pax Americana*):

> In such an order, production in particular countries becomes connected through the mechanisms of a world economy and linked into world systems of production. The social classes of a dominant country find allies within other countries. The historic bloc underpinning particular states become connected through the mutual interests and ideological perspectives of social classes in different countries, and global classes begin to form.
>
> (Cox 1987: 7)

At one level, this formulation of the role of classes in the international system appears to be very similar to that presented by Becker and Sklar. The crucial difference (underplayed by Cox in the previous passage), however, lies in the emphasis placed by Cox and the neo-Gramscians on the concept of *hegemony* represented by specific *historic blocs*. For although the theorists of postimperialism make passing references to cultural and educational forms of transnational socialisation, the neo-Gramscians adopt this label precisely through their extrapolation onto the international arena of the Italian communist's reflections on the role of culture (understood in the broadest sense) in sustaining an antisocialist hegemony in his own country. Thus, for transnational historical materialism, world orders are maintained not only through the dull compulsion of the market and the coercive powers of the state, but also by way of the consent elicited through ideological and institutional forms such as transnational foundations, think-tanks, pressure-groups and multilateral agencies. It is in this sense that institutions emanating from civil society such as the Trilateral Commission or the Davos World Forum become organic representations of a transnational ruling class (Gill 1990; van der Pijl 1998a: chap. 4).

This necessarily sketchy survey of the postimperialist and neo-Gramscian analyses of class in international relations will have hopefully demonstrated their almost exclusive focus on the agency of ruling classes in twentieth-century international relations. Despite their differing methods and conclusions, my claim has been that these two theories offer one avenue for exploring the interface between class and globalisation. It is a perspective that interprets globalisation as a process consciously engineered by international ruling classes, either through the convergence of interests mediated through multinational corporations (postimperialism) or through the more complex ideological and institutional mechanisms that characterise hegemonic world orders (transnational historical materialism). In this respect, they both privilege the *subjective* role of class in the process of globalisation, and are thus open to the charge of underestimating the centrality of objective relations of production in the global reproduction of class antagonisms. Such a 'charge' can be substantiated with reference to two assumptions inherent in the postimperalist and neo-Gramscian analyses.

First and foremost, both these perspectives treat class, and especially the ruling class, as a virtually autonomous entity that is free to determine the historical conditions of its own development. Consequently, they both overlook one of the central tenets of the Marxist conception of class, namely the mutual constitution of classes in the process of exploitation. Postimperialists assume that the interests of the corporate international class will eventually be satisfied simply by virtue of this group being at the summit of the hierarchy of the multinational corporation. Similarly, transnational historical materialists derive their notion of hegemonic world orders through reading back into history moments of apparent stability in the international system. In both cases, there is little or no space for class struggle in the construction of either corporate international class nor hegemonic historic blocs, nor indeed for the possibility of counter-hegemonic blocs seizing the 'historical day' (e.g. through revolutions). Yet such ruling-class coalitions emerge in the process of confrontation with exploited classes which may, or may not, be resolved through the 'doctrine of domicile' or the establishment of a hegemonic world order, but which are certainly the product of crises generated by such a clash of class interests. In other words, in as far as we can speak of the rise of an international ruling class and its attendant hegemonic institutions, these phenomena must be explained as a dynamic response to the resistance and contestation displayed by the exploited classes; a resistance that often produces favourable results for the exploited classes.

The insistence upon the centrality of relations of production in the formation and reproduction of classes is important because it underlines a second and related shortcoming in the postimperialist and neo-Gramscian analyses, namely their assumption that the international self-organisation of classes expresses a higher, and therefore determinate, stage of capitalist globalisation. Again, this is an unqualified generalisation which is aimed at identifying commonalities among the texts in question, and not at imposing some purported homogeneity in their formulations and conclusions. Nonetheless, it can be said that both postimperialism and transnational historical materialism tend to overemphasise the institutional and ideological self-representation of the ruling class on a global scale at the expense of the constitution of these classes within local contexts. On this account, national class fractions become subordinated to the more powerful and globally organised transnational class fractions. In his contribution to this volume, for example, William Robinson insists that '[t]he capturing of local states by agents of global capitalism resolves the institutional contradiction ... between transnational capital and national states, that is, local state practices are increasingly harmonized with global capitalism' (Robinson, this volume: 221). The approach adopted here, on the contrary, suggests that if we start from the premise that classes are constituted internationally through the process of exploitation and not exclusively through their capacity of global self-expression, the relationship between the local and the global becomes much more dynamic, thus allowing for instances where the bourgeoisie mediates its interests on a global scale *through* inter-state institutions, and in defence of very particular local privileges. From this perspective, many of the policies adopted by what Robinson calls 'The new managers of the neo-liberal national states, from Clinton and Blair, to Cardoso and Mbeki' could actually be seen as defending local, national class interests through the multilateral institutions of global class rule such as the IMF and the World Bank. The emphasis here, therefore, is upon the need for the capitalist class to guarantee its own reproduction through the exploitation of the working class – an objective it pursues both at the national and the international level, but which it need not necessarily resolve through its organisation as a global transnational *class-for-itself* as Robinson suggests.

Class as an object of globalisation

I have thus far concentrated on class analyses of globalisation that focus on the ruling class as the key agent in this process. The critical overview offered above argued that postimperialist and neo-Gramscian accounts of class and globalisation are flawed, first, because they obscure the primacy of social relations of production in the constitution of antagonistic classes, and, second, because they consequently reify the power of a putative international ruling class in designing a world after its own image.

I now turn to a set of writings on the post-war international organisation of production which again, without always invoking the concept, are essentially about globalisation. These analyses claim that the crisis of the long post-war boom during the 1970s ushered in a radical shift in the methods and sites of global capitalist exploitation and accumulation. In contrast to the perspectives analysed in the previous section, the class-based theories of globalisation presented on the one hand by Fröbel, Heinrichs and Kreye (on the new international division of labour), and, on the other, by authors inspired by the so-called 'Regulation School' such as Hoogvelt (on 'flexible accumulation'), are explicitly concerned with the international dimensions of class-formation within the sphere of *production*. Moreover, they emphasise the effects of global restructuring upon *exploited classes*. It is in these two senses that I take these theories to represent an approach to globalisation that sees class as the *object* (albeit not always the passive one) of this process.

Perhaps the most influential analysis of the effects on labour of the post-1973 crisis is that of Fröbel *et al.* on the 'new international division of labour' (1980). Through a rich empirical investigation into the international relocation of German industrial capital to the so-called newly industrialising countries during the 1970s, Fröbel and his colleagues argued that the world economy was experiencing a qualitative shift in the mechanisms of capital valorisation and accumulation. Productive capital was being relocated from the core of the capitalist world economy to its periphery, thereby generating export-oriented capitalist development in several peripheral economies and fostering structural unemployment in the heartlands of the system. This global shift was predicated upon three interconnected preconditions: the availability of a world-wide 'reserve army of labour' – chiefly though not exclusively originating from Latin America, Asia and Africa; the development of technological innovations which introduced greater flexibility at all stages of the production process; and the consequent horizontal (geographical) and vertical (social) fragmentation of capital and labour.

The relevant conclusions of this study with regard to class and globalisation were somewhat contradictory. On the one hand, Fröbel *et al.* recognised that this relocation of capital was reproducing an industrial working class in the periphery which might eventually ally itself politically with the proletariat of the advanced capitalist states. On the other hand, the authors of the study insisted that the new international division of labour was intensifying the relations of dependent development between core and periphery in the world-capitalist economy. In the absence of a clear response within Fröbel *et al.*'s own book, it may be justified to turn to one of their contemporary followers who has in recent years reformulated the new international division of labour thesis in the context of globalisation. For A. Sivanandan 'Capital is still dependent on exploiting workers for profit, only now the brunt of that exploitation has shifted to the underdeveloped countries of the Third World, and the increasing intensity of exploitation there more than compensates for its comparative loss at the centre' (1990: 181).

Although Sivanandan's statement is conceptually and empirically contestable,[11] it does raise a central question as to the relationship between class and globalisation, namely: have the processes associated with globalisation fragmented classes vertically and horizontally in such a way as to render the categories of capital and labour redundant in the analysis of global capitalism? My own answer to this question is negative, although I shall endeavour to qualify it in the closing section of this chapter. But for our purposes it might be interesting to pause briefly on two perspectives that answer affirmatively.

The first of these is defended from the ambit of development studies by Ankie Hoogvelt. In her study on *Globalisation and the Postcolonial World* (1997), Hoogvelt argues that under post-Fordist conditions of 'flexible accumulation' capital–labour relations have altered beyond the recognition of any Marxist theory:

Under conditions of flexible production two things happen: capital fragments into a thousand splinters of production capacity blurring the
distinction between ownership of working capital and labour, and the
output of labour is paid at the point of delivery. ... Thus the *casualisation of
labour*, through part-time employment, if-and-when contracts, through self-
employment and piecemeal work and so on, are all social changes that are
being brought into place almost everywhere in the world. [...] The point is
that there is an historical trend towards forms of production organisation in
which *capital no longer needs to pay for the reproduction of labour power*.

(Hoogvelt 1997: 112)

In a similar vein, though from a different angle, Robert W. Cox argues that
'Recent developments in the late twentieth century suggest ... a movement
toward the unification of capital on a world scale, while industrial workers and
other subordinate classes have become fragmented and divided' (1987: 358).
Despite initially grounding his analysis of class on the sound basis of relations of
production, Cox inexplicably shifts to a definition of class based on arbitrary
technocratic and occupational categories. Thus, on his account, the ruling class
becomes fragmented into '(1) Those who control big corporations operating on a
world scale, (2) Those who control big nation-based enterprises and industrial
groups, and (3) Locally based petty capitalists' (1987: 358). The exploited classes
are further divided into 'a middle stratum of scientific, technical, and supervi-
sory personnel', 'established workers', 'nonestablished workers', 'new industrial
labor forces in the industrializing Third World countries' and 'peasants and
marginals' (1987: 368).

For all their differences, what these arguments amount to is the idea that globalisation as it was defined earlier in this chapter has fragmented capital and
labour in such a way as to make them irrelevant in the analysis of contemporary
society. The division of labour both *within* specific production chains and *between*
different sites of production, so the argument runs, has made capital unaccount-
able to any law of expanded reproduction and labour far too splintered to
combat its own exploitation in any significant form.

There are two counter-arguments to be made here which will hopefully feed
into the claims made in the next and concluding section of this chapter. First,
assuming for the moment that the empirical basis of Hoogvelt's analysis of a
'flexible regime of accumulation' reflects the experience of the *majority workers in
the world economy*, the fact remains that no amount of casualisation will do away
with the fundamental antagonism between capital and labour. On the contrary,
the kind of flexible and deregulated relations of exploitation that Hoogvelt holds
to represent the end of the capital–labour relation, in fact reveal the clash of
interests between direct producers and appropriators in the starkest light: the
capitalist is here simply being allowed to revert to the extraction of absolute as
opposed to relative surplus-value; but it is good surplus-value all the same!

Second, Cox's descriptive taxonomy of social classes operating under global
capitalism raises the issue once again as to the explanatory value of the Marxist

understanding of class. In the *Communist Manifesto*, Marx and Engels remind us that 'Capital is ... not a personal, it is a social power' (1967: 91). Though class certainly arises in the context of inter-personal relations inside and outside the workplace, these everyday experiences are in significant ways expressions of a wider set of social structures predicated upon a mode of production that divides society into one collectivity made up of individuals that can only offer to sell their labour-power as a means of subsistence, and another collectivity which, through its ownership or control of the means of production, lives off the surplus labour of others. In essence, these two groups are what Marx and Engels called the working class and the bourgeoisie, respectively. Social theorists have divided society in an infinite number of other ways, as do Cox and Hoogvelt; the point is whether such alternative gradations *explain* anything about the dynamics of contemporary capitalist society. My claim thus far has been that they don't, primarily because they take contingent divisions among capitalists and workers as expressions of structural, and therefore necessary, relations of exploitation. Presented as descriptions of the complex forms taken by social relations of production across the world, such exercises in the subdivision and fracturing of capital and labour are empirically useful and relevant. Once such taxonomies are abstracted out and granted theoretical purchase, however, they explain very little about the nature of contemporary capitalism and the class antagonisms it engenders. A Marxist understanding of class, on the other hand, does explain the dynamics of contemporary capitalist society because it is able to identify the source of an irremovable condition for the existence of this mode of production: the generation of the very surplus-value that nourishes its own reproduction. The international expansion of capitalism and the current process of globalisation which it has spurred have certainly transformed the mechanisms of surplus-value extraction and capitalist accumulation, thereby conditioning the social structures and processes in most societies across the world. But such a global reproduction has not altered the fundamental exploitative relations of production that characterise capitalism. Indeed, in many parts of the world, pre-capitalist forms of exploitation coexist and are often articulated with global capitalism. In the last section of this chapter I shall offer some general reflections on class and globalisation which I hope address further this productive tension between capital's abstract 'laws of motion' and its concrete historical manifestation in different social formations across the world.

Conclusions: class, globalisation and the persistence of non-capitalist relations

There can be little doubt that the forms of global capitalist reproduction have undergone significant changes since the end of the long post-war boom. Clearly, technological innovations in the accumulation and circulation of capital, the extended reach of institutions of 'global governance', the development of export-based economies in the once peripheral regions of world capitalism, and not least the absence of viable alternatives to capitalism since the collapse of communism have, among other factors, affected the global organisation of capitalism. As David Harvey has lucidly argued:

> We need some way, therefore, to represent all the shifting and churning that has gone on since the first major post-war recession of 1973, which does not lose sight of the fact that the basic rules of the capitalist mode of production continue to operate as invariant shaping forces of historical-geographical development.
>
> (Harvey 1990: 121)

This chapter has defended the view that it is through an analysis of class struggles within capitalism that we can explain the ongoing processes of globalisation. Thus, I have argued that it is the abstract (though, of course, no less real) confrontation between capital and labour that holds the key to an analysis of capitalism on a world scale. The difficulties for Marxists, however, emerge in the process of providing a concrete account of such class struggles. And it is here that I would revert to the claim flagged in the introduction to the effect that capitalism has historically reproduced itself in articulation with other non-capitalist modes of production. Far from 'creating a world after its own image' as Marx and Engels once predicted, the global expansion of capitalism has tested the adaptive mechanisms of capital so as to produce what Eric Wolf (1982: chap. 10) called a 'differentiated' mode of production. The implications of all this for the interface between class and globalisation are twofold.

First, analytically, it presents Marxists with the challenge of considering how capital grafts its own logic of exploitation upon pre-existing institutions and social structures such as sovereign political communities, households, ethnic, religious or caste hierarchies and, most notably, sexual differentiation. For an investigation into the actual historical formation of classes on a world scale reveals how class is *experienced* in the Thompsonian sense (i.e. both objectively and subjectively) in conjunction with other social hierarchies. At one important level, these hierarchies are all subsumed under the single logic of capitalist surplus value extraction: that defined by the social relation between direct producers and appropriators. Yet the way this determinant social relation is experienced on a quotidian basis is filtered through manifold historical and cultural legacies, many of which are international in nature. It is this complex interface between the universality of capitalist social relations and their specific manifestation in different socio-historical contexts which arguably defines international class-formation and reproduction.

Such an intricate social crystallisation of class is by no means static. The dynamic nature of capitalism allows for a transformation of these hierarchies through the collective organisation of classes in ways which often reinforce the capitalist ideal of a free exchange between capital and labour. Thus, for example, it is only through the collective struggle of black and female workers against racial and sexual discrimination in the workplace that something closer to a pristine and unencumbered capitalist exploitation obtains today in most advanced capitalist countries. But in many other regions of the world, global capitalism is either unable to destroy the 'natural economy' or only too capable of accommodating non-capitalist forms of oppression and exploitation in ways that complicate the identification of classes along the capital–labour axis. Again, it is precisely these heterogeneous variations in class formation and reproduction that call for the distinction between the abstract definition of classes within the structure of a given mode of production and their concrete expression in contingent socio-historical settings.

The basic point emerging out of all these consideration is as follows: capitalism has historically articulated itself internationally in myriad ways, producing variegated expressions of the overarching antagonism between capital and labour. This antagonism has been mediated through the institutions of the sovereign state and through pre-capitalist hierarchies of sex, ethnicity, caste, colour and so forth. In as much as the processes of globalisation are a reflection of the class antagonisms arising out of such complex social hierarchies, they often reinforce, rather than undermine, these divisions. Contrary to most views of class and globalisation that highlight the radical *break* in modes of capitalist exploitation, I posit a *continuity*, indeed a persistence of the old, pre-capitalist modes of exploitation within global capitalism.

The second and final implication of viewing capitalism as a 'differentiated' or 'articulated' mode of production, even under conditions of globalisation, concerns the formulation of viable socialist alternatives. I start from the premise that socialist politics involves the self-organisation of exploited classes for the purposes of transcending capitalism and constructing viable, genuinely democratic socio-economic and political structures. I also assume that such a project must necessarily be international in scope and organisation, and therefore draw on the rich tradition of socialist internationalism. The foregoing discussion on class and globalisation has suggested that the Marxist notion of class, both *in-itself* and *for-itself*, today pervades most social relations across the world. Yet it plainly does so in complex and contradictory ways that only a socialist movement conscious of the interaction between the universal and the particular expressions of class antagonism would be capable of translating into a real alternative to capitalism. What this means is that neither the views on class and globalisation that objectify exploited classes in such a way as to render them simple victims of history, nor those views that take as given the subjective power of transnational ruling classes, can offer comprehensive and feasible socialist alternatives to capitalism. Moreover, we would do well to avoid seizing on any and every single movement that contests the existing world order as representing a socialist alternative. Exploited classes *do* resist and organise against their perceived oppressors, but neither do they necessarily offer alternatives attractive to socialists (e.g. the various religious fundamentalist attacks on 'globalisation'), nor do they necessarily represent a systematic confrontation with capitalism (e.g. the EZLN's (Zapatista National Liberation Army's) confused programme against 'global neo-liberalism'). Such perspectives 'from below' often fail to theorise the intricate nature of capitalist power structures 'from above'. On the other hand, socialist analyses of world politics that place all their emphasis on allegedly hege-monic institutions like the World Bank or the International Monetary Fund (IMF) also miss the crucial, and often conflictive, link between these organisa-tions and other seemingly subordinate entities such as states and classes.

A viable world-wide socialist alternative must therefore strive to bridge this gap between an exclusive focus on localised forms of resistance and views that reify global hegemonic orders. It must develop a class analysis of world politics premised on the complex and variegated reproduction of capitalism through the mediation of states and the attendant oppressive ideologies such as racism and sexism. Such an analysis would speak to the concerns of socialist organisations – trade unions, political parties, and other groups – that are daily combating the global articulation of capitalism. It would also hopefully seek to reformulate the basic tenets of socialist internationalism which as a theoretical principle and a political practice, for the better part of this century, grappled with the very concerns that globalisation theorists now seem to be so enchanted by.

Notes

1   I am indebted to Hannes Lacher, Shirin Rai, Mark Rupert, Hazel Smith and Benno Teschke for their extensive comments and penetrating criticisms of an earlier version of this chapter. I have ignored some of their insights at my own peril.
2   See the essays collected in Gill (1993). Individual works associated with this approach include Cox (1987); Gill (1990); Holman (1996); Overbeek (1996); Robinson (1996); Rupert (1995); van der Pijl (1998a, 1998b). For critical overviews of the neo-Gramscian approach see Burnham (1992) and Scherrer (1998). For the programmatic statements of 'postimperialism' see Becker *et al.* (1987).
3   This understanding of class and globalisation bears a strong resemblance to that expounded by Burnham (1994: 221–31).
4   In this chapter, the term 'articulation' is used in the sense developed by the so-called 'articulation of modes of production' approach. Representative texts include: Althusser and Balibar (1970); Rey (1973); and the essays in Wolpe (1980). For a comprehensive survey of this approach see Foster-Carter (1978).
5   Like most generalisations about Marx and Engels's work, this statement requires some nuancing. For reasons of space, I cannot go into the vexed issue of the status of land-owners and ground-rent under capitalism.
6   In his correspondence with the Russian socialist Vera Zasulich, for example, Marx emphasises that the investigation of the capitalist system carried out in *Capital* was premised on the historical experience of Western Europe, thereby suggesting that a 'late Marx' may have come to re-evaluate the place of the peasantry in the project of socialist transformation (see Shanin 1983).
7   There is no space here to justify fully this contentious reading of the Thompson–Anderson dispute. In essence, however, my claim is that Anderson mistakenly ascribes to Thompson's definition of class the need of a fully fledged, for-itself consciousness, whereas for Thompson, to 'act, think and struggle in class ways' can mean, as his study of eighteenth-century English 'class struggle without class' suggests, that collectivities often formulate their objective class position in a language and form different to the for-themselves working-class movements of the nineteenth and twentieth centuries. The real difference between Anderson and Thompson's defi-nition of class has been neatly summarised by Ellen Wood: 'Where Thompson's critics see structures as against processes, or structures that undergo processes, Thompson sees structured processes' (1995: 79).

8 See the contributions by Halliday and Sutcliffe in this volume for the argument that, in describing very similar phenomena, the term 'imperialism' displays greater theoretical purchase than 'globalisation'.
9 Some of the more recent neo-Gramscian work, for example by Gill (1993), Overbeek (1996) and others, does explicitly address globalisation.
10

> [M]eaning that individual subsidiaries of an international business group may operate in accordance with the requirements of divergent and conflicting policies pursued by the governments of their respective host states [...] Positing a mutuality of interest, the doctrine of domicile justifies transnational corporate expansion while it also legitimizes large-scale foreign investments in the eyes of the host country.
>
> (Sklar 1987: 29)

11 The rate of exploitation is arguably higher in advanced capitalist economies than in the less developed ones, while it is at the very least a matter of debate whether most Third World countries have historically suffered from 'underdevelopment' as opposed to 'maldevelopment', or even the absence of a sustained capitalist development.

Bibliography

Althusser, L. and Balibar, E. (1970) *Reading Capital*, London: New Left Books.
Anderson, P. (1983) *Arguments within English Marxism*, London: New Left Books.
Becker, D. *et al.* (eds) (1987) *Post-imperialism: International Capitalism and Development in the Late Twentieth Century*, Boulder, CO: Lynne Rienner.
Becker, D. and Sklar, R. (1987) 'Why Postimperialism?', in Becker *et al.* (eds), *Postimperialism*.
Bottomore, T. (ed.) (1991) *A Dictionary of Marxist Thought*, Oxford: Blackwell.
Burnham, P. (1991) 'Neo-Gramscian Hegemony and the International Order', *Capital & Class*, 45, Autumn: 73–93.
—— (1994) 'Open Marxism and Vulgar International Political Economy', *Review of International Political Economy*, 1, Summer: 221–31.
Cox, R. (1987) *Power, Production and World Order*, New York: Columbia University Press.
Elster, J. (ed.) (1986) *Karl Marx: A Reader*, Cambridge: Cambridge University Press.
Foster-Carter, A. (1978) 'The Modes of Production Controversy', *New Left Review*, 107: 47–77.
Fröbel, F. *et al.* (1980) *The New International Division of Labour*, trans. P. Burgess, Cambridge: Cambridge University Press.
Gill, S. (1990) *American Hegemony and the Trilateral Commission*, Cambridge: Cambridge University Press.
—— (ed.) (1993) *Gramsci, Historical Materialism and International Relations*, Cambridge: Cambridge University Press.
Harvey, D. (1990) *The Condition of Postmodernity*, Oxford: Blackwell.
Holman, O. (1996) *Integrating Southern Europe*, London: Routledge.
Hoogvelt, A. (1997) *Globalisation and the Postcolonial World*, London: Macmillan.
Katznelson, A. and Zolberg, A. (eds) (1986) *Working-Class Formation*, Princeton, NJ: Princeton University Press.
Kaye, H. and McClelland, K. (1990) *E.P. Thompson: Critical Perspectives*, Philadelphia, PA: Temple University Press.

Labica, H. and Bensussan, G. (1982) *Dictionnaire critique du marxisme*, Paris: Presses Universitaires de France.

Marx, K. (1977) *The Eighteenth Brumaire of Louis Bonaparte*, Moscow: Progress Publishers.

—— (n.d.) *The Poverty of Philosophy*, Moscow: Foreign Languages Publishing House.

Marx, K. and Engels, F. (1967) *The Manifesto of the Communist Party*, Harmondsworth: Penguin.

Overbeek, H. (1996) *Neo-Liberalism and Global Hegemony: Concepts of Control in the Global Political Economy*, London: Routledge.

Rey, P.-P. (1973) *Les alliances de classes*, Paris: François Maspero.

Robinson, W. (1996) *Promoting Polyarchy*, Cambridge: Cambridge University Press.

Rupert, M. (1995) *Producing Hegemony*, Cambridge: Cambridge University Press.

Scherrer, C. (1998) 'Neo-gramscianische Interpretationen internationler Beziehungen', in U. Hirschfeld (ed.), *Gramsci-Perspektiven*, Hamburg: Argument.

Shanin, T. (ed.) (1983) *Late Marx and the Russian Road: Marx and the 'Peripheries' of Capitalism*, London: Routledge & Kegan Paul.

Sivanandan, A. (1990) *Communities of Resistance*, London: Verso.

Sklar, R. (1987) 'Postimperialism: A Class Analysis of Multinational Corporate Expansion', in Becker *et al.* (eds), *Postimperialism*.

Thompson, E.P. (1963) *The Making of the English Working-Class*, London: Victor Gollancz.

—— (1978a) *The Poverty of Theory*, London: Merlin Press.

—— (1978b) 'Eighteenth-century English Society: Class Struggle Without Class?', *Social History*, 3, May: 133–65.

van der Pijl, K. (1984) *The Making of an Atlantic Ruling Class*, London: Verso.

—— (1998a) *Transnational Classes and International Relations*, London: Routledge.

—— (1998b) 'Internationale Klassenverhältnise', in M. Bader *et al.* (eds), *Die Viederentdeckung der Klassen*, Hamburg: Argument.

Wolf, E. (1982) *Europe and the People Without History*, Berkeley, CA: University of California Press.

Wolpe, H. (ed.) (1980) *The Articulation of Modes of Production*, London: Routledge & Kegan Paul.

Wood, E.M. (1986) *The Retreat From Class: A New 'True' Socialism*, London: Verso.

—— (1995) *Democracy Against Capitalism: Renewing Historical Materialism*, Cambridge: Cambridge University Press.

11 Capitalist globalization and the transnationalization of the state

William I. Robinson

World capitalism has been undergoing a profound restructuring since the 1970s. Many have come to refer to this process as globalization, although what this concept exactly means, the nature, extent and importance of the changes bound up with the process, is hotly debated.[1] In my view, globalization is a concept useful intellectually and enabling politically. It helps us to organize empirical information on the restructuring of capitalism in such a way as to provide explanation on the nature and direction of world social change at the dawn of a new millennium, and therefore to gain a better grasp on the prospects for emancipatory social action. In this chapter I will analyse capitalist globalization and develop an historical materialist analysis of the transnationalization of the state. Some of what Marx had to say about the world in his day no longer applies but the method of historical materialism as knowledge grounded in praxis is not restricted to particular historical circumstances. Indeed, historical materialism is emancipatory precisely because it allows us to cut through the reification that results from naturalizing historical arrangements and reveals the historical specificity of existing social forms.

I will argue here that the nation-state is an historically specific form of world social organization that is in the process of becoming transcended by capitalist globalization. The debate on globalization has increasingly centred on the relation of the nation-state to economic globalization. But the issue of globalization and the state has been misframed. Either the nation-state (and the inter-state system) is seen as retaining its primacy as the axis of international relations and world development in a dualist construct that posits separate logics for a globalizing economic and a nation-state based political system, or the state is seen, as in diverse 'end of the nation-state' theses, as no longer important. Rejecting these frames by critiquing and moving beyond this global–national dualism, I call for a return to an historical materialist conception of the state, and on this basis explore three interrelated propositions: (1) economic globalization has its counterpart in transnational class formation and in the emergence of a transnational state (henceforth, TNS) which has been brought into existence to function as the collective authority for a global ruling class; (2) the nation-state is neither retaining its primacy nor disappearing but becoming transformed and absorbed into this larger structure of a TNS; (3) this emergent TNS institutionalizes a new class relation between labour and capital world-wide. Exploring these issues is of major import for popular struggles and socialist politics in the new century. Globalization is anything but a peaceful process. It has involved protracted and bloody social conflict. As an open-ended process, it is highly contested from below and subject to alterations in its course. But strategies for an alternative 'globalization from below' must part from a critique that identifies how this process has unfolded, the contradictions it confronts, and new sites of political contestation, such as a TNS.

This chapter is divided into five parts. The first discusses globalization as a new stage in the development of world capitalism. The second calls for a break with the Weberian conception of the state that underlies much discussion of globalization and develops the concept of a TNS. The third situates the rise of a TNS in the context of a new class relation between global capital and global labour. The fourth reviews empirical evidence for the rise of a TNS between the 1960s and the 1990s. Finally, the fifth refers by way of conclusion to the prospects for emancipatory social action in light of the preceding. I should note, as a caveat, that space constraints preclude a full discussion of the theoretical and analytical issues at hand. The propositions advanced here are of course tentative in nature and require further exploration elsewhere.

Globalization: the latest stage of capitalism[2]

Periodization of capitalism is an analytical tool that allows us to grasp changes in the system over time. In my view, globalization represents an epochal shift, the fourth in the history of world capitalism. The first, mercantilism and primitive accumulation, was ushered in with the birth of capitalism out of its feudal cocoon in Europe and outward expansion. The second, competitive, or classical capitalism, marked the industrial revolution, the rise of the bourgeoisie, and the forging of the nation-state. The third was the rise of corporate (monopoly) capitalism, the consolidation of a single world market and the nation-state system into which world capitalism became organized. The first epoch ran from the symbolic dates of 1492 through to 1789, the second to the late nineteenth century, and the third into the early 1970s. Globalization as the fourth (the *current*) epoch began with the world economic crisis of the 1970s and the profound restructuring of the system that has been taking place since. It features the rise of transnational capital and the supersession of the nation-state system as the organizing principle of capitalist development. As an epochal period globalization constitutes not a new process but the near culmination of the centuries-long process of the spread of capitalist production relations around the world and its displacement of all pre-capitalist relations. The system is undergoing a dramatic intensive expansion. The era of the primitive accumulation of capital is coming to an end. In this process, those cultural and political institutions that fettered capitalism are swept aside, paving the way for the total commodification or 'marketization' of social life world-wide.

Economic globalization has been well researched.[3] Capital has achieved a newfound global mobility and is reorganizing production world-wide in accordance with the whole gamut of political and factor cost considerations. This involves the worldwide decentralization of production together with the centralization of command and control of the global economy in transnational capital. In this process, national productive apparatuses become fragmented and integrated externally into new globalized circuits of accumulation. Here we can distinguish between a *world economy* and a *global economy*. In the earlier epochs each country developed national circuits of accumulation that were linked to each other through commodity exchange and capital flows in an integrated international market (a world economy). In the emerging global economy, the globalization of the production process itself breaks down and functionally integrates these national circuits into *global* circuits of accumulation. Globalization, therefore, is unifying the world into a single mode of production and bringing about the organic integration of different countries and regions into a global economy and society. The increasing dissolution of space barriers and the subordination of the logic of geography to that of production, what some have called 'time–space compression', is without historic precedence. It compels us to reconsider the geography and the politics of the nation-state (Robinson 1998). As we shall see, the TNS embodies new social practices and class relations bound up with this global economy.

The political reorganization of world capitalism has lagged behind its economic reorganization, with the result that there is a disjuncture between economic globalization and the political institutionalization of new social relations unfolding under globalization. Nevertheless, as the material basis of human society changes so too does its institutional organization. From the seventeenth-century treaties of Westphalia into the 1960s, capitalism unfolded through a system of nation-states that generated concomitant national structures, institutions, and agents. Globalization has increasingly eroded these national boundaries, and made it structurally impossible for individual nations to sustain independent, or even autonomous, economies, polities, and social structures. A key feature of the current epoch is the supersession of the nation-state as the organizing principle of capitalism, and with it, of the inter-state system as the institutional framework of capitalist development. In the emerging global capitalist configuration, transnational or global space is coming to supplant national spaces. There is no longer anything external to the system, not in the sense that this is a 'closed' system but in that there are no longer any countries or regions that remain outside of world capitalism, any pre-capitalist zones for colonization, or autonomous accumulation outside of the sphere of global capital. The internal social nexus therefore is now a global one. Such organic social relations are always institutionalized, which makes them 'fixed' and makes their reproduction possible. As the organic and internal linkage between peoples become truly global, the whole set of nation-state institutions is becoming superseded by transnational institutions.

Globalization has posed serious difficulties for theories of all sorts. The embedded nation-state centrism of many extant paradigms, in my view, impedes our understanding of the dynamics of change under globalization (Robinson

1998). My propositions regarding the integration of the entire superstructure of world society is a conception of the current epoch that differs from that of world system analysis, which posits a world system of separate political and cultural superstructures linked by a geographic division of labour, and from many Marxist analyses, which see the nation-state as immanent to capitalist development. The notion that the continued internationalization of capital and the growth of an international civil society has involved as well the internationalization of the state has been recognized by a number of traditions in the social sciences. And the interdisciplinary literature on globalization is full of discussion on the increasing significance of supra- or transnational institutions. However, what these diverse accounts share is a nation-state centrism that entraps them in a global–national dualism. They assume phenomena associated with a TNS to be international extensions of the nation-state system. The conception is one of *inter*national institutions created by nation-states individually or collectively as mechanisms to regulate the flow of goods and capital across their borders and to mediate inter-state relations. Here I distinguish between *inter*national and *trans*national (or global). The former is a conception of world dynamics founded on an existing system of nation-states while the later identifies processes and social relations that tend towards superseding that system.

Conceptualizing a transnational state apparatus: from Weber to Marx

The question of the state is at the heart of the globalization debate. But this debate has been misinformed by the persistent conflation of the nation-state and the state. The two are not coterminous. Here we need to distinguish analytically between a number of related terms: nation, country, nation-state, state, national state, and transnational state. Nation-states are geographical and juridical units and sometimes cultural units, and the term is interchangeable as used here with country or nation. States are power relations embodied in particular sets of political institutions. The conflation of these two related but analytically distinct concepts is grounded in a Weberian conception of the state that informs much analysis of this subject, even analyses by many Marxists. For Weber, the state is a set of cadre and institutions that exercise authority, a 'legitimate monopoly of coercion', over a given territory. In the Weberian construct, the economic and the political (in Weberian terms, 'markets and states') are externally related, separate and even oppositional, spheres, each with its own independent logic. Nation-states interact externally with markets (Weber 1978: 353–4). Consequently, globalization is seen to involve the economic sphere while the political sphere may remain constant, an immutable nation-state system. State managers confront the implications of economic globalization and footloose transnational capital as an external logic (see, *inter alia*, Vernon 1971; Strange 1996; Sassen 1996; Boyer and Drache 1996). This state–market dualism has become the dominant framework for analysis of globalization and the state, and is closely related to the global–national dualism. Globalization is said to be overstated or even imaginary since nation-states 'have more power' than is claimed, or because there are 'national' explanations that explain phenomena better than globalization explanations (see, *inter alia*, Weiss 1998; Hirst and Thompson 1996; Gordon 1988). In this construct, what takes place 'within' a nation-state becomes counterposed to what takes place in the global system. In these recurrent dualisms, economic globalization is increasingly recognized but is analysed as if it is independent of the institutions that structure these social relations, in particular, states and the nation-state. Separate logics are posited for a globalizing economy and a nation-state based political system.

The way out of these antinomies is to move beyond Weber and return to a historical materialist conception of the state. In the Marxist conception, the state is the institutionalization of class relations around a particular configuration of social production. The separation of the economic from the political for the first time under capitalism accords each an autonomy – and implies a complex relationship that must be problematized – but also generates the illusion of independent externally related spheres. In the historical materialist conception, the economic and the political are distinct moments of the same totality. The relation between the economy, or social production relations under capitalism, and states as sets of institutionalized class relations that adhere to those production relations, is an *internal* one. It is not possible here to revisit the theoretical debates that have raged since the revival of interest in the state in the 1960s – which have remained inconclusive and open-ended (but see, *inter alia*, Jessop 1982; Held 1989; Clarke 1991). Note, however, that (1) Marxist theories on the relative autonomy of the state, whether emphasizing a 'structuralist' or 'instrumental' subordination of the state to economically dominant classes, do not posit an *independent* state as a separate sphere with its own logic (in Marx's words, there is no state 'suspended in mid-air' (Marx 1978: 607)). The task of analysis is to uncover the complex of social processes and relations that embed states in the configuration of civil society and political economy; (2) there is nothing in the historical materialist conception of the state that *necessarily* ties it to territory or to nation-states (see also Hannes Lacher's chapter in this volume). That capitalism has historically assumed a geographic expression is something that must be problematized.

States as coercive systems of authority are class relations and social practices congealed and operationalized through institutions. In Marx's view, the state gives a political form to economic institutions and production relations.[4] Markets are the site of material life while states spring from economic (production) relations and represent the institutionalization of social relations of domination. Consequently, the economic globalization of capital cannot be a phenomenon isolated from the transformation of class relations and of states. In the Weberian conception, states are by definition territorially bound institutions and therefore a TNS cannot be conceived as long as the nation-state system persists. Weberian state theory reduces the state to the state's apparatus and its cadre and thereby reifies the state. States are not actors as such. Social classes and groups are historical actors. States do not 'do' anything *per se*. Social classes and groups acting in and out of states (and other institutions) 'do' things as collective historical agents.

State apparatuses are those instruments that enforce and reproduce the class relations and practices embedded in states. The institutional structures of nation-states may persist in the epoch of globalization, but globalization requires that we modify our conception of these structures. A TNS apparatus is emerging under globalization *from within* the system of nation-states. The material circumstances that gave rise to the nation-state are presently being superseded by globalization. What is required is a return to an historical materialist theoretical conceptualization of the state, not as a 'thing' but as a specific social relation inserted into larger social structures that may take different, and historically determined, institutional forms, only one of which is the nation-state.

To summarize and recapitulate: a state is the congealment of a particular and historically determined constellation of class forces and relations, and states are always embodied in sets of political institutions. Hence states are: (a) a moment of class power relations; (b) a set of political institutions (an 'apparatus'). The state is not one or the other; it is both in their unity. The separation of these two dimensions is purely methodological (Weber's mistake is to reduce the state to 'b'). National states arose as particular embodiments of the constellations of social groups and classes that developed within the system of nation-states in the earlier epochs of capitalism and became grounded in particular geographies. What then is a transnational state? Concretely, what is the 'a' and the 'b' of a TNS? It is a particular constellation of class forces and relations bound up with capitalist globalization and the rise of a transnational capitalist class, embodied in a diverse set of political institutions. These institutions are transformed national states plus diverse international institutions that serve to institutionalize the domination of this class as the hegemonic fraction of capital world-wide.

Hence, the state as a class relation is becoming transnationalized. The class practices of a new global ruling class are becoming 'condensed', to use Poulantzas' imagery, in an emergent TNS. In the process of the globalization of capital, class fractions from different countries have fused together into new capitalist groups within transnational space. This new transnational bourgeoisie or capitalist class is that segment of the world bourgeoisie that represents transnational capital. It is comprised of the owners of the leading world-wide means of production as embodied principally in the transnational corporations and private financial institutions. What distinguishes the transnational capitalist class from national or local capitalist fractions is that it is involved in globalized production and manages global circuits of accumulation that give it an objective class existence and identity spatially and politically in the global system above any local territories and polities.

The TNS comprises those institutions and practices in global society that maintain, defend, and advance the emergent hegemony of a global bourgeoisie and its project of constructing a new global capitalist historical bloc. This TNS apparatus is an emerging network that comprises transformed and externally integrated national states, *together with* the supranational economic and political forums and that has not yet acquired any centralized institutional form. The rise of a TNS entails the reorganization of the state in each nation – I will henceforth

refer to these states of each country as *national states* – and it involves simultaneously the rise of truly supranational economic and political institutions. These
two processes – the transformation of nation-states and the rise of supranational
institutions – are not separate or mutually exclusive. In fact, they are twin dimensions of the process of the transnationalization of the state.

The TNS apparatus is multi-layered and multi-centred, linking together functionally institutions that exhibit distinct gradations of 'state-ness' and which have
different histories and trajectories. The supranational organizations are both
economic and political, formal and informal. The economic forums include the
International Monetary Fund (IMF), the World Bank (WB), the World Trade
Organization (WTO), the regional banks, and so on. Supranational political
forums include the Group of 7 and the recently formed Group of 22, as well as
more formal forums such as the United Nations (UN), the European Union
(EU), and so on. They also include regional groupings such as the Association of
South East Asian Nations (ASEAN), and the juridical administrative and regulatory structures established through regional agreements such as the North
American Free Trade Agreement (NAFTA) and the Asia-Pacific Economic
Cooperation (APEC) forum. These supranational planning institutes are gradually supplanting national institutions in policy development and global
management and administration of the global economy. The function of the
nation-state is shifting from the formulation of national policies to the administration of policies formulated through supranational institutions. However, it is
essential to avoid the national global duality: national states are not external to
the TNS but are becoming incorporated into it as component parts. The supranational organizations function in consonance with transformed national states.
They are staffed by transnational functionaries that find their counterparts in
transnational functionaries who staff transformed national states. These *transnational state cadres* act as midwives of capitalist globalization.

The TNS is attempting to fulfil the functions for world capitalism that in earlier
periods were fulfilled by what world-system and international relations scholars
refer to as a 'hegemon', or a dominant capitalist power that has the resources and
the structural position that allows it to organize world capitalism as a whole and
impose the rules, regulatory environment, etc., that allows the system to function.
We are witnessing the decline of US supremacy and the early stages of the
creation of a transnational hegemony through supranational structures that are
not yet capable of providing the economic regulation and political conditions for
the reproduction of global capitalism. Just as the national state played this role in
the earlier period, the TNS seeks to create and maintain the preconditions for the
valorization and accumulation of capital in the global economy, which is not
simply the sum of national economies and national class structures and requires a
centralized authority to represent the whole of competing capitals, the major
combinations of which are no longer 'national' capitals. The nature of state practices in the emergent global system resides in the exercise of transnational
economic and political authority through the TNS apparatus to reproduce the
class relations embedded in the global valorization and accumulation of capital.

The power of national states and the power of transnational capital

As class formation proceeded through the nation-state in earlier epochs, class struggle world-wide unfolded through the institutional and organizational logic of the nation-state system. During the nation-state phase of capitalism, national states enjoyed a varying but significant degree of autonomy to intervene in the phase of distribution and surpluses could be diverted through nation-state institutions. Dominant and subordinate classes struggled against each other over the social surplus through such institutions and fought to utilize national states to capture shares of the surplus. As a result, to evoke Karl Polanyi's classical analysis, a 'double movement' took place late last century (Polanyi 1944), made possible because capital, facing territorial, institutional and other limits bound up with the nation-state system, faced a series of constraints that forced it to reach an historic compromise with working and popular classes. These classes could place redistributive demands on national states and set some constraints on the power of capital (these possibilities also contributed to the split in the world socialist movement and the rise of social democracy). Popular classes could achieve this because national states had the ability to capture and redirect surpluses through interventionist mechanisms. The outcome of world class struggles in this period were Keynesian or 'New Deal' states and Fordist production in the cores of the world economy and diverse multiclass developmentalist states and populist projects in the periphery ('peripheral Fordism'), what Lipietz and others have called the 'Fordist class compromise' (Lipietz 1992).

In each of these cases, subordinate classes mediated their relation to capital through the nation-state. Capitalist classes developed within the protective cocoon of nation-states and developed interests in opposition to rival national capitals. These states expressed the coalitions of classes and groups that were incorporated into the historic blocs of nation-states. There was nothing transhistoric, or predetermined, about this process of class formation world-wide. It is now being superseded by globalization. What is occurring is a process of transnational class formation, in which the mediating element of national states has been modified (on transnational classes, see, *inter alia*, van der Pijl 1998; Sklair 1995; Gill 1990; Robinson 1996a; Robinson and Harris, 2002). As national productive structures become transnationally integrated, world classes whose organic development took place through the nation-state are experiencing supranational integration with 'national' classes of other countries. Global class formation has involved the accelerated division of the world into a global bourgeoisie and a global proletariat and has brought changes in the relationship between dominant and subordinate classes. Specifically, by redefining the phase of distribution in the accumulation of capital in relation to nation-states the global economy fragments national cohesion around processes of social reproduction and shifts the site of reproduction from the nation-state to transnational space. The consequent liberation of transnational capital from the constraints and commitments placed on it by the social forces in the nation-state phase of capitalism has dramatically altered the balance of forces among classes and social groups in each nation of the world and at a global level towards the transnational capitalist class and its agents. (Indeed, the restraints on accumulation imposed by popular classes world-wide in the nation-state phase of capitalism was what drove capital to transnationalization in the first instance.)

The declining ability of the nation-state to intervene in the process of capital accumulation and to determine economic policies reflects the newfound power that transnational capital acquired over popular classes. Different classes and groups contest (national) state power but real power in the global system is shifting to a transnational space that is not subject to 'national' control. This structural power of transnational capital over the direct power of national states has been utilized to instil discipline or to undermine policies that may emanate from these states when they are captured by popular classes or by national fractions of local dominant groups, as popular forces that won state power in Haiti, Nicaragua, South Africa, and elsewhere in the 1970s–1990s discovered. This appears as an institutional contradiction between the structural power of transnational capital and the direct power of states (see, e.g., Gill and Law 1989). But this is a structural contradiction internal to an evolving capitalist system, at whose core are class relations, as the inner essence of a condition whose outward manifestation is an institutional contradiction. One set of social relations reflects a more fundamental set of social relations. On the surface, the structural power of capital over the direct power of states is enhanced many times over by globalization. In its essence, the relative power of exploiting classes over the exploited classes has been enhanced many times over, at least in this momentary historic juncture.

The newfound relative power of global capital over global labour is becoming fixed in a new global capital–labour relation, what some have called the global casualization or informalization of labour, or diverse contingent categories, involving alternative systems of labour control associated with post-Fordist 'flexible accumulation' (on the crisis of Fordism/Keynesianism and restructuring, see, *inter alia*, Kolko 1988; Harvey 1990; Cox 1987; Lipietz 1987; Lash and Urry 1987). Central to this new capital–labour relation is the concept of a restructuring crisis. The crisis of the long post-war boom in the 1970s ushered in a radical shift in the methods and sites of global capitalist accumulation, resulting, in Hoogvelt's analysis, in a transformation in the mechanisms of surplus value extraction (Hoogvelt 1997). These new systems of labour control include subcontracting and contract labour, outsourcing, part-time and temporary work, informal work, home-work, the revival of patriarchal, 'sweatshop', and other oppressive production relations. Well-known trends associated with the restructuring of the labour–capital relation taking place under globalization include 'downward levelling', deunionization, 'ad hoc' and 'just-in-time' labour supply, the superexploitation of immigrant communities as a counterpart to capital export, the lengthening of the working day, the rise of a new global 'underclass' of supernumeraries or 'redundants' subject to new forms of social control and even to genocide, and new gendered and racialized hierarchies among labour.

These new relations have been broadly discussed in the globalization literature. What interests us here is the larger social and political context in which they are embedded, and the extent to which states and nation-states continue to mediate these contexts. State practices and the very structure of states are negotiated and renegotiated in specific historic periods through changes in the balance of social forces as capitalism develops and classes struggle. Capital began to abandon earlier reciprocities with labour from the 1970s onwards, precisely because the process of globalization has allowed it to break free of nation-state constraints. These new labour patterns are facilitated by globalization in a dual sense: first, capital has exercised its power over labour through new patterns of flexible accumulation made possible by enabling 'third wave' technologies, the elimination of spatial barriers to accumulation, and the control over space these changes bring; second, globalization itself involves the culmination of the primitive accumulation of capital world-wide, a process in which millions have been wrenched from the means of production, proletarianized, and thrown into a global labour market that transnational capital has been able to shape. In this new capital–labour relation, labour is increasingly only a naked commodity, no longer embedded in relations of reciprocity rooted in social and political communities that have historically been institutionalized in nation-states.

The dissolution of the 'welfarist' or Keynesian 'class compromise' rests on the power acquired by transnational capital over labour, which is objectively transnational but whose power is constrained and whose subjective consciousness is distorted by the continued existence of the system of nation-states. Here we see how the continued existence of the nation-state serves numerous interests of the transnational capitalist class. For instance, central to capitalism is securing a politically and economically suitable labour supply, and at the core of all class societies is the control over labour and disposal of the products of labour. Under capitalist globalization, the linkage between securing labour and territoriality is changing, and national labour pools are merging into a single global labour pool that services global capitalism. The global labour supply is, in the main, no longer coerced (subject to extra-economic compulsion) due to the ability of the universalized market to exercise strictly economic discipline, but its movement is juridically controlled. Here, national borders play a vital function. Nation-states are about the configuration of space, what sociologist Philip McMichael (1996) has called 'population containment zones'. But their containment function applies to labour and not to capital. Globally mobile capital is not regulated by centralized national political authorities but labour is. The inter-state system thus acts as a condition for the structural power of globally mobile transnational capital over labour which is transnational in its actual content and character, but is subjected to different institutional arrangements and to the direct control of national states.

How then is the newfound relative power of global capital over global labour related to our analysis of the transnationalization of the state? Out of the emerging transnational institutionality the new class relations of global capitalism and the social practices specific to it are becoming congealed and institutionalized. For instance, when the IMF or the WB condition financing on enactment of new labour codes to make workers more 'flexible', or on the roll-back of a state-sponsored 'social wage' through austerity programmes, they are producing this new class relation. Similarly, the types of practices of national states that became generalized in the late twentieth century – deregulation, fiscal conservatism, monetarism, tax regressivity, austerity, etc. – produce this relation, resulting in an increase in state services to, and subsidization of, capital, and underscoring the increased role of the state in facilitating private capital accumulation. With this comes a shift in income and in power from labour to capital. These outcomes generate the broader social and political conditions under which the new capital–labour relation is forged.

But now we need to specify further the relationship of national states to the TNS. Capital acquires its newfound power *vis-à-vis* (*as expressed within*) national states, which are transformed into transmission belts and filtering devices. But national states are also transformed into proactive instruments for advancing the agenda of global capitalism. This assertion that transnational social forces impose their structural power over nations and the simultaneous assertion that states, captured by transnational fractions, are proactive agents of the globalization process, only appear as contradictory if one abandons dialectics for the Weberian dualist construct of states and markets and the national–global dualism. Governments are undertaking restructuring and serve the needs of transnational capital not simply because they are 'powerless' in the face of globalization, but because a particular historical constellation of social forces now exists that presents an organic social base for this global restructuring of capitalism. Hence it is not that nation-states become irrelevant or powerless *vis-à-vis* transnational capital and its global institutions. Rather, power as the ability to issue commands and have them obeyed, or more precisely, the ability to shape social structures, shifts from social groups and classes with interests in national accumulation to those whose interests lie in new global circuits of accumulation.

The contradictory logics of national and global accumulation are at work in this process. Class fractionation is occurring along a new national/transnational axis with the rise of transnational corporate and political elites (for discussion, see Robinson 1996a, 1996b; Robinson and Harris, 2000). The interests of one group lie in national accumulation, including the whole set of traditional national regulatory and protectionist mechanisms, and the other in an expanding global economy based on world-wide market liberalization. The struggle between descendant national fractions of dominant groups and ascendant transnational fractions was often the backdrop to surface political dynamics and ideological processes in the late twentieth century. These two fractions have been vying for control of local state apparatuses since the 1970s. Transnational fractions of local elites have ascended politically in countries around the world, clashing in their bid for hegemony with nationally based class fractions. In the 1970s and the 1980s incipient transnationalized fractions set out to eclipse national fractions in the core capitalist countries of the North and to capture the 'commanding heights' of state policy-making. From the 1980s into the 1990s, these fractions became ascendant in the South and began to vie for, and in many countries to capture, national state apparatuses. National states, captured by transnational social forces, internalize the authority structures of global capitalism. The global is incarnated in local social structures and processes. The disciplinary power of the global capitalism shifts actual policy-making power within national states to the global capitalist bloc, which is represented by local social forces tied to the global economy. Gradually, transnational blocs became hegemonic in the 1980s and 1990s within the vast majority of countries in the world and began to transform their countries. They utilized national state apparatuses to advance globalization and established formal and informal liaison mechanisms between the national state structures and TNS apparatuses.

By the 1990s the transnational capitalist class had become the hegemonic class fraction globally. This denationalized bourgeoisie is class conscious, and conscious of its transnationality. Its interests are administered by a managerial elite that controls the levers of global policy-making and exercises transnational state power through the multilayered configuration of the TNS. But this transnational bourgeoisie is not a unified group. 'The same conditions, the same contradiction, the same interests necessarily called forth on the whole similar customs everywhere', noted Marx and Engels in discussing the formation of new class groups. 'But separate individuals form a class only insofar as they have to carry on a common battle against another class; otherwise they are on hostile terms with each other as competitors' (Marx and Engels 1970: 82). Fierce competition among oligopolist clusters, conflicting pressures, and differences over the tactics and strategy of maintaining class domination and addressing the crises and contradictions of global capitalism make any real internal unity in global ruling class impossible. In sum, the capturing of local states by agents of global capitalism resolves the institutional contradiction discussed above between transnational capital and national states, that is, local state practices are increasingly harmonized with global capitalism. But this only intensifies the underlying class and social contradictions. Before discussing these contradictions, let us reconstruct in brief the emergence of a TNS in the latter decades of the twentieth century, tracing *how* the transnational capitalist class sought to institutionalize its interests within a TNS.

Some empirical reference points: the emergence of a transnational state: 1960s–1990s

Under the political–military canopy of US supremacy, national capitals began a new period of internationalization and external integration in the post-Second World War period. Escalating international economic activity unfolded within the institutional framework of the nation-state system and the cross-border regulation of 'international regimes', in particular, the Bretton Woods system. As multinational corporations extended their reach around the world they sought to evade the central bank controls associated with the Bretton Woods system by depositing their capital in foreign currency markets. Economic internationalization thus brought the massive spread of dollars and other core country currencies around the world. Eurodollar deposits ballooned from just $3 billion in 1960 to $75 billion in 1970 – prompting the Nixon administration to abandon the gold standard in 1971 – and then climbed to over $1 trillion in 1984. The collapse of the Bretton Woods system of fixed currency exchange and national economic regulation via capital controls was the first step in the liberation of embryonic transnational capital from the institutional constraints of the nation-state system.

Liquid capital became accumulated in offshore capital markets established by nascent transnational banks seeking to evade the regulatory powers of national states. In the 1970s the transnational banks began to recycle this liquid capital through massive loans to Third World governments. International bank lending jumped from $2 billion in 1972 to $90 billion in 1981, before falling to $50 billion in 1985 (Strange 1994: 112). These newly liberated global financial markets began to determine currency values, to destabilize national finances, and to undermine the national macro-economic management of the earlier Keynesian regime of capitalism. By the early 1990s some $1 trillion in various currencies was being traded daily, all beyond the control of national governments (ibid.: 107). The dramatic loss of currency control by governments meant that state managers could no longer regulate the value of their national currency. The power to influence state economic policy-making passed from these state managers to currency traders, portfolio investors, and transnational bankers – precisely, the representatives of transnational finance capital – by virtue of their ability to move funds around the world. Offshore capital markets grew from $315 billion in 1973 to over $2 trillion in 1982, and by the end of the 1970s, trade in currencies was more than eleven times greater than the value of world commodity trade. And because this global movement of liquidity created unpredictable conditions of profitability, transnational corporations reduced their risks by diversifying their operations around the world, thus accelerating the entire globalization process and the political pressures for a TNS apparatus.

As transnational corporate and political elites emerged on the world scene in the 1980s they made explicit claims to building and managing a global economy through restructured multilateral and national institutions. They pressured for the dismantling of Keynesian welfare and developmentalist states and the lifting of national controls over the free movement of globally mobile capital. They pushed for public sectors and non-market community spheres to be opened up to profit making and privatized (what Marx termed the 'alienation of the state' (Marx 1959: 754–5)), and set about to impose new production relations of flexible accumulation. The transnational bourgeoisie also became politically organized. The formation in the mid-1970s of the Trilateral Commission, which brought together transnationalized fractions of the business, political, and intellectual elite in North America, Europe, and Japan, was one marker in its politicization. Others were: the creation of the Group of 7 forum at the governmental level, which began institutionalizing collective management of the global economy by corporate and political elites from core nation-states; the transformation of the OECD, formed in the 1950s as a supranational institution by the twenty-four largest industrialized countries to observe their national economies, into a forum for economic policy coordination and restructuring; and the creation of the World Economic Forum, which brought together the top representatives of transnational corporations and global political elites.

The diverse activities, strategies, and power positions of global elites as they sought practical solutions to the problems of accumulation around the world gradually converged around a programme of global economic and political restructuring centred on market liberalization – the so-called 'Washington consensus' (Williamson 1993). This programme became cohesive in the 1980s. The global elite set out to convert the world into a single unified field for global capitalism, amidst sharp social struggles and multiple forms of resistance from subordinate groups and also from dominant groups not brought into this emerging global capitalist bloc. It pushed for greater uniformity and standardization in the codes and rules of the global market – a process similar to the construction of national markets in the nineteenth century but now replicated in the new global space. The G-7 in 1982 designated the IMF and the World Bank as the central authorities for exercising the collective power of the capitalist national states over international financial negotiations (Harvey 1990: 170). At the Cancun Summit in Mexico in 1982, the core capitalist states, led by the United States, launched the era of global neoliberalism as part of this process and began imposing structural adjustment programmes on the Third World and the then Second World. Transnational elites promoted international economic integration processes, including the NAFTA, the EU, and the APEC, among others. They created new sets of institutions and forums, such as the WTO, the Multilateral Agreement on Investment (MAI), and so on.

In this process, the existing supranational institutions, such as the Bretton Woods and the UN institutions, were not bypassed but instrumentalized and transformed. The reformed Bretton Woods institutions took the reins in organizing global economic restructuring, especially through neoliberal programmes. Similarly, the UN conference system helped achieve consensus on reshaping the world political and economic order, while UN agencies such as the United Nations Development Programme and the UN Conference on Trade and Development began to promote the transnational elite agenda of economic liberalization. Speaking before the World Economic Forum in 1998, UN Secretary General Kofi Annan explained how the UN seeks to establish the international security and regulatory environment, and the social, political and ideological conditions, for global markets to flourish:

> [The UN agencies] help countries to join the international trading system and enact business-friendly legislation. Markets do not function in a vacuum. Rather, they arise from a framework of rules and laws, and they respond to signals set by Governments and other institutions. Without rules governing property, rights and contracts; without confidence based on the

rule of law; without an overall sense of direction and a fair degree of equity and transparency, there could be no well-functioning markets, domestic or global. The UN system provides such a global framework – an agreed set of standards and objectives that enjoy worldwide acceptance. A strong United Nations is good for business.

(Annan 1998: 24)

The Uruguay Round of world trade negotiations that began in 1986 established a sweeping new set of world trade rules to regulate the new global economy based on: (1) freedom of investment and capital movements; (2) the liberalization of services, including banks; (3) intellectual property rights; (4) a free movement of goods. On the conclusion of the Uruguay Round the GATT created the WTO, in 1995, to supervise this new 'free trade' regime. Although its powers are far from absolute, the WTO is perhaps the archetypical transnational institution of the new era. The WTO assumes unprecedented powers to enforce the GATT 'free trade' provisions. It has independent jurisdiction, its rules and rulings are binding on all members, and has the power to sanction, to overrule state and local powers, and to override national regulatory powers. The theoretical import here is that the WTO is the first supranational institution with a coercive capacity not embedded in any particular nation-state but rather directly in transnational functionaries and the transnational corporate elite.

By the late 1990s the TNS as an institution attempting to impose its authority on a fluid and spatially open process of capital accumulation was assuming some powers and historic functions that the nation-states had lost in organizing collective action to facilitate and reproduce this process in the global economy. The creation of a capitalist superstructure which carries out at the transnational level functions indispensable for the reproduction of capital, especially those that national states are unable to perform, is not to say that a TNS has fully become consolidated as a fully functioning political, administrative, and regulatory structure. There is no clear chain of command and division of labour within the TNS apparatus, or anything resembling, at this time, the type of internal coherence of national states, given the embryonic stage of this process. Instead of a coherent TNS there seem to be multiple centres and partial regulatory mechanisms. Moreover, diverse institutions that comprise a TNS have distinct histories and trajectories, are internally differentiated, and present numerous entry points as sites of contestation.

Nonetheless, the TNS has developed mechanisms to assume a growing number of functions traditionally associated with the national state, such as compensation for market failure (e.g. IMF bailouts), money creation (e.g. EU currency), legal guarantees of property rights and market contracts (the powers of the WTO), and the provision of public goods (social and physical infrastructure), and so on. Despite this expanded TNS activity, there are numerous functions that the TNS has not been able to assume, such as reining in on speculation and excesses that so characterize the frenzied 'casino capitalism' of the global economy (Strange 1986). Identifying these functions of the TNS does not imply functional analysis so long as the conditions under which these functions are unfulfilled are specified and problematized, as I do later on, and provided as well that analysis of historic change demonstrates the mechanism of agency or how a determined outcome could have been otherwise.

It is out of the process summarized here that a TNS apparatus began to emerge, not as something planned as such, but as the political consequences of the social practice and class action of the transnational capitalist class in this historic juncture, and as an apparatus that is not replacing but emerging out of the pre-globalization infrastructure of world capitalism. But the transnational elite has also operated through an array of *private* transnational business associations and political planning groups that have proliferated since the 1970s and point to the expansion of a *transnational civil society* as part of the globalization process and parallel to the rise of a TNS. They include such well-known bodies as the Trilateral Commission, the International Chamber of Commerce, and the World Economic Forum. A more complete study on the TNS than is possible here may explore the relationship between the TNS and transnational civil society, employing Antonio Gramsci's notion of an *extended (or enlarged) state* incorporating both political society (the state proper) and civil society. The matter of transnational civil society is of great significance since the TNS exists as part of a larger totality and because the practices of an emerging global ruling class take place at both levels. This ruling class is attempting to establish the hegemony of a new global capitalist historic bloc at the broader level of an extended state (Robinson 1996a).

Far from the 'end of the nation-state', as a slew of recent studies has proclaimed (see, *inter alia*, Guehenno 1995; Ohmae 1996), we are witness to its transformation into 'neo-liberal national states'. As component elements of a TNS, they perform three essential services: (1) adopt fiscal and monetary policies which assure macro-economic stability; (2) provide the basic infrastructure necessary for global economic activity (air and sea ports, communications networks, educational systems, etc.); and (3) provide social order, that is, stability, which requires sustaining instruments of direct coercion and ideological apparatuses.[5] When the transnational elite speaks of 'governance' it is referring to these functions and the capacity to fulfil them. This is made explicit in the World Bank's *World Development Report* for 1997, *The State in a Changing World*, which points out that the aegis of the national state is central to globalization. In the World Bank's words, 'globalization begins at home' (1997: 12). But the functions of the neo-liberal state are contradictory. As globalization proceeds, internal social cohesion declines along with national economic integration. The neo-liberal state retains essential powers to facilitate globalization but it loses the ability to harmonize conflicting social interests within a country, to realize the historic function of sustaining the internal unity of nationally conceived social formation, and to achieve legitimacy. The result is a dramatic intensification of legitimacy crises, a contradiction internal to the system of global capitalism.

Concluding remarks: transnational mobilization from below to counter transnational mobilization from above

So what is to be done? Smash the TNS and attempt a return to nation-state projects of popular social change? The problem with such propositions is that globalization, although it involves agency as much as structure, is *not* a project conceived, planned and implemented at the level of intentionality. I think we need to look forward rather than backward. Such historic processes cannot be reverted as such, but they can be influenced, redirected, and transcended. This returns us to my opening affirmation that historical materialism is emancipatory precisely because it reveals the historical specificity of existing forms of social life. Emancipatory projects operate *in* history. As Marx would have us recall, we do make our own history, but we do not make it just as we please, 'but under circumstances directly found, given and transmitted from the past'.

It is not inevitable that a new transnational elite will consolidate its economic and political hegemony. A major economic crisis or collapse could stymie the process or push it into unforeseen directions. Transnational capital currently enjoys an unprecedented structural power over popular classes world-wide, but this is an historic conjuncture and not a fixed feature of the system. The confidence exuded by the transnational bourgeoisie in the latter decades of the twentieth century – with its 'end of history' thesis and so on – is giving way to fear of looming crisis as contradictions *internal* to global capitalism have become increasingly manifest. The world recession of the 1990s exposed the fragility of the world monetary system and caused rising alarm and growing fissures in the inner circles of the global ruling class. As the decade drew to a close a rising chorus of voices from within the global elite called for centralized global financial regulation and numerous proposals were put forward for achieving it, ranging from the creation of a world central bank to the transformation of the IMF into a veritable 'lender of last resort'. These developments highlight the attempt by the transnational capitalist class to achieve some regulatory order given the inability of an incipient TNS to stabilize the system.

Capitalism has always been a violent and unstable system fraught with contradictions. All of the contradictions germane to the capitalist system are rising to the surface in the new epoch of globalization, in particular, overaccumulation and world-wide social polarization. In the past, these contradictions have led to periodic crises that tend to result each time in a reorganization of the system. Imperialism, for instance, allowed core countries to displace to the colonial world, momentarily, some of the sharpest social antagonisms that capitalism generated, while Keynesian absorption mechanisms such as credit creation postponed overaccumulation crises. But many if not all of capitalism's recurrent crises have been mediated by the nation-state. Under globalization the national state is less able to address these manifold crises, yet the emergent TNS is similarly ill-equipped to resolve them, especially those of overaccumulation and social polarization. Even if the global financial system can be brought under regulation, the mechanisms simply do not exist for absorption strategies, nor does the system provide a material basis for a project of legitimation.

It is not clear in the new epoch how the contradictions of the system will be played out, but certainly new opportunities for emancipatory projects are on the horizon. To speak of globalization as the culmination of capitalism's extensive enlargement and its accelerated conquest of pre-capitalist spheres is to posit that there are a series of world historic dynamics and of contradictions that are being modified or supplanted by these new circumstances. The system will not be defeated by challenges from outside its logic such as those of the former Soviet bloc countries and Third World liberation movements. Rather, defeat will be from within the global system itself. The contradictions between capitalist and pre-capitalist classes, for instance, are increasingly irrelevant. Resistance to capitalist colonization from without is giving way to resistance to capitalism from within. The universal penetration of capitalism through globalization draws all peoples not only into webs of market relations but also into webs of resistance.

To defend the relevance of Marx and the continuing vitality of historical materialism is not to say all of what Marx had to say is still applicable to the conditions humanity faces in the new millennium. To the contrary, any such proposition becomes dogma, intellectually sterile and politically disabling. Marx and Engels's argument that 'the proletariat of each country must, of course, first of all settle matters with its own bourgeoisie', is now outdated. 'Its own bourgeoisie' is now transnational; each 'national' bourgeoisie is as well the bourgeoisie of the proletariat of numerous countries. Popular classes in the age of globalization need to transnationalize their struggles. The mobilization of the transnational bourgeoisie from above can only be countered by a transnational mobilization from below. Working and popular classes whose fulcrum has been the nation-state needs must transpose to transnational space their mobilization and their capacity to place demands on the system. This means developing the mechanisms – alliances, networks, direct actions and organizations – that will allow for a transnational resistance. It also means developing a transnational socialist ideology and politics, and targeting the TNS as contested terrain.

Acknowledgements

I would like to thank James R. Maupin, Gioconda Espinosa, Jeffrey Mitchell, George Lambie, Leslie Sklair, Kees van der Pijl, Hazel Smith, and Mark Rupert for their comments on earlier drafts of this chapter. The content and all of its inevitable shortcomings are of course my sole responsibility.

Notes

1   The literature on globalization is burgeoning – too vast to reference here – although a transnational institutionality, such as I examine in this chapter, remains underexplored. For basic studies, see, *inter alia*, Waters (1995); Sklair (1995); Holton (1998).

2   This section advances major propositions that cannot be explored here due to space limitations. A more elaborate treatment of my conception of globalization is found in Robinson (1996a, 1996b, 1998); Burbach and Robinson (1999).
3   Works on the global economy are voluminous. On the globalization of production, which is of most concern here, see, *inter alia*, Dicken (1998); Howells and Wood (1993); Burbach and Robinson (1999).
4   Marx and Engels (1970 [1846]) note:

> Since the state is the form in which the individuals of a ruling class assert their common interests, and in which the whole civil society of an epoch is epitomized, it follows that the state mediates in the formation of all common institutions and that the institutions receive a political form.
>
> (80)

Marx's discussion on so-called primitive accumulation in *Capital*, Book VIII, highlights the role of the state in facilitating the conditions for new economic and social relations. Here I want to highlight the role of the TNS in facilitating the conditions for the new types of relations developing under globalization.
5   The World Bank's 1997 annual report was a virtual blueprint for the transformation of national states along these lines.

Bibliography

Annan, K. (1998) Address by the UN Secretary at the World Economic Forum, Davos, Switzerland, 31 January, reprinted in part as a paid advertisement by the Pfizer Corporation in *The Economist*, 28 March–3 April 1998, p.24.

Boyer, R. and Drache, D. (eds) (1996) *States Against Markets: The Limits of Globalization*, London: Routledge.

Burbach, R. and Robinson, W. (1999) 'The Fin de Siècle Debate: Globalization as Epochal Shift', *Science and Society*, 63: 10–39.

Clarke, S. (ed.) (1991) *The State Debate*, London: Macmillan.

Cox, R. (1987) *Production, Power, and World Order*, New York: Columbia University Press.

Dicken, P. (1998) *Global Shift*, 3rd edn, New York: Guilford.

Gill, S. (1990) *American Hegemony and the Trilateral Commission*, Cambridge: Cambridge University Press.

Gill, S. and Law, D. (1989) 'Global Hegemony and the Structural Power of Capital', *International Studies Quarterly*, 33: 475–99.

Gordon, D. (1988) 'The Global Economy: New Edifice or Crumbling Foundations', *New Left Review*, 168: 24–65.

Guehenno, J.-M. (1995) *The End of the Nation State*, St Paul, MN: University of Minnesota Press.

Harvey, D. (1990) *The Condition of Postmodernity*, Oxford: Blackwell.

Held, D. (1989) *Political Theory and the Modern State*, Stanford, CA: Stanford University Press.

Hirst, P. and Thompson, G. (1996) *Globalization in Question*, Oxford: Polity Press.

Holton, R. (1998) *Globalization and the Nation-State*, London: Macmillan.

Hoogvelt, A. (1997) *Globalization and the Postcolonial World*, Baltimore, MD: Johns Hopkins University Press.

Howells, J. and Wood, M. (1993) *The Globalisation of Production and Technology*, London and New York: Belhaven Press.

Jessop, B. (1982) *The Capitalist State*, Oxford: Martin Robertson.

Kolko, J. (1988) *Restructuring the World Economy*, New York: Pantheon Books.

Lash, S. and Urry, J. (1987) *The End of Organized Capitalism*, Cambridge: Polity Press.

Lipietz, A. (1987) *Mirages and Miracles: The Crises of Global Fordism*, London: Verso.

—— (1992) *Towards a New Economic Order: Postfordism, Ecology and Democracy*, New York: Oxford University Press.

Marx, K. (1959) *Capital*, Vol. I, Moscow: Foreign Language Publishing House.

—— (1978) *The Eighteenth Brumaire of Louis Napoleon*, in R. Tucker (ed.), *The Marx–Engels Reader*, 2nd edn, New York: Norton.

Marx, K. and Engels, F. (1970 [1846]) *The German Ideology*, New York: International Publishers.

McMichael, P. (1996) *Development and Social Change*, Thousand Oaks, CA: Pine Forge Press.

Ohmae, K. (1996) *The End of the Nation State*, New York: Free Press.

Polanyi, K. (1944) *The Great Transformation*, Boston, MA: Beacon Press.

Robinson, W. (1996a) *Promoting Polyarchy*, Cambridge: Cambridge University Press.

—— (1996b) 'Globalisation: Nine Theses of Our Epoch', *Race and Class*, 38: 13–31.

—— (1998) 'Beyond Nation-State Paradigms', *Sociological Forum*, 13: 561–94.

Robinson, W. and Harris, J. (2000) 'Toward a Global Ruling Class?: Globalization and the Transnational Capitalist Class' 64(1): 11–54.

Sassen, S. (1996) *Losing Control? Sovereignty in an Age of Globalization*, New York: Columbia University Press.

Sklair, L. (1995) *Sociology of the Global System*, Baltimore, MD: Johns Hopkins University Press.

Strange, S. (1986) *Casino Capitalism*, Oxford: Oxford University Press.

—— (1994) *States and Markets*, London: Pinter Press.

—— (1996) *The Retreat of the State*, Cambridge: Cambridge University Press.

van der Pijl, K. (1998) *Transnational Classes and International Relations*, London: Routledge.

Vernon, R. (1971) *Sovereignty at Bay*, London: Longman.

Waters, M. (1995) *Globalization*, London: Routledge.

Weber, M. (1978) *Economy and Society*, 2 vols, G. Roth and C Wittich (eds), Berkeley, CA: University of California Press.

Weiss, L. (1998) *The Myth of the Powerless State*, Ithaca, NY: Cornell University Press.

Williamson, J. (1993) 'Democracy and the "Washington Consensus"', *World Development*, 21: 1329–36.

World Bank (1997) *The State in a Changing World*, Washington, DC: World Bank.

12 Historical materialism, globalization, and law

Competing conceptions of property

A. Claire Cutler

Intellectuals on the right and left are challenging the continuing relevance of Marxism, socialism, and the historical materialist tradition. Liberal triumphalism is sounding the death knell for socialism and progressivist histories. Indeed, Francis Fukuyama contemplates the 'end of history' in the 'end point of mankind's ideological development and the universalization of Western liberal democracy as the final form of human government' (1989: 3). The globalization of the market is thus associated with the universalization of liberalism and democracy. Others on the left challenge the relevance of Marxism and the concepts of class analysis and mode of production for understanding the proliferation of 'identities' reflecting fundamental political differences and even irreconcilable interests (Polan 1984: 77; Held 1989: 135–9). Anthony Giddens identifies important gaps in Marxism, including forms of politics, like the environmental, human rights, and peace movements, that cannot be understood from the perspective of class alone (1990a, 1990b: 20–2). Yet others question the ability of the Marxist 'metanarrative' to capture the increasingly fragmentary and diverse nature of global capitalism with its postmodern culture and post-Fordist political economy (but see Jameson 1991: 399; Harvey 1990: 388).

This chapter makes a case for the continuing and, indeed, pressing analytical and practical relevance of historical materialism. Historical materialism is conceived of as a 'critique of capitalism' that insists on the 'historical specificity of capitalism' and 'approaches capitalism in a way exactly antithetical to the current fashions: the systemic unity of capitalism instead of just post-modern fragments, but also historicity – and hence the possibility of supersession – instead of capitalist inevitability and the end of History' (Wood 1995: 2–3). Moreover, as Ellen Meiksins Wood further notes, this involves taking into account major transformations that have occurred in capitalism and 'a constantly renewed critique of the analytical instruments designed to understand it' (1995: 4). This chapter hopes to contribute to greater understanding of contemporary transformations in capitalism and to assist in the development of the analytical foundations of historical materialism. The analysis suggests that the concepts of class and mode of production continue to be relevant, but must be adapted to accommodate transformations in both class and productive relations associated more generally with the globalization of capitalism. However, the focus is not on globalizing capitalism, class relations, nor the mode of production *per se*. Rather, the focus is on the role that law plays in the global transformation of class relations and the mode of production. Indeed, it argues that the law is not neutral in impact and that a significant challenge for historical materialism is recognizing the significance of law. The focus on law is important for a number of reasons. First, law is ubiquitous, domestically, internationally, and transnationally. Increasingly legal regimes codify and regulate our social, political, and economic lives. In the economic realm, particularly, the ubiquity of law is ever more apparent in the deepening of legal disciplines on trade, investment, and financial relations (Cutler 2000). Second, law links local and global political and economic orders, in complex ways (see Cutler 1999a). For example, when GATT disciplines are enacted into domestic law they become part of the lawyers' stock-in-trade, losing their international character as they become part of the domestic legal order. Or when codes or sets of uniform rules, which are developed by private transnationally organized bankers, insurers, maritime shippers or the like, are transmitted to governments for enactment into domestic law, the transnational–local link becomes obscured by the move to legislate nationally and domestically (Cutler 1999b). The rules of private and public international law thus form a juridical link between local and global political-legal orders. Third, the globalization of law is an integral aspect of the globalization of capitalism. The law globalizes rules that facilitate transnational patterns of capital accumulation, attenuating certain regulatory capacities of states, while advancing others. Thus the ability of states to regulate production, trade, and finance for national policy purposes is subordinated to the need for states to act as market participants or 'competition states' in the search for ever expanding market opportunities (Cerny 1997; also Scheuerman 1999). The globalization of law is integral to the internalization of neoliberal discipline by elites and its reproduction in local laws and in the growing corpus of transnational economic law. Globalized law advances the interests of a transnational class whose members function as the 'organic intellectuals' for the globalization of capitalism (Gramsci 1971: 3–23). This class advances a particular legal culture informed by neoliberal values and the privileging of private ordering as the most natural, efficient, consensual, and just manner of regulating international commercial and productive relations (Cutler 1995). In the economic and commercial realms particularly, the law that is being globalized is essentially American or Anglo-American in origin, promoting the values of neoliberal regulatory orders (Wiegand 1996; Cutler 1999c). These values and beliefs are in turn embodied in legal rules that provide the foundation for the expansion of property relations based on the private appropriation of surplus value.

However, the political significance of the law, in terms of determining 'who gets what', is lost on most analysts (but see Gardner 1980). In general, neither conventional nor Marxist analysts of politics and international law capture the political nature and distributional function of law. For surprisingly similar reasons, they both miss the crucial role played by law in the globalization of capitalism. This chapter thus argues that there is a need to problematize the nature and role of law and hopes to advance critical analysis of law by identifying two competing conceptions of property. These conceptions reflect the dialectical relationship between capital and labour and the tension between national and transnational productive relations. Understanding their significance thus sheds light on important aspects of class and productive relations, the analytical foundations of historical materialism.

Moreover, understanding the tension between competing conceptions of property also informs our understanding of significant qualitative transformations in the mode of production. Globalization operates dialectically to disembed and displace certain processes of national capital formation in favour of transnational capital formation.[1] One conception of property is associated with national patterns of capital accumulation, while a competing conception relates to transnational patterns of accumulation. The latter works to facilitate the denationalization of productive relations. In providing new legal forms, *ad hoc*, informal, and private methods for settling commercial disputes, the law both adjusts to post-Fordist changes in production and facilitates the creation of new productive relations.[2] It does so by providing security of possession for increasingly denationalized, deterritorialized, and even dematerialized property relations. However, while legal innovations enable the development of new business techniques, expanding the possibilities for productive relations into new spaces (or non-spaces), they also threaten the security of capital. It is difficult to protect intangible property, like intellectual property and property in information and new technology. Thus, new forms of security and discipline must be developed to make the law safe for capitalism.[3] Hence, we see an opposing tendency in the enhanced surveillance and enforcement capacities of states and efforts to reterritorialize and renationalize certain property relations. States, in turn, work in harmony with the interests of transnational capital as they deepen and internalize neoliberal discipline. Competing conceptions of property underlie these opposing tendencies and thus provide critical insight into the dialectical nature of the mode of production of global capitalism.

In addition to providing analytical insights, these competing conceptions provide very practical insights into the possibilities for emancipatory politics — for the clarification of alternate world orders and the promotion of change in social relations.[4] They signal sites in which contemporary capitalism is being contested and where there are very specific openings for human agency to affect real change. Recognition that law is not neutral in effect, when coupled with the recognition that it is made and can be unmade by human action, provides new avenues for emancipatory politics.

Before addressing these competing conceptions of property, it will be useful to consider the inadequacy of both conventional and critical approaches to legal theory. To that end, the next section addresses the limitations of liberal and Marxist analyses, arguing for a more critical understanding of law. The following section presents two competing conceptions of property and links them to changes in class and productive relations more generally. The final section addresses important analytical dimensions of class and the mode of production. It makes a case for the urgent need for historical materialism to develop its understanding of the role of law in constructing and reproducing the foundations for global capitalism.

Law and the analytical foundations of historical materialism

For liberal and Marxist analysts alike, the political and distributional dimensions of law are minimized and are, as a result, under-theorized. For conventional legal and political analysts, liberalism and formalism block the recognition of the social and political dimensions of law (Silbey 1997). Indeed, law, politics, economics, and society, both globally and locally, are regarded to be separately constituted and existing domains. The liberal distinction between public and private spheres – between politics and economics – assists in constructing these separations by confining politics to the public realm (Cutler 1997, 1999a). Commercial law is regarded like markets as existing externally, as some private and neutral order that is created and endowed with objectivity and, hence, authority by legal formalism. Legal formalism posits law to constitute an objective and neutral order, comprised of laws created through positive legislative methods and ascertainable through the application of reason.[5] For domestic law, judges apply the law – they do not make it. Legislatures create the law and are limited by the constitutional principles and practices of responsible government. For international law, the law is traced in origin to the consent of states, as evidenced in positivist sources like treaties and in customary law, where consent is implied. In both realms, the authority of law is thus traced by liberal theory to the natural acts of free willing agents in a highly individualistic and atomistic world and is endowed with legitimacy through allegedly consensual acts of choice that are consistent with the laws of nature (Cutler 1999a). The possibility for the law to exhibit bias or to serve unrepresentative interests or undemocratic ends is ruled out by presumptions of the law as a natural, neutral, and consensual order. The challenge for conventional legal theory is to recognize that law is not external, but internal to and constitutive of social, political, and economic worlds and is thus inescapably implicated in the politics of 'who gets what'.

However, more important in my mind is the challenge for historical materialism.[6] For many Marxists, the separation between economics and politics appears as a differentiation between the base and superstructure of capitalism, similarly obscuring the crucial role of law in constituting, reflecting, and reproducing the dominant mode of production. According to Marx, legal relations derive from the 'material conditions of life' and not from the 'human mind'. Relations of production form the 'real foundation, on which rises a legal and political superstructure and to which correspond definite forms of social consciousness. The mode of production of material life determines the social, political, and intellectual life processes in general' (Marx 1983a: 159–60). Law, as a product of political and intellectual life therefore, takes its place as part of the superstructure, or does it? In addressing law and historical materialism Marx attempts to displace the 'illusion that law is based on the will' divorced from material interests as part of a criticism of the nature attributed to law by liberal political economy (Marx 1983b: 184). Liberal political economy posits the law governing commercial relations to be based upon the free will of contracting parties. However, in discussing how civil law evolved and facilitated exchange among medieval merchants and later the bourgeoisie, Marx clearly suggests that law was linked to the mode of production. While he does not address how, it is clear that he regarded the law as serving and advancing the interests of the powerful through the establishment of the institution of private property as an unassailable right, 'independent of the community' and based 'on the private will, the arbitrary disposal of things' (Marx 1983b: 184). This illusion then led to the further development of new property relations and property rights, suggesting that law works to expand the possibilities for relations of production.

Such a view finds support in Marxist criticisms of the prevalent theoretical understandings of domestic law. These critics argue that 'law, or rather the legal ground rules that structure bargains between competitive/cooperative groups, plays a "larger" "causal" role in distribution than is allotted either in conventional marxist or conventional liberal accounts' (Kennedy 1991: 332). For some Marxists, distribution is determined by the relations of production, which, though rendered in legal form, are said to merely reflect the underlying material conditions. The way in which legal rules structure the bargaining process, alternatives to the bargaining process, and ultimately the distribution of income between capital and labour, is thus obscured.[7] For the liberal, law plays a major role in the form of 'the rule of law', a defining element in the liberal conception of a good society. But the content of the background of the legal rules is seen to flow either as a matter of logic from regime-defining first principles (rights of bodily security, private property, freedom of contract) or from the will of the people, or from both together in some complex combination. The distributive issue is present, but understood as a matter of legislative intervention (e.g. progressive taxation, labour legislation) to achieve distributive objectives by superimposition on an essentially apolitical private law background (Kennedy 1991: 333).

The challenge for historical materialism is to show how the law relates to the mode of production and to class relations. Ellen Meiksins Wood's analysis of the nature of the separation between economics and politics and the base–superstructure distinction sheds useful light on ways of thinking about these relationships. Wood observes that E.P. Thompson's insight that the law, although in some respects is an element of the superstructure, is in others 'deeply imbricated within the very basis of productive relations', 'is a different way of understanding the base itself, as it is embodied in actual social practices and relations' (Wood 1995: 74). It is worth quoting at length her description of this way of understanding, which she calls 'Political Marxism'.

Bourgeois political economy, according to Marx, universalizes capitalist relations of production by analysing production in abstract from its specific social determinations. Marx's approach differs from theirs in his insistence that a productive system is made up of its specific social determinations – specific social relations, modes of property and domination, legal and political forms. This does not mean simply that the economic 'base' is reflected in and maintained by certain 'superstructural' institutions, but that the productive base itself exists in the shape of social, juridical and political forms – in particular forms of property and domination. ...

'Political Marxism', then, does not present the relation between base and superstructure as an opposition, a 'regional' separation, between a base 'objective' economic structure, on the one hand, and social, juridical and political forms, on the other, but rather as a continuous structure of social relations and forms with varying degrees of distance from the immediate processes of production and appropriation, beginning with those relations and forms that constitute the system of production itself. The connections between the 'base' and 'superstructure' can then be traced without great conceptual leaps because they do not represent two essentially different and discontinuous orders of reality. ...

Some legal and political institutions are external to the relations of production even while helping to sustain and reproduce them; and perhaps the term 'superstructure' should be reserved for these. But relations of production themselves take the form of particular juridical and political relations – modes of domination and coercion, forms of property and social organization – which are not mere secondary reflexes, nor even just external supports, but *constituents* of these productive relations. The 'sphere' of production is dominant not in the sense that it stands apart from or precedes these juridical-political forms, but rather in the sense that these forms are precisely forms of production, the *attributes* of a particular productive system.

A mode of production is not simply a technology but a social organization of productive activity and a mode of exploitation is a relationship of power.

(Wood 1995: 22–7)

Wood continues that the whole point of this understanding is to present productive relations in their 'political aspect', being the aspect in which they are 'actually *contested* as relations of domination, as rights of property, as the power to organize and govern production and appropriation'. This is a 'practical' objective for the point is to 'illuminate the terrain of struggle' by viewing modes of production 'as they actually confront people who must *act* in relation to them' (1995: 25). This is, indeed, the challenge for historical materialism today. It is both analytical and practical, for the continuing practical significance of historical materialism will turn on the adequacy of its analytical foundations. The potential practical costs for emancipatory politics of failing to analytically capture the nature and role of law today as both an attribute and a constituent element of the mode of production are huge. There is a homology between the rhetoric of legal globalization and neoliberal discipline; both are advancing class interests that do not fit easily into conventional Marxist analysis that tends to focus on the mode of production as nationally based and conceives of class in terms of national formations.[8] Indeed, the law advances the interests of a transnational class and articulates processes of transnational capital formation. As a result the law is working an unprecedented expansion of private corporate power in the world. The law is a significant element of neoliberal discipline and the expansion of private power in ways that both expand capital transnationally and threaten domestic aspects of capital formation. We see law working dialectically, to increase the mobility and expand the scope of processes of capital accumulation, while simultaneously creating a predominantly state-based protective, disciplinary network. The argument advanced here is that this dialectic is linked fundamentally to a tension between two competing conceptions of property, which both reflect and constitute competing political and social relations of production. The mode of production as thus conceived is 'not a "total system"', but includes 'a variety of counterforces and new tendencies within itself, of "residual" as well as "emergent" forces, which it must attempt to manage or control (Gramsci's concept of hegemony). Were those heterogeneous forces not endowed with an effectivity of their own, the hegemonic project would be unnecessary.' Capitalism thus 'produces differences and differentiation as a function of its own internal logic' (Jameson 1991: 406).

Contemporary efforts of corporate and government elites, of a transnational *mercatocracy* or a transnational merchant class[9] to create a transnational and global legal order, are best analysed as responses to developments and challenges that are internal to the changing nature of the capitalist mode of production. The globalization of the rule of law is an integral aspect of neoliberal discipline, which is expanding the private sphere of capital accumulation, while constraining potentially democratizing influences (Gill 1995b). Indeed, notions of 'a rule of law' advance the rhetoric of globalization, which posits that the expansion of private corporate authority and private property rights are natural, organic, efficient, and ultimately more just means of adjusting to the challenges posed by globalization (see Cutler *et al.* 1999; and Scheuerman 1999). We will turn now to consider two competing conceptions of property.

Two conceptions of property

It has been noted that the 'idea of property is rather like an iceberg. It is more complicated than it looks, and much of its significance is submerged' (Minogue 1980: 10). Indeed, property laws and their underlying theories of entitlement define key elements in the material constitution of societies. In a famous essay Morris Cohen theorizes that 'the essence of private property is always the right to exclude others' (1927–8: 12). While, as will become evident, this overstates the extent to which real property (land) has been characterized historically by excludability, the right of excludability also involves both a protective and an acquisitive function.

> The extent of the power over the life of others which the legal order confers on those called owners is not fully appreciated by those who think of the law as merely protecting men in their possession. Property law does more. It determines what men shall acquire. Thus, protecting the property rights of a landlord means giving him the right to collect rent, protecting the property of a railroad or a public service corporation means giving it the right to make certain charges. Hence the ownership of land and machinery, with the rights of drawing rent, interest, etc., determines the future distribution of the goods that will come into being – determines what share of such goods various individuals shall acquire.
>
> (Cohen 1927–8: 13)

Cohen continues in the same passage that the acquisitive element of property in fact determines the distribution of 'future social product', including the powers to tax the future social product and to command the services of a great many people in business enterprises. These distributional and authoritative powers, he argues, are 'the essence of what historically has constituted political sovereignty'. Cohen thus directly links private property and sovereignty, two concepts generally regarded as belonging to two different legal/political orders. Sovereignty is most often regarded as a conception bound up with the public sphere and its public law and politics. Private property, in contrast, is associated with the private sphere of economy, civil society, and private law. Indeed, distinctions between private and public, economics and politics, and markets and states, obscure the distributional and authoritative dimensions of private property (see also Cutler 1997).

Today, two conceptions of property compete for recognition. They provide very different rationales for the sovereignty of private property, giving rise to competing theories of entitlement.

First conception: property as 'bundles of rights'

One conception posits property to be 'bundles of rights', wherein ownership is not absolute, but contingent, conditional, fragmented, and based upon diffuse and overlapping claims to authority. This conception is associated generally with the feudal mode of production and property relations that were paternalistic, protective, and embodied an organic view of society. During the feudal period, the law regulating local political economies embodied this conception and advanced and protected property rights that were generally consistent with securing and reproducing the private power of local authorities, both secular and religious.

Under the feudal mode of production[10] relations of distribution and authority, while less absolute and more contingent, were more transparent in terms of their historic origins and lineage in customary law and practice. Perry Anderson describes the feudal mode of production as

> dominated by the land and a natural economy, in which neither labour nor the products of labour were commodities. The immediate producer – the peasant – was united to the means of production – the soil – by a specific social relationship. The literal formula of this relationship was provided by the legal definition of serfdom – *glebae adscripti* or bound to the earth: serfs had juridically restricted mobility.
>
> (Anderson 1974a: 147)

They did not own the land they worked, nor did they control it. A class of feudal lords controlled land privately, extracting value from the peasants through coercive political and legal arrangements. These arrangements included labour services, rents in kind or customary dues owed to the individual lord by the peasant. The peasant owed duties to his lord, while the lord in turn held his property under duties to a superior noble to whom he owed knight-service, military service or the like. So it went up the feudal hierarchy, as Appendix A illustrates.

The absence of a distinction at this time between private and public realms reflects the conditions of the feudal, pre-capitalist world, when 'locating authority' posed many problems (see Cutler 1999b). Local political authorities shared 'authority' with other political and religious authorities in a system mediated by customary laws and historic entitlements. As one historian notes:

> the dominant note of the period was authority. The social organization was a hierarchy of controls: the individual, if such there was, owed allegiance to priest and bishop of Holy Church, to lord and Baron of Feudal order, to gild and town of a rising third estate. The foundations of obedience, which underlay all human activity, were established by churchmen.
>
> (Hamilton 1931: 1136–7)

Indeed, the multiple and overlapping sources of authority are evident in the ambiguity of the social foundations of the period. The feudal mode of production was 'characterized by a complex unity ... a juridical amalgamation of economic exploitation with political authority' (Anderson 1974a: 147). Political sovereignty was 'never focussed in a single centre. The functions of the state were disintegrated in a vertical allocation downwards, at each level of which political and economic relations were ... integrated. This parcellization of sovereignty was constitutive of the whole feudal mode of production' (Anderson 1974a: 148). Although Anderson (1974b: 19) describes the feudal mode of production as 'an organic unity of economy and polity', it was not territorially centralized; nor was it fixed. In addition, fractures in the social foundation were evident in resistance from those at the interstices of society, the tensions between town and manor, and the search for public authority resulting from ambiguity as regards political authority (Anderson 1974a: 148–9, 152). In feudal society the right to rule was neither territorialized nor centralized, but diffuse and ambiguous. Due to the absence of a distinction between public and private to provide the foundation for social unity or political authority, the feudal mode of production gave rise to 'a constant struggle to establish a "public" authority outside the compact web of private jurisdictions' (1974a: 152). While commercial developments in merchant communities in parts of Europe gave rise to a system of commercial law, the law merchant (*lex mercatoria*), that operated largely independent of the feudal political economy, this was a general exception to the paternalistic and authoritarian protection in local markets of just prices, quality controls, and the enforcement of merchant offences aimed at providing security of market supplies (see Cutler 1995; and Rosenberg 1994).

Appropriately, the feudal system of property rights embodied similar ambiguity and indeterminacy of ownership. As Cohen (1927–8: 9) observes, the 'essence of feudal law ... is the inseparable connection between land tenure and personal homage involving often rather menial services on the part of the tenant ...'. Moreover, a 'multiplicity of estates, tenures and customary arrangements' embodied these personal obligations:

> [l]and could sustain multiple overlapping claims by many individuals and casual or regular uses by many others. The primary relations of an individual to a parcel of land, what lawyers called the 'right', could be maintained without physically excluding others. Indeed, land had little value to the rightful holder if others were entirely excluded.
>
> (Seipp 1994: 87)

The suggestion here is that excludability was not a dominant characteristic of the feudal land tenure system. Insofar as the property relation pointed to the person who had capacity to bring actions in court and to initiate transactions out of court, excludability probably approximated the proprietary nature of one's relations with goods and animals rather more than with land.

> In the practical arrangements of life in late medieval England, it was goods and animals, not land, that came closest to what Blackstone [a leading jurist of the eighteenth century] would later call 'that sole and despotic dominion ... in total exclusion of the rights of any other individual in the universe'.
>
> (Ibid.)

If one consults the depiction of the feudal land tenure system in Appendix A, the various and overlapping claims to the same piece of land seem to work against notions of absolute excludability and illustrate why the feudal system is described in terms of 'bundles of rights'.

Importantly, the word 'ownership' 'in terms of an immutable legal idea' was not used much by English medieval lawyers who tended to speak of real property (land) in terms of uses and rights. This was a direct result of the feudal land tenure system, by which land was held, as opposed to owned, on a particular use or tenure. This dates to 1066 with the Norman conquest of England when the lands of England were declared to be the property of the Crown and tenancies or rights to use were granted to a few Norman families. This worked a renegotiation of landholding arrangements. All land was held ultimately by the King who then parcelled out tenancies in chief to a few Norman families in return for various services. They in turn parcelled out their holdings to tenants in return for services, creating the chain of tenures through the process of subinfeudation (Baker 1990: 257).

On the European continent, in contrast to England, the reception of Roman law in the sixteenth and seventeenth centuries provided notions of unconditional and absolute ownership. This was an important development, replacing medieval conceptions of conditional and contingent property rights and facilitating the centralization of political control. The law merchant drew on Roman sources as well, facilitating the development of notions of absolute and unconditional property. In England, where Roman law was not received, the imprint of Roman notions of ownership was nevertheless felt through the gradual incorporation of the law merchant into English private commercial law (see Cutler 1995, 1999a). These were significant developments because they formed the foundation for commodity relations that were crucial to the transition from feudalism to capitalism in the West (Anderson 1974b: 26). The Roman law distinction between civil law (*jus*), regulating private and economic relations among citizens, and public law (*lex*), regulating relations between the state and its subjects, assisted in this transition. The recognition of two distinct private and public spheres facilitated 'commodity exchange in the transitional economies of the epoch', while at the same time enhancing the consolidation and 'concentration of aristocratic power in a centralized state apparatus' (Anderson 1974b: 27). Increasingly, property came to be regarded as part of the private sphere where exclusivity and excludability became the litmus test of ownership. In England, the enclosure movement of the sixteenth century, enclosing large estates in land, displaced customary manorial tenants with more lucrative sheep raising. This marked the beginning of the end of the traditional rights of 'common' to pasture field animals, replacing the collective cultivation of manorial lands with private and individual management and holdings. As the distinctions between the public and private realms took shape, it became increasingly more difficult to conceptualize property in terms of overlapping 'bundles of rights'.

Second conception: property as the 'ownership of things'

The second conception posits property to be the 'ownership of things', contemplating a more absolute and exclusive form of ownership. This accompanied the advent of local and national capital accumulation and political theories that facilitated the dismantling of feudal entailments and restraints on the transmissibility of land and the commodification of property relations in general. While the transition from feudal structures of authority to centralized and absolutist states facilitated the development of notions of absolute and exclusive ownership, the advent of the liberal state and liberal theories of political economy effected the transformation of property to the 'ownership of things' (see Macpherson 1978). Central to this transformation was the erosion of the fusion of the polity and economy. This organic unity was transformed into separate spheres of civil society and political jurisdiction with the growing territorialization, localization, and centralization of political authority in the absolutist state. The right to rule came to be located in centralized states, which gradually worked an erosion and eventually the disappearance of the law merchant as an autonomous legal order. In international law, the recognition of separate private and public realms translated into the distinction between public and private international law: public international law applied to states and their international relations, while private international law applied to private individual and corporate actors. The law merchant was incorporated into domestic legal systems and there reconfigured as private international trade law.

However, the separation of the public and private spheres was neither simultaneous nor uniform in Europe. It occurred at different times and in different institutional and legal contexts. In addition, the advancement of capitalism and the demise of the feudal order were necessary to complete the separation between politics and economics. Significantly, capitalism broadened the scope of politics, but narrowed the scope of economics.

> The 'polity' in traditional states is limited to the active participation of the few, whose policies and internal conflicts mainly determine the distribution of authoritative resources. With the arrival of modern capitalism, a definite sphere of the 'economic' – as 'the economy' – comes into being. Traditional states, of course, had economies in the sense that their existence depended upon the generation and distribution of allocative resources. But the modern 'economy' is a (relatively) distinct sphere of activities from other institutional sectors in capitalist societies. 'Distinct' in this context has to be understood as 'insulated' from political life, not as cut off from it. 'Politics', on the other hand, has a broader definition in modern societies (that is, in nation-states), encompassing the mass of the population.
>
> (Giddens 1987: 67–8)

A significant transformation occurred with the transition to a capitalist mode of production. Under a capitalist mode of production,[11] as distinct from the feudal or mercantilist modes of production, the relationship between owners and producers – between capital and labour – 'assumes a purely economic form', distinct from feudal tribute or mercantilist domination (Rosenberg 1994: 84). It is crucial to note, as I argue elsewhere (Cutler 1997, 1999b), that the separation of economic exchange relations from political relations under capitalism is not simply a separation of different and independent spheres. As Justin Rosenberg (1994: 85) notes, it is a distinction that is '*internal* to the mode of production'. This distinction has not effected an 'evacuation of relations of domination from the realm of production' (Rosenberg 1994: 84). Rather, as Giddens (1987: 68) observes, the distinction has 'insulated' economic relations from political control. Ellen Meiksins Wood captures the essential nature of this separation:

> the differentiation of the economic and the political in capitalism is, more precisely, a differentiation of political functions themselves and their separate allocation to the private economic sphere and the public sphere of the state. This allocation reflects the separation of political functions immediately concerned with the extraction and appropriation of surplus labour from those with a more general communal purpose ... the differentiation of the economic is in fact a differentiation within the political sphere.
>
> (Wood 1995: 31)

As noted earlier, Wood persuasively argues that modes of production take the form of distinct 'juridical and political relations', which she identifies as 'modes of domination and coercion, forms of property and social organization' that are 'constituents of the productive relations themselves' (Wood 1995: 27). Under feudalism, power was diffuse, parcellized, and privatized because the 'instruments of appropriation' were controlled by private feudal lords. Wood argues that under the capitalist mode of production the privatization of political power was effected by the 'complete expropriation of the direct producer and the establishment of absolute private property' and centralized public power. The state 'divested the appropriating class of direct political powers and duties not immediately concerned with production and appropriation, leaving them with private exploitative powers purified, as it were, of public, social function' (Wood 1995: 39). The capitalist mode of production transformed political powers into economic powers and defined the latter as a separate 'apolitical' sphere.

In law, property as 'ownership of things' became the template of modern conceptions of property. This in turn reflected a number of related assumptions concerning the exclusivity, commodifiability, objectivity, and individuality of private ownership.[12] As Thomas Grey notes,

> [i]t is not difficult to see how the idea of simple ownership [thing-ownership] came to dominate classical liberal legal and political thought. First, this conception of property mirrored economic reality to a much greater extent than it did before or has since. Much of the wealth of the preindustrial capitalist economy consisted of the houses and lots of freeholders, the

land of peasant proprietors or small farmers, and the shops and tools of artisans. ... Second, the concept of property as thing-ownership served important ideological functions. Liberalism was the ideology of the attack on feudalism. A central feature of feudalism was its complex and hierarchical system of land tenure. To the rising bourgeoisie, property conceived as a web of relations among persons meant a system of lord, vassal, and serf from which they were struggling to free themselves. On the other hand, property conceived as the control of a piece of the material world by a single individual meant freedom and equality of status. Thus Blackstone denounced the archaisms of feudal tenure. The French Civil Code marked the culmination of a revolution that abolished feudal property. Hegel wrote that the abolition of feudal property in favor of individual ownership was as great a triumph of freedom as the abolition of slavery. Jefferson contrasted the free allodial system of land titles in America with the servile English system of feudal tenure.

(Grey 1980: 74)

Moreover, property as 'thing-ownership' was more consistent with the treatment of private property as a natural right, as posited by theories justifying private property. One theory drew upon Locke's *labour theory* of property wherein property in a good follows from the mixing of one's labour with nature, while another drew on the views of Hegel and Kant and regards property as an extension of one's *person* and *personality* (Grey 1980: 74; see also Cohen 1927–8). Both theories posit private property in things to be a natural and organic right. Moreover, the law served to objectify this condition as feudal restrictions on the transmissibility of land were progressively removed and land became commodified along with other things (Polanyi 1944). This marked the constitution of the private sphere of capital accumulation as the sphere of autonomy, individuality, and freedom from want, carving private property and its law out of the domain it had once shared with polity (Horowitz 1982; and Klare 1982).

Significantly, as part of this transformation, commercial law was privatized. Nationally, commercial relations between individuals were regulated by a growing corpus of law which conceptualized property as thing-ownership. Internationally, the law merchant was privatized and neutralized of political content as it became a component of *private* international trade law.[13] As such it was regarded as a body of commercial law and practice, operating neutrally among market participants, deemed to be of equal bargaining power. This facilitated the consolidation of nationally based capitalism by providing the legal framework for the emergence of market society. Its laws and procedures provided the security of ownership required for domestic capital accumulation, while also providing a juridical link with other states. Importantly, too, it provided the ideological framework for the recognition of private corporate power as the legitimate authority for regulating international commercial relations.

Theorizing class and the mode of production: property in disintegration or rebirth?

The notion of property as 'thing-ownership' came under attack in the United States by legal realists seeking to establish the legal foundation for both the welfare and the regulatory state.[14] In addition, the growth of corporations and corporatist forms of association expanded notions of ownership. The attack on property as thing-ownership began with the 'dephysicalization' of property by severing property from *things* and attaching it to abstract *rights* and with the erosion of the exclusivity of property.[15]

> Property, howsoever owned, meant that one stood in a certain relationship to others, a relationship which could be broken down into powers, privileges, duties, rights, immunities and so on. Thus both the elements of physicalism (property as thing) and absolutism (property as exclusivity) in Blackstone's concept of property were subject to attack.
>
> (Edgeworth 1988: 97)

These attacks reconstituted property as a 'bundle of rights'. Welfare rights, along with other forms of wealth created by the expansion of governments' regulatory powers and the development of new corporate forms and claims to property, developed new bases of entitlements. These emerged as property in the 1960s and were declared to be a 'new property' (Reich 1964: 733). Government-generated wealth in the form of social insurance, government contracts and other corporate-generated wealth, like franchises, equities in corporations, the right to privately provided services and utilities, came increasingly to be regarded as part of the complex 'bundle of rights' that constitute private property. The proliferation of new corporate forms of organization along with novel methods of finance and investment created bases of entitlement that were no longer linked to things physical or material. Property as a 'bundle of rights' enabled corporate reorganization and, indeed, the reconstitution of capital in non-physical and non-exclusive ways. Corporations operating transnationally devised new methods of transacting, spreading their operations over multiple jurisdictions and creating complex webs of corporate rights and entitlements (see Cutler *et al.* 1999).

Importantly, this conception of property was

> inextricably bound up with a specific politics. '[L]egal realists' were, by and large, staunch interventionists as far as the economy was concerned. ... So the attack on the Blackstonian desocialised concept of property was also an attack on the anti-regulatory character of the U.S. Supreme Court's constitutional jurisprudence of the time.
>
> (Edgeworth 1988: 97–8)

Indeed, legal realists regarded these as fundamentally progressive social moves. However, critics on both the left and right have criticized this development for expanding corporate power in America. Some note that corporations have probably benefited more than individuals by the 'new property' because they have responded with new and varied uses of the Bill of Rights to protect against state intervention and to expand the range of corporate entitlements (Meyer 1990).

This diffusion, fragmentation, and deterritorialization of corporate power has been characterized as a 'remedievalization' of the political economy (Bull 1977; Strange 1996). In my view, however, this characterization obscures more than it clarifies. These developments reflect only one dimension of the dialectical transformations occurring. Moreover, they are not reversions to an earlier, feudal mode of production, but constitutive of a new mode of production. The fragmenting tendencies of 'bundle of rights' conceptions of property may evoke images of medieval politico-legal relations, however they are being advanced by a systematic and global unification movement organized by a transnational merchant class. Emphasis on the fragmentary nature of corporate property relations thus risks obscuring the underlying unity of the mercatocracy. In addition, these fragmenting tendencies pose clear risks for property and capital and are being met by countervailing forces that seek to unify and stabilize property protections through reassertions of territoriality and nationality. These contradictory tendencies flow from the internal logic of capitalism; they are the mechanisms that ensure the continued reproduction and expansion of capital, revealing tensions between national and transnational forces and between related competing conceptions of property. Property as 'ownership of things' speaks to processes of national capital accumulation and control, whereas property as 'bundles of rights' frees capital from national limitations and enables transnational expansion. However, enforcement remains a prerogative of states, so capital is driven back to thingness and the state for its protection. But the attempt to treat intangible property as 'things' poses problems. These problems are so severe that some are led to the conclusions that the concept of property is in disintegration and that we are moving into a fundamentally different mode of production.

For some, the dephysicalization of property is a transformation internal to the contemporary mode of production associated with a transition to a *mode of information* characteristic of post-industrial or post-Fordist and late capitalist society (Edgeworth 1988: 98–9; also Castells 1989). This, Brendan Edgeworth argues, is driving the concept of property 'to the margins of political and economic discourse' and undermining the notion of *labour* 'as the central concept of critical theory':

> First, the modern economy is now structured along increasingly complex
> corporate lines. Whereas in times past the means of production were in the
> main family farms, artisans' workshops and traders' personal effects, today
> the huge limited liability company is the definitive form of economic organi
> zation. The legal nature of such organizations comes to resemble less and
> less thing-ownership. Ownership itself fragments by virtue of the separation
> of the formal ownership of share capital by shareholders and the control of

the day-to-day business operations by a managerial class. As a result company law effectively operates as a mechanism to allow for complex and variegated bundles of rights to be created and combined. As well, the absolutely central role of essentially anonymous financial institutions in the economy further complicates the notion of ownership. These bundles of rights come to be even further removed from any determinate thing or things and it becomes progressively more difficult to identify a particular owner or owners. Moreover, an increasing share of economic wealth resides not in tangibles but in intangible intellectual property.

(Edgeworth 1988: 98)

Thomas Grey (1980: 74) also argues that the 'disintegration' of the concept of property as a central organizing or crucial category is a result of 'a process internal to the development of capitalism itself'. The expansion of corporate property, forms of association, and finance based upon new theories of entitlement have been central to this process. He argues that the disintegration of property is eroding the moral foundations of capitalism because the traditional rationales of private property, like labour and personality theories, attach to property as things and not as bundles of rights. However, for Grey this is not ultimately fatal for class analysis. He argues that other rationales of private property and capitalism survive (enhanced efficiency and wealth and the protection of individual liberty) and that the bundle of rights conception, while masking the existence of private economic power, does not change the 'view that capitalist society is fundamentally divided into two sharply distinct and opposing classes, the bourgeoisie and the proletariat' (Grey 1980: 81). Thus, Grey, although positing the 'disintegration' of property, does not go as far as Edgeworth in questioning the extent to which capitalism has lost or is losing its materialist basis in class-based productive relations. Moreover, although Grey's article was published almost twenty years ago, his view is arguably even more relevant today. When one considers contemporary developments in the area of intellectual property it is clear that bundle of rights thinking has not impaired the expansion of capitalism nor undercut its material base. Indeed, to the extent that fragmented ownership has facilitated the reconstitution of capital and its relation to the state, such thinking has enabled the transnational expansion of capital. Rather than in disintegration, property is being reconstituted. In the area of intellectual property, clearly the intangible nature of the property lends itself to bundle of rights thinking and is reflective of many of the attributes said to accompany postmodern or late capitalist property. Here, critics assert the inadequacy of intellectual property law concepts, like copyright and patents to accommodate the increasingly dephysicalized and deterritorialized nature of intellectual property. John Barlow (1994: 8) has observed about the challenge posed by digitized property that '[l]egal efforts to keep the old boat floating are taking three forms: a frenzy of deck chair rearrangement, stern warnings to the passengers that if she goes down, they will face harsh criminal penalties, and serene, glassy-eyed denial'. He argues that digital technology is erasing the physicality of intellectual property and with it the legal jurisdiction of states. While in the past copyright and patent secured property in the vehicle giving expression to thought, now, with the technological ability to transmit ideas without making them physical, it is the ideas themselves that we seek to appropriate, for which copyright and patent laws are ill-suited.

One might ask how is it that there has been such an expansion in information technology given the seeming inadequacies in intellectual property law concepts. The answer lies in part in a contrary tendency. While intellectual property is indeed intangible, and is probably the archetypical form of dephysicalized and deterritorialized property, its protection remains very exclusive, physical, and territorial. Moreover, intellectual property rights 'represent governmental authority to exclude' and are expanding the power of corporations claiming such rights (Gerber 1996: 466). Indeed, the emerging intellectual property regime is reasserting a territorial notion of rule quite out of synch with what is argued to be the deterritorialization of the postmodern or late capitalist moment. Intellectual property rights emerged out of and are associated with first world corporate interests and recent developments in the construction of an intellectual property regime suggest that despite their intangible character, their enforcement remains very much linked to physical space through legal jurisdiction (Bawa 1997; also Sell 1999).

So, too, transnational corporations, which operate in multiple territorial locations and are generally averse to the development of legal regimes that hamper their freedom to relocate production processes, actively support the development of strong national laws that attach civil liability on the basis of nationality and territoriality. Corporations can manipulate the rules governing nationality and use their corporate status strategically to shield themselves against liability coming from the actions of foreign subsidiaries, foreign shareholders and creditors, and injured third parties, like consumers. Indeed, many suggest that the intensification of interjurisdictional competition for incorporations is producing a 'race to the bottom' as jurisdictions engage in the competitive deregulation of corporate standards (Blackburn 1994; Charney 1991). The problem is particularly acute in the case of rules of corporate nationality and conflict of laws that allow corporations to use their subsidiaries as shields against liability for environmental disasters, hazardous waste disposal, or wrongs suffered by foreign shareholders.[16]

The move to reterritorialize and renationalize property is evident as well in the global sweep of private arbitration services that, while replacing national adjudication with private processes, remain very much dependent upon national control for the recognition and enforcement of arbitration awards (Cutler 1995; Dezalay and Garth 1996).

These contrary tendencies in the enforcement of property reflect a strategic use of property rights and are linked to broader developments in the global political economy. These developments are reconstituting property, capital, state, and class relations in a manner consistent with a globalizing corporate ideology and business culture. This ideology and culture is being advanced by private international regimes (see Cutler 2002) and by a transnational mercatocracy through the principles and practices of the modern law merchant. The modern law merchant is a central mechanism for the globalization of disciplinary neoliberal norms. These forces are restructuring state–society relations through globalized production and finance and through competitive deregulation. Stephen Gill identifies the globalization of the state with the 'restructuring of state and capital on a world stage towards a more globally integrated and competitive market-driven system' which transforms the state 'so as to give greater freedom to the private aspects of capital accumulation in the extended state at the local, national and transnational levels' (Gill 1995b: 85). Indeed, there has been a general decline in the corporate control functions of states and an expansion of their role in facilitating and enabling corporate activities (Muchlinski 1995). In some instances, states are experiencing a loss of control in relation to corporations, whereas in others state enforcement of property and contract rights and the ability of states to shield corporations from liability are strengthening the enforcement powers of states. Corporations are clamouring to incorporate in state jurisdictions like the United States', which offer handsome damage awards and well-developed procedural protections.

These trends appear to be out of synch with the deterritorialization and dephysicalization of property. However, they are consistent with the idea of flexible accumulation and the need to adjust property relations to changing terms of global competition. Property, like the chameleon, can change colour as the needs of capital dictate. Law is one of the mechanisms of flexible accumulation. David Harvey offers the following explanation of what he regards as a 'central paradox' of postmodernity:

> the less important the spacial barriers, the greater the sensitivity of capital to the variations of place within space, and the greater the incentive for places to be differentiated in ways attractive to capital. The result has been the production of fragmentation, insecurity, and ephemeral uneven development within a highly unified global space economy of capital flows. The historic tension within capitalism between centralization and decentralization is now being worked out in new ways.
>
> (Harvey 1990: 295–6)

The reassertion of territoriality and exclusivity in the enforcement of certain corporate property rights is part of the process by which capital and state are readjusting to the contemporary crisis of late capitalism. For Harvey, it is a crisis of overaccumulation. I believe that it is a crisis of legitimacy in that neither national nor international law is attempting to restrain the influence of expanding corporate power.[17] However one characterizes the crisis, the expansion of corporate power and authority is a central element. This expansion is being driven by a transnational mercatocracy comprised of both private and public authorities who are deeply committed to the globalization of the rule of law (Cutler 1999c). Significantly, it is a particular sort of law and a particular rhetoric of globalization. The law facilitates the expansion of capital through permissive rule structures that grant merchants great freedom to transact and through mandatory enforcement procedures operating through the agency of the state. States, in turn, have taken up their enforcement role enthusiastically as part of the restructuring process. The rhetoric of the globalization of law constitutes a number of narratives or stories that

> not only describe how social relations are organized globally; they also construct ethical claims about the way the world should be organized and how social relations should be governed. Each globalization narrative reveals a particular construction of justice and its possibilities.
>
> (Silbey 1997: 211)

One narrative frames globalization as a triumph of reason over nature, while another emphasizes the triumph of global markets over national and regional particularisms. Silbey describes the latter thus:

> [it] communicates clear moral lessons, the most important of which is that private property rights are paramount and should be inviolable. The major actors or characters in this story are private persons. This means that states should cease engaging in economic activity and state-owned productive enterprises should be privatized. In this political and moral economy, national borders should cease being barriers to trade; all national economies should be open to trade. Exchanges and engagements in this moral universe are marked solely by market prices (which are the means of rewarding good action and punishing bad). Public regulation of private enterprise, as an alternative to price regulation, should cease. As a corollary to the dominant role of prices as the major form of communicating participation in the market economy, domestic prices should conform to international prices and monetary policies should be directed to the maintenance of price and balance of payments stability. These are the universal constants – the morality – of market economics.
>
> (Silbey 1997: 215)

The law's role in this story is to render liberal market morality into legal norms, which, through the globalization of the rule of law, are transmitted throughout the world, creating for some the promise of a unifying global commercial code, common law, or transnational *lex mercatoria* (Cutler 1999c). These norms promote the private regulation of commerce as the most natural, neutral, efficient, and just method possible (Cutler 1995). However, 'the question of globalization raises the issue of globalization for whom and for what purposes' (Gill 1997: 205). Echoing Robert Cox's view that theory always serves someone's purpose, Stephen Gill (1997: 206) notes that increasing social polarization, 'a sense of political indifference, government incompetence, and a decay of public and private responsibility and accountability' are aspects of the contemporary crisis. In my view, the basic contradiction between globalization and democratization portends a legitimacy crisis wherein 'the ruling class has lost its consensus, i.e. is no longer "leading" but only "dominant". ... The crisis consists precisely in the fact that the old is dying and the new cannot be born' (Gramsci 1971: 275–6). Globalized law functions to expand the hold of powerful corporations through the global reproduction of first world corporate normative structures, which are then enforced through the instrumentality of states. The complicity of states in advancing the interests of transnational capital is a crucial element in the restructuring of property, capital, and class relations. Bundle of rights notions of property facilitate the expansion of corporate power in novel ways, quite in keeping with contemporary trends in communication and information technologies. However, the delinking of property from territory, save for purposes of enforcement, contributes to the disengagement of law and state, paving the way for transnational legal norms to evolve relatively free from democratic controls. When coupled with the reassertion of property as exclusivity, the globalization of law advances a rhetoric of equality, efficiency, and justice while creating global regimes of private protectionism and exclusivity of ownership. The growing disjunctures of law and fact and of the rhetoric of globalization and the material conditions of the global political economy are important aspects of the crisis of late capitalism. The corporate world is responding to intensified competition brought about by processes of globalization with very specific and limited attempts to relink property with territory, state, and law. Corporations are contesting the impact of globalization through manipulating the laws governing intellectual property and the foreign liabilities of transnational corporations and strengthening territorial links for purposes of protection and enforcement. However, the corporate-state monopoly of protective and enforcement measures is nowhere preordained nor inevitable. Indeed, these areas provide important and potentially fertile sites of contestation for consumers, investors, purchasers, and inventors to organize efforts to re-democratize the processes through which property rights and their underlying theories of entitlement are constructed and protected. This is evident in the field of intellectual property where novel claims by indigenous peoples to ownership of cultural property are challenging the corporate/statist monopoly of intellectual property and effecting a fundamental reconsideration of the nature of property rights protected by intellectual property laws.[18] Similar challenges to the laws governing corporate liability from consumer groups, environmentalists, and human rights and labour activists would assist in expanding the responsibilities of transnational corporations under national and international laws. The vocal opposition of labour and consumer groups to the Multilateral Agreement on Investment, which attempted to limit the restrictions that states could place on foreign corporations, and mounting criticism of the privileged position of corporations under the North American Free Trade Agreement and the Canada–US Free Trade Agreement indicate openings for resistance and challenge to corporate power (Cutler 2000).

Such efforts might work powerful and urgently needed correctives to the expansion of private power and authority in the world. The law can be used by the disenfranchised and dispossessed as a powerful instrument of change once the mythology of its inherent objectivity and neutrality is displaced by the sort of critical analysis provided by historical materialism.

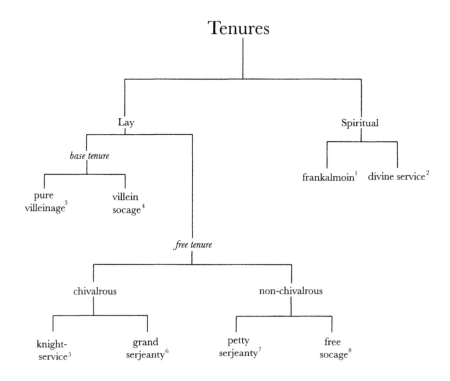

1 Tenure 'in free alms' with no specified services, but general duty of performing divine service.
2 Certain service, such as saying mass on certain days, finding a chantry chaplain, or distributing alms.
3 Uncertain villein services, e.g. copyhold (an estate subject to customs of the manor), by the virge (a type of copyhold).
4 Certain villein services, e.g. tenure in ancient demesne (differs from copyhold in certain privileges).
5 Military service, including castleguard (guarding the castle) and scutage (payment in lieu of service).
6 Certain non-military service to the king's person.
7 Service of rendering something to the king. According to some definitions it must have a military use.
8 Of two kinds: (i) common socage, the only form of tenure apart from frankalmoin and grand serjeanty remaining after 1925; (ii) customary socage, e.g. gavelkind, burgage (payment of certain rent).

Appendix A Types of tenure

Source: Adapted from J.H. Baker (1990) *An Introduction to English Legal History*, 3rd edn, London: Butterworth, p.282.

Notes

1 Jameson (1991: 4, 38) refers to the contemporary mode of production as a 'decentered global network' of 'multinational capitalism', but it is unclear whether he is referring to a fundamentally interstate system or a transnational system. For transnational capital formation see Gill and Law (1993), also Robinson (1996, 1998), van der Pijl (1984, 1997).

2 Harvey (1990: 147) associates post-Fordism with enhanced capital mobility and flexibility, which he refers to as 'flexible accumulation' ('flexibility with respect to labour processes, labour markets, products, and patterns of consumption'; the emergence of new sectors of production, new financial services and markets; and intensified rates of technological, commercial and organizational innovation) and the resulting time-space compression as the time horizon for decision-makers shrinks.

3 I would like to thank Warren Magnusson, a colleague at the University of Victoria, for this crucial insight.

4 I here adopt the emancipatory goals associated with critical theory in the works of Robert Cox (1996).

5 Singer (1988: 496, 499) notes that the term legal formalism has been used in many ways to denote mechanical jurisprudence; the belief that a legal system could be reduced to a small number of general principles; that the principles can be rigidly separated; that the process of applying the principles to generate conclusions is a logical, objective, and scientific process of deduction; and that the legal standards applied are objective. Legal formalism was associated with the classical era of legal scholarship which

> started with the notion of a self-regulating market system, a private sphere insulated from government interference, influence and control. It then added the belief in a formalistic method of legal reasoning. ... Judicial method was seen as scientific, apolitical, principled, objective, logical, and rational. Legal argument was pervaded with a sense of certainty. This sense of certainty, coupled with a commitment to the self-regulating market ideal, allowed classical judges to nullify hundreds of pieces of regulatory legislation to protect 'property', 'freedom of contract', and 'liberty'. They seldom recognized that their own definition of property and contract embodied forms of regulation of exactly the sort that was being struck down. Nor did they recognize that their own definitions of property and contract embodied forms of government regulation and involvement in the market system.

6 Drawing on this now familiar distinction made by Cox (1996: 88–9), I would argue that the challenge for conventional theory is not as significant as that for historical materialism because the former tends to be 'problem-solving theory', while the latter represents 'critical theory' engaged in emancipatory politics.

7 Kennedy (1991) identifies rules governing the rights to organize, to secondary boycott, to picket; the rules governing dismissal, sabotage blacklisting; labour torts and the enforcement of contracts, contractual remedies, and the like, as examples of laws with distributional consequences.

8 See Robinson (1996, 1998) for analysis of the largely national-based nature of Marxist theorizing about class and productive relations. For important exceptions, see van der Pijl (1984, 1997) and Gill and Law (1993).

9 I derive the term *mercatocracy* from the medieval *lex mercatoria*, Latin for the law merchant, which was an autonomous body of private law that governed the commercial activities of medieval merchants. Today, the modern law merchant forms the ideological core of transnational capitalism.

10 The concept 'mode of production' is here being used in the terms formulated by Robert Cox (1989: 39):

Production here is to be understood in the broadest sense. It is not confined to the production of physical goods used or consumed. It covers also the production and reproduction of knowledge and of the social relations, morals, and institutions that are prerequisites to the production of physical goods. ... Production is both a social process and a power relationship.

11 Marx defines the capitalist mode of production thus:

[t]he specific economic form, in which unpaid surplus-labour is pumped out of direct producers, determines the relationship of rulers and ruled. ... It is always the direct relationship of the owners of the conditions of production to the direct producers ... which reveals the innermost secret, the hidden basis of the entire social structure, and with it the political form of the relation of sovereignty and dependence, in short, the corresponding specific form of the state.

(quoted in Rosenberg 1994: 84)

12 Edgeworth (1988: 89) identifies these four properties in the works of modern theorists like Locke, Hegel, and Kant. He also criticizes Macpherson's interpretation of the movement from feudal to modern property rights for linguistic essentialism and historicism, in assuming the existence of a single dominant conception of property at different historical times. However, it would appear that while there was indeed considerable variation on the themes of exclusivity and absolute property, as Seipp (1994) so clearly shows as regards the early common law and Patrick Atiyah (1979) shows in the context of later common law, it is difficult to deny that the prevailing notions of Anglo-American property were premised on what was regarded as an objective right of an individual to exclude others from the enjoyment of commodities or things.

13 In Cutler (1999a) I analyse the evolution of international maritime transport law in the context of the construction of two separate regimes of private and public international maritime laws. I argue that the private international legal regime created and sustains an exploitative regime of private protectionism that serves the interests of powerful maritime shipping, insurance, financial, and legal corporations.

14 Legal realism was a movement that emerged in the United States, primarily at Yale and Columbia, as a reaction to legal formalism. Legal formalism, or 'classical legal thought', dominated jurisprudence from the late nineteenth century to about the 1930s and is known for its strengthening of business corporations. Legal realists attacked the public/private distinction in domestic law in an effort to expose the political dimensions of private law concepts. They were interested in limiting the power of corporations and in creating a more powerful, centralized administrative state. However, after the war, legal realism was itself suspect as being anti-democratic (see Fisher *et al.* 1993).

15 Edgeworth (1988: 97) attributes this move to Wesley Hohfeld who conceived of law in terms of abstract legal relations and jural correlatives (Hohfeld 1913).

16 Notes, 'Liability of Parent Corporations for Hazardous Waste Cleanup and Damages', *Harvard Law Review*, 99 (1986): 986–1003; also Ismail (1991).

17 In Cutler (2001), I argue that the doctrine of international legal personality functions to obscure the expansion of corporate power and authority in the world, producing a disjuncture between law and fact. The disjuncture lies in the theoretical insignificance of corporations as 'subjects' of law in the face of their overwhelming factual power and authority. This disjuncture portends a crisis of legitimacy in international law because the law is incapable of theorizing its 'subject' in any meaningful way. See also Twining (1996).

18 See Doucas (1995), and the efforts of indigenous peoples to change international law
    evident in the 'Initiatives for Protection of Rights of Holders of Traditional
    Knowledge, Indigenous Peoples and Local Communities', Roundtable on Intellectual
    Property and Indigenous Peoples, World Intellectual Property Organization, Geneva,
    23 and 24 July 1998, *WIPO/LNDIP/RT/98/4A* and *The Mataatua Declaration on
    Cultural and Intellectual Property Rights of Indigenous Peoples*.

Bibliography

Anderson, P. (1974a) *Passages from Antiquity to Feudalism*, London: Verso.
—— (1974b) *Lineages of the Absolutist State*, London: Verso.
Atiyah, P. (1979) *The Rise and Fall of Freedom of Contract*, Oxford: Clarendon Press.
Baker, J.H. (1990) *An Introduction to English Legal History*, 3rd edn, London: Butterworth.
Ball, C. (1996) 'The Making of a Transnational Capitalist Society: The Court of Justice,
    Social Policy, and Individual Rights Under the European Community's Legal Order',
    Harvard International Law Journal, 37 (Spring): 307–88.
Barlow, J. (1994) 'The Economy of Ideas', *Wired*, March: 8–12.
Bawa, R. (1997) 'The North–South Debate Over the Protection of Intellectual Property',
    Dalhousie Journal of Legal Studies, 6: 77–119.
Blackburn, T. (1994) 'The Unification of Corporate Laws: The United States, the European
    Community and the Race to Laxity', *George Mason Independent Law Review*, 3 (1): 1–95.
Bull, H. (1977) *The Anarchical Society*, New York: Columbia University Press.
Castells, M. (1989) *The Informational City*, Oxford: Blackwell.
Cerny, P. (1997) 'The Paradoxes of the Competition State: The Dynamics of Political
    Globalization', *Government and Opposition*, 32 (2): 251–74.
Charney, D. (1991) 'Competition among Jurisdictions in Formulating Corporate Law
    Rules: An American Perspective on the "Race to the Bottom" in the European
    Communities', *Harvard International Law Journal*, 32 (2): 423–56.
Cohen, M. (1927–8) 'Property and Sovereignty', *The Cornell Law Quarterly*, 13: 8–30.
Cox, R. (1989) 'Production, the State, and Change in World Order', in E. Czempiel and
    J. Rosenau (eds), *Global Changes and Theoretical Challenges*, Lexington, MA: D.C. Heath.
—— (1996) 'Social Forces, States, and World Orders', in R. Cox with T. Sinclair,
    Approaches to World Order, Cambridge: Cambridge University Press, pp.85–123.
Cutler, C. (1995) 'Global Capitalism and Liberal Myths: Dispute Settlement in Private
    International Trade Relations', *Millennium*, 24 (3): 377–97.
—— (1997) 'Artifice, Ideology, and Paradox: The Public/Private Distinction in Interna-
    tional Law', *Review of International Political Economy*, 4 (2): 261–85.
—— (1999a) 'Private Authority in International Trade Relations: The Case of Maritime
    Transport', in C. Cutler, V. Haufler and T. Porter (eds), *Private Authority and International
    Affairs*, New York: SUNY Press, pp.283–329.
—— (1999b) 'Locating "Authority" in the Global Political Economy', *International Studies
    Quarterly*, 43: 59–81.
—— (1999c) 'Public Meets Private: The Unification and Harmonization of Private Inter-
    national Trade Law', *Global Society*, 13 (1): 25–48.
—— (2000) 'Globalization, Law, and Transnational Corporations: A Deepening of
    Market Discipline', in S. McBride and T. Cohn (eds), *Power in the Global Era*,
    Basingstoke: Macmillan, pp.53–66.
—— (2001) 'Critical Reflections on the Westphalian Assumptions of International Law
    and Organization: a Crisis of Legitimacy', *Review of International Studies*, 27 (2): 133–50.

—— (2002) 'Private Interactional Regimes and Interfirm Cooperation', in R. Hall and T. Biersteker (eds), *The Emergence of Private Authority in Global Governance*, Cambridge: Cambridge University Press.

Cutler, C., Haufler, V. and Porter, Tony (eds) (1999) *Private Authority and International Affairs*, New York: SUNY Press.

Dezalay, Y. and Garth, B. (1996) *Dealing in Virtue: International Commercial Arbitration and the Construction of a Transnational Legal Order*, Chicago, IL: University of Chicago Press.

Doucas, M. (1995) 'Intellectual Property Law – Indigenous Peoples' Concerns', *Canadian Intellectual Property Review*, 12: 1–5.

Edgeworth, B. (1988) 'Post-Property? A Postmodern Conception of Private Property', *University of New South Wales Law Journal*, 11: 87–116.

Fisher, W., Horowitz, M. and Reed, T. (eds) (1993) *American Legal Realism*, Oxford: Oxford University Press.

Fukuyama, F. (1989) 'The End of History?', *The National Interest*, 16: 3–18.

Gardner, J. (1980) *Legal Imperialism: American Lawyers and Foreign Aid in Latin America*, Madison, WI: The University of Wisconsin Press.

Gerber, D. (1996) 'Intellectual Property Rights, Economic Power, and Global Technological Integration', *Chicago-Kent Law Review*, 72: 463–76.

Giddens, A. (1987) *The Nation-State and Violence*, Berkeley, CA: University of California Press.

—— (1990a) *The Consequences of Modernity*, Cambridge: Polity Press.

—— (1990b) 'Modernity and Utopia', *New Statesman*, 3(125): 20–2.

Gill, S. (1995a) 'Globalisation, Market Civilisation, and Disciplinary Neoliberalism', *Millennium*, 24 (3): 399–423.

—— (1995b) 'Theorizing the Interregnum: The Double Movement and Global Politics in the 1990s', in B. Hettne (ed.), *International Political Economy*, Halifax: Fernwood Publishing pp. 65–99.

—— (1997) 'Globalization, Democratization, and the Politics of Indifference', in J. Mittelman (ed.), *Globalization*, Boulder, CO: Lynne Rienner.

Gill, S. and Law, D. (1993) 'Global Hegemony and the Structural Power of Capital', in S. Gill (ed.), *Gramsci, Historical Materialism and International Relations*, Cambridge: Cambridge University Press, pp.93–124.

Gramsci, A. (1971) *Selections from Prison Notebooks*, Q. Hoare and G. Smith eds and trans., London: Lawrence & Wishart.

Grey, T. (1980) 'The Disintegration of Property', in J. Pennock and J. Chapman (eds), *Property, Nomos: Yearbook of the American Society for Political and Legal Philosophy*, New York: New York University Press.

Hamilton, W. (1931) 'The Ancient Maxim *Caveat Emptor*', *Yale Law Journal*, 40 (8) (June): 1153–87.

Harvey, D. (1990) *The Condition of Postmodernity*, Oxford: Blackwell.

Held, D. (1989) *Political Theory and the Modern State*, Cambridge: Polity Press.

Hohfeld, W. (1913) 'Some Fundamental Legal Conceptions as Applied in Judicial Reasoning', *Yale Law Journal*, 23: 16–59.

Horowitz, M. (1982) 'The History of the Public/Private Distinction', *University of Pennsylvania Law Review*, 130: 1423–8.

Ismail, H. (1991) 'Forum Non Conveniens: United States Multinational Corporations, and Personal Injuries in the Third World: Your Place or Mine?', *Boston College Third World Law Journal*, 11: 249–76.

Jameson, F. (1991) *Postmodernism or the Cultural Logic of Late Capitalism*, London: Verso.

Kairys, D. (ed.) (1982) *The Politics of Law: A Progressive Critique*, revised edn, New York: Pantheon Books.

Kennedy, D. (1991) 'The Stakes of Law, or Hale and Foucault', *Legal Studies Forum*, 15 (4): 327–68.

Kennedy, D.W. (1994) 'Receiving the International', *Connecticut Journal of International Law*, 10 (Fall): 1–26.

Klare, K. (1982) 'The Public/Private Distinction in Labour Law', *University of Pennsylvania Law Review*, 130: 1358–1422.

Macpherson, C. (ed.) (1978) *Property: Mainstream and Critical Positions*, Toronto: University of Toronto Press.

Marx, K. (1983a) 'A Contribution to the Critique of Political Economy', in E. Kamenka (ed.), *The Portable Karl Marx*, New York: Penguin Books.

—— (1983b) 'Law and the Materialist Conception of History', from *The German Ideology*, vol. 1, in E. Kamenka (ed.), *The Portable Karl Marx*, New York: Penguin Books.

Meyer, C. (1990) 'Personalizing the Impersonal: Corporations and the Bill of Rights', *The Hastings Law Journal*, 41: 577–667.

Minogue, K. (1980) 'The Concept of Property and its Contemporary Significance', in J. Pennock and J. Chapman (eds), *Property, Nomos: Yearbook of the American Society for Political and Legal Philosophy*, New York: New York University Press.

Muchlinski, P. (1995) *Multinational Enterprises and the Law*, Oxford: Blackwell.

Polan, A. (1984) *Lenin and the End of Politics*, London: Methuen.

Polanyi, K. (1944) *The Great Transformation*, Boston, MA: Beacon Press.

Reich, C. (1964) 'The New Property', *Yale Law Journal*, 73: 733–91.

Robinson, W. (1996) 'Globalisation: Nine Theses on our Epoch', *Race & Class*, 38 (2): 13–31.

—— (1998) 'Beyond Nation-State Paradigms: Globalization, Sociology, and the Challenge of Transnational Studies', *Sociological Forum*, 13 (4): 561–94

Rosenberg, J. (1994) *The Empire of Civil Society*, London: Verso.

Scheuerman, W. (1999) 'Economic Globalization and the Rule of Law', *Constellations: An International Journal of Critical and Democratic Theory*, 6 (1) (March): 3– 25.

Seipp, D. (1994) 'The Concept of Property in the Early Common Law', *Law and History Review*, 12 (1) (Spring): 29–91.

Sell, S. (1999) 'Multinational Corporations as Agents of Change: The Globalization of Intellectual Property Rights', in C. Cutler, V. Haufler and T. Porter (eds), *Private Authority and International Affairs*, New York: SUNY Press.

Silbey, S. (1997) 'Let Them Eat Cake: Globalization, Postmodernism, Colonialism, and the Possibilities of Justice', *Law and Society Review*, 31 (2): 207–35.

Singer, J. (1988) 'Legal Realism Now', *California Law Review*, 76: 465–544.

Strange, S. (1996) *The Retreat of the State*, Cambridge: Cambridge University Press.

Twining, W. (1996) 'Globalization and Legal Theory: Some Local Implications', *Current Legal Problems*, 49: 1–42.

van der Pijl, K. (1984) *The Making of an Atlantic Ruling Class*, London: Verso.

—— (1997) 'Transnational Class Formation and State Forms', in S. Gill and H. Mittleman (eds), *Innovation and Transformation in International Studies*, Cambridge: Cambridge University Press, pp.115–33.

Wiegand, W. (1996) 'Americanization of Law: Reception or Convergence?', in L. Frieden and H. Schuker (eds), *Legal Culture and the Legal Profession*, Boulder, CO: Westview Press, pp.137–52.

Wood, E. (1995) *Democracy Against Capitalism: Renewing Historical Materialism*, Cambridge: Cambridge University Press.

13 The politics of 'regulated liberalism'

A historical materialist approach to European integration

Hazel Smith

In this chapter I want to take the approach of historical materialism drawn from the work of Karl Marx, and argue for its cogency, pertinence and relevance in the explanation and understanding of the processes of European integration.[1] I argue that this approach has much more to offer than it has been given credit for in the discipline of international relations or the sub-disciplines of European integration studies (see Smith 1994). I go on to argue that it is one of the few approaches that can illuminate the interrelated social, political and economic dynamics of European integration. In this chapter I specifically investigate the Amsterdam treaty as marking an institutionalisation of the latest 'stage' of European integration and I particularly focus on what I term the 'rights' agenda of Amsterdam. This is because a key objective of the Amsterdam treaty was to promote individual rights in the context of the Union's increasing institutionalisation of commitments to uphold 'the principles of liberty, democracy, respect for human rights and fundamental freedoms, and the rule of law' (Article 6).[2] It is not immediately obvious why this would be so, given that the impetus behind further European integration remains overtly that of an elite-led politico-economic project designed to consolidate 'Europe' as a zone of increasing profitability and to ensure that relations between states remain anchored in a stable and predictable network of intergovernmental relationships.[3] Amsterdam therefore presents us with a non-trivial intellectual (and political) problem. Why would the elites who control the European integration process bother? The argument is that capital is not giving up rights to workers but gaining them for itself. The seeming rights of workers in production are actually rights for capital in exchange. Likewise, potential political rights for workers are also actual economic rights for capital. I go on to argue that the liberal democratic project associated with the European integration should be conceived as the politics of regulated liberalism.

The rights agenda is likely, however, to be problematic for capital. There is an essential and often very apparent contradiction set up in practice by the 'granting' of rights in one sphere at the same time as the often systematic abrogation of what seem to be the same rights in other spheres. To take a current example, in the Amsterdam treaty the Council 'may' take action against racial discrimination in the context of Community law. This would essentially permit the Council to take action against racial discrimination in employment. Yet even these weak provisions against racial discrimination have a normative value and draw into sharp relief the actual discrimination against Black people in the EU. Rights not to be racially discriminated against at work in Britain can be set against for instance the widely disseminated revelations of the Stephen Lawrence inquiry of the deep-seated institutional racial discrimination in the British Metropolitan police force. Given that human individuals are much more than their capacity to work, the rights talk of Amsterdam could help to expose the contradictions of the project of European integration – and also provide a legitimating discourse for the pursuit of an emancipatory version of rights talk and practice outside the sphere of commodified labour exchange.

I conclude by arguing that historical materialism satisfies explanatory, normative and emancipatory criteria and that its use opens up a fruitful research agenda in terms of the theoretical study of European integration.

Historical materialism and liberal democracy

In many senses, Marx's views on what we understand today as liberal democracy can be read off from his critique of liberal constitutionalism. These views are very straightforward. Political emancipation, which can be achieved with the installation of liberal constitutional regimes, 'represents a great progress' (Marx 1978a: 35). Indeed it represents the ultimate form of emancipation 'within the framework of the prevailing social order'. But political emancipation does not of itself imply human emancipation. In many ways for Marx, political emancipation implies a diminution or alienation of individual emancipation. This is because human rights agendas, as evinced in the various declarations of the 'Rights of Man' associated with the American and the French revolutions, were understood by Marx as a recognition that 'man' in civil society had become shorn of political subjectivity. The rights agenda for Marx split off man in civil society, as an egoistic, individualised, passive object of political activity, from man as citizen whose exclusive sphere of activity was the state. Here, egoistic means to be:

> an individual separated from the community, withdrawn into himself, wholly preoccupied with his private interest and acting in accord with his private caprice. Man is far from being considered, in the rights of man, as a species-being; on the contrary, species-life itself – society – appears as a system which is external to the individual and as a limitation of his original independence. The only bond between men is natural necessity, need and private interest, the preservation of their property and their egoistic persons.
>
> (Marx 1978a: 43)

This is partly because, Marx argues, within capitalist social relations civil society constitutes a separate sphere of activity from the state and, because the state is also constituted as the political sphere, activities within civil society are correspondingly constituted as 'non-political', even 'natural'. Such a situation contrasts with feudal systems of social organisation where, although civil societies existed, they were directly political in that the individual's location in civil society corresponded directly to his or her political status or, as Marx put it, 'his separation and exclusion from other elements of society'. Again by contrast, the state, within feudal social organisation, is perceived as something separate from the political and civil affairs of the people, it appears as 'the *private* affair of a ruler and his servants' (Marx 1978a: 45).[4]

Within capitalist social relations, then, conscious political activity is concentrated in the sphere of the state while in civil society egoistic man is 'passive', an object of political activity, as opposed to a political subject. For Marx, political emancipation in many real senses reduces human freedoms. 'Political emancipation is a reduction of man, on the one hand to a member of civil society, an *independent* and *egoistic* individual, and on the other hand, to a citizen, to a moral person' (ibid.: 46).[5] Liberty for Marx then as one of the 'Rights of Man' is 'the right of self-interest. ... It leads every man to see in other men, not the *realization*, but rather the *limitation* of his own liberty' (ibid.: 42).[6] The 'equality' aspects of the rights of man were simply dismissed as of 'no political significance. It is only the equal right to liberty ... namely that every man is equally regarded as a self-sufficient monad' (ibid.: 42). As for Marx's notion of democracy, this was something far from today's notions of liberal, representative democracy. Democracy for Marx entailed human emancipation, not just political emancipation. In democracy the '*political state is annihilated*' (Marx 1978b: 21).[7] By this Marx means the state as something separate from the people disappears and 'the constitution, the law, the state itself ... is only the self-determination of the people, and a particular content of the people' (ibid.). Democracy for Marx then closely corresponds with a system defined by the actualisation of human emancipation.

> Human emancipation will only be complete when the real, individual man has absorbed into himself the abstract citizen; when as an individual man, in his everyday life, in his work, and in his relationships, *he has become a species-being; and when he has recognized and organized his own powers (forces propres) as social powers so that he no longer separates this social power from himself as political power.*[8]
>
> (Marx 1978a: 46)

If the above gives an illustration of how Marx conceives liberalism and democracy, it does not, however, give us much of an indication about the theoretical framework which underpinned the analysis. It also does not allow for much of an insight into how human emancipation can be achieved. For these we have to turn to both *The German Ideology* and *Capital*, the latter the supposedly most economistic of Marx's work but which clearly analyses the social relations of capitalist production in which actual unfreedoms are mutually constitutive of the formal freedoms we today associate with liberal democratic polities (Marx 1986; Marx and Engels 1989).

In *The German Ideology* Marx sketched his understanding of a historical materialist project which was historical in that it understood human individuals to be historically constituted and situated agents. It is materialist – not in the modern sense of the word as consumerist – but in the sense of taking the human individual and 'sensuous' human activity as the analytical focus for explaining human society. Such a materialist philosophy can be contrasted with an idealist philosophy which looks to the life of the mind – separated from material existence – as the primary analytical focus in understanding human beings and their interrelationship in society.

For Marx, in order to explain the fundamental dynamics of any historical epoch, it is necessary to understand the prevailing social relations of production. The production relations Marx analyses are not simply those found in the workplace but all those social activities that together contribute to the production and reproduction of human societies. Production describes the human being's purposeful interrelationship with nature to sustain life and such intrinsically human activity is always for Marx a social activity. Relations of production is such a key concept for Marx because he argues that all human societies are transformed and defined by the introduction of changing instruments of production. Instruments of production include both tools created by human beings – everything from ancient flint axes to modern technology – and social organisation – and their function is to assist human beings create and recreate the environment in which they live. Although Marx defined the framework in which these specific and definite social relations were situated by the term 'mode of production', this did not refer to an economistic analysis of human society. For Marx a mode of production was another term for 'a definite mode of life' (Marx and Engels 1989: 42).

Marx is most well known, however, for his application of the historical materialist framework to analyse modern society which, he argued, could best be understood as constituted through antagonistic relations between major social groups who competed for a share in the wealth created within that historically specific society. This modern society was characterised by Marx as capitalist in its social relations in that its unique dynamics revolved around the creation or 'accumulation' of capital (Marx 1986).[9] The social relations of the production of capital are such that workers are free in the sense that they are no longer tied or connected through rights and obligations to their means of production and subsistence. They must therefore sell their labour-power on the free market for wages in order to be able to physically survive. At the same time, within the production process, the worker creates what Marx calls surplus value. (What is surplus is the value created in the labour process or the process of production that is over and above what it costs to maintain the worker at socially defined subsistence levels.) Surplus value does not accrue to the worker, however, because it is alienated through its purchase in exchange for wages by those who own the means of production, the capitalists. Class conflict is therefore endemic to capitalist relations as workers struggle to claw back some of the surplus value claimed by capitalists who, forced by the ancillary laws of the market to engage in competition with other capitalists, try to cut costs and increase productivity by decreasing the share in surplus value available as a return to workers.

The capitalist therefore 'exploits' the worker through the mechanics of the system itself. Marx stresses that the notion of exploitation does not necessarily imply moral turpitude (which does not mean to say that Marx has many kind words to say about the capitalist). Marx argued that the way that capital is created and expropriated is systematically hidden from those who create value (the worker – who he called the direct producer) through the structures engendered by the mechanics of the capitalist system. This means that workers can conceive of themselves as free – which in fact in law they are as they are free to contract their labour – but that these relations of production hide actual relations of inequality – between those who own wealth or the means of production, the bourgeoisie, and those who do not, who he terms the proletariat, between those who are formally free to sell their labour but in practice are compelled to do so in order to survive, and those who purchase that labour. In the realm of exchange (the market), therefore, where labour-power (the capacity to work) is bought and sold as any other commodity, both worker and owner of capital are equal to each other in law. For Marx, however, it is in the hidden dynamics of relations of production, in which workers are compelled to sell their labour-power, where inequality inheres.

The separation of formal political equality guaranteed by law and actual socio-economic inequality, combined with the tendencies of capitalist social relations to constitute such a relationship as natural and ethical, prompt Marx to sarcastically identify capitalist society as 'a very Eden of the innate rights of man. It is the exclusive realm of Freedom, Equality, Property and Bentham' (Marx 1986: 280). Freedom is given because those who buy and sell commodities, including labour power, enter into agreements voluntarily. Equality is guaranteed because these relationships are formalised in contracts as exchange of equivalents – usually money (itself a commodity in capitalist society) for other commodities. Property is part of the triad of rights in this 'innate Eden' because both the worker as owner of his or her labour-power and the owner of capital 'disposes only of what is his own'. And, for Marx, 'Bentham, because each looks only to his own advantage. The only force bringing them together, is the selfishness, the gain and the private interest of each. Each pays heed to himself only, and no one worries about the others' (1986: 280).

Historical materialism implies therefore that increasing political liberalisation is likely to accompany expanding capitalist relations of production. Political liberalisation implies equality under the law (of the capitalist state) because the system of social relations is constituted by an actual equality of exchange of commodities. The worker is alienated under both the system and the law from rights other than those pertaining to the buying and selling of commodities on the market (he or she has no right to a home for instance or to land). The worker however does establish the right to buy and sell the commodity of their own labour-power and, by entering into social relations where those commodity relationships – built around freedom of exchange – prevail, the worker is constituted within the discourse of capitalist society as a free and equal human being (with other individuals). Liberalism with its ideas of the sovereign individual provides, therefore, the ideological cement for such a system.

In Liberal polities, politics is constituted as a separate sphere from economics in the process of which the state (the political authority) is reified as something separate from the society in which it is embedded. The state is, however, an instance of the overall 'capital relation', that is 'class domination in capitalist society'.[10] The state is not an autonomous entity but neither is it subordinate to the 'needs' or 'requirements' of some abstract process of deterministic economistic or technological development. At its most abstract the state is the political embodiment of a whole complex of fluid class relations of power as defined through the nature of the essential struggle within capitalist social relations between labour and capital and for that matter between capitalist and capitalist. The institutionalisation of the form of the state within and as an apparatus captures to a greater or lesser extent these class conflicts. The state is also the political arena which guarantees as far as it is able the equality of exchange of commodities, including labour-power. In addition, all operational systems of capitalist social relations, whether at the state or the international level, are partially dependent on systems of formal law which institutionalise individual rights. As well as providing an enabling framework for commodity-exchange, legal systems provide sanctions against those members of society who abrogate property rights. The state is not, however, an immutable, transhistorical form – either logically or historically. The capitalist state has thus far provided the most important political appurtenance of capitalist social relations but there is no logical or historical reason why this should continue to be so. (The increasing salience of the European Union, for instance, at least gives cause for rethinking a perhaps hitherto automaticity of state/capital complexes as the way to understand capitalist social relations.)

We should not be surprised to see the promotion of liberal democratising projects as the essential accompanying project of the global spread of capital and its accompanying social relations (see Parekh 1993).[11] Democratisation – in its late twentieth-century liberalist version – is the other side of the coin of globalisation.[12] Democratisation emphasises individual rights and downplays any notion of democracy as equality except in the way Marx understood equality within bourgeois societies – as the equality of self-sufficient 'monads'. Liberal democracy is a real relation of class struggle that, among other things, has played out such as to inscribe democracy as the ability for commodities, including labour-power, to be equally exchanged in the market. Liberal democracy can also be conceived of as more liberal than democratic simply because the dominant understanding of democracy has been transformed in the late twentieth century through the acceptance of the practice of an intensely mediated representative function (see, for example, Huntington 1993).[13] It is representatives who make decisions and it is the role of the citizenry to be accepting of a subordinate role in the decision-making process. The major participatory function is as an individual voter in elections. Voting is an individual 'right' that should be exercised to validate the liberal democratic system. Even this most basic of political rights is, however, differentially, that is unequally, beneficial in modern societies. Some voters will have better access to decision-making (through pressure groups, business influence, wealth, access to media) than others. In this way actual equality in political decision-making is denied while formal political equality is retained.

There are clearly strains in the project of liberal democracy, however, and it is these tensions that allow a space for emancipatory politics. These strains are arguably much more visible in the discourse of democracy as equality than the discourse of liberalism as individual rights. This is because the prevailing inequality of liberal democracy is borne out by the evidence of everyday experience, which is that individuals in liberal democracies are not equal in many meaningful ways. This is reflected in, for instance, the pervasive fear of unemployment and the visible evidence of homelessness, rundown council estates and decrepit hospitals. On the other hand, class struggles for liberal rights which also have the effect to a certain extent of deepening human emancipation have been relatively successful as the rights talk of liberal capitalism has provided the possibility of an uneasy cross-class political convergence around both emancipatory struggle and questions of economic 'efficiency'. For instance, equal pay struggles have provided the focus of both socialist platforms and managerial 'good practice'. This does not, of course, mean that equal pay struggles have been successful to the extent of achieving the emancipation of all women, in that for instance women might be formally receiving equal pay with men but, on the other hand, restructuring of industry has meant that women are often incorporated into workforces on the basis of low paid, part-time, insecure employment with Black women overrepresented in this type of employment.

The point is that the rhetoric of liberal democracy allows the envisioning of an alternative emancipatory project where political rights would be matched by socioeconomic equality. It also permits and legitimises the sorts of politics which take the rights rhetoric as their base but which envisage a broader and deeper vision of an emancipated society. Some have argued that capitalist social relations compel emancipatory projects. One does not have to endorse the idea that capitalist social relations inevitability lead to human emancipation to accept the logic of such a connection. John Hoffman, for instance, argues very strongly that the fundamental pressures for capital accumulation encourage abrogations of workers' rights to allow short-term benefits for individual capitalists. This means that

> If propertyless producers are to enjoy their individual rights, they must seek to exercise *collective* power in order to do so. The market themselves compels them to invoke what Marx calls 'standards entirely foreign to commodity production'.
>
> In other words, equal rights inevitably generates a demand for equal *power*. … For the demand for democracy (and thus for socialism) is a product of capitalism. It can only emerge as workers are compelled to turn the weapons of the bourgeoisie (their abstract rights) against this or that aspect of the capitalist system.[14]

(Hoffman 1991: 40–1)

In all, then, historical materialist analysis intends to cover the hidden dynamics of capitalist society where actual relations of socio-economic inequality are constituted through and by the same process that constitutes formal equality between politically free individuals as the *sine qua non* of that same society. Successful capitalism relies on the contract rather than on coercion for efficient operation. Rights, based on the right of the individual to trade his or her labour-power (capacity to work) on the market, are prioritised while democracy as any form of human emancipation is severely circumscribed by the logic of capitalist production relations. Put another way, freedom in production gives way to freedom (of a sort) in exchange (Smith 1996).[15] Even these limited freedoms, however, provide some space and rhetorical legitimacy for socialist politics which might seek to transcend capitalist–socialist relations which can be, in practice and in lived experience, relations of unfreedom and alienation.

Historical materialist explanations of European integration

Mainstream European integration studies have remained virtually untouched by historical materialist theorising. Peter Cocks made a valiant attempt way back in 1980 which hit the pages of the very respectable *International Organization*. Marxists such as Ernest Mandel (1970) have, however, commented on integration. A very useful, readable and systematic historical materialist analysis of European integration by John Holloway and Sol Picciotto (1980) has been ignored by European integration theorists. One recent noteworthy attempt to offer 'class analysis' of European integration is by Bruno Carchedi and Guglielmo Carchedi (1999: 120) who argue for the EU to be understood as an imperialist actor. European integration is 'a process moved by the interests of (inter)national capital in which, not by chance, popular participation (not to speak of real democratic decision-making power) has been remarkably absent'. Such 'green shoots' of historical materialist analysis appear to be bearing fruit in one aspect of the study of European integration – the study of European monetary integration. Here the work of Bonefeld and Burnham (1996), and Carchedi (1997), offers theoretical analysis utilising the labour theory of value with this work being complemented by empirical work assessing the role and interests of the labour movement in monetary integration (Strange 1997).

Samir Amin (1997) has commented on the EU from a historical materialist perspective but in a parenthetical manner as it refers to his concerns with international inequality. Stephen George (1991) has marshalled the neo-Marxist framework provided by Immanuel Wallerstein to comment on European Political Cooperation. Another group of neo-Marxist international relations scholars, the 'critical theorists' influenced by Robert Cox's innovative interpretation of historical materialism – have seen European integration as a fruitful locus for empirical and theoretical inquiry,[16] reflecting Cox's view that the new Europe could be 'a proving ground for a new form of world order'.[17] The Amsterdam school with its work on capitalist class fractions in the context of its research programme on 'Social Forces in Western European Integration' has also generated some neo-Gramscian inquiries into elite projects within the context of European integration.[18] The focus here has been on the efforts of transatlantic elites (not just west European elites) to combine development of integrated economies of scale as a basis for increased and improved profitability with attempts to establish political integration in Europe, or at least in western Europe. Here we have a very visible potential empirical locus for Marxist theorising that argues for immanent and constitutive relationships between social, economic and political relations of production.

That historical materialism has not made inroads into mainstream EU studies is perhaps surprising. First, the standard introductory textbook in the field of European integration notes that 'many have suggested that ... the Treaty is guided by a clear philosophy or ideology: that of free market, liberal, non-interventionist capitalism' (Nugent 1993: 45). Secondly, the evolution of European integration seems to offer prima-facie support for historical materialist approaches – at least for vulgar versions of them.[19] Thirdly, although even vulgar Marxists have not latched on to a deterministic or functionalist rendering of the relationship between politics and economics in the evolution of the European Union, this has not prevented other schools of theorising from doing so. Both functionalists and neo-functionalists are explicit in their allegiance to models which contain elements of technological tautology (Hodges 1985; Taylor 1996).[20] Neoliberal institutionalists have found European integration a fertile ground for the application of theories which attempt a marriage (sometimes of convenience) between explanations that separate economics from politics as if their analytical abstraction somehow represented real separations of spheres of social activity (Wood 1996: 19–48).

One explanation for the impermeability of European integration studies to historical materialist theories is to point at their general absence in the discipline of international relations in general.[21] Carchedi and Carchedi argue that class analysis has been 'expelled, for obvious ideological reasons, from official and academic discourse [on European integration]' (1999: 120). These obvious reasons include the closeness of the discipline to United States foreign policy theory and practice which perhaps explains the difficulties of publishing during the Cold War. In addition Marxian theorising was associated by many with a discredited political project; Marxian scholarship was not very well distinguished from Marxist-Leninist ideology.[22]

More specifically, what I have termed as the 'institutionalist bias' of the sub-discipline of European integration studies has mitigated against those approaches that do not share the same theoretical prism.[23] I have argued elsewhere that the institutionalist bias, based on two institutionalist fallacies, sets the tone for writing about the EU.[24] Institutionalist fallacy number one is the tendency to narrow down the subject of inquiry in respect of European integration to the study of how the institution makes its decisions. Institutionalist fallacy number two is the conflation of the study of European integration with the institutional practices defined by policy-makers. We can also note a tendency in the institutionalist literature to combine these two biases. In the first category we see the concern with the institutional development of EU policy-making. The study of European integration becomes the historical study of how the internal decision-making procedures have changed over time and why and how these decision-making procedures have been formalised (institutionalised) or not. In the study of EU foreign policy, for instance, the second tendency is manifested in the delimitation of the study of EU foreign policy to the study of either European political cooperation (EPC) or the common foreign and security policy (CFSP). The institutionalist bias is powerful and influential. Those who do not share the bias have had difficulties in being heard.

An explanation of European integration utilising historical materialism, however, would start by locating both outcome and process in the context of the social relations of production in which integration evolves. This chapter attempts more specifically to investigate one specific aspect of European integration, the 'rights agenda' of Amsterdam, and does this within the Marxian framework examined above. If the relationships which Marx argues are constitutive of capitalist social relations hold in our explanation of Amsterdam, then we may also be able to draw some tentative conclusions about the nature of the broader project of European integration. The chapter therefore locates the discussion in the context of two relationships. The first is that of the dynamic relationship of European integration – as a process that involves the progressive opening of markets – to the institutionalisation of political rights. The second contextual framework is that of the contradictory normative project inherent to a capitalist logic which limits individual rights to a politics which is about facilitating capitalist exchange and, at the same time, provides 'the conditions of possibility' for emancipation through the collective exercise of those rights (necessarily, in opposition to the prevailing capitalist social relations).

European integration and the promotion of liberal democracy

The project of European integration has overtly concentrated on market integration since its inception. Many hoped that the processes of economic integration would facilitate problem-solving in more controversial 'political' areas – derived from the famous functionalist 'spill-over' thesis' – but the Community project was, at least overtly, designed to function in 'economic' issue-areas. It is only with the 1987 Single European Act that we first see treaty references to democracy which, since the Maastricht treaty, is considered as an essential characteristic of the Union (Church and Phinnemore 1994: 53). The Maastricht treaty established a very thin form of EU citizenship, granted to EU citizens by virtue of their prior citizenship status within member-states. EU commitments to liberal democracy have been mainly operationalised through the granting of individual rights – with the rights agenda of Maastricht and Amsterdam building on the legacy of social policy rights already established as part of the processes of encouraging market integration.

Market integration was pursued by member-states' governments, supported by United States' governments, who attempted to facilitate harmonisation of both the conditions of exchange (among themselves and in relations with the outside world) and the conditions of production (for exchange). Both together formed the base of the move to the 'common market' predicted by the 1957 Rome treaty. In terms of the conditions of exchange, the common external tariff was the major achievement of the late 1960s, enabling the Community to act as one in international trade terms. Competition rules and the harmonisation of taxation particularly in respect of VAT have been further moves in harmonising conditions of exchange. The moves to implement the single European market – the once famous 1992 project – is another. The introduction of the Euro, which follows a long chain of monetary co-ordination and integration projects since the 1971 Werner report, will also facilitate the integration of capitalist exchange (of goods and money) (Archer and Butler 1996: chap. 4).[25] Harmonisation of the conditions of production has sometimes been more controversial because of the perceived 'legitimate' right of business to operate without 'political interference'. Moves to impose common standards, for instance, including those relating to health and safety and sanitation rules, have sometimes been opposed as an unwarranted interference in what should be the prerogative of 'the market' to decide.

The distinction drawn here between 'production' and 'exchange' does not imply that the two never overlap in practice. In terms of the former, for instance, the production-led Common Agricultural Policy has significant effects on exchange in the shape of world agricultural market prices and conversely, for example, efforts to control imports of third country textiles (exchange) have a significant impact on, among other things, the continued maintenance of uneconomic sweatshop industries within the EU (production). The distinction does, however, allow us to inquire into the other conditions of production that might accompany a project of European integration. Of the three common policies outlined in the 1957 Rome treaty, commercial policy relates to integrating conditions of exchange. The other two – agriculture and transport – relate to production with agriculture, as we have seen, having significant overlaps between the two.[26] Transport policy has not ever been as extensive as the other common policies but the rationale of an integrated transport policy is to provide infrastructural support for industry.

Another factor of production given some thought in the Rome treaty was that of labour. The 1957 Rome treaty spelt out the need for the Community to promote workers' rights including equal pay for equal work by men and women. The 1987 Single European Act introduced provisions designed to improve health and safety at work. The Union's famous Social Charter is specifically designated the 'Charter of Fundamental Social Rights of *Workers*', and was first introduced in 1989 before being institutionalised in the 'Social Chapter' at Maastricht (Archer and Butler 1996: chap. 5). Social Charter provisions included health and safety at work, working conditions, information and consultation of workers, protection of workers made redundant, equality at work between men and women, the integration of persons excluded from the labour market, social security and social protection of workers, representation and the collective defence of the interests of workers and employers, conditions of employment of third country nationals, financial contributions for promotion of employment and job creation.

Any measures undertaken within the framework of the social policy had to take into account, according to a standard textbook on European integration, 'the need to maintain the competitiveness of the Community economy' (Nugent 1993: 407).[27] The Union emphasised the promotion of individual rights based on workplace and market calculations. Clive Archer and Fiona Butler (1996: 105) note that the EU has a 'conventional leaning of social policy toward market and employment issues'. This does not mean to say that all member-state governments were convinced that intervention to promote workers' rights would increase economic efficiency or were convinced to the same degree. There was some general agreement however that social policy was functional for economic integration, and, specifically in the context of the EU project, was judged as necessary for the success of the '1992' project – the completion of the Single European Market (SEM). This should not be taken as a structural-functionalist or teleological argument. This policy was contested within west European elites but eventually prevailed as the philosophy set out most famously by Commission president Jacques Delors in 1985.'The European social dimension is what allows competition to flourish between undertakings and individuals on a reasonable and fair basis. ... Any attempt to give new depth to the Common Market which neglected this social dimension would be doomed to failure' (Delors quoted in Hantrais 1995: 6).

Abroad, the Union progressively institutionalised its promotion of democracy, human rights and the rule of law within the context of its support for market economies. The first treaty reference to these commitments was in the preamble to the 1987 Single European Act (SEA). The 1993 Maastricht treaty provisions on the Common Foreign and Security Policy (CFSP) and the development policy provisions of the Maastricht treaty spelt out the Union's growing commitments in these areas.[28] In 1995 the Commission adopted a further obligation when it issued a communication which stated that an essential element of future contractual relations with third countries would be a reference to respect for democratic principles and human rights.[29] This move to political conditionally is a new feature of EU foreign policy.[30]

There was some contrast in emphasis with the Union's support of democracy and human rights at home and abroad. Domestically the 'rights agenda' placed the accent on liberalism and less on the deepening of democracy (whether defined as more equality or more effective participation in decision-making or both). The 'democratic' deepening that has taken place has been limited to the establishment of Union citizenship in the Maastricht treaty of 1993. The democratic 'right' associated with EU citizenship was limited to the right to vote and stand as a candidate in local and European Parliament elections. Abroad, however, the EU, at least in rhetoric, has supported more emancipatory versions of rights talk. There has been some emphasis on the promotion of human rights in the context of support for liberal democracy. In practice however support for liberal democracy has tended towards support for elections – based on the individual's right to vote. There have been some attempts to encourage the creation of the conditions for 'free and fair' elections which have gone beyond the promotion of elections but much of this work has been overtly geared around the promotion of market economies and the liberalisation of economies.

The 'rights' agenda of Amsterdam

A theme of the Amsterdam treaty was the promotion of citizens' and people's individual rights. Amsterdam builds on the 1993 Maastricht treaty in this respect. Article 2 states that the 'rights and interests of nationals' should be protected through the consolidation of Union citizenship. The same article supports the free movement of persons with the exception of asylum seekers, immigrants and criminals. Article 6 states that the Union shall respect 'fundamental rights' as outlined in the 1950 European Convention for the Protection of Human Rights and Fundamental Freedoms. What makes this different from the similar Maastricht provision is the agreement in Article 7 that permits the Union to take disciplinary action against those member-states in breach of Article 6(1) which reiterates respect for democracy, liberty and human rights. Article 11(1) on the Common Foreign and Security Policy commits the Union to promote democracy, the rule of law, human rights and 'fundamental freedoms'. As part of the provisions on police and judicial cooperation in criminal matters, Article 29 specifies that racism and xenophobia is to be prevented and combated. The treaty also takes a position against discrimination on the grounds of sex, racial or ethnic origin, religion or belief, disability, age and sexual orientation.[31] These provisions would have to be implemented by secondary legislation. In Britain, for example, it is still legal to discriminate on the grounds of age. Another Amsterdam declaration points to the fact that the death penalty is not carried out anywhere in the Union. Another states that the Union will respect religious and non-confessional communities.[32] There are no proposals to improve democracy in the Union either in the institutional sense or in the sense of increasing the ability of European citizens to participate in decision-making. The commitment made in terms of the former was to call a new Inter-Governmental Conference (IGC) to discuss the workings of the institutions one year before the Union achieves a membership of twenty.[33]

Of the initial areas identified by the Westendorp report for action, first, the citizen and the union and, second, democracy and efficiency, action on the former is unproblematically inscribed in the treaty.[34] The Union is consolidated and EU citizenship is maintained. More problematically, because less universally accepted as 'common sense', we could argue that the second agenda item of the Westendorp group was also systematically inscribed into the treaty. This would be so if we found that the treaty institutionalises the prevailing theory and practice of the capitalist social relation and if this relation in some way represents, within the specific historical and social context of early twenty-first century capitalist relations, 'democratic' capitalist relations. This would be so even if liberalism had been conflated with democracy at Amsterdam to the extent that the rights provisions predominate and democratic provisions, in the sense that we conventionally understand them, are absent. It would simply imply a 'new' understanding of what constitutes liberal democracy (and democracy). I understand this idea of liberal democracy as the politics of regulated liberalism.

Explaining Amsterdam

The Amsterdam treaty, signed in October 1997, is characterised by Clive Church and David Phinnemore as the disappearing treaty – partly because of the lack of press attention it has received and partly because their argument is that the enduring legacy of the treaty is likely to be in its codification and simplification of the EC and EU treaties (Church and Phinnemore 1994). Amsterdam, for them, is little more than a pragmatic, tidying-up exercise. For Michel Petite, the judgement is somewhat similar. Amsterdam 'is by no means the last word on European integration [representing] the most that Member States were prepared to agree among themselves at a given moment'.[35] Petite bases his assessment on a comparative analysis of the outcomes of Amsterdam with the ambitions of the Commission as set down in its opinion on the IGC of February 1996.[36] At one level there is not much more to add to the conclusions advanced by Church and Phinnemore and Petite. The Amsterdam treaty was clearly a tidying-up job, it did only achieve modest outcomes and much more work is going to be necessary to cope with the institutional consequences of enlargement.

If all we demand from a theory is a logical cumulation of verifiable and/or falsifiable facts – what we might call in technical language an empirico-analytic approach – then the analysis outlined above provides well-founded and sufficient knowledge. If, on the other hand, we demand to know more, about things that are not immediately accessible from observation, we might want to turn elsewhere. Instead of accepting what Robert Cox (1986) has called a 'problem-solving' approach to theory – that which takes the world as it finds it – we can turn to a critical approach – that which challenges the parameters of the social world it finds. This does not obviate the need for detailed empirical work matched by a process of logical reasoning. On the contrary it demands that this process be undertaken but within the context of a specifically historical and material context. The treaty, in other words, should be assessed in the context of the particular historical and social circumstances out of which it emerges and in terms of its significance for the material life of real 'sensuous' (to use the Marxian term) human beings. The original question set for this chapter was why do elites bother? Why would any fraction of capital accept restrictions on its powers in production? The short answer is as follows. First of all, capital is not giving up rights to workers but gaining them for itself. The seeming rights of workers in production are actually rights for capital in exchange. Likewise, potential political rights for workers are also actual economic rights for capital.

How then is capital gaining power through the formal granting of 'social policy' rights for workers? First of all exchange between equivalents – and therefore predictability in the labour process – is facilitated by the eradication of extraneous handicaps to the maximisation of surplus value from labour-power (obstacles based on discriminatory practices). Second, the pursuit of homogeneity – of moves to incorporate the real 'sensuous' labourer into a commodity or labour as a 'thing' – as a more predictable unit within global accounting processes, are facilitated by the promotion of the worker as an unindividuated individual. Third, the intra-elite conflicts within the EU have explicitly focused their attentions on social policy as a remedy for what has been termed 'social dumping' which is the possibility of individual states within the EU being 'unfairly' competitive (*vis-à-vis* other member states) in attracting global business because they were able to offer cheaper, more easily exploitable labour. Thus social policy was a way of providing the oft-quoted 'level playing field' for European capital (Hantrais 1995: 10).

As we also have already noted, social policy in terms of an explicit reference to the individual as worker was incorporated in the Maastricht treaty in 1993. This common policy was an effort to harmonise one condition of production, which was not the individual themselves but the individual's labour-power (the capacity to work). To remind ourselves, within capitalist relations labour-power is a commodity like anything else which can be bought or sold (exchanged) on the market. It is a commodity which the individual owns and sells (should they obtain employment) in an exchange with those who are in a position to pay wages for it. Arguably, if it makes sense to harmonise the conditions of production, in terms of improving the standards and efficiency of the components in the production process either by direct improvement of those inputs or by environmental support (more efficient transport and telecommunications infrastructure for instance) in order to optimise productivity and competitivity, then it makes just as much sense to maximise the efficiency of that other component of the production process – the labour-power (capacity to work) of the worker. For instance, it is clearly inefficient to permit discrimination on the basis of race if that discrimination results in a person not being employed who is the most able to maximise value in the labour process. Social policy can thereby be seen as explained and produced by and subordinated to the priority of creating the market (production and exchange) conditions for competitive European business. It is part of the process of providing optimum conditions of production for the expenditure of labour-power. This perhaps is not a very controversial conclusion. It does not imply that Commission officials or other decision-makers never act for altruistic motives or that there are not divisions within political elites about the efficacy of intervening in the labour-market as part of a strategy of improving competitivity.

On its own, however, the above explanation can perhaps offer some post-hoc insight but we still need to know why this particular strategy is adopted at this time. This is because capital has historically often found it just as useful to utilise an opposite approach in its battle with labour – which is to exploit differences based on gender, race, age, disability etc. as part of a policy to 'divide and rule', to prevent effective class action. One particular pernicious legacy of this can be found in the current institutional and actual discrimination faced by Black people in all advanced capitalist states today. An explanation can be found, however, in the context of the changing dynamics of social relations, which both inhibit certain options and encourage others.

Historically, the initial stages of capitalist accumulation were characterised by the production of absolute surplus value through the mechanism of outright coercion or force (Holloway and Picciotto 1980: 137). Domestically, the laws of capitalist states either permitted coercion or, except when accompanied by political struggles to enforce extant legislation, were ignored by nascent capitalists. Abroad capitalist states also used force in colonisation projects which also had as their object the maximisation of the production of (absolute) surplus value. Modern capitalist social relations are, however, constituted through and by the production of relative surplus value. This means that profitability relies on 'improvements' (for the capitalist) which are generated through advanced technology and changes in methods of work organisation. Production of relative surplus value is globally organised (hence globalisation) and force is much more difficult to employ for the dominant states. This is partly because force does not always provide an efficacious underpinning for social systems designed to maximise relative surplus value. (This is not always the case – for instance, South Korea, now an OECD member and an advanced capitalist state, relied heavily on military coercion in its capital/state building operations.)

Military force is also not so readily available, partly because of the successful struggle by exploited groups in the 'advanced' capitalist states against conscription and war itself, the campaign against the Vietnam War being one but by no means the only example of such activity. Even policing activities have become more circumscribed and subject to public accountability, again within certain limits, in EU states. For all sorts of reasons then, the guarantee of the capitalist exchange relation has come to be more overtly resident in the legal systems, structures and norms as distinct from within the directly coercive arm of the state. I do not want to suggest here of course that the state has either lost its coercive capacities or that these would never be wielded in times of crisis – only that legal strategies to support the wage/commodity relation predominate in the era of globalisation. The rule of law has always underpinned capitalist relations of production in that contract rights of the free worker to buy and sell their labour on the free market are fundamental rights in capitalist relations. Legal systems in states are kept in place by sanctions but, as importantly, legislation provides powerful norms by which individuals order their lives. I want to suggest here, then, that because of the general weakening of the sanction of force to underpin the process of capitalist exchange, reinforced legal norms which protect the capitalist right to exchange labour-power as a commodity on the market can contribute to the stability sought by capital within the precarious world of globalising capital.

Given the strong normative intent and power of globalised systems of law to promote liberal market morality as 'natural, neutral, efficient and just' – and given that the EU has already acted as an institutional model for regional integration schemes internationally – the potential impact of such legal norms and ideology is considerable.[37]

The rights as outlined in Amsterdam such as the provisions designed to eradicate discrimination on the grounds of sex, racial or ethnic origin, religion or belief, disability, age and sexual orientation are potentially political, not merely economic, rights of workers. Given however that the whole thrust of the integration project is to strengthen the competitivity of European business we might want to ask why it is that capital would have to concede such apparently enormous inroads into its ability to squeeze surplus value out of recalcitrant labour. One answer is to point out that such political rights as legal 'norms' have the effect of stripping workers of extraneous identities to produce the commodity for which capital craves – unfettered labour-power. The legal norms which institutionalise these ostensible rights for workers have then the result of securing actual improved conditions of exchange for capital as well as seeming political advances for workers.

There is a further more practical, more empirical and more mundane argument as to why these ostensible rights for workers in production turn out to be in fact rights for capital in exchange and why political rights for workers turn out to be economic rights for capital. First, the social rights which were institutionalised in the Social Chapter in Maastricht are almost unenforceable. This is partly because they are broadly worded and hugely general and partly because they are meant to be implemented by 'management and workers' together.[38] The emphasis is on implementation through consultation in the context of dialogue (Hantrais 1995: 11). It goes without saying that the deep structural and resource inequalities between these two 'sides' means that the activity of implementing specific rights will hardly be an equitable process.

Second, although the Amsterdam treaty suggests that sanctions can be imposed upon states that offend against 'democracy, rule of law and human rights', given the notion of democracy is as some form of regulated liberalism, and given the prevailing social relations of power are skewed in the direction of capital and not labour, such sanctions are unlikely to be forthcoming in the areas of preserving and extending radical versions of rights. These provisions were in fact designed to provide possible sanctions against ex-Communist states which could become members in any enlargement process. Given the EU's historically specific view of what constitutes rights, it remains likely that such provisions would not be used to maintain the once taken-for-granted collective social provisions in east European societies in, for instance, education and pensions or trade union rights over and against management but instead to insist on further moves to institutionalise the rights of self-interested competitive monads in the war of all against all which constitutes turn-of-the-century western Europe.

Obstacles to even something which could be considered a basic right within the EU, the free movement of workers, are considerable. This is directly the case for refugees, asylum seekers and criminals but is also so in a less obvious way for those who may have the formal right of free movement but who may be prevented from doing so by lack of money or knowledge (languages, unfamiliarity with different national bureaucratic practices) or simply because given the insecurity of capitalist social relations it is easier to stay within a known community than to move out of it. And third, and perhaps most obviously, the rights mentioned at Amsterdam are not really rights at all. Citizenship is a thin version of a right to vote in some elections (although not general elections) and is entirely dependent anyway on the national states deciding who should be granted national citizenship. The rights not to be discriminated against are not actualised – just mentioned as 'future possibilities'.

Politics: from freedoms for capital to emancipation for individuals

At first glance, the politics of the rights agenda seems to set in place a pretty firm structure of capitalist domination. I want to suggest here why this might not be so but first need to consider what the potential political effects of such a structure might be. Holloway and Picciotto have suggested that state intervention within capitalist social relations is designed 'to subject to the law of value, albeit indirectly, activities which for some reason cannot be directly subjected to its operations by individual capitals' (1980: 133). If this is so we might want to consider what activities the European Union undertakes which either the state does not or does less efficiently. One of the differences between the EU and actual, historically developed member-states, is that the EU has not been directly implicated in historic class struggles. In this way it is 'divorced' from class politics. In addition, as we have seen, the system of legal and political norms developed in the EU specifically formalises an abstract conception of the individual as self-interested monad who relates to the European Union in a way which is seemingly separate from any class location with capitalist social relations.[39] In this particular location, then, the European Union, not only is the 'economic' function of the worker separated from 'political' existence, but the worker is at the same time potentially separated from any notion of class solidarity. The undifferentiated, alienated, advanced capitalist individual comes more and more to resemble the 'potato' made famous by Marx in his description of the relations of peasants thrown together by circumstances but without social bonds that could create the possibilities for collective action.[40]

In addition the political project of the European Union rights agenda can only be associated with the promotion of democracy if that notion is no longer equated with any form of political (or human) emancipatory project but simply seen as regulated liberalism. Rights based on the idea of the unindividuated individual are incorporated into legal frameworks and ideologies so that even liberal democracy, not in itself ever a concept or practice which has leant itself to hugely emancipatory projects, becomes further truncated as a synonym for a social and political system whose organising principle is solely that of liberal individualism.

I want to insist, however, on an understanding that being given rights within the European integration process is not for the workers themselves but their labour-power (their capacity to work) as a commodity in the production process. The worker in real life, however (as opposed to his or her existence within the project of the capitalist relations of European integration), is much more than the sum of their labour-capacity. The possibilities of a counter-offensive against the alienating tendencies of the European integration project are therefore buried within that self-same project. For instance, given that ideologies of anti-discrimination – even though these are founded in narrow workplace rights – are established within the project of European integration, these are unlikely to remain located in the workplace arena. A worker, for instance, who is protected from discrimination at work on the basis of race is very likely to carry over the 'rightness' of that anti-discrimination ideology into civic, social and political life. Rights talk generated or sustained through market relations can then provide legitimacy for wider projects of social emancipation. Whether they will do so or not will depend on a number of issues – not least the collective agency of those caught up in the contradictions of these capitalist relations.

There are other implications that flow from an historical materialist interpretation of the Amsterdam treaty in the context of a discussion of European integration and I can only point to some of them here. Peter Burnham (1999) has argued that EMU should be understood as primarily an anti-inflationary strategy designed to maintain European competitivity at the expense of working people (Burnham 1999: 37–54). The 'rights agenda' of Amsterdam should be seen in this context. It does not reduce personal and economic insecurity at work or in the wider society precisely because the prevailing unequal social relations of production do not permit extensive democracy to operate so that the majority (who do not own the means of production) would be able to ensure their interests were represented across Europe.

Conversely the rights provisions of the Amsterdam treaty and of previous treaties, particularly Maastricht, do not represent the actions of a confident capitalist class. It must be the first time in history that for instance citizenship – even in such a truncated form as is on offer in the EU – was given without an immense political battle to achieve it. This is partly a reaction to the 'democratic deficit' problem for the elites who shape the European integration project. Within states, liberal democratic provisions help to obscure real dynamics of inequality. They usually also allow for an element of redistribution of wealth. Within the EU, the rights provisions have failed to provide both political legitimacy for European integration and to supply any redistributive effect to individuals. This may well be problematic for capital given the intensification of the European integration process through the establishment of the Euro. Capital risks fronting an EU-focused economic project very visibly based upon actual inequality (especially given a European recession) with only a threadbare and unconvincing legitimation project unable to absorb the fall-out from working-class reaction to any crisis.

The EU's pursuit of liberal democracy internationally

Historical materialism might also help us explain the puzzle of why the EU insists on introducing human rights and democracy clauses into its agreements with third countries. These clauses have sometimes caused difficulties for the EU in terms of its ability to pursue primary objectives such as the expansion of open free-trade markets. Australia objected to such clauses as did Mexico and it is certain that the United States would do so in any agreement between the two. The rationale becomes clearer if we can understand the rights clauses as being integral to a European integration project which wants to optimise efficiency for all aspects of the processes of production and exchange. This does not mean to say that human rights clauses, if implemented, would not have a significant effect on the lives of many suffering from the abrogation of much more than their rights at work. Two things follow. If the first priority is to maintain open exchange – as with Mexico and China for instance – trade provisions are likely to achieve priority. But in the world of globalisation that implies the spread of the optimum conditions for the expansion of capital, the European Union will continue to promote liberal democracy world-wide as what is being promoted is the politics of regulated liberalism. Globalising capital does not need liberal democracy in any structural-functional sense. As we have seen, the political system of regulated liberalism, in an ontological sense, is constituted by globalising capital.

Why use historical materialist explanations?

Historical materialism, like any other theory, can be judged by how well it satisfies certain criteria which include explanatory power, normative acceptability and, perhaps more controversially, emancipatory potential. By explanatory power, I mean the ability to illuminate aspects of human society that are not immediately available to us through observation. A satisfactory explanatory theory is governed by rules of logic and consistency with an appeal to verification (or the possibility of falsification) by reference to empirical research. Normative acceptability means that due consideration is given to the ethical implications of the theory. Emancipatory theory links the empirical and normative aspects of theorising to social practice whose intention is to bring about the emancipation of the human individual through political change. These criteria are of course contestable but it is nevertheless probably uncontroversial to state that, irrespective of the disagreements as to their respective legitimacy (particularly the last), all three are located within recognisable epistemological traditions.[41]

Historical materialism is both explanatory and normative. It can help us understand the obscure, opaque and contradictory processes of European integration but at the same time it takes a point of view, a perspective. At one level of abstraction, we could say that the theory is judged as against its ethical relationship with the individual in society. The priority is to explain European integration as it affects human lives. These are first-order concerns. But the normative concern is more specific than just with the individual *per se*. The capitalist mode of production is about social relations between men and women who are constituted in classes and who are incorporated within that mode of production in an unequal manner. This is a dynamic system and it is not 'natural' in that all societies have always been constituted in this way and will necessarily continue to be constituted in this way in the future. Human agency is necessary to effect change, and ideas of rights as part of even a weak democratic project – which are, if not generated, supported by the project of European capitalist integration – could encourage European peoples to expect and demand deeper forms of democracy. On the other hand, as Mark Rupert has pointed out, there is no guarantee of automatic emancipatory outcomes in the globalising world. It is equally possible that the sorts of employment insecurity generated as the other side of the 'rights' coin of capitalist integration could provide a space for authoritarian and populist ideologies (Rupert 2000).

In terms of the last criteria for judging theory, the emancipatory criteria, the argument is that the rights agenda of Amsterdam and Maastricht, of the entire European integration project, generates 'conditions of possibility' for the human beings that it affects. Liberal democratising projects legitimate the pursuit of rights within the context of some version of democracy. It would take human agency to demand more democracy and deeper human rights than those proposed by the European integration project. The Green movement in Europe is one example of a group that has mobilised around the institutions of the European Union to promote what has sometimes (although not always) been a very radical vision of human emancipation. This political project has not been confined to the realm of environmental issues but has sometimes expanded to include action and mobilisation around issues such as the promotion of peace internationally (for instance in the 1980s Central America conflict) and wider political participation within the European Union. Historical materialist theories would also suggest that the exploitation which underpins the formal relations of political equality can only be overcome through what used to be termed class struggle. In contemporary parlance what we mean is that it is only the purposeful activity of collective human agency organised around many of the axes of disenfranchisement generated by and through capitalist social relations, the most fundamental being the broad relationship between those who depend on wage labour and those who do not, which can transform and transcend those relations of production.

Conclusion

Historical materialism draws from a labour theory of value whose intellectual heritage is as much John Locke and David Ricardo as Marx and offers explanatory power in terms of its reminder that the relationships of politics and economics, labour and capital, society and technology are not accidental or conjunctural but neither are they structurally determined. Outcomes are shaped by human agency.[42] Historical materialism provides explanatory, normative and emancipatory potential for investigating the project of European integration. It is not an interest-driven theory in that it predicates explanation on an individual who operates in social life through a process of instrumental, preference-optimising rationality. It is a theory instead that argues that individuals both constitute and are constituted by the historically specific societies in which they live. These societies are understood as modes of production which are defined by their social relations. In modern times the social relations of production are capitalist in that the society is constituted through the very specific way that capital is valorised – in respect to the activities of human beings within the labour process. The criteria for judging European integration and the Amsterdam treaty must be as to whether it satisfies the demands and needs of workers and the excluded – in Europe and elsewhere. The theory is emancipatory in that it unfolds the mystifications of the processes of integration and at the same time suggests that the processes of exploitation inherent to it are not natural, inevitable or determined. To finish with an apt Marxian aphorism: 'Men make their own history, but they do not make it just as they please: they do not make it under circumstances chosen by themselves, but under circumstances directly encountered, given and transmitted from the past' (Marx 1990: 15).

Notes

1 This chapter takes as the core of historical materialist thought that developed by Marx (not his apologists or detractors).

2 Clive Church and David Phinnemore have pointed out that the codification of all the EU/EC treaties envisaged by the Amsterdam treaty as consolidating and simplifying exercises has, in some cases, led to more confusion. See Church and Phinnemore, 'Amsterdam: the Disappearing Treaty', mimeo, undated but 1998. In this chapter and unless otherwise specified, I utilise the Amsterdam codification of treaty clauses. I am indebted to Clive Church for his kindness in giving me a copy of his 'Consolidated Version of the Treaty on European Union' (mimeo), as well as a copy of the annex to the Amsterdam treaty entitled 'Tables of Equivalencies Referred to in Article 11 of the Treaty of Amsterdam'.

3 I am very aware that I am begging a good number of questions with this statement. However, it would take another article to trace these relationships and in any case my interpretation is not very controversial. The point is that my investigation of the 'rights agenda' does not preclude either in fact or in logic the legitimacy of other interpretations of the process. This does not mean that every explanation carries equal weight. An investigation of inter-elite motivation and behaviour might say something interesting about those elites but for the purposes of explaining European integration, it is something of a second-order dynamic.

4 Author's emphasis.

5 Author's emphasis.

6 Author's emphasis.

7 Author's emphasis.

8 Author's emphasis.

9 For detail on the social relations of capitalist accumulation see Marx, *Capital Volume 1*.

10 There are of course important debates about what constitutes the nature of the state in capitalist society. The approach of John Holloway and Sol Picciotto seems particularly fruitful to me. They reject both economism and politicism as satisfactory approaches, and discuss the state as 'a particular surface (or phenomenal) form of the

capital relation, i.e. of an historically specific form of class domination'. See Holloway and Picciotto, 'Capital, Crisis and the State', in *Capital and Class*, 2, Summer (1977): 77.

11 For a useful commentary on the liberal component of liberal democracy see Bhikhu Parekh, 'The Cultural Particularity of Liberal Democracy'.

12 There is an appreciation in some of the globalisation literature of the tensions involved between notions of democracy as equality and the constraints set by globalising capital. See for example Lester Thurow, *The Future of Capitalism*. One wide discussion argues that globalisation produces both universalising consumerist homogeneity at the same time as generating essentialist fundamentalisms and that both of these are inimical to democracy. See Benjamin R. Barber, *Jihad Vs. McWorld*. For a discussion which specifically refers to the project of European integration see Philip Resnick, 'Global Democracy: Ideals and Reality'. For a discussion of the tensions between capitalism and democracy see chapter six, entitled 'Pluralism, Corporate Capitalism and the State', in David Held, *Models of Democracy*. Paul Cammack utilises similar premises to those developed in this chapter to provide an excellent discussion of the relationship between capitalism and democracy in a case study on Latin America, reminding us that, in the context of capitalist relations of production, '[O]ne can certainly have meaningful citizenship without democracy'. See Paul Cammack, 'Democratization and Citizenship in Latin America', p.193.

13 For one of the most explicit understandings of democracy as purely procedural see the influential Samuel P. Huntington, *The Third Wave: Democratization in the late Twentieth Century*.

14 John Hoffman, 'Liberals versus Socialists: Who are the True Democrats?', pp.40–1. The quote from Marx is Karl Marx, *Capital*, Volume 1 (London: Lawrence & Wishart, 1970), p.586.

15 I have discussed these relationships more extensively in Hazel Smith, 'The Silence of the Academics'.

16 Although Robert Cox does not work within the framework of the labour theory of value as developed by Marx, he can be credited with introducing into the mainstream of international relations scholarship the idea that historical materialism can be used as a legitimate intellectual resource. See his seminal 'Social Forces, States and World Orders: Beyond International Relations Theory', in Robert O. Keohane (ed.), *Neorealism and its Critics* (New York: Columbia University Press, 1986).

17 Robert Cox, 'Structural Issues of Global Governance: Implications for Europe', in Stephen Gill (ed.), *Gramsci, Historical Materialism and International Relations* (Cambridge: Cambridge University Press, 1993). Cox's work has provided the intellectual foundation for investigation of European integration. See for instance Stephen Gill, 'European Governance and New Constitutionalism: Economic and Monetary Union and Alternatives to Disciplinary Neoliberalism in Europe', *New Political Economy*, 3, 1 (1998): 5–26.

18 One useful critical review from within the perspective of this approach is Magnus Ryner, 'Gramscian International Political Economy as Critical Research on European Regionalism: Contributions and Limitations'. Paper to BISA, December 1997. For an 'external' critique of these approaches see Peter Burnham, 'Neo-Gramscian Hegemony and the International Order', *Capital and Class*, 45, Autumn (1991): 73–93.

19 The discipline of international relations has suffered from caricatured interpretations of historical materialism. See particularly V. Kubalkova and A.A. Cruikshank, 'The "New Cold War" in Critical International Relations Studies', *Review of International Studies*, 12, 3, July (1986); and V. Kubalkova and A.A. Cruikshank, 'A Rambo Come to Judgement: Fred Halliday, Marxism and International Relations', *Review of International Studies*, 15, 1, January (1989).

20 A good survey of integration theory, particularly as pertaining to early theories of European integration, is Michael Hodges, 'Integration Theory'. For a more recent

perspective that adopts the consociationalist interpretation see Paul Taylor, *The European Union in the 1990s*.

21 For discussion of the historical materialist theorising that has emerged in the international relations discipline see Hazel Smith, 'Marxism and International Relations Theory'.

22 See Kubalkova and Cruikshank, 'The "New Cold War" in Critical International Relations Studies', and Kubalkova and Cruikshank, 'A Rambo Come to Judgement: Fred Halliday, Marxism and International Relations'.

23 Those analysts who wish to go further than the institutionalist bias might allow remain obligated to start from within this framework – even if they wish to transcend it. I have developed this critique to evaluate EU foreign policy studies. The argument can be made in respect of European integration studies more generally. See Hazel Smith, 'Actually Existing Foreign Policy – Or Not?: The EU in Latin and Central America', in John Peterson and Helene Sjursen (eds), *A Common Foreign Policy for Europe* (London: Routledge, 1998).

24 Ibid.

25 For details see Clive Archer and Fiona Butler, chapter 4 entitled 'Economic and Monetary Union', in Clive Archer and Fiona Butler, *The European Union: Structure and Process*, pp.83–97.

26 For the EEC treaty see *Treaties establishing the European Communities*, abridged edition (Luxembourg: Office for Official Publications of the European Communities, 1987), pp.115–383.

27 Information on the social charter in this paragraph and quote taken from Neill Nugent, *The Government and Politics of the European Community*.

28 The TEI is reprinted in Martin Holland, *European Community Integration* (London: Pinter, 1993).

29 For discussion see Communication from the Commission to the Council and the European Parliament, *The European Union and the External Dimension of Human Rights Policy: from Rome to Maastricht and Beyond*, Com (95) 567 final, Brussels, 22 November 1995, pp.15–16.

30 There is some useful work on *what* is happening – much less on *why* we see these developments. For the former see Karen Elizabeth Smith, 'The Use of Political Conditionality in the EU's Relations with Third Countries: How Effective?', EUI Working papers, SPS No. 97/7 (San Domenico: European University Institute, Florence, 1997).

31 Michel, Petite *Treaty of Amsterdam*, Annex entitled 'Assessing the Achievements of the Commission's Objectives for the IGC', p.5.

32 Petite, *The Treaty of Amsterdam*, p.9 of 14.

33 Ibid., p.4 of 14.

34 The 'Reflection Group' chaired by Carlos Westendorp met in 1995 and established a menu of areas of involvement for the IGC. The Reflection Group identified the broad areas for IGC involvement as, first, the citizen and the Union, and, second, efficiency and democracy in the Union. The Amsterdam treaty remained faithful to these topics – producing decisions in six areas – freedom, security and justice, the union and the citizen, external policy, the institutions, the management of cooperation (the flexibility provisions) and an agreement to codify and simplify the existing treaties. See *Reflection Group's Report*, SN 520/95 (REFLEX 21), mimeo, 1995.

35 Michel Petite, *The Treaty of Amsterdam*, essay located on http://www.jeanmonnetprogram.org/papers/98/98-2-.html.

36 See Church and Phinnemore for a discussion of how these thematic areas were translated into treaty amendmanets and the consequences of this translation.

37 For discussion of the role of law in globalisation see the Claire Cutler chapter, this volume.

38 The 'Protocol on Social Policy' of the Treaty on European Union is reproduced in Clive H. Church and David Phinnemore, *European Union and European Community*, pp.422–5.

39 John Holloway discusses a similar process in the historical creation of citizens within capitalist states where 'being treated as a citizen is thus a process of abstraction from class – a process of abstract individualism in which class conflicts are transformed into individual problems'. See John Holloway, 'State as Class Practice', *Research in Political Economy*, Vol. 3 (Greenwich, Connecticut: JAI Press, 1980), pp.12–13.

40 The metaphorical allusion is used by John Holloway to describe the creation of political constituencies in representative democracy. See John Holloway, 'State as Class Practice', p.14.

41 Epistemological debates have characterised the discipline of international relations in the last ten years. For my discussion of these in the context of an historical materialist theory of international relations see Hazel Smith, 'The Silence of the Academics: International Social Theory, Historical Materialism and Political Values', *Review of International Studies*, 22, 2, April (1996).

42 For a discussion that argues that modern concepts of the individual, as a bearer of freedom, rights, obligation and justice and which derive from Hobbes and Locke, depend upon a notion of the individual as the possessor and owner of his or her labour, see the seminal C.B. Macpherson, *The Political Theory of Possessive Individualism* (Oxford: Oxford University Press, 1979).

Bibliography

Amin, Samir (1997) *Capitalism in the Age of Globalization*, London: Zed.

Archer, Clive and Butler, Fiona (1996) *The European Union: Structure and Process*, 2nd edn, London: Pinter.

Barber, Benjamin R. (1996) *Jihad Vs. McWorld*, New York: Ballantine.

Bonefeld, Werner and Burnham, Peter (1996) 'Britain and the Politics of the European Exchange Rate Mechanism', *Capital and Class*, 60, Autumn: 5–37.

Burnham, P. (1991) 'Neo-Gramscian Hegemony and the International Order', *Capital and Class*, 45, Autumn: 73–93.

—— (1999) 'The Politics of Economic Management in the 1990s', *New Political Economy*, 4, 1: 37–54.

Cammack, Paul (1994) 'Democratization and Citizenship in Latin America', in Geraint Parry and Michael Moran (eds), *Democracy and Democratization*, London: Routledge.

Carchedi, Bruno and Carchedi, Guglielmo (1999) 'Contradictions of European Integration', *Capital and Class*, special issue, No. 67, Spring: 120.

Carchedi, Guglielmo (1997) 'The EMU, Monetary Crises and the Single European Currency', *Capital and Class*, 63, Autumn: 85–114.

Church, Clive and Phinnemore, David (1994) *European Union and European Community: A Handbook and Commentary on the Post-Maastricht Treaties*, London: Harvester Wheatsheaf.

Cocks, Peter (1980) 'Towards a Marxist Theory of European Integration', *International Organization*, 34, 1.

Commission to the Council and the European Parliament (1995) *The European Union and the External Dimension of Human Rights Policy: From Rome to Maastricht and Beyond*, Com (95) 567 final, Brussels, 22 November.

Cox, R. (1986) 'Social Forces, States and World Orders: Beyond International Relations Theory', in R. Keohane (ed.), *Neorealism and its Critics*, New York: Columbia University Press.

—— (1993) 'Structural Issues of Global Governance: Implications for Europe', in S. Gill (ed.), *Gramsci, Historical Materialism and International Relations*, Cambridge: Cambridge University Press.

George, Stephen (1991) 'European Political Cooperation: a World Systems Perspective', in Martin Holland (ed.), *The Future of European Political Cooperation*, London: Macmillan.

Gill, S. (1998) 'European Governance and New Constitutionalism: Economic and Monetary Union and Alternatives to Disciplinary Neoliberalism in Europe', *New Political Economy*, 3, 1: 5–26.

Hantrais, Linda (1995) *Social Policy in the European Union*, London: Macmillan.

Held, David (1987) *Models of Democracy*, Cambridge: Polity.

Hodges, Michael (1985) 'Integration Theory', in Trevor Taylor (ed.), *Approaches and Theory in International Relations*, Harlow: Longman.

Hoffman, John (1991) 'Liberals versus Socialists: Who are the True Democrats?', in David McLellan and Sean Sayers (eds), *Socialism and Democracy*, London: Macmillan.

Holland, M. (1993) *European Community Integration*, London: Pinter.

Holloway, J. (1980) 'State as Class Practice', in *Research in Political Economy*, vol. 3, Greenwich, CT: JAI Press.

Holloway, John and Picciotto, Sol (1977) 'Capital, Crisis and the State', *Capital and Class*, 2.

—— (1980) 'Capital, the State and European Integration', *Research in Political Economy*, 3: 123–54.

Huntington, Samuel P. (1993) *The Third Wave: Democratization in the late Twentieth Century*, London: University of Oklahoma.

Kubalkova, V. and Cruikshank, A. (1986) 'The "New Cold War" in Critical International Relations Studies', *Review of International Studies*, 12, 3.

—— (1989) 'A Rambo Come to Judgement: Fred Halliday, Marxism and International Relations', *Review of International Studies*, 15 1.

Macpherson, C. (1979) *The Political Theory of Possessive Individualism*, Oxford: Oxford University Press.

Mandel, Ernest (1970) *Europe versus America? Contradictions of Imperialism*, London: New Left Books.

Marx, K. (1978a) 'On the Jewish Question', in Robert C. Tucker (ed.), *The Marx–Engels Reader*, 2nd edn, London: W.W. Norton.

—— (1978b) 'Contribution to the Critique of Hegel's *Philosophy of Right*', Robert C. Tucker (ed.), *The Marx–Engels Reader*, 2nd edn, London: W.W. Norton.

—— (1986) *Capital*, Vol. 1, Harmondsworth: Penguin.

—— (1990) *The 18th Brumaire of Louis Bonaparte*, New York: International.

Marx, Karl and Engels, Friedrich (1989) *The German Ideology*, London: Lawrence & Wishart.

Nugent, Neill (1993) *The Government and Politics of the European Community*, London: Macmillan.

Parekh, Bhikhu (1993) 'The Cultural Particularity of Liberal Democracy', in David Held (ed.), *Prospects for Democracy*, Cambridge: Polity.

Petite, Michel (1998) *The Treaty of Amsterdam*, essay located at http://www.jeanmonnetprogram.org/papers/98/98-2-.html (date accessed 25/07/02).

Resnick, Philip (1998) 'Global Democracy: Ideals and Reality', in Roland Axtmann (ed.), *Globalization and Europe*, London: Pinter.

Rupert, M. (2000) *Ideologies of Globalization*, London: Routledge.

Ryner, M. (1997) 'Gramscian International Political Economy as Critical Research on European Regionalism: Contributions and Limitations', paper presented to British International Studies Association.

Smith, H. (1994) 'Marxism and International Relations Theory', in A. Groom and M. Light (eds), *Contemporary International Relations: A Guide to Theory*, London: Pinter.

—— (1996) 'The Silence of the Academics: International Theory, Historical Materialism and Political Values', *Review of International Studies*, 22, April.

—— (1998) 'Actually Existing Foreign Policy – Or Not?: The EU in Latin and Central America', in John Peterson and Helene Sjursen (eds), *A Common Foreign Policy for Europe*, London: Routledge.

Smith, K. (1997) 'The Use of Political Conditionality in the EU's Relations with Third Countries: How Effective?', EUI working papers, SPS No. 97/7, San Domenico: European University Institute, Florence.

Strange, Gerard (1997) 'The British Labour Movement and Economic and Monetary Union in Europe', *Capital and Class*, 63, Autumn: 85–114.

Taylor, Paul (1996) *The European Union in the 1990s*, Oxford: Oxford University Press.

Thurow, Lester (1996) *The Future of Capitalism*, London: Nicholas Brealey Publishing.

Wood, Ellen (1996) 'The Separation of the "Economic" and the "Political" in Capitalism', in Ellen Wood, *Democracy Against Capitalism: Renewing Historical Materialism*, Cambridge: Cambridge University Press.

14 Historical materialism, ideology, and the politics of globalizing capitalism

M. Scott Solomon and Mark Rupert

Debates surrounding the question of globalization have spawned a variety of responses, ranging from assertions of the imminent demise of the nation-state system to arguments that the concept of globalization generates more heat than light – with some calling into question the very notion of something called globalization (Hirst and Thompson 1996). We enter this debate with the recognition that in a very real sense globalization is the intensification of an old process, the continuing internationalization of commodity production and capital accumulation. However, we approach this question from the tradition of historical materialism, a tradition that brings a unique perspective that is arguably superior to others in its ability to recognize the dynamism that is inherent to capitalism, and the progressive political possibilities which may be latent within it. That is to say, historical materialism approaches the question of globalization not with puzzlement over dramatic changes in forms of accumulation, but fully expecting them. Indeed, as early as 1848 Marx and Engels recognized that 'the bourgeoisie cannot exist without constantly revolutionizing the instruments of production, and thereby the relations of production, and with them the whole relations of society' (*Communist Manifesto*, in Marx 1977a: 224). We understand globalization as exactly this sort of process – not unexpected, to be sure, but hardly predestined. Rather, as we see it, globalizing capitalism is contested and open-ended. On this view, ignoring capitalism's tendencies towards globalization would constitute a scholarly and political error of no less magnitude than acquiescing in the face of representations of its omnipotence and inevitability. Drawing on the resources of historical materialism, it is possible to represent capitalist globalization as a dialectical process: attendant upon globalizing capitalism have been heightened exploitation and class-based social powers, but processes of globalization also bear the potential for various forms of a progressive transnational politics of solidarity, opening up possibilities for alternative future worlds more democratic and less exploitative.

Commentators often point to the increasing and deepening internationalization of production and finance, especially after the dramatic changes of the early 1970s, as the very essence of globalization. We agree that production and finance are essential elements of this story, but see much more at stake. This internationalization is bound up with a host of political and cultural changes.

One element that has been under-theorized is the ideological terrain of global-ization. The increasing integration of global financial and commodity markets has made even the most remote painfully aware of the vagaries of quicksilver capital. However, while markets become more integrated, the various stories people tell themselves to understand these changes vary dramatically. From Buchanan, Haider, and LePen, to the Australian 'One Nation' movement, xeno-phobic backlashes entailing reassertion of economic, cultural or racial nationalisms are an all too common response. While condemnation of racism and xenophobia is obviously necessary, attempting to understand the roots of these political responses is just as vital to a progressive politics. It is unacceptable to merely dismiss such responses in the hope that they will disappear with the next predicted up-tick in asset value, for this amounts to disengagement from the ideological struggles which will determine the form and political significance of 'globalization' (see Rupert 2000).

There is a sense in which 'freedom', as understood under capitalist social rela-tions, entails meaningful historical progress over and against feudal relations of personal dependence and extra-economic coercion, but is nonetheless a self-limiting, contradictory concept, producing effects that might potentially generate political friction, struggle, and transformation. We take Marx seriously when he argues that under capitalism workers are free in a dual sense – free of ownership of the means of production (and thus compelled to sell his or her labour-power) but also juridically free and formally equal (Marx 1977a: 272). 'The sphere of circulation or commodity exchange, within whose boundaries the sale and purchase of labor-power goes on, is in fact a very Eden of the innate rights of man. It is the exclusive realm of Freedom, Equality, Property and Bentham' (Marx 1977a: 280). Freedom, equality, property and Bentham (self-interest) is shorthand for juridically free and equal persons meeting in the market to exchange their property in mutually beneficial transactions – the core of liber-alism's entire (limited) vision of social life. The sarcasm detectable in Marx's justly famous passage reminds us of the irony that although people may appear as juridically free and equal in the sphere of circulation, relations of private ownership within the sphere of capitalist production subvert both equality and freedom. Capitalism creates new historical possibilities even as it negates or distorts their potential for self-development. The profound ironies of capitalist social life are the sources of Marx's critical leverage, and may become crucial sites of political resistance. As it reproduces itself on a more global scale, the janus-faced character of capitalism is no less evident: globalizing capitalism entails manifold contradictions and creates the conditions of existence from which new forms of social organization might conceivably emerge.

This dialectic is not limited to class. Divisions based on gender, nationality, and other forms of identity exist in uneasy, complex relationships to class. To our minds historical materialism is essential to an understanding of this dialectic, but is not by itself sufficient. We argue that historical materialism needs to rethink some of its more economistic assumptions if it wishes to effectively engage the politics of globalization. By doing so we hope to suggest that there are possibilities

for unity *through* difference that can contest the hegemonic project of globalization driven by the dictates of capital accumulation. We have developed a set of
provisional claims that address specific elements of our perspective on globalization. A connecting thread runs throughout our discussions – a refusal to always
and forever privilege class processes, and the concomitant refusal to ignore them.
We understand historical materialism as an open-ended mode of inquiry that is,
to echo Stuart Hall, 'without guarantees'.

Globalization: 'It's the real thing'

While it is possible to exaggerate the novelty and extent of contemporary manifestations of 'globalization', there are real material processes underlying the
emergence of even the most extreme versions of the globalization thesis. These
processes are historically distinct, with a correspondingly unique politics.
Globalizing capitalism has emerged in a particular historical context, and has
been the political project of a transnational historic bloc (van der Pijl 1984,
1998; Cox 1987; Gill 1990; Rupert 1995, 2000). Constructing the institutional
infrastructure of international trade and finance, this historic bloc fostered the
growth of international trade and investment through the post-war decades,
especially within the so-called 'triad' regions. In this context, trade led the post-
war boom, with trade in manufactured goods expanding most dramatically
(Dicken 1992: 18). While exports grew faster than output, foreign investment
grew faster still. Direct foreign investment – and, debatably, transnational
production and intra-firm trade (cf. Dicken 1992: 48–9; Agnew and Corbridge
1995: 169; Perraton *et al.* 1997: 263–4; Henwood 1997: 15; Feenstra 1998;
Bordo *et al.* 1999) – emerged as important forms of transnational economic
linkage. The traditional global division of labour – in which manufacturing
activities were concentrated in the advanced capitalist 'core' areas, while 'peripheral' areas were limited to primary production – was breached as newly
industrializing countries (NICs) emerged as significant producers of manufactured goods for the world economy (cf. Dicken 1992: chap. 2; Gordon 1988).
Finally, excess liquidity, the collapse of the Bretton Woods fixed rate regime, and
the emergence of offshore xenocurrency markets, together resulted in rapidly
growing volumes of foreign exchange trading and speculative international
investment which dwarf the currency reserves of governments and can readily
inundate, or leave high and dry, the financial markets of particular nations
(Wachtel 1990; Agnew and Corbridge 1995: 171–8; Perraton *et al.* 1997:
265–71).

The above suggests that the processes associated with globalization are not
without author, though the significance of these processes remains an open question. Often, the debate around globalization represents itself as an either/or
proposition. Either globalization has resulted in a borderless world of factor
price equalization and the disciplining of all state governments who foolishly
dare to challenge the dictates of the market, *or* globalization is 'globaloney' –
hype and hysteria that are all out of proportion to the degree of openness in the

contemporary global economy (which in some ways may be less open than during the classical Gold Standard period).

We reject the formulation of the globalization question in bipolar 'either/or' terms. Instead, we seek to contribute to the recasting of this debate. While the empirical record suggests that globalization is in fact neither/nor but somewhere in between, the import of globalization cannot be determined by purely empirical measures. We understand globalization not as an event or a condition, nor even an accretion of secular trends, but as the continuation of an ongoing process of social self-production, structured by particular social power relations but pregnant with possible futures, implicitly political, contestable and contested.

Borrowing from Perraton *et al.* (1997) two broad categories of commentary about globalization can be defined. The *hyper-globalization* school (Reich 1991; Ohmae 1990; others) sees changes in global production and finance resulting in a frictionless political economy that leaves states in a reactive mode to the dictates of capital. The *globalization sceptics* (Gordon 1988; Hirst and Thompson 1996; Weiss 1998; Sutcliffe and Glyn 1999) find that most of these claims have been greatly exaggerated and that states and other political actors need not cower in the face of international capital movements. The hyper-globalization school defend their hypothesis by appealing to empirical measures of globally integrated production techniques by TNCs, the internationalization of services, massive and turbulent flows of portfolio investment, large speculative currency flows (vastly outstripping the necessities of foreign trade) and the increasing efforts of states to make their investment environment more solicitous to the demands of investors. There is much to support this thesis. It is undeniable that the post-war order has seen the institutionalization of an open and liberal political economy. Whatever the measure, it is clear that the globalization of finance and production has resulted in a definite quantitative acceleration of interdependence and openness since 1945. The collapse of the Bretton Woods exchange rate system and end of the Cold War haven't slowed this trend, but have accelerated it.

The global sceptics acknowledge as much, but don't see a qualitatively different world. On a variety of empirical measures the current global economy is similar to, or only marginally different from, the close of the nineteenth century. This view sees the enormous disruptions of the First and Second World Wars (and the inter-war period) as aberrations with the modern era a return to the *status quo ante*. Perraton *et al.* have isolated four main objections by the sceptics, paraphrased below:

1 Economic activity is more nationally based than a globalized economy would suggest.
2 Globalization is more accurately internationalization, the interaction of well-defined and quite sovereign territorial units rather than a borderless world.
3 Global flows (as domestic/international ratios) are similar to the end of the nineteenth century.

4   Globalization is often a reflection of regionalization, the heightened interaction of self-contained regions, rather than an increase in globalized flows.

Perraton *et al.* rightly object to many of these assessments because of the imputed end-state such measures suggest. The sceptics conceptualize globalization as some terminus against which current global flows can be measured. Utilizing such a standard insures a diminution of the impact of actually existing globalization by establishing a base-line of the perfectly globalized economy. Perraton *et al.* prefer to conceptualize globalization as a process. We find this analytically superior in that it allows for a more nuanced and subtle assessment of the openness of the global economy. It rejects the either/or option in favour of a continuum, a vision of *relations in process*. It allows for a recognition that the sovereignty of a state can remain largely intact even as certain policy options become increasingly problematic. Importantly for our political purposes, this view sees globalization as an ongoing process that does not have a predetermined end but is in a state of dynamic flux, politically indeterminate.

Globalization and class

Insofar as these material processes represent a continuation of capitalism's long-standing globalizing tendencies, relations of class and class-based social powers are inextricably bound up with these material processes. Historical materialism remains an indispensable resource for critical analyses of these processes, and the political possibilities they may entail.

This is, of course, not a thesis commonly found in popular treatments of globalizing capitalism. In his best-selling book, *New York Times* global affairs columnist Thomas Friedman celebrates what he imagines to be the egalitarian tendencies of this newest capitalism, creating 'super-empowered individuals' and, in effect, erasing distinctions of class: 'For the first time in American history both Joe Six-pack and Billionaire Bob are watching CNBC to see how their shares in the market are faring' (Friedman 1999: 105). 'Soon', Friedman gushes, 'everyone will have a virtual seat on the New York Stock Exchange' (1999: 58). Despite hallucinogenic liberal triumphalism of this sort, the classical Marxian concept of class based upon relationship to the means of production seems to us no less relevant than it was in Marx's lifetime. Friedman's flights of fantasy notwithstanding, by the late 1990s the ownership of wealth in the USA was more unequal than at any time since the late 1920s. According to Federal Reserve data for 1998, the wealthiest 10 per cent of Americans owned over 82 per cent of stock and 86 per cent of bonds owned by individuals (including indirect ownership through mutual funds), as well as over 91 per cent of business assets. Like a black hole, capitalist wealth is increasingly concentrated, massive and dense closer to the core: ownership of these financial and business assets is even more disproportionately concentrated in the wealthiest *half of 1 per cent* of the population, who owned over 31 per cent of stocks, more than 32 per cent of bonds, and almost 55 per cent of business assets (Henwood 2000: 3). To these relations of class correspond particular kinds of social power. Owners of the means of production may be socially empowered as *employers* and as *investors*, and both aspects of capitalist class power are enhanced by the reality and the ideological constructions of globalizing capitalism.

Again, let us take the USA as an example. Data generated by Kravis and Lipsey (1992) suggest that even while the USA (as a territorial entity) lost around one-third of its share of world exports of manufactures between 1966 and 1986–8, USA-based multinationals maintained their global share by shifting their production for world export markets towards majority-owned foreign affiliates (MOFAs), whose export share increased over this period. 'In 1986–88, US multinationals were exporting more from their overseas affiliates than they were from the United States' (Kravis and Lipsey 1992: 194). Evidence such as this seems to suggest that over the last several decades transnational production for world markets has to a significant degree displaced export production from within the territorial USA. Nominally American multinational firms have maintained their global competitive position, but their US workers now produce less for world markets while workers employed by their foreign affiliates produce more. Further indicative of this tendency, employment in the manufacturing MOFAs of USA-based firms grew from 2.4 million in 1966 to almost 4.1 million in 1987, an increase of about 70 per cent. Although direct foreign investment by US-based firms has remained heavily concentrated in the developed market economies, after 1966 employment by US MNCs engaged in manufacturing in the newly industrializing countries – especially in Brazil, Mexico, and Asia – grew almost five times as rapidly as did such employment in the developed countries. This suggests that US-based MNCs may have sought to transfer some of their more labour-intensive manufacturing activities to these areas (Dicken 1992: 51–3, 59–67). Further, internationalized production has dramatically affected manufacturing within the USA: the import content of US-finished manufactures has increased eightfold – from 3 per cent throughout most of this century and as late as 1963, to 24 per cent in 1985 (Held *et al.* 1999: 174). Reflecting the increased significance of multinational firms as mediators between the USA and the world economy, Dicken claims that intra-firm trade now constitutes more than half of all US trade, an argument buttressed and extended by Feenstra (Dicken 1992: 48–9; Feenstra 1998; but compare Henwood 1997).

Employers are fully aware of the fearful dependence of working people upon their jobs, and in an era of increasingly transnationalized investment and production are prepared to exploit this economic insecurity as a source of workplace power. Employers now commonly threaten to close plants and eliminate jobs when they are faced with unionization drives or new collective bargaining situations. According to one of the most comprehensive and systematic studies of unionization campaigns in the post-NAFTA period, this type of workplace extortion has taken a variety of forms:

> specific unambiguous threats ranged from attaching shipping labels to equipment throughout the plant with a Mexican address, to posting maps of

North America with an arrow pointing from the current plant site to Mexico, to a letter directly stating that the company will have to shut down if the union wins the election.

Between 1993 and 1995, such threats accompanied at least half of all union certification elections in the USA (Bronfenbrenner 1997: 8–9). In the words of one auto worker contemplating his future in a transnationalized economy, the threat of runaway jobs 'puts the fear in you' (quoted in Rupert 1995: 195); and, of course, it is intended to do so.

Bronfenbrenner's study demonstrates effectively the importance of perceptions about globalization. After the passage of NAFTA the bargaining environment changed not necessarily because of actual plant movement (although some of that has occurred) but because of *the widely perceived possibility* of plant movement. A plant that effectively forestalls an organizing drive by such threats (however realistic) achieves an outcome that is not measurable in terms of capital movement, employment changes, etc. Yet, the outcome of this conflict has been dramatically affected by the liberalization of trade and investment through the NAFTA agreement. However great or little the job creation/destruction of NAFTA, the political environment that workers face has changed, and their bargaining power has been effectively attenuated. There seems to be sufficient cause in their minds to understand globalization as a credible threat to their job security and their livelihoods. To the extent that they become embedded in popular common sense, ideological constructions of 'footloose capital' – along with its evil twin, the discourse of 'competitiveness' in a seamless global economy – enhance the effective power of capital relative to working people.

These shifting relations of power have had measurable effects. Real wages of working people have been in a long-term decline since the early mid-1970s, with growth in real wages lagging further and further behind productivity growth. Reflecting shifting power relations within the historical structures of contemporary capitalism, we suspect that these processes are likely to be only temporarily retarded by the 1990s 'boom' – the longest business cycle expansion in US history but relatively feeble in its effects on the economic and political circumstances of working people (Bernstein and Mishel 1999). This intensified exploitation of workers is a large part of the explanation for higher corporate profits, a record-setting stock market, and extravagant growth in executive compensation. In an environment where the rewards to corporate managers and investors have far outstripped the wages of working people, it should not be surprising to discover that inequalities of wealth are at historically high levels (Henwood 2000; also Wolff 1995: 7; and Mishel *et al.* 1997: 278–81).

Increasing inequality in the USA mirrors global processes. As more states embrace and deepen neoliberal market-driven policies, the world economy becomes increasingly polarized. According to the United Nations Development Report of 1999, the income gap between the globe's richest and poorest quintiles 'was 74 to 1 in 1997, up from 60 to 1 in 1990 and 30 to 1 in 1960'. By the late 1990s, the fifth of the world's population living in the highest income countries had 86 per cent of world GDP, 82 per cent of world market exports, 68 per cent of foreign direct investment, and 74 per cent of the world's telephone lines; while the poorest fifth had only about 1 per cent of each of these (UNDP 1999: 3). Evidence such as this points towards the emergence of an unprecedentedly hierarchic global political economy, which concentrates power and wealth effectively in the hands of the wealthiest people in the richest countries.

Employers and investors in the USA, and globally, have enjoyed the fruits of their enhanced social power. But this power is not confined within the boundaries of the 'economy'; it has broader political manifestations as well. 'Even in a society whose government meets the liberal democratic ideal, capital has a kind of veto power over public policy that is quite independent of its ability to intervene directly in elections or in state decision making' (Bowles and Gintis 1986: 88). Even if members of the owning class were somehow unable or unwilling to access political influence through manipulation of their relationships with particular politicians or officials, they would nonetheless be uniquely privileged by virtue of their structural situation and social powers. Insofar as the state under capitalism depends for its economic vitality upon the investment activities of a class of 'private' owners of the social means of production, it is effectively subject to their collective blackmail. If a state fails to maintain conditions of 'business confidence' (Block 1977: 16), or if it enacts policies which appear threatening to the interests of the owning class, investors may subject the state to a 'capital strike' – driving up interest rates, depressing levels of economic activity, throwing people out of work, exacerbating the fiscal crisis of the state and endangering the popular legitimacy of the incumbent government. Thus are market values enforced upon governments which claim to be responsive to popular democratic pressures. 'The presumed sovereignty of the democratic citizenry fails in the presence of the capital strike' (Bowles and Gintis 1986: 90).

Ideologies of globalization can also operate so as to constrain further the (already limited) possibilities of democratically enacted public policy. The volume and speed of foreign exchange trading and international capital flows has heightened the disciplinary effect of a threatened capital strike. Governments are increasingly obliged to weigh carefully their welfare, fiscal and monetary policies against the interests of investors who may exit *en masse* in response to expectations of lower relative interest rates or higher relative inflation rates. Intensifying this disciplinary effect is an ideology of globalization which prioritizes the interests of investors. The particular interests of the owning class are represented as if they were the general interests of all: 'since profit is the necessary condition of universal expansion, capitalists appear within capitalist societies as bearers of a universal interest' (Przeworski quoted in Thomas 1994: 153). In this ideological construction, the social and moral claims of working people and the poor are reduced to the pleadings of 'special interests' which must be resisted in order to secure the conditions of stable accumulation. In William Greider's apt summary,

Like bondholders in general, the new governing consensus explicitly assumed that faster economic growth was dangerous – threatening to the stable financial order – so nations were effectively blocked from measures that might reduce permanent unemployment or ameliorate the decline in wages. … Governments were expected to withdraw more and more benefits from dependent classes of citizens – the poor and elderly and unemployed – but also in various ways from the broad middle class, in order to honor their obligations to the creditor class …

(Greider 1997: 298, 308)

To the extent that state managers understand the world in terms of ideologies of hyper-globalization (e.g. Reich 1991) this very real disciplinary power is intensified to the point that consideration of effectively pro-worker or environmentally friendly policies is precluded, and policies may be specifically designed to attract and hold (putatively footloose) capital by offering the most favourable business climate possible.

Historical materialism and critique

These material processes of globalizing capitalism are not prescripted and ineluctable, but contradictory and contestable. They may be interpreted in different ways, and their political effects and possibilities will be mediated by the social meanings attached to them. Historical materialist critiques imply that capitalism's abstraction of politics from the economy and the naturalization of a civil society of abstract individuals are historical conditions which are open to question and hence potentially to transformation. This transformation would necessarily entail (but not necessarily be limited to) the re-politicization and democratization of the economy and of civil society, such that they cease to be pseudo-objective and apparently natural conditions which confront isolated individuals as an ineluctable external 'reality'. Rather, they would become explicitly political – sites for, and objects of, reflective dialogue and contestation, mutable aspects of a broad process of social self-determination.

Accepting in broad outline Marx's analysis of the structure and dynamics of capitalism (e.g. 1971: 201–2), Antonio Gramsci resisted more mechanical and economistic interpretations of Marx. For Gramsci, progressive social change must be produced by historically situated social agents whose actions are enabled and constrained by their social self-understandings (1971: 164–5, 326, 375–777, 420). Popular 'common sense' then becomes a critical terrain of political struggle (1971: 323–34, 419–25). Gramsci's theorization of a social politics of ideological struggle – which he called 'war of position' to distinguish it from a Bolshevik strategy of frontal assault on the state (1971: 229–39, 242–3) – contributed to the historical materialist project of de-reifying capitalist social relations (including state-based conceptions of politics) and constructing an alternative – more enabling, participatory, democratic – social order out of the historical conditions of capitalism. Gramsci's project entailed addressing popular common sense, making explicit the tensions and contradictions within it as well as the socio-political consequences of these, in order to enable critical social analysis and transformative political practice.

From this perspective, we have found non-teleological conceptions of historical materialism to be politically congenial. Stuart Hall's vision of 'marxism without guarantees' foregrounds the significance of ideological struggle. Without presuming a pre-determined outcome, Hall is seeking to understand the conditions and processes through which ideological self-understandings are formed and reformed within particular historical circumstances. We understand Hall to be suggesting that class relations are human social products, contradictory and contested, and in no sense 'exogenous' or simply pre-given. Like all social structures, the class-based organization of production does not (re-)produce itself automatically but through the actions of concretely situated social agents, agents whose self-understandings and political horizons may be shaped by ideologies which foreground social identities other than class. 'It is therefore possible', Hall tells us,

> to hold both the proposition that material interests help to structure ideas and the proposition that position in the social structure has the tendency to influence the direction of social thought, without also arguing that material factors univocally determine ideology or that class position represents a guarantee that a class will have the appropriate forms of consciousness.
>
> (Hall 1988: 45)

Hall's Gramsci is one who sees history as a complex and contradictory story of social self-production under specific social circumstances; it is, in Gramsci's words, a process of 'becoming which ... does not start from unity, but contains in itself the reasons for a possible unity' (Gramsci 1971: 355–6).

We understand this to mean that the class-based relations of production under capitalism create the *possibility* of particular kinds of agency, but these possibilities can only be realized through the political practices of concretely situated social actors, practices which must negotiate the tensions and possibilities – the multiple social identities, powers, and forms of agency – resident within popular common sense. Insofar as Marx's social ontology posits the *internal relation* of human beings, their social relations, and their natural environment, we would suggest that various non-class social determinations are always already present within processes of social self-production, and that these should be explicitly addressed in an effective anti-capitalist politics.

Critique of competitiveness ideology

Ideologies of globalization which centre around *competitiveness* – whether cast in terms of competition among abstract individuals in a market, or in terms of economic, cultural or racial nationalisms – effectively reinforce the class-based powers available to the owners of capital, and divide and disempower non-owners.

A crucial terrain of struggle for contestations of 'common sense', and an important correlate of globalization, is the relentless discourse of 'competitiveness'. Nation-states and municipalities offer subsidies and tax incentives in order to remain competitive in the market of firm placement. Firms lay-off workers, cut wages, and seek out production sites with lower wage or lax environmental and labour standards (among other things) in the name of competitiveness. Workers feel compelled continually to sharpen skills and improve their marketability, or more often work longer hours for less pay, because it appears as self-evident that something called the international economy (and hence, the domestic economy) is a very competitive place and, therefore, their livelihoods are continually at risk.

The explosion, since the mid-to-late 1970s, of both popular and academic literature that relates to competitiveness demonstrates two things. First, there is something going on that encourages authors and academics to think about and make prescriptions about competitiveness. Second, the variety of approaches in the literature reveal much agreement about something called competitiveness requiring a response from states, firms, and workers and very little agreement about what this response should be.

What is interesting about the competitiveness issue is the importance of the actions taken in its name when there seems so little agreement on what competitiveness is or should be. Communities are devastated, vast numbers of workers are laid-off and very many more feel their livelihoods imperilled, and states, counties, and municipalities forego significant public revenues, all in the name of this quite nebulous concept of competitiveness. While commentary varies dramatically, investors seem to be of one mind about what competitiveness means. A seemingly guaranteed strategy for a dramatic increase in the value of a large firm's stock is the announcement of lay-offs in the name of international competitiveness (Henwood 1997). While profit rates soar, firms plead that competitiveness compels them to cut jobs and wages. There can be no clearer indication of how class interests diverge around the issue of 'competitiveness'.

The notion of competitiveness is sufficiently indeterminate to mean nearly all things to all people. No less an authority than the eminent economist Paul Krugman (1994) has argued competitiveness is 'a dangerous obsession'. Krugman argues that nation-states don't compete meaningfully in any economic sense. Krugman is right but for the wrong reasons. States *do* compete. They don't compete *qua* firms but *for* firms – competing in various ways to secure an attractive environment for capital. While it is true that states do not compete in the same fashion as firms, Krugman doesn't demonstrate the irrelevance of competitiveness discourse by such a conclusion. Krugman's argument demonstrates something important – the notion of competitiveness has resonance regardless of its accuracy in describing the reality of competitive pressures on nations, firms, plants or workers. Even in the absence of acute competitive pressure, the rhetoric of competitiveness fosters an environment that heavily favours the owners of capital and challenges attempts at solidarity. When workers, states and communities are pitted against each other in a 'race to the bottom' or in movements towards downward harmonization, the competition is not between firms but between the owners of the means of production and those whose income is derived from labour. On this view, competitiveness can be understood as a rhetorical tool in the competition over the division of surplus.

From competitiveness to solidarity?

Resistance to the globalizing powers of capital may be enabled by ideologies of transnational solidarity, grounded in – if not wholly determined by – capital's increasingly transnational subsumption of labour, and the intensified exploitation this entails. The globalization of production has increased the need for ideologies of resistance that are global as well. A new internationalism seems to be recognizing the necessity of rethinking traditional forms of labour organization and the irreducibility of class, race, and gender. Theoretical work envisioning new possibilities of international organizing have recognized as much. DeMartino's (2000) 'Social-Index Tariff Structure' (SITS) policy approach suggests that trade be discouraged with social tariffs to the extent that competitive advantage is gained by worker repression, environmental degradation, exploitation of women and children, and prison and slave labour. The SITS approach seeks to establish criteria that allow trade to flourish, but only trade that does not gain advantage through exploitation. Kidder and McGinn (1995) have suggested that transnational worker networks (TWNs) be encouraged in place of bureaucratic structures that may be too rigid to move quickly or embrace multifaceted movements. TWNs are conceived as loose coalitions that can form around broadly progressive themes in order to check the suzerainty of transnational capital without succumbing to one-dimensional struggles. In the wake of NAFTA, cross-border solidarity efforts have mushroomed. The Coalition for Justice in the Maquiladoras, a loose-knit coalition of maquiladora workers and progressive, grass-roots groups from Mexico, Canada, and the United States, exemplify a TWN that is truly transnational. Moody's (1997) vision of a transnational social movement unionism is likewise encouraging, rethinking traditional labour politics in an environment of transnational production. All of these approaches recognize that exclusively local resistance to globalization is insufficient and ultimately self-defeating.

There are early but significant signs of a growing internationalism in labour solidarity. An important example of a truly global campaign was the Ravenswood Aluminum campaign in the early 1990s. Herod (1995) and Juracvich and Bronfenbrenner (1999) have documented the extensive reach of this campaign. Ravenswood Aluminum Corporation (RAC), located near Ravenswood, West Virginia, locked out its unionized workforce (United Steel Workers of America, USWA) in 1990 in order to break the union. The corporate ownership of RAC is complicated, but it included Marc Rich an American with vast holdings in firms in forty countries. Rich was indicted in 1985 for tax evasion, fraud, and other federal violations and fled to Switzerland from where he managed his investments (until his recent pardon by the outgoing Clinton administration).

The USWA and AFL-CIO took a multifaceted approach to the lockout and included a strong international dimension in their campaign. Linking up with the International Metalworkers Federation (IMF), the International Confederation of Free Trade Unions (ICFTU), and a host of other national and international labour groups and secretariats, the campaign organized resistance to all manner of Marc Rich's business dealings. From organizing public relations pressure embarrassing Rich to organizing mass demonstrations to prevent Rich from acquiring recently privatized firms in Eastern Europe, the international campaign made RAC a significant thorn in the side of Marc Rich. End-user boycotts were organized and heads of state including Vaclav Havel and Michael Manley weighed in on the side of labour when Rich attempted to acquire firms in their countries. The campaign was effective in industrialized as well as developing countries. The lockout was ended with a new contract in the spring of 1992. The contract provided for dismissal of replacement workers, reinstatement of locked-out workers with full seniority and wage and pension increases.

The effectiveness of the RAC campaign demonstrates the possibility of international resistance to capital. Herod argues that an important insight of the RAC campaign is the willingness of the participants to define community in a broad, not parochial, sense (1995). Local resistances to globalization choose to define community geographically, not in terms of interests or identity. Importantly, the RAC campaign utilized global resources and both thought and acted globally in the face of globally active capital. Further, labour groups were active on the basis of *international solidarity*. Herod (1997) has demonstrated that labour has always been international in a sense, but that far too often it was focused on securing national labour goals and frequently acted *against* international solidarity. The new internationalism aspires to be more truly international in its struggles.

Another interesting development in the new internationalism has been the willingness of industrialized and developing countries' labour unions to act cooperatively. Estrada-Levinson and Frundt (1995) have argued that international efforts were crucial to Guatemalan organizing of its Coca-Cola bottling plant, and continues to be important in the attempted organization of maquiladora processing plants. A further development that heightens the necessity for international solidarity has been the large number of immigrants that often find themselves forced into unskilled factory work in hostile environments. Exploring an example of this phenomenon demonstrates the importance of international solidarity even where it seems least likely to occur.

The Peerless Clothing corporation is one of the largest manufacturers of men's suits in North America.[1] Peerless' factory in Quebec employs roughly 2,400 workers, over 80 per cent immigrants from Bangladesh, Pakistan, Vietnam, Laos, Guatemala, Cambodia (Kampuchea) and other countries. Peerless actively recruits immigrants for their assumed docility in the face of management pressure, their willingness to accept sub-par wages for the industry and the assumed disunity that such a polyglot workforce seems to represent. Peerless utilizes a company union called Fraternite. Many of the workers at

Peerless have found the company union to be ineffective in addressing grievances. Importantly, the grievances of labour at Peerless are not solely centred around wages, but also are concerned with racism and sexual harassment in the workplace.

A campaign was launched by UNITE in November of 1995 to organize the workers under an independent union. As could be expected, initially language difficulties were problematic for organization. However, UNITE, combined with others sympathetic to the campaign, were able to form a coalition of activists and trade unionists centred around bridging language barriers. Trade unionists were actually flown from Bangladesh to assist in organizing the Bengali-speaking workers (in the dead of winter no less!). The trade unionists were women affiliated with BIGWU, a Bangladeshi trade union. Sympathizers from Guatemala, Bangladesh, Vietnam, Sri Lanka and the Philippines among others have either visited or participated locally (emigrants) in the campaign. This kind of activity is a unique example of an outside-in approach in that Peerless is not a global firm, but it is being confronted by an international force.

While these examples only scratch the surface of new forms of resistance in the face of new forms of exploitation, they demonstrate that international solidarity is a very real possibility. While these forms of solidarity often emanate from class struggles, they are not wholly determined by class. The dramatic events at the Seattle meetings intended to inaugurate a new round of WTO talks testify to the potential of a transnational and multifaceted resistance to elements of globalization. While the real effects of the decidedly indeterminate negation of 'the battle in Seattle' remain to be seen, it serves as further evidence of the nascent transnational resistance to capitalist globalization. The global expansion of solidarity networks may be the corollary to the global expansion of production and exchange.

Unity through difference?

This cosmopolitan project of resistance is complicated, however, by the situation of productive activity within a nexus of relations which – as Marx steadfastly maintained – is at once natural and social. We believe this implies that at the point of production, where the necessary social interchange with the natural world takes place, various historically specific social determinations are *already present*. These may entail a variety of 'extra-economic' or non-class-based social identities and power relations variously articulated with class.

Construction of democratizing projects which would challenge the globalizing social powers of capital, then, requires the formulation of ideologies of globalization which speak to the complex social situations in which the world economy's waged and un-waged workers find themselves. If such projects are to forge a unified resistance to globalizing capitalism, they must find ways to articulate class-based identities with other social identities and powers already resident and active within the popular common sense of working people in various parts of the world.

This implies negotiation with issues of gender, race, postcoloniality, and other facets of identity politics. A strong case can be made that processes of class formation within the US political economy have been integrally related to construction of racial identities and systems of white dominance (Goldfield 1997). Indeed for at least five hundred years, racialized identities and ideologies of racial hierarchy have been used to justify the domination and exploitation of peoples of colour by Europeans and North Americans (Stavrianos 1981; Hall 1996). We recognize that this history poses serious issues for any project of transnational political solidarity, if it is to avoid replacing one structure of Western white male power with another. We believe that historical materialism has much to learn on this score from struggles over race and postcoloniality within the feminist movement (Gabriel and Macdonald 1994; Pettman 1996; Eschle 2001). While it is beyond the scope of this chapter to engage substantively with these debates (see Rupert 2000), we want at least to acknowledge their relevance to an historical materialism which projects its emancipatory horizons on a global scale.

We conclude that progressives in the age of globalizing capitalism cannot afford to presume the emergence of a simple and homogeneous identity such as 'global proletariat'. Rather, a political movement must be built through the recognition that those exploited and dominated by globalizing capitalism share a potential unity in view of their common structural relation to capital, but that this commonality is embedded in and mediated by manifold social relations which mark them off as meaningfully different. We are arguing, in other words, that a democratizing transnational social movement can only be constructed through the negotiation of difference, and that ideological struggles to construct a common political project must recognize and respect these differences if they are to attain their object.

Note

1   The information presented here was acquired by Scott Solomon in interviews with Josh Remis and Sam Luebke of UNITE during December 1996.

Bibliography

Agnew, John and Corbridge, Stuart (1995) *Mastering Space*, London: Routledge.

Bernstein, J. and Mishel, L. (1999) *Wages Gain Ground*, Washington, DC: Economic Policy Institute.

Block, Fred (1977) 'The Ruling Class does not Rule', *Socialist Revolution*, 33 (May–June): 6–28.

Bordo, Michael D., Eichengreen, Barry and Irwin, Douglas A. (1999) 'Is Globalization Today Really Different than Globalization a Hundred Years Ago?', *NBER Working Paper # 7195*.

Bowles, S. and Gintis, H. (1986) *Democracy and Capitalism*, New York: Basic Books.

Bronfenbrenner, Kate (1997) 'We'll Close!: Plant Closings, Plant-Closing Threats, Union Organizing and NAFTA', *Multinational Monitor* (March): 8–13.

Cox, Robert (1987) *Production, Power, and World Order*, New York: Columbia University Press.

DeMartino, G. (2000) *Global Economy, Global Justice*, London: Routledge.

DeMartino, George and Cullenberg, Stephen (1994) 'The Single-Industry Tariff Structure: An Internationalist Response to Economic Globalization', *Review of Radical Political Economics*, 26: 76–85.

Dicken, Peter (1992) *Global Shift*, 2nd edn, New York: Guilford.

Eschle, Catherine (2001) *Global Democracy, Social Movements, and Feminism*, Boulder, CO: Westview.

Estrada-Levinson, Deborah and Frundt, Henry (1995) 'Toward a New Internationalism: Lessons from the Guatemalan Labor Movement', *NACLA Report on the Americas*, 28(5):16–21.

Feenstra, Robert C. (1998) 'Integration of Trade and Disintegration of Production in the Global Economy', *Journal of Economic Perspectives*, 12: 31–50.

Friedman, Thomas (1999) *The Lexus and the Olive Tree*, New York: Farrar, Straus & Giroux.

Gabriel, C. and Macdonald, L. (1994) 'NAFTA, Women, and Organizing in Canada and Mexico: Forging a Feminist Internationality', *Millennium*, 23: 535–56.

Gill, Stephen (1990) *American Hegemony and the Trilateral Commission*, Cambridge: Cambridge University Press.

Goldfield, Michael (1997) *The Color of Politics*, New York: New Press.

Gordon, David (1988) 'The Global Economy', *New Left Review*, 168 (March/April): 24–64.

Gramsci, Antonio (1971) *Selections from the Prison Notebooks*, Q. Hoare and G. Smith (eds), New York: International Publishers.

Greider, William (1997) *One World, Ready or Not*, New York: Simon & Schuster.

Hall, Stuart (1988) 'The Toad in the Garden: Thatcherism among the Theorists', in C. Nelson and L. Grossberg (eds), *Marxism and the Interpretation of Culture*, Urbana, IL: University of Illinois Press, pp.35–73.

—— (1996) 'The West and the Rest', in S. Hall *et al.* (eds), *Modernity*, Oxford: Blackwell, pp.184–227.

Held, D., McGrew, A., Goldblatt, D. and Perraton, J. (1999) *Global Transformations*, Oxford: Polity.

Henwood, Doug (1997) 'Does Globalization Matter?', *In These Times*, 31 March: 14–16.

—— (2000) 'Wealth News', *Left Business Observer*, 94 (5 May).

Herod, Andrew (1995) 'The Practice of International Labor Solidarity and the Geography of the Global Economy', *Economic Geography*, 26: 76–85.

—— (1997) 'Labor as an Agent of Globalization and as a Global Agent', in Kevin Cox (ed.), *Spaces of Globalization: Reasserting the Power of the Local*, New York and London: Guilford, pp.167–200.

Hirst, Paul and Thompson, Grahame (1996) *Globalization in Question*, Cambridge: Polity.

Juravich, T. and Bronfenbrenner, K. (1999) *Ravenswood: The Steelworkers' Victory and the Revival of American Labor*, Ithaca, NY: Cornell University Press.

Kidder, Thalia and McGinn, Mary (1995) 'In the Wake of NAFTA: Transnational Workers Networks', *Social Policy*, Summer: 14–21.

Kravis, I. and Lipsey, R. (1992) 'Sources of Competitiveness of the United States and of its Multinational Firms', *Review of Economics and Statistics*, 74 (2): 193–201.

Krugman, Paul (1994) 'Competitiveness: A Dangerous Obsession', *Foreign Affairs* (March/April): 28–44.

Marx, Karl (1977a) 'The Communist Manifesto', in D. McLellan (ed.), *Karl Marx: Selected Writings*, New York: Oxford University Press.

—— (1977b) 'Results of the Immediate Process of Production', in *Capital, Volume I*, trans. B. Fowkes, New York: International Publishers, pp.948–1084.

Mishel, Lawrence, Bernstein, Jared and Schmitt, John (1997) *The State of Working America, 1996–97*, Armonck, NY: M.E. Sharpe.

Moody, Kim (1997) *Workers in a Lean World*, London: Verso.

Moody, K. and McGinn, M. (1992) *Unions and Free Trade: Solidarity vs. Competition*, Detroit, MI: Labor Notes Books.

Ohmae, Kenichi (1990) *The Borderless World: Power and Strategy in the Global Marketplace*, London: HarperCollins.

Ong, Aihwa (1987) *Spirits of Resistance and Capitalist Discipline*, Albany, NY: SUNY.

Perraton, J. *et al.* (1997) 'The Globalization of Economic Activity', *New Political Economy*, 2: 257–77.

Pettman, Jan Jindy (1996) *Worlding Women: A Feminist International Politics*, London: Routledge.

Reich, Robert (1991) *The Work of Nations*, New York: Knopf.

Rupert, Mark (1995) *Producing Hegemony*, Cambridge: Cambridge University Press.

—— (2000) *Ideologies of Globalization*, London: Routledge.

Stavrianos, L.S. (1981) *Global Rift*, New York: Morrow.

Sutcliffe, Bob and Glyn, Andrew (1999) 'Still Underwhelmed: Indicators of Globalization and Their Misinterpretation', *Review of Radical Political Economics*, 31 (1): 111–31.

Thomas, Paul (1994) *Alien Politics: Marxist State Theory Retrieved*, London: Routledge.

United Nations Development Programme (1999) *Human Development Report*, New York: UNDP, Oxford University Press.

van der Pijl, K. (1984) *The Making of an Atlantic Ruling Class*, London: Verso.

—— (1998) *Transnational Classes and International Relations*, London: Routledge.

Wachtel, Howard (1990) *The Money Mandarins*, Armonck, NY: M.E. Sharpe.

Weiss, Linda (1998) *The Myth of the Powerless State*, Ithaca, NY: Cornell University Press.

Wolff, Edward N. (1995) *Top Heavy*, New York: Twentieth Century Fund.

Index